The English Lakes

The Langdales (in 1898)

The Hills
The People
Their History

(An illustrated walking guide)

Ramshaw & Adams

The English Lakes

Index to the Maps and the Areas covered

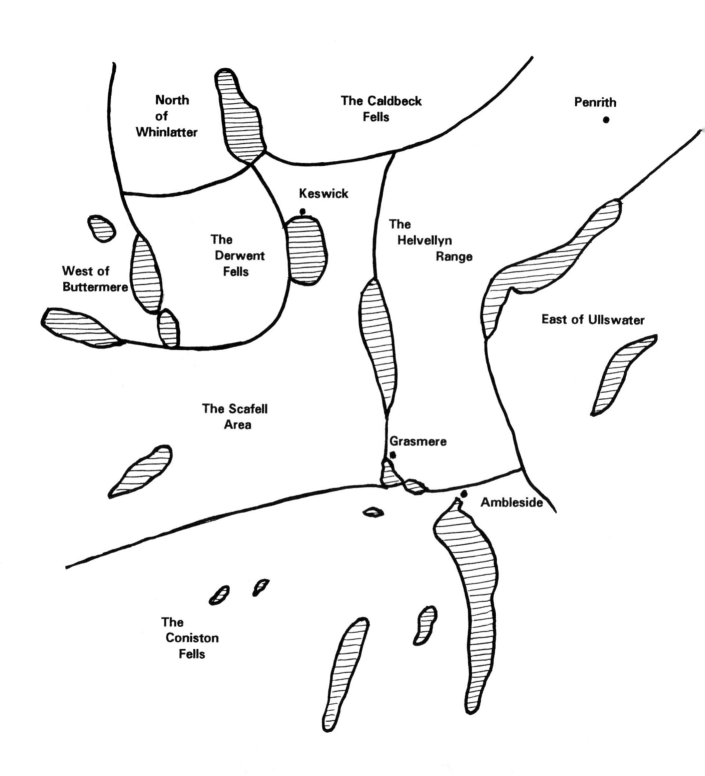

North
of
Whinlatter

The Caldbeck
Fells

Penrith

Keswick

The
Helvellyn
Range

The
Derwent
Fells

West of
Buttermere

East of Ullswater

The Scafell
Area

Grasmere

Ambleside

The
Coniston
Fells

The English Lakes

About this Book

This new guide to the Lake District has been compiled with the needs of all visitors in mind. For convenience the district has been divided up into eight areas as shown opposite. The information on each area is arranged in two sections.

Section 1   For the Walker

The first section includes a general description of the area with information on viewpoints, the nature of the terrain, areas to avoid etc.. Suggested walks are described but the reader can use the 3D type pictorial maps and the comprehensive A-Z guide to the fells to plan his or her own routes, bearing in mind the general advice given. The O.S. maps referred to in the text are the 1:25000 Outdoor Leisure Maps Numbers 4,5,6 and 7.

Section 2   Local History

The second section deals in some detail with the local history of the area. Where applicable, points of historical interest are indicated in the first section, as shown in this example:

" leading one to the head of Scale Force waterfall (**LH 2**). "

(page 42, line 4)

This example, from the **'West of Buttermere'** notes in the book, refers to the second item in the **'West of Buttermere, Local History'** section on page 46.

Access and Country Code

The description of a route in this book does not necessarily imply a right of way. Please respect the country code. **DO NOT** climb over or damage walls, fences or hedges. **DO NOT** deposit litter, take it home with you. Take care not to frighten livestock. **DO** follow marked paths wherever possible, using stiles and gates. **DO** close gates after you and **DO** keep your dog under close control, **ON A LEAD** (if he is not fully trained to stay by you and completely ignore sheep).

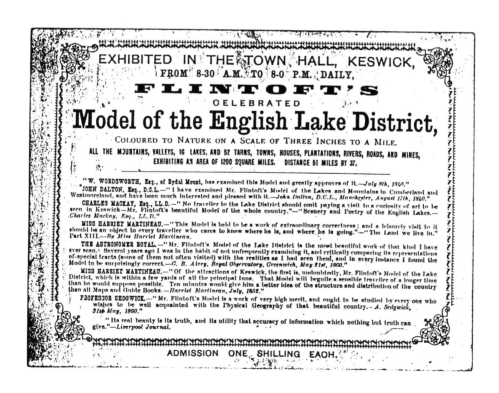

The English Lakes

About the Authors and the Illustrator

John Adams and David Ramshaw are Science teachers who live and work in Carlisle. Therefore they have ample opportunity to explore the Lake District.

Dave is an obsessive fellwalker who has already worn out two dogs on the fells and is now into his third and fourth. Dave wrote the walk descriptions and researched much of the local history and folklore of the area.

John is the map man. He is also a fellwalker but not quite so obsessive. John's idea of heaven is crawling along in a long abandoned lead or copper mine. John created the pictorial maps which are a novel feature in this book and he is also responsible for the A-Z guide to the fells. This is John's second book. His first publication **'Mines of the Lake District Fells'** was published by Dalesman in 1988.

Most of the illustrations in the book have been drawn by Dave Lush who, apart from being a Science teacher, is a talented artist, musician and amateur juggler.

British Library Cataloguing in Publication Data
Ramshaw David & Adams John,
The English Lakes-The Hills-The People-Their History
1. English Lakes, Hill- walking, Local history

ISBN 0 9522098 0 2

First published in Great Britain in 1994 by

P3 Publications
13 Beaver Road, Carlisle, Cumbria
CA2 7PS
Tel. 0228 43302

**If you have difficulty obtaining copies of this book
please phone or write to the address above**

Printed in Great Britain by
The Amadeus Press Ltd.
Huddersfield
HD2 1YJ

The English Lakes

Contents

Bassenthwaite Lake and Skiddaw

Safety on the Hills and on the Lakes

On the Hills - It is essential that anyone intending to venture onto the hills is properly equipped for the conditions that they may encounter. The following items of equipment are, in our opinion, the minimum necessary for a fine weather trip onto the Lakeland Fells:

Strong walking boots, woollen trousers or breeches **(not cotton jeans)**, windproof anorak with hood, spare sweater, gloves, extra emergency food, first aid kit, map, compass, torch, whistle, a survival bag and of course a rucksack to put them all in.

The response of a randomly-selected group of people to a physical challenge
(Courtesy of the Open University)

More information: a free leaflet is available, from the Information and Visitor Centres throughout the National Park, entitled 'Enjoy the Hills in Safety'.
The proximity of the lakeland mountains to the Irish Sea and the prevailing westerly winds can lead to sudden and dramatic changes in the weather. It is all too common to set out for the tops in warm and pleasant conditions to be confronted, sometime later, with driving rain and a cold blustery wind. Do **NOT** get caught out. Go properly equipped.

The National Park Ranger Service provides a recorded fell top weather report, which is updated twice daily. The number to call is Windermere **(05394) 5151.** If you are unlucky enough to get

6

into difficulties use the international distress signal to attract attention. This consists of six blasts on a whistle, or six flashes of a torch, or six shouts. Wait one minute before repeating the signal. For mountain or mines rescue dial 999 and ask for 'Police,' who will contact the local rescue team.

First Aid

No fellwalker should consider venturing onto the fells without:

(a)   a basic first aid kit
(b)   basic first aid knowledge

The former can be built up from items supplied by your local chemist and the latter by attending a course offered by one of the recognised organisations. e.g. St. John's Ambulance, Red Cross, or St. Andrew's Association in Scotland.

Statistically the most likely First Aid situations will fall into the eight categories listed below:

1. Minor cuts and bruises
2. Sprains
3. Blisters
4. Insect bites and stings

5. Minor burns and scalds
6. Splinters
7. Headaches and stomach upsets
8. Sunburn

There follows a suggested First Aid kit that will deal with the above and allow you, with the addition of First Aid knowledge, to give First Aid in more serious situations which can occur.

Contents of Kit

adhesive dressing strip 30 cm x 30 cm
tube antiseptic cream
tube insect repellant
tube Anthisan
paracetamol tablets
milk of magnesia tablets
crepe bandage 7.5 cm x 4.5 m
open wove bandage 5 cm x 5 m
five medi-prep antibactericidal wipes
triangular bandage
safety pins

reel zinc oxide plaster
two 5 cm sq. Melolin dressings
10 cm sq. Melolin dressing
moleskin or similar for blisters
medium sterile unmedicated dressing
small bottle (e.g aspirin) of Calamine lotion
glucose tablets
small capsule of salt
small scissors
tweezers

The items above can be packed carefully, if some of the unnecessary packaging is removed, into a soft plastic container, used for keeping food fresh, with a self sealing lid. Paracetamol tablets and others can be placed in a small film capsule suitably cleaned and labelled. **Don't forget to restock after use.**

The English Lakes

Safety on the Lake

The Lake District National Park Authority publishes a range of free information leaflets which are available at visitor centres. There is a leaflet on water safety as well as leaflets for individual lakes which give localised information on water sport facilities including safety aspects. Below is a summary of the main rules to follow when boating on the lakes.

1. Wear a life jacket
2. Supervise children on or near the lake
3. Don't overload your boat
4. Beware of the cold water
5. Beware of steeply shelving shores
6. Watch out for broken glass

Inflatables drift quickly and should be tethered to the shore when used by unaccompanied children.

If you see anyone in difficulties CONTACT THE POLICE AT ONCE

If you are in real difficulties STAY WITH YOUR BOAT, SHOUT AND SIGNAL FOR HELP

D LUSH.

The Derwent Fells

General

This popular walking area, bounded by Derwentwater to the east with Buttermere and Crummock Water to the west, has something to offer everyone. The proximity of Keswick and the ease of access to the fells ensures that the area is often very busy in high season. This will be obvious to anyone who has ever tried to walk on Cat Bells on a sunny Bank Holiday Monday. For those who are fortunate enough to live within easy access of the district such expeditions are best left for a fine winter's day. Then one can experience the beauty of the surroundings with fewer companions and perhaps the added charm of a mantle of snow.

In the centre of the district lies the Vale of Newlands, now a rural backwater, which gives little indication of its former industrial importance as a silver, lead and copper mining area. The name Newlands derives from the draining of a tarn, 'Husaker Tarn', by the monks of Furness who thus acquired the *new lands* of Newlands valley for cultivation. The name of the tarn survives with Uzzicar Farm in the valley. Indeed, the Derwents are rich in local history some of which is recounted in the local history section at the end of this chapter. Although the Derwents do not boast the highest tops in the Lake District

they present some of the most pleasing and dramatic views. The fells tend to be steep sided and appear to rise almost vertically from lake level to summit, thus enhancing their grandeur. An excellent example of this is Grasmoor, when viewed from Lanthwaite Green. Incidentally, Grasmoor is the highest mountain in the area at 852 m.

Walking

The Derwents offer a large variety of walking including several horseshoes or 'rounds', an exciting gulley scramble or two and gentler low level routes suitable for families. The popularity of the area has ensured that all of the main routes are well worn and easily visible. This has the advantage of making it less likely that one will get lost, but the disadvantage that paths sometimes become dangerously eroded on steep descents such as that from Eel Crag to Coledale Hause **(F)**. The main rounds are summarised below.

The Coledale Round
Total climbing about 3600 ft, 1100 m

Several variations are possible depending on which tops you wish to visit and whether you wish to avoid road walking at the end of the day. Here are two suggestions:

The Derwent Fells

Route 1 - Stoneycroft **(H)** to Braithwaite
via Causey Pike, Coledale Hause
and Grisedale Pike.
(7 miles)

(plus 3 miles back to Stoneycroft, partly along the road).This can of course be avoided if your party has two cars and leaves one at Braithwaite.

In clear weather this route provides impressive views and varied walking which includes gentle sloping ridges, steep pulls and a rocky scramble to the summit of Causey Pike. As you traverse the ridge leading up to Crag Hill, Force Crag Mine **(E)**, with its extensive workings, is clearly visible in the valley below. This mine, one of the oldest in the district, was also the last mine to operate in the National Park. Zinc and Barytes were mined, mainly at weekends, by a small group of enthusiasts. Unfortunately, the lease ran out in 1991 and the mine has now closed.

Take care when descending the steep northern edge of Eel Crag **(F)** to Coledale Hause. The path down through the crags can be avoided by descending the grassy slope to the west from the summit of Crag Hill onto the path leading north from Whiteless Pike to Coledale Hause. From Coledale Hause take the path to the right which bears steeply up to the summit of Grisedale Pike. As you start your climb, note the fenced off hole in the ground to the right of the track. This is the top of an open stope above No. 7 level of Force Crag Mine. If you detour to look down into the stope, please do **NOT** be tempted to throw stones into the hole as there may be someone below. Members of the local mine exploration society spend many happy hours underground exploring the disused ore mines of the Lake District. From the summit of Grisedale Pike you will be treated to fine views of the Causey Pike ridge in the foreground and Borrowdale and the Langdale Pikes in the background. The descent down the ridge of Sleet How to Braithwaite is enjoyable in this direction, but I would not recommend coming up this way as it is a long hard slog. The path near the end of the ridge has been rebuilt and diverted to reduce erosion. Please keep to this new path, which leads directly to the car park near the bottom of the pass.

Route 2 -Braithwaite back to Braithwaite
via Stile End and Sail to join Route 1
(8 miles)

Take the road leading up past the Coledale Inn **(C)** and follow the well graded path which leads round Stile End. This eventually joins the mine road leading to the site of the old cobalt mine, which lies high on the north face of Sail. When you reach the ridge turn right to join Route 1.

Shorter Walks

Several shorter walks can easily be devised around the Causey Pike Ridge. For example one can park at the Quarry car park at Rigg Beck Bridge **(I)** and follow the path beside the beck which climbs up to the hause between Ard Crags and Sail. Alternatively, if feeling more energetic, one can leave this path after half a mile and bear left up onto the Ard Crag ridge. As you climb towards the hause note the wooded area high on the side of Causey Pike just below Scar Crags. These clumps of stunted trees are the remnants of an ancient oak forest which covered the whole area, prior to the arrival of the German Miners seeking fuel for their smelters **(LH 4)**.

From the hause there is a steep climb up to the ridge followed by a pleasant stroll over

Mediaeval Oak Forest
(between Ard Crags and Causey Pike)

10

The Derwent Fells

LUSH.

The Hobcarton Round

Causey Pike to Rowling End from where you can drop down the fellside back to Rigg Beck Bridge. The views over the vales of Keswick and Newlands from this ridge are truly excellent and not to be missed.

Route 3 - Grisedale Pike via Ladyside Pike
and Hopegill Head
Return via Hobcarton End

Total climbing about 2100 ft   (640 m)
(6 miles)

The Thornthwaite Forest Guide Map available at the Whinlatter Visitor Centre, would be useful at the beginning and end of the walk when following the forest tracks.
Car Parking is available at the Forestry Commission Fellwalkers' car park, Hobcarton Plantation **(A)**.

This is one of my favourite walks offering fine ridge walking with excellent views of Scotland, the Solway and the Cumbrian Coast to the north and west. The route takes in the summits of Ladyside Pike, Hopegill Head and Grisedale Pike which, in good conditions, are ideal viewpoints for the hills to the south and

east. The route starts 900 ft (274 m) up Whinlatter Pass thus enabling the summit of Grisedale Pike at 2595 ft (790 m) to be reached with approximately 2100 ft (640 m) of climbing. This is best done on a fine summer evening when the sun is beginning to sink over the Solway. On leaving your car follow the track which rises to the west and takes you towards the Swinside Plantation. The object here is to reach the ridge leading up to Ladyside Pike. The forest guide map is useful here as you can follow the numbered marker posts. On leaving the forest at the end of the track **(B)** follow the fence up onto the ridge. As you reach the ridge there is a stile in the top corner of the fence at the bend in the fallen down wall. A steep climb following the line of the collapsed wall now leads to the cairn at the summit of Ladyside Pike. Continue on to Hopegill Head. In wet weather take care on the exposed slate slabs leading to the summit. The angle at which the bedrock lies makes it slippy in wet conditions and treacherous if icy. If you stay close to the edge of the ridge you can look down into the spectacular crags and gullies rising from the valley below. The view from the summit of Hopegill Head well repays the effort of getting there. To the west the ridge of Whiteside leads off towards Lanthwaite Green. To the south and below is seen Coledale Hause rising to the high pass between Eel Crag and Grasmoor, which gives access to Whiteless Pike and Buttermere beyond.

The Ascent of Hopegill Head
(from Ladyside Pike)

Beware however, as you may be literally standing on a volcano. It is to be hoped that, while perched on Hopegill Head, you do not experience the *'eruption'* of Whiteside reported by the locals in 1908 **(LH 3)**. Pressing on, follow the path down and to the left which closely skirts the head of Hobcarton Crags. This is particularly important in mist if you are to avoid ending up on Coledale Hause. After

dropping down about 300 ft the path rises again to the summit of Grisedale Pike, marked by its cairn and old iron fence post.

From here it is downhill all of the way. Begin your descent by following the path east for about 100 yds down towards Braithwaite. Bear sharp left at the old iron fence post marking the start of the ruined wall, which runs north down the ridge to Grisedale Gill. In misty or poor weather conditions this wall provides a good emergency descent into Hospital Plantation and to the road over Whinlatter Pass. However, to complete our horseshoe, we must bear left 100 yds or so along the wall in order to follow the left hand ridge to Hobcarton End (bearing 340 degrees magnetic). Turn left in this direction immediately after descending a steep little scramble, where there is a second iron fence post adjacent to the wall. The path here is indistinct or absent completely due to the rocky nature of the ground. Continue your descent keeping to the line of the ridge and, as you lose height, the path becomes visible once more, meandering through the grass and heather towards the small cairn at Hobcarton End. Turn right at the cairn and follow the ridge path as it drops down into the forest running parallel to the road below. On entering the forest follow the path in an easterly direction, dropping down to the forest track north of marker post 41. This part of the route may be difficult due to recent tree felling and planting. Once on the forest track follow it northwards and then round to the west, as you gradually descend on your return to the fellwalkers car park.

Hobcarton Gully (D)

An exciting evening walk is afforded by an ascent to Hopegill Head via Hobcarton Gully. From the Fellwalkers' car park **(A)** follow the forest track to the head of the valley under Hobcarton Crags. The gully is steep and loose but devoid of any major problems, if reasonable care is taken. On a fine summers evening it is ascended in deep shadow and, when you emerge at the summit of Hopegill Head into brilliant sunshine, the experience is, to say the least, quite unforgettable.

The Derwent Fells

Suggested routes
from Lanthwaite Green (G)

Route 4 - Hopegill Head via Liza Beck
Coledale Hause and Sand Hill
Return via Whiteside Ridge.
Total Climbing about 2100 ft (640 m)
(5 miles)

The path which follows the Liza Beck up to Coledale Hause although probably the easiest route to Hopegill Head is anything but boring. The steep sided valley gives dramatic views of the screes of Grasmoor to the right and the craggy Whiteside Ridge to the left. This valley was the scene of a tremendous waterspout described by Mr Gilpin in the 1760's **(LH 5)**. The return route along the Whiteside ridge is a pleasant stroll, although care should be taken when descending the steep path down from the end of the ridge via Whin Ben back to Lanthwaite Green.

Route 5 - Coledale Hause via Rannerdale
Whiteless Pike and Whiteless Ridge
Return via Liza Beck
or Whiteside Ridge
Total Climbing 2000 - 2500 ft (610 - 762 m)
(7 - 8 miles) depending on route

On a good day this route affords spectacular views of the surrounding fells and coastal plain with the advantage of nicely graded paths. From the car park at Lanthwaite Green follow the road south for one mile to Cinderdale Common car park **(J)**. There is no need to walk along the road as there are adequate sheep tracks on the common to the left of the road. From Cinderdale follow the track which leads southwest up the narrow valley between Rannerdale Knotts and Whiteless Pike to the Hause **(L)**, which overlooks Buttermere and the Newlands valley. A sharp left turn at this point takes you up onto the Whiteless Ridge which is followed all the way up to the plateau between Crag Hill and Grasmoor. A gentle descent now follows to Coledale Hause from where you have a choice of routes back to Lanthwaite Green. If short of time you can drop down to the left and follow the path beside the Liza Beck. Alternatively carry on, up and over Sand Hill, to Hopegill Head and

Grasmoor 'Direct'

return along the Whiteside ridge, with its fine views over the Solway.

Grasmoor Direct

Experienced walkers with an evening to spare may wish to try their hand at ascending Grasmoor directly via Lorton Gully, which faces directly onto the car park at Lanthwaite Green.

There are several difficult pitches but it is possible without artificial aids. However this gully scramble is difficult (3 star rating) and should not be attempted by those who dislike exposure, or are lacking in agility. It is possible to bypass the most difficult sections by climbing out to the left. Towards the top of the gully take the left hand branch, which comes out on the ridge path about two thirds of the way up the mountain. This poorly marked path up the northwest corner of the face of Grasmoor is itself quite a good scramble and a good alternative for the more sane fellwalker.

•••❖•••

The fells in the southeast of the area are better known and more popular than those in the northwest. Here one has a choice of several testing 'rounds' of varying length, as well as

13

some beautiful low level walking along the river Derwent into Borrowdale. A good starting point for the high level routes is the car park at the northern end of the Cat Bells ridge. Coming from Portinscale on the road to Grange, cross the cattle grid at Hawes End and then bear right onto a minor track. The car park lies directly below the ridge about 100m along this track.

Cat Bells - Maiden Moor - High Spy Dalehead

Route 6 - Return via Hindscarth Ridge
Total Climbing about 2750 ft (840 m)
(10 miles)

Route 7 - Return via Robinson
Total Climbing about 3250 ft (990 m)
(13 miles)

Route 6

Cat Bells must be one of the most popular hills in the Lake District due to its modest height and the beautiful panoramic views it provides. How many of today's regular fellwalkers, I wonder, were introduced to the beauties of the area with an expedition up Cat Bells in their younger years?

However, as you climb the ridge beyond Cat Bells onto Maiden Moor you will soon leave the crowds behind. As you cross the Hause after leaving the summit of Cat Bells the path to the right leads down past Yewthwaite Mine to Little Town. The ridge ahead rises steadily to the summit of Maiden Moor, giving views to the left into the Borrowdale valley and behind you a fine open vista of Derwentwater and Keswick, with Bassenthwaite Lake and Skiddaw beyond. To your right note the large bare spoil heaps of Goldscope Mine **(K)** on the side of Hindscarth. Vegetation cannot flourish on these heaps due to the high concentration of lead and copper in the soil. For a brief description of the colourful history of this ancient mine, which dates back to Elizabethan times, see **(LH 4)**.

From the top of Maiden Moor the ridge dips slightly before rising gently to the top of High Spy and then dropping steeply down to the swampy bowl containing Dalehead Tarn **(N)**. If short of time or energy, one can return along the valley bottom, between Hindscarth and High Spy, by following the stream which drains Dalehead Tarn. A steep climb follows to

On Grange
(an estate agent's dream ?)

It matters little where you build a house in Grange, it is sure to have a pleasant outlook, and is never in the way of its neighbour; for the land over which the dwellings are so picturesquely dribbled, is all fertile dingles, and knolls, and nest-like nooks mixed with bloomy orchards, flower gardens and scattered tufts of wood; and there are several mansions thereabout, whose green shades and ornamental grounds give a park-like tone to the skirts of the village.

D. LUSH

Edwin Waugh : Rambles in the Lake Country (1882)

the summit of Dalehead overlooking Honister Crag and its extensive quarry workings. Green slate was mined here for many years and the crag contains vast underground caverns. The remains of the old cableway and several tunnel entrances can be seen on the crag face opposite.

From Dalehead top continue along Hindscarth Edge to the summit of Hindscarth. As you traverse the edge note the classic 'U' shaped glaciated valley to your right, a reminder of the manner in which the district was sculpted to its present form by the last ice age. On a clear day the descent to the Newlands valley, down the ridge past Goldscope Mine to Little Town, is unforgettable. On reaching Little Town, a road walk can be avoided by joining the path to the right of the road which contours round Cat Bells back to the car park, from which the walk started.

Route 7

Follow Route 6 to Hindscarth edge and then continue in a northwesterly direction along Littledale Edge. A steep climb of about 500 ft. will bring you to the summit of Robinson, an ideal vantage point for surveying Fleetwith Pike, Haystacks and the fells behind Buttermere. The names of the Lake District

Robinson
(from the east ridge)

Fells can usually be traced back to our Celtic or Norse ancestors. The name 'Robinson' is more recent dating back to Edward VI and the dissolution of the monasteries. A certain Richard Robinson purchased forfeited estates in the area at that time. Over the years 'Robinson's Fell' has just become plain Robinson. The descent down the ridge from Robinson to the Newlands valley is every bit as pleasing to the eye as that previously described. On reaching Little Town follow **Route 6** back to your car.

Low Level Walks

Route 8 - Portinscale to Grange along the western side of Derwentwater

One can walk from Portinscale to Grange along the Lakeside. Public footpaths wind their way through the woodlands of Fawe, Brandlehow and Manesty parks. As you walk through Brandlehow Park it is hard to realise that this was once the site of an extensive lead mine. A few spoil heaps are now the only visible remains of the industrial past of this beautiful area. The site of the Borrowdale Mineral

Ascending Robinson in Winter

The Derwent Fells

Spring, or Salt Well, is also to be found near here. **(LH 1)**.

Route 9 - Grange to Rosthwaite
(or Seatoller)
via Castle Crag **(M)**

The path from Grange follows the access road for Hollows Farm to the campsite in Dalt Wood which lies directly below High Spy. From here several paths follow the meanderings of the river through the woods towards Rosthwaite. If you wish to visit Castle Crag, site of an ancient fort and hermitage **(LH 2)**, then you must follow the main track south which leads out of the wood through a farmgate. This track climbs the low pass between Castle Crag and the lower slopes of High Spy. Although only reaching a maximum of about 500 ft. above the valley, the views from this path are excellent. A short distance past Castle Crag, at point **(O)** on the map, the path down to Rosthwaite bears off to the left and eventually rejoins the riverside path at a footbridge. The return trip to Grange from Rosthwaite can be made along the riverside path thus avoiding any further climbing towards the end of the day.

Time and weather permitting a pleasant extension to this walk is achieved by continuing from point **(O)** south towards Seatoller, at the foot of the Honister Pass. The path contours round the fell below Riggindale Quarries giving fine views to the left of the Borrowdale valley below. Return along the riverside path past Longthwaite Youth Hostel thus rejoining the path to Grange.

* * * * *

Lakes to Visit
Derwentwater, Buttermere, Crummock Water, Loweswater

Nearest Towns
Keswick, Cockermouth

Places to Visit
Cars of the Stars (Motor Museum), Keswick
Cumberland Pencil Museum, Keswick
Keswick Museum and Art Gallery
Blue Box Theatre by the Lake

Recommended Country Inns in the Area

Good food and good ale

Coledale Inn	Braithwaite
Borrowdale Hotel	Borrowdale
Scafell Hotel	Rosthwaite
Kirkstile Inn	Loweswater

•••••✿•••••

Derwentwater from Friar's Crag

The Derwent Fells, Local History

1. Borrowdale Mineral Spring

A saline spring with medicinal properties was discovered and used by the early German miners. The Salt Well, as it became known, was mentioned in 1615 in the 'Great Deed of Borrowdale' when the well was sold together with the land. The site of the well, in the field in front of Manesty House, is now unfortunately neglected. However, this spring was once very popular and featured in Thomas Short's 'History of Mineral Waters' which was published in 1740. The benefits of Barrowdale Well, as it was then known, are reproduced for your education at the end of this section (page 29). Salt water is also to be found in an old mineshaft in the field adjacent to the well.

2. Castle Crag and Hermits

Castle Crag is the site of an old British hill fort which was used by the local inhabitants for their protection. This was necessary after the departure of the Romans left them vulnerable to other invaders. West, writing in 1779, tells us that much freestone, both red and white, was quarried out of the ruins. He also records that an iron bow and two masses of smelted iron were taken out of them, evidence for iron age occupation. In more recent times Castle Crag has been used as a slate quarry, as is readily evident when one climbs up and investigates.

There are ancient records of a hermit living on Castle Crag, but we know far more of the 20th century hermit; one Millican Dalton. Millican was an early refugee from the rat race of the city. He was born at Nenthead near Alston in 1867 and worked at a shipping office in London until the age of thirty. A lover of the simple life, he then gave up his job to become a professional camper and guider leading organised tours in the Lake District, Scotland and Switzerland. When in England, he divided his time between Epping Forest and the Lake District, spending three months every summer in a man-made cave on Castle Crag. He soon became quite famous being known as *'The Professor of Adventure'* and would give instruction in the art of raft building and sailing as well as rock climbing. Millican was a colourful character. He made his own clothes and equipment, wore shorts, a slouch hat with pheasant's feather, and a tweed coat. He was also a strict vegetarian and a Quaker. The picture of Millican on his raft on the Derwent was even sold to tourists as a postcard. The hermit of Castle Crag finally died in 1947 at the age of 80. One memorial to Millican still exists; one that was wrought by his own hand. At the entrance to the upper cave, his sleeping quarters known as *'The Attic,'* one can still see the carving on the wall of his favourite saying: Don't !! Waste Worrds ' Jump to Conclusions !

(To get the intended meaning put an 'or' between Worrds and Jump). Millican's Cave is to be found on the lower eastern slope of Castle Crag, in the woods and near to the riverside path between Grange and Rosthwaite.

3. Eruption of Whiteside (1908)

In recent years Cumbria has experienced the occasional ground tremor indicating that some geological activity still exists in the area. However, if contemporary records are to be believed, these pale into insignificance when compared to the eruption of Whiteside in 1908. In July and August of that year the local people experienced a series of frightening rumblings and shakings of the ground over a three week period. The source of the disturbance was eventually located as coming from within Whiteside. Then, on the evening of August 14th, as Mr W.C. Hope of Cornhow was leading hay, Whiteside spoke again. The mountain gave a great groaning rumble and instinctively Mr Hope looked over at it. He got the shock of his life when he saw what looked like a great cloud of smoke rising. Then, through the cloud, came bounding a number of large boulders which he thought had been shaken off the side of the mountain. Whiteside has not erupted again since that day and no satisfactory explanation of its long protracted rumblings has ever been given, although it was suggested that they might be the sign of a slumbering volcano beginning to stir once more. So, perhaps you should not linger too long on Hopegill Head.

4. Goldscope and the German Miners

Mention is made in a 13th century land inventory of a gold, silver, copper and lead mine in the Derwent Fells. Large scale working of the mine, however, commenced with the arrival of the German Miners in 1564. They worked the mine for copper and obviously found it profitable as they called the mine *'Gottesgab'* or God's Gift. Over the years this has become distorted to the present *'Goldscope'*. The Germans were not well received by the locals, who were jealous of their prosperity and ability to attract the local girls. They were frequently attacked and occasionally murdered. Eventually, however, they became integrated into the community, as can be seen from the names on some of the gravestones in the grounds of Newlands church. Thomas Percy, Earl of Northumberland, on whose property Goldscope and several other mines lay, was also ill disposed to the mining activities. He received no benefit from the operations of the 'Mines Royal Company' and obstructed their activities whenever possible. His conflict with the Crown led to litigation and eventually armed rebellion. He was finally executed for insurrection and his head was displayed on one of the gates of York. The mining of copper at Goldscope petered out with the development of Coniston as a copper mining centre. For the first half of the nineteenth century lead was mined with little success under a number of different owners. Then, in 1852, the great lead vein was discovered and the mine really did become God's gift as, in a twelve year period, about 5000 tons of lead ore was raised, which also yielded 22000 ozs of silver.

5. Waterspout of 1760

John Gilpin in his book 'Observations relative chiefly to Picturesque Beauty' (1772) describes a terrible *'waterspout,'* possibly a cloudburst, which devastated the area of Lanthwaite Green on the 9th September 1760 at about midnight. The waterspout originated high on the watershed of Grasmoor, sweeping down the steep valley between Grasmoor and Whiteside

In Gilpin's words :

"charging itself with all the rubbish it found there it made its way into the vale. At the foot of the mountain it was received by a piece of arable ground; on which its violence first broke. Here it tore away trees, soil and gravel; and laid bare, many feet in depth to the naked rock. Over the next ten acres it seems to have made an immense roll; covering them

with so vast a bed of stones that no human art can ever again restore the soil. When we saw the place, tho twelve years after the event, many marks remained, still flagrant of this scene of ruin."

Gilpin goes on to describe how the village of Brackenthwaite had a wonderful escape from catastrophe as the current was deflected by a projection of the native rock on which the houses were built. The energy of the deluge was finally dissipated in the river Cocker, causing widespread flooding.

6. The Borrowdale Cuckoo and other Tales

The folk of Cumberland and Westmorland generally used to think of the Borrowdale people as rather simple and unsophisticated. In the same way that an Englishman tells Irish jokes, or a German tells jokes about the Swiss, so the Burghers of Keswick told tales about the inhabitants of Borrowdale. Harriet Martineau related several of these in her book 'English Lakes' published in 1855.

To preserve these stories for posterity I reproduce three of them in full below:

It is said that an old Borrowdale man was once sent a very long way for something very new, by some innovator who had found his way into the dale. The man was to go with horse and sacks (for there were no carts, because there was no road) to bring some lime from beyond Keswick. On his return, when he was near Grange, it began to rain; and the man was alarmed at seeing his sacks begin to smoke. He got a hatful of water from the river; but the smoke grew worse. Assured at length that the devil must be in any fire that was aggravated by water, he tossed the whole load over into the river.

That must have been before the dalesmen built their curious wall; for they must have had lime for that. Spring being very charming in Borrowdale, and the sound of the cuckoo gladsome, the people determined to build a wall to keep in the cuckoo, and make the spring last forever. So they built a wall across the entrance, at Grange. The plan did not answer; but that was, according to the popular belief from generation to generation, because the wall was not built one course higher. It is simply for want of a top course in that wall that eternal spring does not reign in Borrowdale.

Another anecdote shows, however, that a bright wit did occasionally show himself among them. A "statesman" (an "estateman," or small proprietor) went one day to a distant fair or sale, and brought

home what neither he nor his neighbours had ever seen before; - a pair of stirrups. Home he came jogging, with his feet in his stirrups; but, by the time he reached his own door, he had jammed his feet in so fast that they would not come out. There was great alarm and lamentation; but, as it could not be helped now, the good man patiently sat his horse in the pasture for a day or two, his family bringing him food, till the eldest son, vexed to see the horse suffering by exposure, proposed to bring both into the stable. This was done; and there sat the farmer for

Keeping in the Cuckoo

several days, - his food being brought to him, as before. At length, it struck the second son that it was a pity not to make his father useful, and release the horse; so he proposed to carry him, on the saddle, into the house. By immense exertion it was done; the horse being taken alongside the midden in the yard, to ease the fall: and the good man found himself under his own roof again, - spinning wool in a corner of the kitchen. There the mounted man sat spinning, through the cleverness of his second son, till the lucky hour arrived of his youngest son's return, - he being a scholar, - a learned student from St Bees. After duly considering the case, he gave his counsel. He suggested that the good man should draw his feet out of his shoes. This was done, amidst the blessings of the family; and the good man was restored to his occupations and to liberty. The wife was so delighted that she said if she had a score of children, she would make them all scholars, - if only she had to begin life again.

7. The Great Deed of Borrowdale

The manor of 'Barrowdale', (Dale of the Castle), had been granted to the monks of Furness Abbey by the Derwentwater family. At the dissolution of the monasteries the property reverted to the Crown and was later sold by James I to two Londoners. For reasons unknown these two worthies promptly sold the estate to the tenants for less than a single year's revenue and the contract for this sale, dated 1613, became known as 'The Great Deed of Borrowdale.'

Origins of Keswick

The name **Kesewic** first appears in writing in a document about 1234 relating to the purchase of land by William de Derwentwater from the monks of the Furness Abbey. Part of the deal gave the monks *'leave to have a mill dam on William's land of Kesewic'*.This is simply *'Kese wic'* or the cheese dairy of the Derwentwater Estate. So Keswick originated from a cheese farm near Crosthwaite.

Weather Lore

The Borrowdale Sop

The Borrowdale Sop is a small cloud that rises at times at the head of Borrowdale near Piers Ghyll. Gradually growing larger it floats away down the Derwent Valley over Styhead Tarn. If it goes over towards the vale of St John the weather will continue to be fine, but if it takes the direction of Langdale, rain will follow within the next twenty-four hours. (See Page 101)

Seathwaite in Borrowdale

Sty Head Tarn above Seathwaite has consistently been the wettest place in England, over many years, with an average rainfall of more than 170 inches or 4.3 m. In 1954 a total annual rainfall of 257 inches or 6.5 m was recorded near Sprinkling Tarn, at the head of Grains Ghyll.

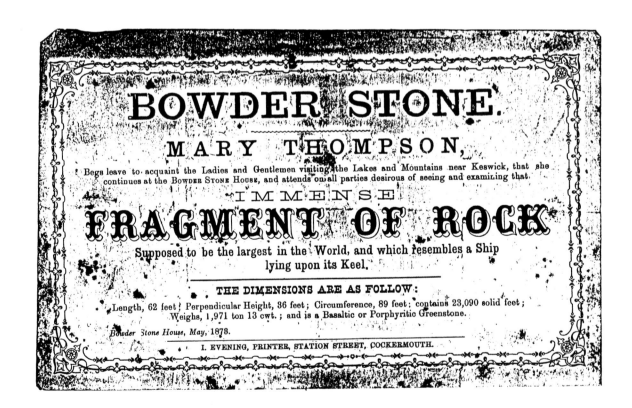

20

Hiſtory *Of Purging Waters from Marine Salt only.*

IT's not an account of all thoſe Waters in this large diſtrict we intend, this would lead to give a Hiſtory of the Brine Pits, *Wiches* and *Salt works*, but theſe not being reckoned Medicinal mineral Waters, I ſhall give a few of thoſe reputed and uſed as ſuch and firſt.

Barrowdale Well, near *Grange*, three Miles from *Keſwick* in *Cumberland*, it lies in a Level near a Moſs; it was found at firſt by Miners digging in Queſt of Ore, and ſprings out of the hard blew-ſtone which conſtitutes all thoſe awfull Mountains, and terrible precipices called *Fells*. being a kind of *Lapis ſciſſilis*, is pretty ſolid of a blewiſh Colour, and much of it will bear a pretty good Gloſs in poliſhing. It's a rough, ſevere purge to ſtrong Conſtitutions, heats the Body much excites a Thirſt, being a meer Brine of inland Salt, ſo ſtrong as it would well bear the Expence of a Salt work there, for ſcarce a 22d part of the German Ocean is Salt, but a 16 of this is pure Salt, and might be brought to a much richer Brine, were the freſhes made out of it, which drain into it at preſent, being a kind of pond; there grows no Graſs as far as this Water reaches. But a Gallon of *Middlewich Cheſhire* ſtrong *Brine* leaves fifty Ounces of Salt, and a Gallon of the weak *Brine* 45 and half ounce: But however harſh a vomit and Purge *Barrowdale* Well is, it wants not it's Cuſtomers and Admirers, and indeed in Dropſical, cacochymic, cachectic, diſorders; foulneſs of the Stomach, ſlipperyneſs of the Bowels from Relaxations, or much Mucus, ſome icteritious diſorders, it is of Service to ſeveral. There are ſeveral of this ſort in *Lancaſhire*, ſome weaker, others ſtronger; as one or two on *Dudden Sands*, *Minehead*, the neweſt *Cartmall* Well, below the *Carters houſe*, one beyond *Drigg*, another near *Edgermont*, *Whalney*, with ſeveral more. --------- As to the Brine Pits of *Middlewich*. they are from 10 to 35 Yards deep, and ſometimes they bore 28 or 30 Yards lower before the Brine burſts up, before which the VVorkmen hear a

M

great

Essay towards a Natural, Experimental and Medicinal History of the Mineral Waters of England. Thomas Short, 1740

The Caldbeck Fells

General

The small group of fells between the Solway and the Helvellyn range lie in what is still a relatively quiet corner of the Lake District. The only two high mountains in the area; Skiddaw and Blencathra (or Saddleback), form the western and southern ramparts of the group. To the west Skiddaw rises above the Keswick-Bassenthwaite road and to the south mighty Blencathra looms above the Keswick-Penrith road at Threlkeld. The area between these giants is less well known and consists of smooth grassy topped mountains linked by narrow valleys and occasional steep ravines. In the past these hills were an important mining area and became known, during the reign of Elizabeth the first, as her treasure chest. Unlike many parts of the district, mining continued here well into this century. Sandbeds barytes mine closed in 1963 and Carrock tungsten mine in 1982. The base for the industry associated with the area was the, now quiet, village of Caldbeck, once a hive of industry with its mines and mills. The feeling of the time when Caldbeck was a centre of commerce is perhaps best summed up by an amateur poet of the period who quoted the following:

"Caldbeck and Caldbeck fells are worth all England else"

The most popular walking areas are of course on the slopes of Skiddaw and Blencathra with their steep rocky ridges providing a variety of possible ascents and descents. However, the smaller fells beyond can provide a wealth of interesting routes, giving expansive views over the Solway to the north and the Eden valley to the east. This, together with the rich industrial and social history of this quiet corner of Lakeland, make the Caldbeck Fells well worth a visit.

A word of warning however. The fells above Caldbeck can give low, relatively easy walking in clear conditions. In mist however, a not infrequent occurrence in these hills, they can be difficult due to their lack of distinguishing features. In addition, the hills, particularly in the Sandbeds and Potts Gill area, are riddled with collapsed barytes workings. New holes appear every year and it is important to be aware of this, or you may take an involuntary trip into an abandoned mine working.

Blencathra or Saddleback

Blencathra, the old name for Saddleback, is thought by some to be of Celtic origin. The Celtic *"Blaen"* meaning *"end"* is found in the first syllable of many local places such as Blencow, Blencogo and Blindcrake (*Blaencrake*), for example. However, others say that the name derives from the Norse personal name Blenigr. Study of the local place names indicates that Celtic inhabitants did survive in the area after the coming of the

The Caldbeck Fells

Norse invaders **(LH7)**. There are seven ridges radiating to the east, south and west of Blencathra. Two of these, Hall's Fell and the Sharp Edge ridge, are precipitous and exciting. All give excellent views of the surrounding countryside. A variety of interesting rounds can be devised depending on the start point. I will describe two examples, one of which takes in adjacent hills.

Route 1   Blencathra from Scales **(K)**

Blencathra via Mousthwaite Combe, and Sharp Edge

return via Hall's Fell 5.5 miles (9 km)
or via Scales Fell 4.25 miles   (7 km)

Total climbing about 2300 ft (701 m)

There is space for several cars beside the bridge at Comb Beck. Turn off the A66 at the White Horse Inn, (Scales), and follow the very narrow fell road past the telephone box at the eastern corner of the Inn. In about 500 yds the road crosses Comb Beck. Park your car here.

The route begins at the stile, which is situated at the top of the slope just west of the bridge. The path follows the fence through a boggy area of reeds before becoming much drier and well worn as it rises and contours round Mousthwaite Comb onto the White Horse col **(I)** which links Scales Fell to Souther Fell. As you climb the col, note the spoil heap above and to the left of the path. This marks one of the levels of Saddleback Old Mine, which was last worked over one hundred years ago. On a clear day the col is a good place to pause a while and take in the view. To the south is Matterdale and the Helvellyn Range beyond. Note the old railway viaduct in the valley below, a monument to the old Penrith - Keswick - Cockermouth line; a victim of Dr Beeching's cuts, although the Penrith Keswick section did not close until 1972. The path of the line from Keswick to Threlkeld is now a public footpath and is a good alternative walk for a wet day or when one is not feeling energetic enough to take to the tops. To the west in front of us is the mass of Blencathra with the stark outline of Sharp Edge, our immediate goal, clearly visible. The route now is a comfortable stroll westwards which gradually climbs towards the head of the river Glenderamakin. In one mile the main path turns sharp left to follow and ford Scales Beck as it tumbles down from Scales Tarn. A short steep climb brings the tarn into view dwarfed by the surrounding cliffs below Sharp Edge. According to old folklore the sun never shines on Scales Tarn, an obvious reference to the steepness and proximity of the surrounding fells.

The wild beauty of Scales Tarn has been recorded many times in a host of different guide books. Writers in the eighteenth century often showed fear and horror when confronted by rugged hills for the first time and their guides make amusing reading. An account of a journey over Sharp Edge is given in the history section **(LH8)**, but perhaps you should not read it until after you have completed the crossing yourself. Sharp Edge lives up to its name if you stick to the summit of the ridge and ignore the path which traverses to the right of the edge. In dry weather and with good footwear the crossing is quite straightforward. There is only one point where a feeling of exposure may create a problem for certain individuals, but it is soon past. At the

Sharp Edge from the east

23

The Caldbeck Fells

Crossing Sharp Edge, as viewed from the west

risk of holding up the queue waiting to cross, this is the best spot for taking a spectacular photograph with your companion in the foreground and Scales Tarn, about 700 ft almost vertically below, in the background. In wet conditions care must be taken, especially when climbing up the steep rocky cliff, having crossed the edge proper. The rock is very smooth from countless pairs of boots and can be very greasy at times. In winter when icy, or in high winds, the edge should be avoided altogether. There have been many accidents here over the years through people attempting to cross in poor conditions. Anybody reading this who has been put off by the foregoing paragraph can reach Blencathra top by climbing the steep grassy slope to the south of the tarn. Those stalwarts who wish to continue should follow the path which leads northwards up onto the small col between Sharp Edge and Brunt Knott. From here

traverse the horizontal section of the edge keeping to path or ridge according to your wont. A steep scramble follows up to the summit plateau of Blencathra. There are a variety of routes that can be followed but take care because much of the earth and rock is eroded due to overuse. On reaching the plateau take the path which follows the ridge south as it gently rises to the highest point just above Hall's Fell. Look out for the two large white stone crosses on the plateau (LH3).

At the time of writing there is no cairn to mark the summit of Blencathra, there is just a low mound of scattered slates. If you arrive on a good day in the middle of the season beware of the extremely tame sheep who are not above mugging tourists for their sandwiches. Only on Place Fell and Pillar have I encountered sheep more tame than on Blencathra. Once, whilst sitting eating my sandwiches, a woolly head suddenly appeared over my left shoulder and grabbed my sandwich, just as I was about to take my first bite.

Sheep mugging a Tourist

Return by Hall's Fell

The ridge descending immediately to the south of the summit is Hall's Fell Ridge; a craggy and spectacular route which leads directly down to Threlkeld village. At the bottom of the ridge the path encounters Gatesgill Beck. On reaching the old weir (L), a relic of Threlkeld Lead Mine, turn left and follow the path east along the fellside just above the drystone wall. The route takes us past Doddick and Scales Farms, fording Scaley Beck en route and eventually leads up the fell a short way before meeting up with our outward route at Mousthwaite Comb. The last part of this path may be rather indistinct. If this is so, just follow the fence which skirts the field marked 'sheepfold' on the 1:25000 map; (English Lakes NE sheet), until you intersect the Mousthwaite Comb path.

Return via Scales Fell

From the summit of Blencathra retrace your steps east for about 100m to the point where the path to Sharp Edge bears to the left as it follows the ridge above Scales Tarn. Continue due east over the brow of the ridge and follow the well worn path, which descends steeply at first and then more gradually, down the shoulder of Scales Fell. On your right are the steep cliffs above the narrow valley between Doddick and Hall's Fells and to your left the terrain descends more gently to Scales Tarn and the River Glendermakin. From this vantage point the stark outline of Sharp Edge can be clearly seen; its cliffs appearing to rise vertically from the tarn below. The path follows the ridge to its end where it becomes a broad convex plateau. At this point there is little evidence of a path and one must strike out down the broad face of the fell in an easterly direction until you arrive at a lower path which contours south along the ridge above Mousthwaite Comb, forty metres or so above our ascent route. This path splits just above the 'sheepfold field' fence mentioned earlier (J), the left fork descending into Mousthwaite Comb, the right fork being the path from Hall's Fell.

Route 2   Blencathra from Mungrisedale via Bowscale Fell, Bannerdale Crags and Atkinson Pike

return via Scales Fell and Souther Fell,
(pronounced 'Sutrah')
Total Climbing about 2700 ft (823m)
9 miles   (14 km)
Start point   Mungrisedale village (F)

Threlkeld

The name Threlkret or Threlkeld, is said to have come from a Viking named Thorgell who, in the tenth century, conquered the Cimbric people and settled in this fair valley. Centuries before this, as early as 553, St Kentygern reared the cross at this place and preached to the inhabitants. This cross, we are told, stood for centuries near the 'Priest's Acre'.

Edmund Bogg 1898

This derivation of the name is at odds with the explanation given by **Mc Intyre** see (**LH7**). The visit of St. Kentigern, otherwise known as St. Mungo, is enshrined in the name of the nearby hamlet of Mungrisedale.

The Caldbeck Fells

This route is an excellent proposition for a full day round which takes in Blencathra but also encompasses the scenic valley of Bannerdale with its spectacular crags. Bowscale Fell and Souther Fell, although not of great height in themselves, make an excellent platform for appreciating the remoteness and beauty of the surrounding hills. Limited parking is available in the Cul de Sac; adjacent to the telephone kiosk just north of the Mill Inn. From here follow the road towards Caldbeck through the village as far as the junction signposted "Caldbeck " straight ahead and "Hutton Roof" to the right. A few yards past the junction a field gate, giving access to the rear of some cottages, leads one onto the lower southern slopes of Bowscale Fell (E). A rough fell path climbs steeply northwards up the end of the ridge. This soon becomes an easier gradient as the ridge broadens and curves to the west. As you climb westwards towards the rounded summit of the fell the valley of Mosedale lies below to the right with Carrock Fell, crested by its iron age fort (LH5), beyond. To your left is Bannerdale with the ridge of land aptly named *The Tongue* protruding into the valley. Beyond, lie the steep crags above Bannerdale where birds of prey make their home.

There are two cairns marking subsidiary summits along the ridge. Just after the second cairn, by diverting a little to the right, you can look down upon Bowscale Tarn nestling in its tiny valley high on the northern side of Bowscale Fell. There is a folk tale dating back several centuries which tells of two immortal fish which swim in Bowscale Tarn. Wordsworth recalls the tale in his song at the feast of Brougham Castle:-

> "-Both the undying fish that swim
> in Bowscale Tarn did wait on him;
> The pair were servants of his eye
> In their immortality;
> They moved about in open sight,
> To and fro for his delight -"

Beyond the tarn, in Mosedale, the scars left by Carrock Tungsten Mine are still to be seen although the surface buildings were cleared away only a few years ago. The ground now rises gently to the summit cairn of Bowscale Fell; which is about 500 m to the southwest

of the second cairn. From here panoramic views are to be had in all directions. In particular, the route ahead to the south drops gently to follow the escarpment of Bannerdale Crags; beneath which lies Bannerdale Lead Mine (LH1). Beyond Bannerdale Crags the path continues south to the miniature col at the source of the River Glendermakin (G). There follows a steep climb up the shoulder of Atkinson Pike with Sharp Edge to the left and Skiddaw in the distance on the right. Several cairns mark the summit of Atkinson Pike. The *'monument'* mentioned on the 1:25000 leisure map is a large cross laid out in white stones, (LH3). Continuing south across the broad top of Blencathra, the summit, above Hall's Fell, is reached in a further quarter of a mile. To return to Mungrisedale via Scales and Souther Fells, follow the path east from the summit down the shoulder of Scales Fell to the col above Mousthwaite Comb (I). There follows a steady climb of about 100 metres up onto the Souther Fell ridge.

This is a truly haunted mountain and it is a brave soul who would climb it on midsummer's eve. In 1735 on that night a ghost army was seen and heard marching over the summit of the mountain (LH10). Continue along the summit of Souther Fell to its end where it drops steeply down to the rear of the

Bannerdale Crags from Bowscale

26

The Caldbeck Fells

Mill Inn at Mungrisedale. Exiting from the open fell can be a problem here, as the field behind the inn has a *'Private Keep Out'* notice in it and, although there is an obvious path down the ridge, there is no obvious route to the road. A low fence round the field to the right of the *'private'* one can be stepped over and the field crossed to reach the road immediately south of the inn. As this is obviously a well used route it would be sensible if a representative of the planning board would get together with the local landowner and negotiate an agreed route off the fell. An important point about this walk is that, on a hot day, it ends where one can adequately slake one's thirst and appease one's appetite.

Skiddaw (The Shooters' Hill)

The lower slopes of Skiddaw were probably a hunting ground for the Norse settlers of the ninth and tenth centuries who gave the mountain the name *'Skytja-haugr,'* shooters'hill. Written evidence supports this as the name was recorded as *'Skithoc'* in 1231, and *'Skythouc'* a little later. In fact the eastern slopes of the mountain, down as far as Skiddaw House **(LH9)**, eventually became known as Skiddaw Forest. An easily accessible mountain, Skiddaw, with its bare rounded summit, was an important beacon station in

The Ullock Pike Ridge

years gone by **(LH2)**. Indeed it is possible to drive a landrover to the top, a fact which might make many think of it as a boring mountain. However, there are several interesting and taxing routes to the summit from which the uninterrupted views in all directions are magnificient. Skiddaw has been one of the chief sources of inspiration to the Lakeland poets who have written more about this hill than any other in the district. For more historical information on this well loved mountain see the local history notes at the end of this section.

I will only describe one route over Skiddaw, which avoids the main tourist track from Keswick over Latrigg, and takes one over the more remote northern foothills.

Route 3 Skiddaw via Ullock Pike
  Return via Birkett Edge and Dash Falls
  Total climbing about 2600 ft (792 m)
  (8.5 miles)
  Start point **(D)** on the Orthwaite road

There is a small layby carpark on the Orthwaite road about a quarter of a mile from the junction with the Keswick-Bassenthwaite road. A few yards east of the layby a stile indicates the path which climbs up onto the Ullock Pike ridge. There are several tracks leading across the field towards the ridge. The most direct route follows a line of stunted trees before rising to the wall at the top of the field. However, one should follow the way-marked route with the yellow arrows. The ridge rises gently at first, gradually becoming more narrow and steep as Ullock Pike is approached. To the west Sale Fell and Ling Fell lie in the foreground with Cockermouth and the West Cumbrian Coast beyond. To the east lie the massive northern slopes of Skiddaw with the smaller Uldale Fells behind. In about two miles the ridge levels out as the summit of Ullock Pike is reached.

From here it is a pleasant stroll along the narrow curving ridge of Longside Edge to Carlside. If the weather is fine and clear pause a while here and feast on the view to the south. Directly below us, it seems, lies Keswick nestling at the northern end of Derwentwater. From here the noise and bustle of visitors is missing. It looks a pleasant place to be. Beyond the lake to the south can be seen the jaws of Borrowdale, with the *'tonsil'* of Castle Crag in the centre (See the picture on page 17). On either side of Derwentwater are enclosing mountains; Catbells and High Spy to the west, Castlerigg and Watendlath Fell to the east. From Carlside our path turns northeast as it climbs the *'Skiddaw slates'* towards the summit of the mountain. This is the hardest part of the route being a steep ascent of just under half a mile over broken loose slates. Eventually the path levels out as the summit ridge is gained, leaving a pleasant stroll of half a mile to the summit cairn and shelter. Skiddaw, being the highest mountain in the area, commands spectacular views from its summit. This and the accessibility of the summit to packhorses carrying fuel, made it an obvious location for a signalling station in years gone by.

The summit of Skiddaw is one of the few mountains in the Lake District where cloud conditions occasionally arise such that one can observe a Brocken Spectre, so named as the phenomena was first recorded as being seen on Mount Brocken in the Harz Mountains in Germany. I have personally observed and

Brocken Spectre on Skiddaw
31st May 1991

photographed Brocken Spectres on Skiddaw and Helvellyn in the Lake District and on Ben Nevis and Buchaille Etive Mor in Scotland. They are best seen when the sun is low in the sky and casts your shadow onto cloud or mist

The Giant of the Brocken

I once witnessed with three companions an atmospheric phenomena on this mountain, rare in England, but not unfamiliar it is said on the Harz Mountains in Germany, where its occurrence is supposed to have given rise to the superstitious legends of the Giant of the Brocken. We set out late in a fine August night to reach the top of Skiddaw before sunrise: there was no moon, but the stars shone brilliantly, and as we rose up the steep hill-side overhanging Applethwaite, the lake and the valley became slowly more and more distinct. As often happens after the finest nights, the floating vapours were suddenly condensed, and by the time we reached the table-land near the top, we were enveloped in a thick white mist, cold and uncomfortable, which confined our sight to a circle of a few yards diameter. One of the party was a short distance in advance, when a ray of sunshine darted through the mist, and he saw a figure walking ten or fifteen yards distant from his side. Taking it for granted that this was one of his companions, whom he had supposed at some distance, he vented some expression of disappointment; and receiving no answer, repeated and repeated it again. Still there was no answer, though the figure kept steadily advancing with even steps. At last he stopped, half angry, and turned quite round to look at his silent companion, who did the same, but receded as he approached; and it became evident that the figure, apparently dimly seen through the mist, was his own shadow reflected upon it. It was then surrounded by a bright halo, and as the light became stronger, grew less and less distinct. The rest of the party came up in time to witness this remarkable appearance with some modification. On reaching the ridge of the mountain, our figures, of superhuman size, appeared to be projected on the mist in the direction of the Solway.

From **'The Penny Magazine'**, July 31st 1837

lying below you. A rainbow coloured halo is seen around the shadow. Above is an early 19th century description of the appearance of a Brocken Spectre on Skiddaw. Leaving the summit on the return trip the route leads due north along the narrow ridge which eventually broadens as it descends towards Dash Farm. In about a mile a fence is encountered which soon turns northeast to avoid Dead Crags; which lie directly on the line of descent. The path follows the fence (useful in mist) over Bakestall and Birkett Edge; which lie to the east of the crags. An alternative, slightly shorter, route is to follow the depression of Dead Beck, lying to the west of Dead Crags, past the disused mine workings. There is no clear path to Dead Beck. From the first bend in the fence, where the ridge broadens, continue due north down the slope. Dead Beck is the depression lying directly between Cockup on the left and Dead Crags on the right. Both routes eventually intersect the bridleway which leads from the Orthwaite road to Dash Farm and Skiddaw House. Turn west onto this track which will take you back to the road. A brisk one and a half mile walk along the road towards Keswick will bring you back to your car.

Route 4   Great Sca Fell
              via Longlands Fell
              and Lowthwaite Fell

          Return via Frozen Fell Gill
              and Trusmadoor

          Total climbing 1520 ft (463 m)
                  (5 miles)

This delightful little round gives one a taste of the remote Uldale Fells, with an unexpected surprise in the form of a beautiful little valley hidden between the adjacent hills of Meal Fell and Frozen Fell. There is parking for about three cars at Longlands **(A)** adjacent to the newly built water pumping station. Access to the fell is over the stile beside the gate which lies just east of the pumping station. There is no definite path up the fellside although there is a clear path along the base of the fell; our return route. Strike up the shoulder of the hill in a south easterly direction and, in about half a mile of climbing, the summit of Longlands Fell is achieved. To the west the small lake of Overwater is seen in the foreground with Binsey beyond. Braefell, higher than our present vantage point, lies across the gill to

the east. From the summit of Longlands Fell it is a pleasant stroll south down to a small col and then up onto the adjacent Lowthwaite Fell.

As each vantage point is gained it is well worth looking back to see how the view to the west and east is improving with the height gained. This is especially true if the walk is attempted on a fine summer's evening when the sunsets over the Solway can be exceptional. From Lowthwaite Fell we turn southeast, dropping again, before climbing up

Hay Knott from Brae Fell
showing marks left by smelter chimney

to the top of Little Sca Fell with Great Sca Fell just beyond. This is the highest point on the walk and, if there is time, a small diversion to the east will allow a view down into Silver Gill and Roughton Gill **(B)**, scenes of intense mining activity in the last century. It is hard to imagine that over a hundred years ago the Roughton Gill valley provided work for over one hundred miners. The view below would be of mine buildings, ore crushers, steam driven water pumps and, at the northern end of the valley, a lead smelter. The line of the smelter

The Caldbeck Fells

chimney up the side of Hay Knott can still be seen.

From the summit of Great Sca Fell descend the southern slope into Frozen Fell Gill and follow the sheep track to the left of the stream, which takes you down into a delightful narrow valley. This sheltered little vale has everything, a narrow gorge, grassy banks and small stunted trees. The stream meanders along, gently dropping as it finds a path between the hills. Notice the interesting folding in the layered rocks on the northern side of the gorge **(C)** as it winds its way round the base of Meal Fell. In half a mile an exit appears on the right hand side of the valley between Great Cockup and Meal Fell.

This miniature pass is Trusmadoor and gives passage through to the western flanks of Lowthwaite and Longlands Fell. The rest of the walk is a pleasant descent to the north from Trusmadoor. Keep to the right on reaching the valley bottom and follow the path alongside Longlands Beck which leads back to the start point.

Lakes to visit - Bassenthwaite, Ullswater

Nearest Towns-Carlisle, Cockermouth, Keswick

Places to visit -Carlisle Castle
Tullie House Museum, Carlisle
Priest Mill, Caldbeck
Caldbeck Mining Museum,
This small but excellent museum is dedicated to the miners of the Lake District and houses an extensive display of photographs, plans, original mining tools and minerals. The museum is the result of many years of exploration of the Lake District mineral mines by the joint proprietors of the museum and their friends.

Recommended Country Inns in the area
Good food and good ale

The Old Crown, Hesket Newmarket
(The landlord brews his own beer)
Indian food, a speciality
The Mill Inn, Mungrisedale
The Sportsman Inn, Troutbeck

A Ride up Skiddaw

Having engaged a guide, and with horses accustomed to the labour, we began to ascend this tremendous mountain by a way which makes the summit five miles from Keswick. Passing through bowery lanes, luxuriant with mountain ash, holly and a variety of beautiful shrubs to a broad, open common, a road led us to the foot of Latrigg. - A narrow path now wound along steep green precipices, the beauty of which prevented what danger there was from being perceived. - Soon after, we rose above the steeps which had concealed Derwentwater, and it appeared, with all its enamelled banks, sunk deep amidst a chaos of mountains, and surrounded by ranges of fells not visible from below. On the other hand, the more cheerful lake of Bassenthwaite expanded at its entire length. Having gazed a while on this magnificent scene, we pursued the path. - At length, as we ascended, Derwentwater dwindled on the eye to the smallness of a pond, while the grandeur of its amphitheatre was increased by new ranges of dark mountains, no longer individually great, but so from accumulation - a scenery to give ideas of the breaking up of a world. - Not a tree nor bush appeared on Skiddaw, not even a stone wall anywhere broke the simple greatness of its lines. Sometimes we looked into tremendous chasms, where the torrent, heard roaring long before it was seen, had worked itself a deep channel, and fell from ledge to ledge, foaming and shining amidst the dark rock.- At length, passing the skirts of the two points on Skiddaw which are nearest Derwentwater, we approached the third and loftiest and then perceived that their steep sides, together with the ridges that connect them, were entirely covered near the summits with a whitish shivered slate, which threatens to slide down them with every gust of wind. - The air on this summit was boisterous, intensely cold, and difficult to be inspired, though below the day was warm and serene.

Mrs Ann Radcliffe, "Description of the Scenery in a Ride over Skiddaw". Condensed from:-
'A Guide to the Lakes' by **T. West**. (Ninth edition published in 1807. Pages 306 - 11.)

Priest Mill, Caldbeck

The Caldbeck Fells, Local History

1. Bannerdale Lead Mine

At the head of the valley under Bannerdale Crags lies a small rather insignificant lead mine. There are two reasons for mentioning it here:

(a) Probably because of its remoteness, the mine building, although minus a roof, is still in quite good condition. According to Richard Hewer this consists of a smithy and office and the hearth in the smithy still contains coal and ashes. The mine is not thought to have been worked after 1870.

(b) This is the only mine in the district, apart from the famous wad mine of Seathwaite in Borrowdale, where graphite has been found. The graphite level is quite high up on the crags and its output is said to have been used in the making of pencils.

2. Beacon station on the summit of Skiddaw

For hundreds of years beacons have been lit on the summit of Skiddaw to warn of Scots raiders, pirates on the coast, the approach of the Spanish Armada, and also in celebration of national events. Skiddaw was one of the northern outposts of a network of such beacons which covered the whole country. The neighbouring beacons in West Cumberland, as it then was, were on Black Combe, Boothill, Muncaster Fell, St. Bees Head, Workington Hill and Moota Hill.

Skiddaw, because of its broad summit, required two beacons to be maintained, a not inconsiderable task considering the height and remoteness of the summit from supplies of wood. It was Macaulay in the last century who wrote a patriotic poem which described how the news of the sighting of the Spanish Armada was passed from beacon to beacon until the whole country was warned. The last two lines read as follows :-

"Til Skiddaw saw the fire that burned on
Gaunt's embattled pile
and the red glare on Skiddaw roused
the burghers of Carlisle"

The Royal Observer Corps, who were recently stood down in the Defence Review, were the modern equivalent of the beacon watchers of old.

D. Thomson, an observer with Bedford Group ROC, who has researched the beacon sites mentioned in the poem, puts *'Gaunt's embattled pile'* as the hill in the middle of Lancaster. It is most unlikely that a beacon in Lancaster could have been seen from Skiddaw and much more likely that the message followed the coast from Lancaster to Beacon Hill, Barrow then on to Workington via Black Combe, Muncaster, Boothill and St. Bees Head. The glow from Workington, across the Solway Plain, would be the signal to put the torch to Skiddaw's two beacons. The beacons were again primed for use at the beginning of the nineteenth century when a French invasion was expected but failed to materialise. The most recent bonfire on Skiddaw was in celebration of the Queen's Silver Jubilee in 1977. Unfortunately, I can vouch for the fact that the burghers of Carlisle never saw that glow, neither did the people of Keswick. The five hundred or so people on the summit that night, including the narrator, had difficulty seeing the fire from more than fifty yards distant. The weather was foul with continuous driving rain and sleet. But, needless to say, everyone enjoyed the camaraderie and the experience in spite of the elements. I will remember that night for a long time, not least for the fact that, whilst leading a party on the descent towards Dash Farm in pitch blackness, we strayed from our compass bearing and ended up above Dead Crags. My friends lost no time in pointing out to me that the fell on which this occurred, was called 'Cockup' and just across the way, beyond the crags, was Great Cockup!!

Large Cross on Blencathra

3. Crosses of Blencathra (H)

There are two stone crosses made from large pieces of white quartz-like rock set into the ground on the plateau between the summit of Blencathra and Atkinson Pike. The larger of these was built as a labour of love over many years by Harold Robinson of Threlkeld. Harold, who died in 1988 aged 80, climbed Blencathra sometimes twice a day, each time carrying a stone for the cross. This large white cross was built in memory of Mr Straughan, a great friend of Harold's, who was unfortunately killed while on active service in 1942. Mr Straughan in civilian life was the gamekeeper at Skiddaw House, (LH 9). Harold was a dedicated walker and fellrunner. According to his brother Sid, who still lives in Threlkeld, he preferred walking to using public transport. He regularly walked to Maryport and back, a distance of some forty miles. Harold's fellrunning tradition has been passed down to the present generation in the form of Kenny Stuart; the Threlkeld runner aiming for Olympic Titles, who is related to the Robinson family. The smaller cross, which is set into the slope of the rise towards the summit of the mountain, is thought to have been built by persons unknown from stones robbed from the larger cross. It is, of course, of more recent origin than the large cross.

4. Hermit of Skiddaw

Skiddaw can boast a hermit as can various other hills in the district. About 1864 a Scotsman from Banffshire, one George Smith, came to the mountain and built himself a hut on a ledge of Skiddaw Dodd, now covered by Dodd Wood. McIntyre describes how George, in order to enter his lair, had to climb a wall and then drop down through a hole into the interior of the dwelling. His table was a stone and he slept on a bed of leaves. He wore no hat, coat or shoes, washed his single shirt in the water of the beck and let it dry upon his back. He frequently ate his meals uncooked, and was so partial to whisky that he sometimes found himself in the hands of the police. His ostensible means of livelihood was the painting of portraits, but as he often refused payment for these, his survival was somewhat of a mystery. Alas, his home was eventually destroyed by the nineteenth century version of our 'yobs' and George went to live in Keswick. He suffered from religious mania, however, and was finally removed to an asylum in his native Banffshire, where he most probably died.

The ascent of Skiddaw is long but easy: a lady may ride to the top and down again without even dismounting. **Penny Magazine, July 31st 1837** A reference to Mrs Anne Radcliffe, no doubt !

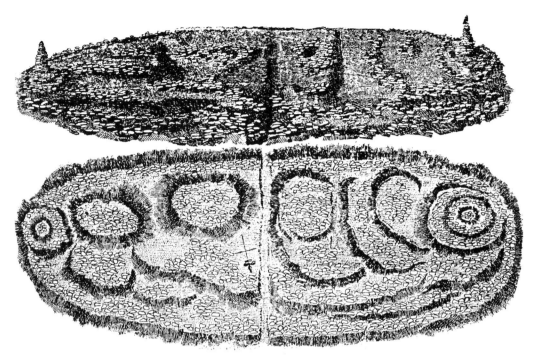

Early Nineteenth Century Impression of Carrock Fort

5. Iron Age Fort on Carrock Fell

The summit of Carrock Fell is the site of the largest and most strategically placed iron age fort in the district. Remains of other forts are to be seen at Castle How, Peel Wyke on Bassenthwaite, at Dunmallet on Ullswater, at Mardale Castle Crag, at Borrowdale Castle Crag and at Reecastle Crag above Lodore Beck in Borrowdale. Prior to the Roman invasion, Cumbria was ruled by the Brigantes and Carrock Fort was possibly the capital of this tribe. It is also probable that the fort was partially dismantled by the Romans, so that it could not be used against them. It is difficult to make out much of the detail of the original fort from the remains as they stand today. The artist's impression shown is from a guide book published in the early nineteenth century when, presumably, the remains were more upstanding than they are today. The fort is eight hundred feet long by three hundred and seventy feet wide. It seems, that in the middle of the last century, people were not so sure of the origins of the monument on Carrock Fell. John Pool indicates this in his poem

'A Tour of Carrock Fell'

In the ancient parish of Caldbeck,
Where Alpine regions, range,
Ther's none more famed than Carrock,
For noted things and strange:
In April, on a Monday,
In eighteen-sixty-two,
I ventured then to climb it,
To have a distant view,
In company with two shepherds,
To the summit, I did stroll;
What I saw, and what they told me,
May be written in a scroll.
To mount its rugged sides
Is not an easy task;
But we did it very easily,
Without a spirit flask.
We talked of nature's beauties,
And drank of "Mountain View";
We had it clear as crystal,
As it gurgled fresh and new.
There's "Brandy Well" at the bottom,
And "Cold Kail" by the way,
And a hundred other little springs,
That flow by night and day.
We talked of nature's Maker,
His wisdom and his love;
We sent a prayer of thanks
To him that reigns above.
Thus lingering as we went,
Before we reached the top,
About two hours had gone,
When the summit made us stop.

Our attention's first attracted
By a curious circular wall,
The stones are piled together,
In sizes great and small:
The enclosure is four acres,
And of an oval shape;
Some say "it was a battery
For soldiers to escape:"
Others say: it was for judges,
Who gravely read the law,
And punished all the criminals
For deeds done down below;"
And others tell of worshippers,
Who met in ancient time;
Who chaunted on the summit,
As being near the land sublime.
Ther's a heap of stones collected,
And placed about the middle,
But to tell the why and wherefore
Would seem to be a riddle.
Tel - why the wall around?
And spaces where to enter?
For judge, for priest, for soldier,
Now - which did dare to enter?
-------------- etc..

6. John Peel - made famous by a song

John Peel, the famous huntsman, was born at Park End in Caldbeck. The date of his birth is not known but he was baptised in St. Kentigern's Church, Caldbeck on the 24th September 1777. He fell in love, while still quite young, with Mary White of Uldale and they were to be wed. However, when the banns were called in church, her mother objected on the grounds:-

"Ther far ower yung"

John, however, was not to be so easily thwarted. Soon after, he followed the example of his parents before him, and eloped with Mary to Gretna Green on his mare *"Binsey, "*where they were wed over the blacksmith's anvil. Mrs White soon forgave them and, accepting the situation, endowed the couple with land worth several hundred pounds a year. From then on John never looked back. He worked the land covered by the present Blencathra Foxhounds and soon built up a local reputation as a hunter of note. He hunted with his hounds at least twice a week, wearing his coat of *'gray'* made from the local Herdwick wool. It is often said that John Peel hunted on foot as do the Lakeland huntsmen of today. Undoubtedly he did hunt on foot at times, especially

John Peel

in his earlier years, but his greatest hunts were on horseback. Indeed John maintained his famous pack of twentyfour hounds and two hunting horses for about fifty five years. John, unlike the huntsmen further south, did not hunt in scarlet as is depicted in some portraits. Like his fellow Cumbrians, he wore a coat of *'Hodden Gray,'* often known locally as *'Skiddaw Gray.'*

Even before his friend, John Graves, wrote the song that eventually immortalised his name, he became famous for his prowess as a huntsmen. He is reputed to have lived on a diet of porridge and milk for breakfast followed by only one other meal; of vegetables and meat, later in the afternoon. He must have been extremely fit to have run with the hounds over so many years. He often covered upwards of twenty miles in a day over very difficult country with its stone walls, peat bogs, undulating fields and craggy hills. In middle age John Peel became very friendly with John Woodcock Graves who, one winter night in 1832, whilst reminiscing with Peel, put pen to paper and wrote the now famous song. It was John's autobiography which included details of his friendship with Peel that provided the wealth of detail about how the song came to be written thus:-

"We were then both in the heyday of manhood, and hunters of the olden fashion; meeting the night before to arrange earth stopping, and in the morning to take the best part of the hunt - the drag over the mountains

in the mist - while fashionable hunters still lay in the blankets. Large flakes of snow fell that evening. We sat by the fireside hunting over again many a good run, and recalling the feats of each particular hound, or narrow neck-break 'scapes, when a flaxen-haired daughter of mine came in saying, 'Father what do they say to what granny sings ?'

Granny was singing to sleep my eldest son - now a leading barrister in Hobart Town - with a very old rant called 'Bonnie (or Canny) Annie.'

The pen and ink for hunting appointments being on the table, the idea of writing a song to this old air forced itself upon me, and thus was produced, impromptu,

'D'ye ken John Peel with his coat so gray.'

When Peel heard the song he smiled, through a stream of tears, and John Graves jokingly said to him: 'Bye Jove, Peel, You'll be sung when were both run to earth.' "

It was many years later however before the song became widely known in its present form. John Peel died at Ruthwaite, near Ireby, on Monday 13th November 1854. The song "D'ye ken John Peel" only became nationally famous after it was polished up, with Grave's approval, by one George Coward, who was preparing a book of "Songs and Ballads of Cumberland."

The first verse and chorus of the song follow:

D' ye ken John Peel with his coat ..so gray ?

D' ye ken John Peel at the break of the day ?

D' ye ken John Peel when he's
                  far, far a..way ?
With his hounds and his horn
                  in the morn..ing ?
Twas the sound of his horn brought
                  me from my bed.
And the cry of his hounds has me
                  off..times led;
For Peel's view hol..loa would
                  wa..ken the dead,
Or a fox from his lair in the morn..ing.

7. Norse influence - evidence from the place and mountain names

The names of the places and valleys around Blencathra indicate that the indigenous Celts survived the invasions of the Angle and the Norsemen. A document of 1278 relating to a dispute between Lord Thomas de Derwentwater and William de Threlkeld calls the river Glenderamakin by the name *'Glenermakan.'* McIntyre suggests that this is the Celtic *'Glyndyfr-Mcchyn;'* 'the river of the swine.' Similarly *'Glenderterra'* (Glenderterray in an old boundary role) looks like *'Glyndyfr-derw'* or Oak-dale river. The place names in the easily accessible and more fertile valleys such as at Threlkeld are undoubtedly Norse in origin. Threlkeld, for example, is from the Norse *'Thraela Kelda'* which means The *'Thralls'* or Bondsman's Well. The Norsemen soon worked their way higher into the country to establish their sheep runs. Thus we have Berrier (Bergherge in a document of 1166), the *'erghe'* or mountain pasture of the rocks. *'Scales'* is from *'skalar,'* (huts) and Bowscale from *'boll-skala,'* (farmstead huts). All of these lie on the lower slopes of Blencathra. It would appear, from the retention of the Celtic names in the more remote areas, that the Norse settlers allowed the British inhabitants to remain as serfs to work their farms.

8. Sharp Edge, Blencathra - as seen by an early fellwalker.

Visitors to the area in the eighteenth century often went in fear and awe of the mountains. A good example is the account following of an ascent of Sharp Edge from Scales Tarn by Mr Green; the narrator, and Mr Jonathan Otley, a well known Lakeland character of the late 18th century.

"-we crossed the stream which issues from the tarn and commenced the steep ascent at the foot of Sharp Edge. We had not gone far before we were aware that our journey would be attended with peril. The passage gradually grew narrower and the declivity on each hand awfully precipitious. From walking on it we were reduced to the necessity either of bestriding the ridge or of moving on one of its sides with our hands lying over the top, as security against tumbling into the tarn on the left or into a frightful gully on the right, both of immense depth. Sometimes we thought it prudent to return; but that seemed unmanly and we proceeded thinking with Shakespeare that 'Dangers retreat when boldly they are confronted.'"

These terrifying descriptions in the guide books of the time obviously reflected and probably affected the ordinary person's attitude to these wild places. Another account of an excursion of four people from Threlkeld to the summit of Blencathra describes how, as they climbed from the valley, one of the party was

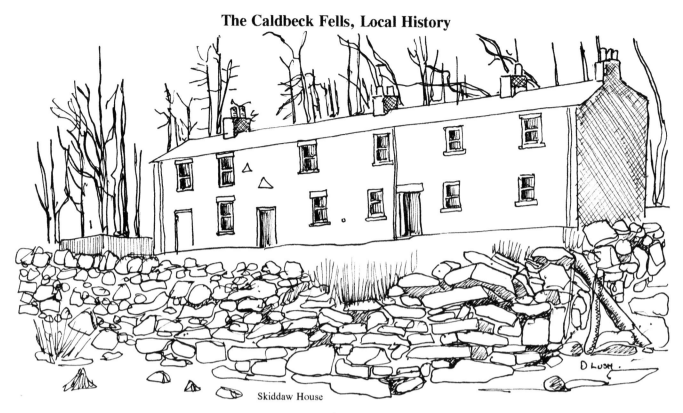

Skiddaw House

so *"astonished with the different appearance of objects in the valley beneath,"* that he chose to return home. Before they had gone much further another of the four was suddenly taken ill and *"wished to lose blood to calm him down."* However he was persuaded to continue as far as Scales Tarn where the party, now reduced to three, *"contemplated the scene with a westruck wonder."* Not surprisingly perhaps, the potential blood letter refused to continue and was left at the tarn. His companions made their way to the summit up the steep slope to the south of Scales Tarn. On returning, by way of Sharp Edge, the narrator described his impressions as follows:

'We walked back by the side next to the lake, but to look down from thence was so terrible, I could not endure it a moment. We perceived from thence, that my companion, whom we had last left, was laid upon the ground; I pressed the guide to hasten to him, but he refused, alleging that a fog was rising, and it would be very hazardous for me to explore my way alone down the mountain: in a short time we were enveloped in a very dense vapour, so that we were obliged to keep near each other; the sudden change was almost incredible. It was with difficulty that my guide regained the passage, or dry bridge, which we missed on several attempts; and one incautious step would have plunged us into the horrid abyss.'

No further mention is made of the hapless bloodletter so I presume they met up with him on the way down. There was obviously a shortage of Mountain Leadership courses in those days. It goes without saying that you should not abandon people in distress half way up a mountain.

> *"On stern Blencartha's perilous height*
> *The winds are tyrannous and strong;*
> *And flashing forth unsteady light*
> *From stern Blencartha's skiey height,*
> *As loud the torrents throng!*
> *Beneath the moon in gentle weather*
> *They blend the earth and sky together.*
> *But o! the sky and all her forms how quiet!*
> *The things that seek the earth how full of*
> *noise and riot!"*

Coleridge

9. Skiddaw House and the Cumbria Way

Situated in an isolated grove of trees on the north east of Sale How and lying approximately midway between Bassenthwaite village and Threlkeld, Skiddaw House is an unexpected sight in such remote terrain. The house was originally built for the gamekeepers and shepherds who worked on the Lonsdale Estate. Remains of grouse butts can be seen about half a mile to the northwest of the house. Today Skiddaw House has been converted into a youth hostel for walkers on the Cumbria Way. The Cumbria Way is a modern long distance path which traverses the Lake District from north to south using many of the old bridleways. As it rises from Keswick up on to Latrigg and traverses round Lonscale Crags towards

36

Skiddaw House the path follows what is probably the old sled route from Lonscale Quarries. This would be used to transport the stone and slate which was used to build Crosthwaite Church and other buildings in Keswick from the twelfth century onwards.

Mosedale seen from Skiddaw House

10. Spectre Army of Souther Fell

Stories of ghosts and unexplained visions are plentiful when one delves into local history. Few, however, are so well corroborated with dates, times and named observers as the story of the spectre army seen on Souther Fell. There are several versions of this happening in the eighteenth century. One of the most detailed is that of Harriet Martineau in her 'Guide to the English Lakes' of 1855.

I quote from her account :

"On Midsummer eve 1735 a farm servant in the employ of William Lancaster of Blake Hills Farm, half a mile east of Souther Fell, saw the east side of the mountain, near the summit, covered with troops, which pursued their onward march for over an hour. They came, in distinct bodies, from an eminence in the north end, and disappeared in a niche in the summit. When the poor fellow told his tale he was insulted on all hands; as original observers usually are when they see anything wonderful. Two years after, also on Midsummer's eve, Mr Lancaster saw some men there, apparently following their horses, as if they had returned from hunting. He thought nothing of this; but he happened to look up again ten minutes after, and saw the figures now mounted, and followed by an interminable array of troops, five abreast, marching from the eminence and over the cleft, as before. All the family saw this, and the manoeuvres of the force, as each company was kept in order by a mounted officer who galloped this way and that. As the shades of twilight came on, the discipline appeared to relax, and the troops intermingled, and rode at unequal paces, 'til all was lost in darkness. Now, of course, all the Lancasters were insulted, as their servant had been: but their justification was not long delayed. On the Midsummer day of the fearful 1745, twenty six persons, expressly summoned by the family, saw all that had been seen before and more. Carriages were now interspersed with the troops; and everybody knew that no carriages ever had been, or could be, on the summit of Souther Fell. The multitude was beyond imagination; for the troops filled a space of half a mile, and marched quickly 'til night hid them, - still marching.' There was nothing vaporous or indistinct about these spectres. So real did they seem that some of the people went up, the next morning, to look for the hoof-marks of the horses; and awful it was to them to find not one foot-print on heather or grass. The witnesses attested the whole story on oath before a magistrate; and fearful were the expectations held by the countryside about the coming events of the Scotch rebellion.

It now came out that two other persons had seen something of the sort in the interval, viz., in 1743, - but had concealed it to escape the insults to which their neighbours were subjected. Mr Wren, of Wilton Hill, and his farm servant, saw, one summer evening, a man and his dog on the mountain, pursuing some horses along a place so steep that a horse could hardly, by any possibility, keep a footing on it. Their speed was prodigious, and their disappearance at the top of the fell so rapid, that Mr Wren and the servant went up, the next morning, to find the body of the man who must have been killed. Of man, horse or dog thay found not a trace: and they came down and held their tongues. When they did speak, they fared not much better for having twentysix sworn comrades in their disgrace."

So look for ghosts if you will on Souther Fell but don't expect anyone to believe you if you see them.

****

D. LUSH.

West of Buttermere

General

The small group of fells bounded by Buttermere, Crummock Water and Ennerdale range from low rolling hills at the northwest corner to the steep and rugged cliffs of Red Pike and High Stile which tower above Buttermere. The area can be conveniently split into two parts. Most of the higher fells lie on a ridge which rises north of Ennerdale and takes in Great Borne, Starling Dodd, Red Pike, High Stile and High Crag. The route along this ridge forms part of the renowned Ennerdale Horseshoe, perhaps the toughest round in Lakeland. The remainder of the area consists of lower rounded hills, which are dominated by Blake Fell and Mellbreak. These hills should not be overlooked because of their lower stature. Some of the finest and most unexpected views of the area are to be found around Cogra Moss and Mellbreak.

Walking

The higher fells above Buttermere offer a challenge to the more energetic walker whilst, in contrast, the forest tracks around Cogra Moss are ideal for an easy introduction to the delights of hill walking. Between these extremes there is fine walking to be had on and around Mellbreak including the spectacular Scale Force waterfall.

Selected Walks

Route 1.　　　　　Cogra Moss **(F)**
A circular walk around the Cogra Basin which follows mine and forestry tracks

Total climbing about 400 ft　　(122m)
(5 miles)

This little known tarn, used as a reservoir and fished by Cockermouth Angling Club, lies under the northern face of Knockmurton Fell, the iron mountain. The southern slopes of the fell still bear the scars left by the haematite miners of the Kelton and Knockmurton Mine which was worked from 1853 to the early

West of Buttermere

1900's. This is a good introductory walk for youngsters or friends yet to be convinced about the pleasures of hill walking. The route takes the walker into some quite dramatic scenery without a lot of effort being required.

Park your car at the point where the old mine railway crosses the road **(H)** and climb over the stile onto the disused railway embankment. Our route leads along the top of the embankment, with a slight detour to avoid the fenced off bridge (Danger!). The path follows the embankment to the point where it merges with the gated Forestry Commission track **(G)**. A hundred years ago this area would have been a hive of industry as iron ore was lowered down the hill to be loaded onto waiting ore wagons for transport by rail to West Cumbrian ironworks. Now little remains but the railway embankment and the spoil heaps, which mark the mine entrances high up the fellside.

This part of the route, although of historic interest, is rather dull to the eye and gives no warning of what is to come. Go through the gate or climb the stile and follow the track which now leads up through the forest and soon levels off to reveal a breath-taking view of the Cogra Basin. Two hundred feet below is Cogra Moss surrounded by wooded slopes which climb steeply up the western flanks of Blake Fell and Sharp Knott. The forest road contours round this enclosed valley giving spectacular views of the small lake below and the flatter land to the west. Follow the track round until a fork is reached below Sharp Knott **(C)**. As this is about half way round and the highest point on the route, it is a good place for a refreshment stop.

To continue, take the left hand track which gradually turns south as it drops down between High How and Bield towards the Moss. At the next sharp turn right leave the main track and follow the firebreak 100 m west to the fence at the edge of the wood. The fence can now be followed downhill to the waterside where a fisherman's path will take you round the lake, over the spillway and onto the access road to the moss **(F)**. To avoid a road walk take the track east along the southern edge of the Moss. In about half a mile, at the end of the old iron fence, a steep track forks right climbing up through the wood

round the eastern flank of Knockmurton Fell. This sheltered little track will take you back to the point where you first observed the Cogra Basin. The forestry road can now be retraced back to your car.

Access from Ennerdale, Bowness Knott (L)

Route 2.   Red Pike from Ennerdale
via Great Borne and Starling Dodd
Return via Gillerthwaite
Total Climbing about 2500 ft   (762 m)
(10 miles)

This route, as far as Red Pike, is the first seven miles of the Ennerdale Horseshoe previously mentioned. Park your car in the Forestry Commission car park at Bowness Knotts on the north side of the lake. Unfortunately we must begin by retracing our steps. Follow the road back towards Ennerdale Bridge for about a mile until a bridle path signposted 'Floutern Tarn' appears on the right hand side of the road. Follow this path north and then east as it gently climbs the shallow valley between Banna Fell and Herdus. In just over a mile a brow is reached which overlooks Floutern Tarn, immediately below, with Crummock Water in the distance beyond. Believe it or not it was once proposed to bring a rail link up into this wild place to serve the iron mines around the tarn. Luckily nothing came of the proposal, the iron mines closed down and the land reverted to its present untamed state.

To your right a fence climbs the steep northern slope of Steel Brow leading to the summit of Great Borne. Leave the Floutern Tarn track at this point, climb the stile and follow the track up by the fence. After a steep scramble you will emerge onto the broad boggy summit plateau of Great Borne. The rather indistinct path meanders in a south easterly direction, gradually rising to the summit cairn of the mountain. From here the broad ridge leads gently down and then up again connecting Great Borne to the slightly higher top of Starling Dodd, one and a half miles ahead. From here the Dodd is rather unimpressive as a peak, hardly appearing to rise above the general level of the ridge. The grandeur of the view lies in the vastness of the open top with the higher peaks of Red Pike and High Stile rising in the background. On a good day the rest of the walk is a gentle stroll across the wide ridge to Starling Dodd and Little Dodd, followed by a more strenuous climb to the ironstone summit of the aptly named Red Pike. Apart from the final climb up to Red Pike the track follows the old boundary fence along the crest of the ridge. This can be useful in mist. The return route involves a steep drop down into Ennerdale from the summit of Red Pike. A path, cairned near the summit, drops away to the southwest leading one down through a gap in the forest and reaching the forestry road at High Gillerthwaite. From here it is a two mile stroll along the lakeside track back to Bowness Knotts car park.

Access from Buttermere Village (J)

Route 3.   Red Pike, High Stile, High Crag
        Return by Scarth Gap
                and Lakeside Path

        Total Climbing about 2300 ft   (704 m)
            (7 miles)

                or
Route 4.   As above but return by
        Scale Force Waterfall (I)
        Total Climbing about 2150 ft   (655 m)
            (5.5 miles)

Park your car in the large car park adjacent to the Fish Hotel at Buttermere **(LH 1)** and follow the farm access road leading towards the lake. Take the main track to the footbridge below Burtness Wood at the northwestern end of Buttermere Lake. After crossing the bridge go through the gate or climb the stile into Burtness Wood. You can now follow the excellent path, recently rebuilt by the National Trust, which winds up through Burtness Wood towards Bleaberry Tarn. On leaving the wood the path traverses to the west across the lower slopes of High Stile before crossing Sour Milk Gill, just below the tarn. A warning should be issued here. If descending by this route do **NOT** be tempted to take a short cut and follow the Sour Milk Gill Gorge down to Buttermere. Several people, some of them experienced fell walkers, have come to grief in recent years. Keep to the recommended route and stay alive. The rather eroded path now

The eroded path onto the Dodd
Red Pike, Buttermere

leads steeply up onto Dodd; the eastern buttress of Red Pike, which rises to the north of Bleaberry Tarn. From here it is a less strenuous pull up to the saddle and hence round onto the summit of Red Pike.

On a fine still day this is a pleasant place to linger. There are panoramic views in all directions. The valleys radiate outwards like the spokes of wheel with Ennerdale to the west, Loweswater and Crummock Water to the north, the Newlands Valley with Derwentwater and Keswick beyond to the northeast, and Buttermere below us to the east. Having feasted your eyes on the view and your stomach on your sandwiches, you must decide on the return route.

Route 3. Return via High Stile and High Crag

This is an exhilarating ridge walk which includes two miles of the Ennerdale Horseshoe from Red Pike to just beyond High Crag. Follow the ridge path south from the summit of Red Pike as it takes you down forty or fifty metres before rising again to the craggy and boulder strewn top of High Stile. At 807 m this is the highest point on the ridge. The route now drops down onto the narrow col between High Stile and High Crag. To your left the buttresses of Eagle and Grey Crags **(K)** tower above Burtness Comb, a favourite haunt of rock climbers. Many of Lakeland's pioneer rock climbers developed their expertise on these crags. One of the more notable of these, W Peascod, pioneered the climb 'Eagle Front' up the face of Eagle Crag. This still ranks as possibly the hardest and best route in the district. Unfortunately eagles are no longer to be found on Eagle Crag. They were not

Eagle Crag, Buttermere

frightened away by the rock climbers, rather they were persecuted by the local folk. According to Edward Bogg, eagles have not nested on Eagle Crag since about 1800. Around that time one John Vicars of Borrowdale twice robbed nests of their young and eventually shot both parents.

From High Crag a very eroded, loose and rather dangerous path drops steeply down to the lower top of Seat. This would be a good place for the National Trust to put to use their excellent path repairing skills. No doubt they will in time. At the bottom of this steep section we have a choice of routes. One path drops down to the left of Seat and meets the Scarth Gap track lower down Buttermere Fell. The other path, the main one, carries on over Seat and down onto the col of Scarth Gap. The Scarth Gap track can then be followed north to the southern end of Buttermere. On reaching the lake, follow the track along the western shore which takes you through Burtness Wood and back to Buttermere village.

Route 4. Return via Scale Force **(I)**

This shorter route home follows the ridge path northwest as it drops down, above Lingcomb Edge, from the summit of Red Pike. In about half a mile the main path turns southwest towards Starling Dodd but our route continues in a northerly direction along Lingcomb Edge,

Scale Force
Buttermere

dropping gently to a large cairn above Blea Crag. About 100 yds before the cairn a good cairned path drops gently down into the valley between Gale Fell and the Blea Crag Ridge. This path converges on Scale Beck leading one to the head of Scale Force Waterfall (LH 2). The main path drops into the narrow gorge carrying Scale Beck on the right hand side of the stream. The gorge follows a vein of ironstone thus explaining the deep red colouration of the soil and rocks on the path. Indeed the path actually passes over the spoil heaps of old iron workings as it emerges at the foot of the gorge. The main drop of Scales Force waterfall, Lakeland's longest at 172 ft, is best seen from the bottom of the gorge. The roar of the water can be heard as you descend the path but it would be difficult to view from above without risking life and limb due to the depth and sheerness of the drop. Unfortunately a large rock outcrop blocks a full view of the falls from the bottom and the iron ladder, originally set in it to overcome this obstacle, has long since disappeared. This obstacle can be scaled with difficulty by the determined and agile photographer but, beware, it is slippery and potentially dangerous in wet weather.

Apart from the spoil heaps of old iron working in this area there is evidence of early settlement in the form of earthworks (LH 4). The path now bears east towards Crummock Water. There are several possible routes but the driest path contours round the base of Blea Crag keeping well above Scale Beck. This path is well marked with small cairns as it turns southeast above the western shore of Crummock Water. Follow this path for a mile until you can fork left down the farm access road which leads back to Buttermere village.

Access from Loweswater

Route 5   Mellbreak from Park Bridge,
                  (Loweswater) (E)
                  Return via Mosedale
           Total climbing about 1330 ft (405 m)
                      (4.5 miles)

This is only one of several short but scenic walks which are possible in this area. Suitable for an afternoon or evening in summer or a short day walk in the winter. Mellbreak is a dramatic mountain, although its summit is only about 400 metres above the surrounding terrain. Its precipitious sides make it appear much higher. Seen from the Kirkstile Inn it looms like a giant sugarloaf above the village. There is limited parking beside Park Bridge so, on a busy day, it may be necessary to use the car park at Maggies's Bridge (B) near the southern end of Loweswater. The first part of the route takes us along the bridle path which passes through Low Park and contours round the northern face of Mellbreak just above Flass

Mellbreak from Loweswater village

Wood. This track continues on into Mosedale, the valley between Mellbreak and Hen Combe. As you contour round the mountain a grassy track will be seen which bears off to the left and climbs up to the screes at the northwest corner of the mountain. Follow this track which winds its way up the steep and broken hillside called Raven Crag on the 1:25000 map. It is invariably windy up here but the views can be spectacular. At the top of the crag, where the path becomes less steep and turns south up towards the summit, detour to the east for a few yards for a sheltered viewpoint overlooking Crummock Water. From here excellent views are to be had of

West of Buttermere

Grasmoor, Whiteside and Hopegill Head to the east. Directly below is Crummock Water stretching away to the south with Buttermere beyond. Refreshed after a well earned break, the rest of the walk to the first summit of Mellbreak is a relatively easy plod south along the ridge, which broadens out considerably as the summit cairn is reached. However we are still not at the highest point on Mellbreak. The second summit, half a mile further south across the broad plateau, is three metres higher than our present vantage point. In our walk across to this, our second goal, we must first descend and then re-ascend fifty metres or so across a rather marshy depression. This extra effort is well rewarded by fine views of the fells to the west of Ennerdale with Dale Head and Fleetwith Pike rising beyond Buttermere Lake.

The return journey involves retracing your steps into the depression between the two summits. Then, bearing northwest, follow the line of the stream which rises here and flows down into Mosedale. There are two paths, one drops straight down into the valley just north of the stream, the other contours north along the side of the mountain only gradually losing height. I would recommend the latter route as it is more interesting and varied. Both paths eventually rejoin the bridleway on which we commenced the expedition. From here it is a short brisk walk back to the car, with the promise of a pint and a bar meal at the Kirkstile Inn to end a perfect day.

This walk can easily be extended if more time is available. For example, from the top of Mellbreak one could descend into Mosedale and follow the track west up to Floutern Tarn. From the tarn climb the ridge to the north leading up into Gavel Fell and on to Blake Fell. This route gives views to the west of Knockmurton Fell with Cogra Moss below. From Blake Fell follow the ridge which falls away to the northeast onto Carling Knott **(A)** **(LH 4)**. From the summit of Carling Knott take care to avoid the crags to the east and descend the northwestern flank to the track above Holme Wood. Turn left along this wide grassy track and, about two hundred metres before the track crosses Holme Beck, a stile is reached giving access over the wall into Holme Wood. A leafy track now leads diagonally

The Post Office Gillerthwaite, a hundred years ago
Sir Rowland Hill and his penny post scheme - over the page - >

down through the wood to the southern shore of Loweswater. From here just follow the footpath and farm road in an easterly direction back to Loweswater village. This area, owned by the National Trust, is criss-crossed by several scenic and sheltered paths which meander through the woods and the area around the lake. It is ideal for a family afternoon out.

*****

Lakes to visit

Buttermere, Cogra Moss, Crummock Water, Ennerdale Water, Loweswater

Nearest Towns

Cockermouth, Egremont, Keswick, Whitehaven, Workington

Places to visit

Cumberland Toy and Model Museum, Cockermouth
Helena Thompson Museum, Workington
Maryport Maritime Museum
Senhouse Roman Army Museum, Maryport
Whitehaven Museum
Wordsworth's House, Cockermouth

Recommended Country Inns
(Good Ale and Food)

The Kirkstile Inn   Loweswater
The Fish Hotel   Buttermere

Sir Rowland Hill and his Penny Post

Sir Rowland Hill visited Buttermere before the introduction of his penny post scheme. He saw a young woman at a cottage door refuse a letter that the postman had brought. Thinking that she could not afford the high postal rates then prevailing, Sir Rowland spoke to her, but was informed that there was no need for his concern. The letter was from her brother who was working at Penrith and he and his sister had agreed that, if he were able to come for a holiday at Martinmas, he should put a cross on the right hand corner of the envelope; if he were unable to do so, on the left hand corner. The cross, the maiden blushingly informed Sir Rowland, was on the right hand corner so her brother would be coming at Martinmas. According to this account the Buttermere folk were certainly careful with their money. **(W.T. McIntyre in the Cumberland News 1939).**

However **Morris Danesborough**, writing in **Cumbria Magazine**, maintains that this story is untrue. Sir Rowland did visit Lakeland in 1823 and kept his family informed of his whereabouts and state of health by a similar method to that described in the tale above. He is purported to have sent copies of old newspapers to his family, having previously franked the wrappers with the names of M.P.'s (who were allowed to send so many letters free of charge). The postmark indicated the place visited and the name of the M.P. indicated his state of health. The names of Liberal M.P.'s showed that he was in good fettle whilst those of Tory members that he was not so well.

The tale of the Buttermere girl originates from an anecdote of Coleridge in **Letters, Conversations and Recollections of S.T. Coleridge.** Coleridge describes passing a cottage near Keswick where a postman was demanding a shilling for a letter: The woman refused to pay and the postman was about to take the letter away when Coleridge paid the fee. The woman told him that the letter was from her son and that its arrival was sufficient to tell her that he was well. The woman had no intention of paying and when the letter was opened it was found to be blank. Such frauds were in fact very common and Sir Rowland Hill mentioned Coleridge's experience in a pamphlet on post office reform published in 1837. Distortions of the story eventually led to the version given earlier where Coleridge became Sir Rowland and the son became her brother. The distorted version was given even more credence when it was described by **Miss Harriet Martineau** in her book
'A History of England during the Thirty Years' Peace,' published in 1849

LUSH

West of Buttermere, Local History

1. The Beauty of Buttermere

Mary Robinson, known as 'The Beauty of Buttermere,' became famous in the late 18th century as a result of an account given of her by the author of "A Fortnight's Ramble to the Lakes in Westmorland, Lancaster and Cumberland" (1792), see below. Unfortunately this brought her to the attention of one John Hatfield, a dashing rogue and impostor, who left a trail of unpaid bills and fraudulent transactions wherever he went. John, later known as the Keswick impostor, took up residence at the Queen's Head Keswick in July 1802. He then proceeded to woo Mary, the innkeeper's daughter at Buttermere, and eventually married her using the assumed name of Alexander Augustus Hope, brother of the Earl of Hopetoun. The wedding took place at Lorton Church on October 2nd 1802, the groom having concealed the fact that he already had a wife and two children at Tiverton.

Alas, soon afterwards, his crimes caught up with him. The notice of his wedding in a Scottish newspaper brought his debtors on his trail. He was arrested, arraigned at Carlisle and sentenced to death for forgery. Even in those times this penalty was considered to be exceptionally harsh and, not surprisingly, he appealed. There was widespread public sympathy for his plight but the expected reprieve was not forthcoming and John Hatfield was publicly hanged at the Sands, Carlisle, on Saturday September 3rd 1803. Mary, who by this time was expecting a child, eventually got over this experience. She was married to a local statesman and lived to a ripe old age. Contemporary accounts of the hanging, which took place on the island between Eden Bridges at Carlisle, describe John's perfect manners and bravery as he calmly accepted his fate:

"As soon as the carriage door had been opened by the under-sheriff, he alighted with his two companions. A small dung-cart, boarded over, had been placed under the gibbet, and a ladder was placed against it, which he instantly ascended. He was dressed in a black jacket, black silk waistcoat, fustian pantaloons, shoes and white cotton stockings. He was perfectly cool and collected. At the same time, his conduct displayed nothing of levity, of insensibility, or of hardihood. He was more anxious to give proof of resignation than of heroism. His countenance was extremely pale, but his hand never trembled. He immediately untied his neck handkerchief, and placed a bandage over his eyes. Then he desired the hangman, who was extremely awkward, to be as expert as possible about it, and that he would wave a handkerchief when he was ready. The hangman, not having fixed the rope in its proper place, he put up his hand and turned it himself. Then he requested the jailer would step on the platform and pinion his arms a little harder saying

that, when he had lost his senses, he might attempt to lift them to his neck. The rope was completely fixed about five minutes before five o'clock: it was slack, and he merely said, 'May the Allmighty bless you all.' Nor did he falter in the least, when he tied the cap, shifted the rope, and took the handkerchief from his neck. Having taken leave of the jailer and sheriff, he prepared himself for his fate. He was at this time heard to exclaim, 'My spirit is strong, though my body is weak.' Great apprehensions were entertained that it would be necessary to tie him up a second time. The noose slipped twice, and he fell down about eighteen inches. His feet at last were almost touching the ground, but his excessive weight, which occasioned this accident, speedily relieved him from pain. He expired in a moment and without any struggle."

The Life of John Hatfield (1846).

Dramatic as this true life situation was, the popular press at the time had to embellish it. About 1841 a novel was published in three volumes for the circulating library entitled "James Hatfield and the Beauty of Buttermere" by Robert Cruickshank. The description of the hero's demise in the novel illustrates the free use of artistic licence in these matters. According to the novel, John (James in the book) was accompanied to the scaffold by his friend Mr Fenton; the curate of Lorton. Mr Fenton, overcome with the situation, promptly collapsed and died. As he fell to the ground he was caught and supported by the hangman's victim. This of course brought cries from the crowd for the hanging to be stopped, as it was obviously a sign from heaven. To no avail. As the trapdoor dropped, Mary appeared, distraught, at the foot of the scaffold.

Apparently this story still has an appeal today. Only recently the Cumbrian author Melvyn Bragg has written a novel around this tale.

There follows an extract from a Lakeland guide, first published in 1792, in which the author, Joseph Budsworth, describes his first encounter with the girl who was to become known as 'The Beauty of Buttermere.' In his book Mary is referred to as 'Sally of Buttermere.'

"Her mother and she were spinning woollen yarn in the back kitchen; on our going into it, the girl flew away as swift as a mountain sheep, and it was not

until our return from Scale Force, that we could say we first saw her; she brought in part of our dinner,

Sally Robinson

and seemed to be about fifteen. Her hair was thick and long, of a dark brown, and though unadorned with ringlets, did not seem to want them; her face was a fine contour, with full eyes, and lips as red as vermillion; her cheeks had more of the lily than the rose and although she had never been out of the village, (and, I hope, will have no ambition to wish it) she had a manner about her which seemed better calculated to set off dress, than dress her. She was a very Lavinia, "seeming when unadorn'd, adorn'd the most." When we first saw her at her distaff, after she had got the better of her first fears, she looked an angel, and I doubt not but she is the "reigning lily" of the valley."

(A Rambler, 1792)

2. Cruelty to Animals in the 1790's

Unfortunately cruelty to our domestic animals is not a new phenonemon. In the book mentioned above the author describes his visit to Scale Force Waterfall. He recounts that they saw local people hurling dogs over the 172 ft fall for 'sport.' He and his party were most disturbed at this and urged the locals to desist. This, thankfully, they did whilst expressing surprise because other visitors had previously enjoyed the spectacle. It was apparently laid on as a spectator sport for visitors. His moving account of how the poor wretched creatures (those that survived the fall) "limped away looking bewildered at the treatment they had received from their owners," showed a compassion that was sadly lacking in the local Buttermere folk.

3. Deaths in a flood at Loweswater

There have been many lives lost over the years in the district due to both natural and man-made calamities. One such happening at Loweswater was recounted by Edmund Bogg in 1902:

"Many years ago a small reservoir, or tarn, on the hill above the lake, burst, and came rolling in one huge wave towards the lake; a farm stood in its path, and one of the occupants, a girl who was outside the house, saw the dark mass of water sweeping downwards. Darting into the house, she informed the inmates (the master and a female) of the occurrence. These two had just reached the outside of the door in their endeavour to escape, when the wave caught them both, swept them into the lake, and their bodies were never discovered, whilst strange to say, the girl, who was first to discover the inundation, was saved by the water forcibly banging the door in her face and holding her prisoner, when she was in the act of following the other persons."

The small dam was across Crabtree Beck and provided water for Loweswater lead mine which is situated in Kirkhill Wood, immediately west of the Kirkstile Inn.

Loweswater
showing Crabtree Beck

4. Early Inhabitants

There is evidence that stone age man inhabited this remote corner of our district. Two great tumuli are to be found on the summit of Carling Knott (A), marking the tombs of the people living around Loweswater long ago. Also, about one quarter of a mile NNE of Floutern Tarn is the remains of one of their pit dwellings. It appears that these early people ventured high on the fells as, in 1868, a stone hammer was found on the side of Mellbreak about 1700 ft above sea level. Later inhabitants were probably responsible for the large earthwork (D) about half a mile south of Loweswater village on the track to Mosedale. This three sided rampart of earth

Stone age man on Mellbreak ?

about three feet high and measuring 136 ft by 70 ft was probably a fort built by Romanised Britons to defend themselves after their abandonment by Rome. According to MacIntyre the name 'Loweswater' indicates that the area was occupied by Norse invaders in the 10th century. Written records of the name appeared as *Laweswater* (1188), *Lowswater* (1190), and *Lousewatre,* (1343). The early name 'Lawes' is best explained as the possessive form of the Norse personal name Laghi.

Crummock Water

was referred to as Crombokwatre in 1343 and is thought to be from the old English word meaning
'crooked '

North of Whinlatter

General

This extreme northwest corner of the national park has a charm all of it's own. The group of fells encircling Wythop Moss, although small compared with their neighbours further south, are well worth a visit. This is one of the few areas in the Lake District where one can still find solitude.

Walking

All of the fell tops offer relatively easy, safe walking. The only crags to be avoided lie directly above Whinlatter Top and to the east of Barf. Due to the remoteness of the area paths are often not well defined and occasionally disappear and reappear, so the walker must be prepared for this. The map only shows paths where they are well defined and easy to follow.

Access

Access to the tops may be gained from :
1. Whinlatter Forest - The forest is criss-crossed by forest tracks which are all open to walkers. Several of these tracks give access to the adjacent tops of Broom Fell and Lords Seat, both of which provide open vistas of the surrounding fells and the coast to the west. (Forest track map available at Whinlatter Visitor Centre **(M)**, see below)

2. Beckstones (I) - Here one has the choice of two routes to the top of Barf. The first, which follows Beckstones Gill, is a relatively straightforward but rewarding walk. The second which takes one past the famous white painted Bishop Rock, **(LH2)**, is a very stiff scramble over loose scree which gives way higher up to rocky outcrops (2 star rating). The summit gives excellent views of Bassenthwaite, Skiddaw and Keswick. From the car park opposite the Swan Hotel follow the narrow tarmacadam track. The wishing gate that appears to the right of the track is the path to the Bishop rock. For the Beckstones Gill path, continue on a further hundred yards or so until you see a stile on your right just beyond the point where the track crosses the gill.

3. Woodend Brow Picnic Site (H) - From the car park follow the old road north towards Beck Wythop for about 100m. and on your left you will see a public footpath signpost to Wythop Hall. This path winds up through the forest, past the remains of the ill fated silica brickworks **(G)**, **(LH6)**, to Wythop Hall and

Wythop Moss beyond. This is an ideal area to explore for those requiring solitude and remoteness without climbing too high. I would warn you, however, that due to forestry workings, the path up through the forest can be difficult to follow.

4. Wythop Mill (C) - Follow the back road to Cockermouth westwards from the top of the village as it skirts round Ling Fell. As you leave the village bear left in about 100m up Green Lonning; the access track to Highside farm. Before reaching the farm a gate to the left leads one onto the lower slopes of Ling Fell. Follow the rutted track round above Tom Rudd Beck to Wythop Moss at the rear of Ling Fell.

5. Brumston Bridge (D) - Here you have the choice of following the farm road along the north bank of Wythop Beck to Sale Fell and the ruined chapel at Kelsick, **(LH5)**, or you may cross the beck and follow the road left

Bassenthwaite from Barf

towards Wythop Hall. Alternatively, on crossing the bridge, one can take the road to the right. This leads back eventually to Wythop Mill but in a quarter of a mile you may turn left through a gate **(F)** on to Ling Fell.

Two tracks traverse the lower slopes of Ling Fell from here. The track to the left leads to Burthwaite and Wythop Moss whilst the other track, named the copse road on the outdoor leisure map, possibly a mistake **(LH3)**, leads up the north side of the fell. The cairned summit of Ling Fell, isolated as it is, is a fine spot to watch the sun set over the Solway. Sale Fell has a smooth grassy summit with curious depressions and provides good views of Skiddaw to the east and Keswick to the southeast.

6. Scawgill Bridge (K) - Follow the signposted footpath from the bridge towards Spout Force. Just past the disused quarry on the left a stone wall is seen to climb up the fellside to the summit of Greystones. This affords a direct but strenuous route to the tops.

Wythop Moss
This is best skirted or viewed from the adjacent slopes. The moss, being the watershed for the fells that ring it, is invariably wet and boggy and is criss-crossed with ditches and old wire fences. The locals tell me that the moss was well drained before 1930 but that it has been neglected since that time. The remains of an old earth walled reservoir can be seen when one looks down from the summit of Greystones.

*****

Lakes to visit
Bassenthwaite Lake
Nearest Towns
Cockermouth, Keswick
Places to visit
Cumberland Toy and Model Museum
Cockermouth

Spout Force Waterfall **(K)**
This minor but spectacular little waterfall, about 50 ft high, is well worth a visit. It may be approached from either Scawgill Bridge or through the woods from the Forestry Commission car park **(L)** at Darling How.

Whinlatter Visitor Centre **(M)**

This recently refurbished and extended Forestry Commission centre has much to offer be it wet or fine. One can indulge in a range of activities from watching a slide show to going orienteering. There is a permanent exhibition which features, amongst other things, a walk-in tree, computer programmes, a working forest model and a separate audi-visual room with a wide selection of tape/slide shows. There is also a shop selling books, posters and souvenirs, a tea room and a forest study centre for schools and groups. Outside in the forest one can visit the walk-in badger sett, follow a forest trail, or an orienteering course. There are several walks of varying lengths and difficulty, two marked mountain bike routes and five orienteering routes to choose from. In addition there are picnic areas, and a children's playground with giant snakes, mushrooms and a 'caterpillar!'

Wordsworth House, Cockermouth

Jennings Brewery, Cockermouth

Wythop Mill and Coffee Shop, Embleton**(C)**
A working overshot water mill which presently operates vintage woodworking machinery **(LH 8).**

Recommended Country Inns -
(Good Ale and Food)

Coledale Inn, Braithwaite
Wheatsheaf Inn, Embleton

Over the [1643] Doorway.
The Shutter at end Window fallen down.
·X·1874

Kelsick Chapel in 1874

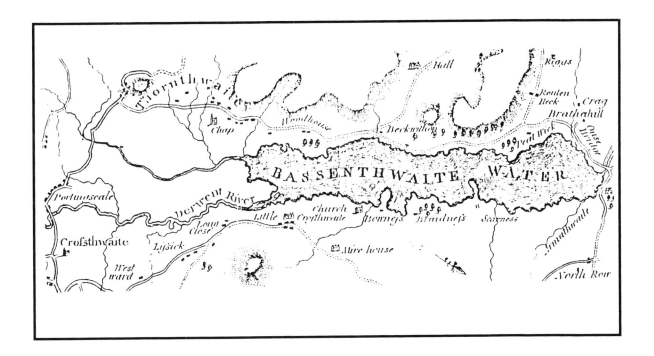

North of Whinlatter, Local History

1. Ancient road between Cockermouth and Keswick

The ancient road from Keswick to Cockermouth ran obliquely from Beck Wythop up the steep ascent of the fell past Wythop Hall and Kelswick before descending into Embleton via Wythop Mill (see copy of old map above). The main reason for following this rather difficult route was probably the marshy nature of the land at Dub Wath on the northwest corner of Bassenthwaite. This area was referred to in a 12th century document as *'the Dubs,'* a Norse word meaning pools of water in marshy ground. The Dubs, which were frequently impassable in wet weather, cut the road to Cockermouth at the northern end of the Wythop range. Travellers were therefore obliged to take the mountain road in preference to the present easier route which skirts the lake past the Pheasant Inn. The old road is now hidden in a modern pine forest but is clearly shown as a public footpath on the 1:25000 map. The path starts at Beck Wythop where there is plenty of parking space on an old unused section of the A66. Follow this old section of road up the slope which bears round to the left of the house at Beck Wythop. Just beyond the house, on the left, there is a public footpath sign which points up through the wood to Lothwaite Side. This is the old coach road, which becomes obvious as you follow it up through Wythop Woods. It is firm and well graded with a stone wall in places on the left to retain the

bank. The road emerges from the wood just below the abandoned farmstead of Lothwaite Side. It then climbs up past the farm before descending through the ancient Chapel Wood, past Kelswick Chapel and down to Wythop Mill.

2. Bishop of Barf (I)

This white painted rock is clearly seen high up the scree on the lower slopes of Barf from the Swan Hotel in Thornthwaite. Tradition has it that in 1783 the newly appointed Bishop of Derry, now Londonderry, was in the area and stayed at the Swan. He apparently wagered that he would ride his horse up the side of Barf and onwards to the summit of Lord's Seat. Unfortunately, on attempting this feat, his horse fell on reaching the height of Bishop rock killing both horse and rider. To commemorate this rather foolhardy enterprise the rock was painted white by patrons of the Swan, who still maintain the Bishop in his pristine white coat to this very day.

The Bishop was laid to rest at the base of the mountain, now marked by the white painted rock known as the Bishop's Clerk. The fee paid to patrons painting the rock was set at one shilling and a quart of ale. According to the present landlord this is now negotiable.

How true this tale is you must judge for yourself. In his book 'Mountain Ascents,' printed in 1886, John Barrow mentions the Bishop's Rock as *'standing*

Bishop of Barf

apart and standing out well due to the fact it has been recently coated with whitewash.' Although he stayed at the Swan he makes no mention of the story just related. What is sure is that the patrons of the Swan Hotel have kept the rock painted white for a very long time.

3. Corpse Road between
Wythop / Embleton and Lorton

The inhabitants of Wythop and Lorton talk about an ancient corpse road which linked the two villages. The routes and reasons for this road however appear to be at odds and so I can only relate what I have been told and leave the reader to decide for himself or herself. One story is that at one time in the past there was no burial ground at Wythop, as Wythop was a township and chapelry within the parochial chapelry of Lorton, and coffins were transported on horseback to High Lorton for internment. This is supported by the fact that some of the pews at Lorton Church were marked *'Wythop Pews.'* The route wound its way from point (**F**) on the map, through Burthwaite, around the edge of the moss, over Widow Hause via Darling How and Skawgill Bridge (**K**) to High Lorton. It is supposed to be possible to see the raised stone resting places for the coffins along the route although I have yet to find them. Possible evidence for this route is the name of the Hause between Broom Fell and Graystones, namely 'Widow Hause.' However the route is long, boggy and arduous and definitely not the shortest route to

Lorton. A possible alternative route is the well-graded path which traverses the northern slope of Ling Fell and labelled the 'Copse road' on the O.S. map. This route is more direct although it does climb rather high up the fell and becomes less distinct at or about Tom Rudd Beck. I suppose that it is possible that the lower slopes of Ling Fell were coppiced in years gone by but I have found no evidence that this was so. Should the Copse Road read Corpse Road ?

The other tale of a corpse road originates in the village of High Lorton which was liable to frequent flooding in the past, whenever Crummock Water filled up too quickly. This constant threat of flooding supposedly caused people to request to be buried at Embleton rather than their native Lorton. The route of this corpse road follows the well graded track from Kirk Fell House (**J**), over Embleton High Common to Embleton Church via Tom Rudd Beck, Highside Farm and Beckhouse to Embleton Church.

4. Embleton Sword

In the early part of the 19th century a Celtic sword, known as the 'Embleton Sword' was found in a field adjacent to Wythop Mill near the great stone, thought to be the site of an old battleground. The sword was in its sheath ornamented with enamels of various colours. The sword was placed in the Peter Crosthwaite Museum, Keswick, but it eventually found its way to the British Museum. The sword is believed to date from the year 50 BC and is probably the best example of its kind in Britain. In 1985, on hearing that the sword was miles from its ancestral home, three apprentices at Workington's British Steel Plant determined to make a steel replica of it. The sword was forged by the apprentices and the scabbard was made and decorated by Mrs P Beaty of Cockermouth. In April of that year, the replica sword, a truly beautiful object, was handed over to the village at a ceremony in St. Cuthbert's Church, where it now resides.

5. Kelswick Chapel (E)

The remains of the old chapel, built in 1473, are still to be seen alongside the track which passes through chapel wood below Sale Fell. Chapel Wood, incidentally, is said to be the oldest surviving oak planting in the British Isles. The chapel, which was rebuilt in 1673, had no vestry, chancel, turret or spire. There was no font or burial ground, hence the need for the corpse road. The Wythop church bell hung in a tree near the east window. This had the disadvantage that the church bell would toll whenever

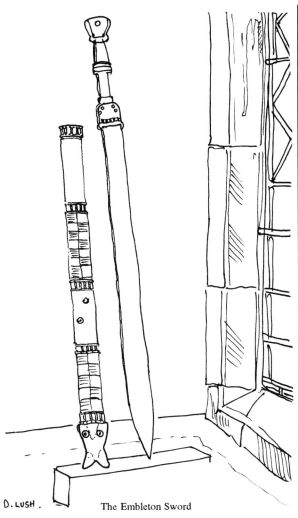

D. LUSH.   The Embleton Sword

A share prospectus to raise £120,000 was floated in 1932 and the building of the works provided work for about 50 men over a two year period. The plant including kilns, a very tall chimney and a crusher were duly completed and an overhead cable way was commenced to link the crusher with the quarry. Meanwhile the kilns were fired up and about 50 tons of bricks were produced in the first few days. Alas that was all that was ever produced. On the next firing the kilns were somehow overheated and they all collapsed. This was rather fortunate for the instigators of the venture as it turned out that there were no workable reserves of quartz in the area. Surprisingly, there was no local money involved. People I have spoken to locally maintain that everyone, including the directors, knew the venture was not viable and that, in fact, it was an example of a swindle known as 'share puffing.' Be that as it may the works have since been pulled down. All that remains are the foundations of the plant and, in the forest, the concrete plinths for the proposed aerial cableway are visible among the trees.

there were gales, striking fear into the god fearing local farmers. The church fell into disuse during the 18th century, was used as a dwelling house for a time, and was eventually pulled down in 1865. In 1866 the chapel was replaced by the new parish church of St. Margaret (**B**) which stands on the north side of Sale Fell alongside the road between Wythop Mill and the Pheasant Inn (**A**). For many years a church service has been held at the site of the old Kelswick chapel on the 3rd Sunday in August. This tradition is still maintained.

6. Silica Brick Works (G)
The visitor walking the remote track past Wythop Hall towards Beck Wythop may wonder at the signs of past industrial activity presented by the remains of the old silica brick works. These ruins mark the site of an ill-fated venture to build a brickworks which would produce fire bricks from the local quartz rock.

Kelswick Chapel
(prior to 1865)
Rev. J Ormiston at the door

7. The Pride of Lorton Vale

Wordsworth wrote:-

"There is a Yew tree, pride of Lorton Vale,
Which to this day stands single, in the midst
of its own darkness,as it stood of yore.
Of vast circumference and gloom profound.
This solitary tree! a living thing,
Produced too slowly ever to decay;
Of form and aspect too magnificent
To be destroyed."

In 1898 Edmund Bogg described the tree as being *"now only a wreck of its former glory."* He continues: *"In its pride and strength the trunk measured twenty four feet in circumference; one of its own branches was some years ago wrenched off right down to the ground. At another time the tree was actually sold for fifteen pounds to a cabinet maker from Whitehaven, and two men began to stub it up, but fortunately a gentleman from Cockermouth, hearing of its proposed destruction, made overtures to the*

Wythop Mill

owner, and thus preserved, though shorn of its ancient dignity, the pride of Lorton Vale."

The tree can still be seen today on the green behind the village hall in High Lorton. Its present condition is much better than that depicted in the drawing of 1898 below. Incidentally the large barn-like building which is now the village hall was originally a bobbin mill and later a well known local brewery now based in Cockermouth.

8. Wythop Mill (C)

There has probably been a mill on this site since pre-Norman times although it was first mentioned in deeds dating back to the 14th century. The mill originally milled corn for the manor of Wythop but in about 1860 it was converted into a timber sawmill. The present overshot waterwheel dates from this time and is used to drive vintage woodworking machinery. There is also a display of old woodworking tools.

The Pride of Lorton Vale

9. Dry Stone Walls

The earliest of these walls, which are so characteristic of English Lakeland, were built to enclose the immediate area around the farmstead and some still standing may date back to the fifteenth or sixteenth century. However, the long outlying walls, which climb the high fells, are of more recent origin. They date back to the late eighteenth and early nineteenth century when the local farmers decided they would prefer their common grazing grounds to be fenced off, so as to reduce the wandering and mixing of their stock. The shortage of building materials, other than the local stone on the high fells, made stone walls the obvious choice. The stone could be quarried, as near the building site as possible, and then ferried by horse drawn sled to where it was needed.

The walls, which rely for their stability on the distribution of weight and the friction between the stones, are built in two parallel layers with a space between. The most important part of the wall is the foundation bed which is made with large stones laid with their length into the wall. At about two foot and four foot in height *'through stones'* are placed to hold the walls together. Finally, the wall is crowned by a row of coping stones, called *'cams.'* which extend the full width of the wall to hold both sides together. These are tilted to run off the water.

Each farmer was allocated a number of acres of the common land according to the size of his farm and the number of his stock. The allocation was one *'cattle gate'* (or fifteen acres) for every hundred sheep or thirty cows.

The building of the walls must have been a tremendous task considering the way they were built straight up the fellside no matter how difficult the terrain. We can only admire the skill and tenacity of these craftsmen who have left such a permanent monument of their endeavours.

Dry Stone Wall near Spout Force, Whinlatter

Red Tarn and Swirral Edge in Snow

The Helvellyn Range

General

Although not the highest, Helvellyn; (The Hill of Willan) is probably the best known mountain in Lakeland. This is, I feel, more likely due to the attraction of the Striding and Swirral Edges than to its own grandeur. Helvellyn is the high point of a meandering ridge which rises in the north at Clough Head (A), traverses the Dodds and Raise to the rounded and rather featureless summit dome of Lakeland's second highest mountain. From here the ridge continues south over Nethermost and Dollywaggon Pikes, dropping briefly to Grisedale Tarn (R), before rising to the stony summit of Fairfield. A gentle descent over Rydal Fell then follows until valley level is reached once more at Rydal Water (X).

This line of mountains can be thought of as the backbone of the Lake District running north to south and separating east from west. Accordingly, they form a fine platform from which to enjoy the beauties of the area. To the west the ground generally drops steeply down to the vales of Grasmere and Thirlmere, giving limited and rather unremarkable access to the tops. In contrast, on the eastern side many subsidiary ridges fall away in a north easterly direction towards the vales containing Ullswater and Brotherswater. These ridges enclose rocky coves and narrow passes, which eventually become picturesque green valleys as they descend to the hamlets of Matterdale, Dockray (C), Glenridding (K), Patterdale and Hartsop. Consequently access to the ridge is easier, more varied and more scenic from the east. However, there are many steep crags and rocky precipices to the east of the summit ridge and care must be taken in poor visibility or winter conditions. Beware of cornices and ice beneath the snow on the ridges in winter. Many people over the years have taken the quick route to Red Tarn from the summit plateau, often with disastrous results.

> A serious young lady from Welwyn
> took a cookery book up Helvellyn.
> While reading the recipes
> She fell down a precipice,
> And that was the end of poor Ellen !

56

The Helvellyn Range

The valleys ringing the Helvellyn range are rich in local history. There are stories of myth and legend in the early border battles. There are tales of the lives of the lake poets; who did so much to popularise and romanticise the Lake District in the early nineteenth century. Finally there is the influence of industry on the people and the landscape. The remains of lead and iron mines still scar the fells, silent reminders of once thriving industries which, before the age of tourism, were the lifeblood of the district. The water industry, in the guise of Manchester Corporation, has also left its mark, (still to be seen in a drought), with the creation of the Thirlmere reservoir during the last quarter of the nineteenth century.

Walking

All grades and lengths of walks can be found in this area. There are several rounds or horseshoe routes which follow the high ridges as well as two ancient packhorse tracks crossing east to west through narrow passes. Apart from these higher paths, there are many delightful family walks around the foothills. These can be found in Matterdale, Gowbarrow Park and Glencoyne to the east, as well as Grasmere, White Moss Common and Rydal to the south. Because of the profusion of paths and possible routes, only a selection of walks will be described. The reader is invited to use the maps to plan alternative ascents and descents.

Walks from Glenridding and Patterdale

Route 1.   Helvellyn via Striding Edge
   (a)   Return via Swirral Edge

      Total climbing about 2630 ft (802 m)
               (7 miles)

   (b)   Return via Lower Man
       White Side and Greenside Mine

      Total climbing about 2830 ft   (863 m)
              (10 miles)

This classic round must be one of the most popular in Lakeland. There is only limited parking on the road leading into Grisedale **(N)**; one possible start point. If there is no room you must park either at Glenridding **(K)** or at Patterdale. If parking at Glenridding then follow the alternative route **(ii)** up to Striding Edge.

(i) Starting from the Grisedale Road

Follow the narrow road leading past the entrance to Patterdale Hall for about a quarter of a mile, when you will arrive at a gate barring vehicles from continuing up the valley. Turn right here for the well worn path which crosses the bridge over Grisedale Beck, before striking steeply up the side of Birkhouse Moor. The gradient soon eases as the route traverses the hillside arriving, in just over a mile, at the summit of Bleaberry Crag. There are two stiles giving access over the wall onto the Birkhouse Moor ridge.

(ii) Starting from Glenridding car park and Visitor Centre.

Cross to the minor road along the south side of Glenridding Beck by the bridge on the main road and follow it past the tea and gift shops alongside the beck. In about 200m you will see a wooden signpost saying 'Lanty's Tarn, either path,' where the path splits. Carry straight on, past the cottage on your right, following the track as it bears left and up the hillside. In a short distance a path diversion is reached with erosion control notices. Please observe them and follow the signpost indicating Striding Edge and Grisedale when you reach the next junction. There are many intersecting paths here and you may consider visiting Lanty's Tarn **(M)**. However our route bears off in a direction just south of west, following the stone wall up the ridge onto Birkhouse Moor. The path is indistinct in places but, as long as you keep the stone wall on your left, you will arrive on the Birkhouse Moor ridge about half a mile northeast of Bleaberry Crag **(L)**. Having attained the ridge you can recover your breath as you stroll southeast towards Helvellyn.

Soon Striding Edge will appear before you with Red Tarn to the right, nestling under the massive northern face of Helvellyn and the steep-sided Swirral Edge. A splendid view at any time, this scene is especially majestic when bedecked by winter snows, (see previous page). As you come on to the edge proper the view down to your left is spectacular. The dark northern face of St. Sunday's Crag looms ominously above the narrow green strip of the Grisedale Valley as it pushes between its two enclosing mountains. The edge itself is an engrossing rocky scramble, quite safe in good conditions, but obviously to be avoided in high winds or when icy. As you cross the edge look for the white memorial plaque commemorating an accidental death in 1858 **(LH 6)**. At the end of the edge an interesting rock chimney descent of about twenty feet marks the start of the final pull up to the rounded summit of Helvellyn, which is endowed with two more memorials **(LH 6)**; a stone wall shelter and an O.S. trig. point. The views to the east are the most delightful to the

---

Brownrigg Well

If the weather is fine, and you have time to linger, you may wish to visit Brownrigg Well in order to slake your thirst or refill your water bottle.

The well is the source of the small stream which emerges from the hillside about three hundred feet below and three hundred yards due west of the trig point on the summit. This stream runs down into Whelpside Gill. However, in the last century, the water from the well was diverted north and down into Mines Gill, where it helped provide water power for Helvellyn Mine. All traces of the dam have gone but the 'leat' which led the water north is still visible as a narrow groove in the hillside.

Mr H Wilkinson of Penrith, writing in Cumbria Magazine in 1954 at the grand old age of 90, described how, in his younger days around 1900-1910, he always stopped at the well to partake of its icy cold water. At that time there was an iron cup, fixed by a chain, provided for the thirsty walker. Regrettably, as you might expect, the cup is no longer there.

Striding Edge
from Helvellyn top

D.LUSH.

---

eye with Red Tarn immediately below and Ullswater stretching away in the background.

(a) Return via Swirral Edge

To return by Swirral Edge follow the ridge path north keeping close to the edge above Red Tarn so as not to miss the path leading onto Swirral Edge. The descent of Swirral Edge must be taken with care. The path, although quite good, is loose in places and some of the boulders are very large. To the left the ground drops away down into Brown Cove, with Keppel Cove and its dried up tarn and broken dams beyond; the cause of the great flood of Glenridding earlier this century **(LH 4)**. High up in the cove can be seen the spoil heaps of Brown Cove Mine; a small lead working, which was probably part of the immensely successful Greenside Mine complex; **(LH 3)**. From the vantage point of Swirral Edge many rail chairs, iron castings which would have supported the rail line within the level, can be seen scattered about the mine entrance. (This information is imparted just to save the curious reader from

Crossing Striding Edge

risking life and limb by descending into the cove to ascertain the nature of these strange regular shaped objects). Eventually the route along Swirral Edge starts to climb up again towards the summit of Catstycam. The name Catstycam or Catchedecam has interesting origins. According to McIntyre it is probably a corruption of Cat-steg-cam, *the steg* (mountain ladder or path) *of the wild cats.* Although this was the haunt of wild cats in days gone by it is unlikely that they inhabit the area now. Our path, however, drops away down to Red Tarn, crossing close by the dam at its northern corner and climbing to rejoin the path of ascent at the summit of Bleaberry Crag.

(b) Return via Lower Man, White Side and Greenside.

From the summit of Helvellyn follow the main path, which descends gently to the northwest, as far as Lower Man, just at the end of the summit plateau. As you descend don't forget to look back for a splendid view of the northwestern side of Swirral Edge as it drops away from the summit ridge.

At Lower Man the path splits. This is a good viewpoint for gazing down into the depths of

Brown Cove. The erratic rocky terrain, with Swirral Edge rising on the right, forms a dramatic picture. One arm of the path continues in a northwesterly direction, as it drops steeply down over the reddish brown rocks of Brown Cove Crags towards the road south of Thirlspot (J). We must follow the other arm as it meanders north along the ridge above Keppel Cove, eventually climbing to the summit of White Side. From White Side the path contours east above Red Screes before zig zagging down between the crags into the lower reaches of Keppel Cove. This area is littered with the signs of old mine workings. There are water leats, an old dam, a weir and an old pipeline as well as several spoil heaps and old levels. In the heyday of Greenside Mine this was the catchment area for the water needed to provide electric power for the winding gear and eventually for an electric locomotive (LH 3).

The large concrete dam with the hole in the base was not responsible for the great flood of Glenridding mentioned earlier. The dam which caused the flood is the smaller earth dam behind it at the southern end of the now dry Keppelcove Tarn. If you climb to the top, note how it was constucted of waste products from the mine site. In particular the reinforcing rods protruding from the concrete consist of discarded drill bits. They are the more modern

Swirral Edge in Winter

type with a hole down the middle through which high pressure water was squirted to keep down the dust. The route now continues northeast, just to the north of the Glenridding Beck; which wends its way down through the mine buildings at Greenside. These now house Helvellyn Youth Hostel and several outdoor activity centres. The mine road can now be followed down to Glenridding village. As you descend note the old explosives building, the landscaped spoil heaps and the rows of miners cottages, all reminders of a bygone age.

Route 2   Fairfield via St Sunday Crag

(a) Return via Grisedale
Total Climbing about 2900 ft (884 m)
(8 miles)

(b) Return via Hart Crag
Total Climbing about 3030 ft (924 m)
(9 miles)

The start point for this walk is the same as for Route 1. Take the road into Grisedale as before and, in about a quarter of a mile, a gate in the wall marks the start of the path up onto Thornhow End (P). This leads across a field before climbing quite steeply up onto the ridge of Birks. Here the gradient eases a little, giving some relief before the pull up to the summit of St Sunday Crag. On a fine day this is a fine place to rest and idly count the ants in the distance as they creep across Striding Edge. At least you are more likely to have the summit of St Sunday Crag to yourself than you are the summit of Helvellyn. Continuing on we must first descend about 150m to Deepdale Hause before encountering the steep rocky scramble on to Cofa Pike, which leads up to the broad rock and grass summit of Fairfield itself. There are good views to be had in all directions from the summit plateau of Fairfield (S) and in clear still conditions it is a pleasant place to be. Unfortunately, in my experience, it is more likely to be windy, wet and covered in cloud. There are four main routes of Fairfield, which are all quite obvious in clear weather, but finding them can be difficult in mist. Care needs to be taken in these conditions as there are steep crags to the east above Deepdale.

(a) Return via Grisedale
(Norse: grys dale, the valley of the pigs)
The path down to Grisedale Tarn leads off due west from the summit cairn above the crags, dropping steeply down to Grisedale Hause. Turn north at the hause and join the ancient pack horse route which connects Grasmere to Patterdale. The track fords Grisedale Beck at the point where it leaves Grisedale Tarn.

Grisedale Tarn features in the legend of King Dunmail (LH 5) who lost his life in the battle of Dunmail Raise. Just past the tarn, on the descent into Grisedale, look for the inscribed brothers parting stone made famous by William Wordsworth's poem in which he laments the loss of his brother John (LH 9).

The Grisedale track descends the northern side of the valley as far as Ruthwaite Lodge climbing hut; an old mine building. Here the main track crosses Grisedale Beck to the south side of the valley. There are two lead mines here in Grisedale, Ruthwaite Lodge and, a little further on, the larger Eagle Crag Mine. Both are ancient dating back to Elizabethan times. Neither has been worked since 1880. Eagle Crag Mine can be seen at close quarters if you continue along the track on the north side of the valley for a further half mile, before crossing to the south side of the beck. To return to the start point continue down the track, which gradually improves, until it becomes a road at Elmhow farmhouse; now an outdoor centre.

The Brothers' Parting Stone

The Helvellyn Range

(b) Return via Hart Crag (the crag of the deer)

This route takes us from the summit of Fairfield, across the hause above Rydal Head to Hart Crag. In fine weather this is no problem but be careful in mist. From the summit cairn you must walk in a southeasterly direction. Keep the edge of the ridge, on your left, in view so as not to miss the path across the hause. About two hundred metres from the cairn you should encounter the Hart Crag path which strikes off almost due east. In mist keep to the south side of the hause just above Rydal Head as there are steep crags on the northern side. Cairns mark the summit of Hart Crag **(T)** and the return path descends in a northeasterly direction to the Hartsop above How ridge.

As you descend on to the ridge look for the Priest's Hole Cave; a large rectangular slot high on the face of Dove Crag; the rocky outcrop southeast of Hart Crag. The Priest Hole is about twenty feet across and about ten feet deep. A small wall across the entrance serves to dissuade sheep from entering. The cave is often used by groups of walkers, or climbers on Dove Crag, as an overnight shelter. If you decide to spend the night there don't forget to record the event in the visitors book which is kept in the tin box inside the cave. The path up to the cave is a rocky scramble from the cove beneath but is well worth the effort. The outlook from the Priest Hole can only be described as an "Eagle's Eye View". It is an unforgettable experience early on a frosty spring morning, when the rising sun cuts through the mist to burn you out of your sleeping bag. The name of the cave probably dates back to the Civil War and religious persecution, although I have found no written evidence for this. The route back to Patterdale follows the long curve of the Hartsop above How ridge, which descends to Deepdale Bridge on the Patterdale-Kirkstone Pass road. The road must now be followed back into Patterdale where liquid refreshment is generally available.

Low level walks around Glenridding

For those wishing to get a taste of the high places without climbing too high there are many paths not rising much more than 700 ft above valley level. A network of such paths criss-cross the lower slopes of Birkhouse Moor in the area of Lanty's Tarn. These routes link Grisedale with the Glenridding valley and are ideal for family walks on a fine day. For a longer expedition follow the path to Greenside Mine; which contours along the southern side of the Glenridding valley at a height of about 1000 ft above sea level. This route provides splendid views of the valley, the old lead workings, with the hills beyond and, if we look back, Glenridding village and Ullswater. To return just follow the mine road down the northside of the valley.

Gowbarrow Park and Aira Force (F)

This National Trust area has adequate parking and a network of well maintained paths which meander through the woods leading to the spectacular Aira Force waterfall. The main fall is a vertical drop of 70 ft. and is well worth seeing when in spate. For those who would

Ruined Shooting Lodge
(Gowbarrow Park)

find difficulty climbing up to the height of the falls from the Ullswater road car park there is limited waiting parking; two hours, opposite the falls on the Matterdale road. If the weather is fine one can venture up on to Gowbarrow Fell or Park; an ideal viewpoint for seeing all of the reaches of Ullswater. A pleasant walk can be had from Gowbarrow **(D)** which follows the low meandering ridge above Swinburn's Park as far as the road, a mile west of Watermillock.

Route 3 A circular walk from Dockray **(C)**

Total climbing about 750 ft
(229 m)
return by Dowthwaitehead
(7.5 miles)

Old Dam in Glencoynedale

These routes which, due to the elevation of the starting point, take the walker to about 2480 ft above sea level with relatively gentle gradients, are ideal for fine lazy days. They also offer more peace and solitude than many other paths in the vicinity. However, a word of warning is necessary. The inexperienced fellwalker will find no difficulty with these routes in clear weather, when reading the map is easy. In mist however, these lower fells are often more confusing than their larger relatives. The summits are rounded, dotted with hillocks, covered in vegetation and often swampy in places. As a result the paths can disappear and reappear, split and rejoin, get confused with sheeptracks etc.. The less experienced walkers, particularly those with children, should only tackle these walks in relatively good weather and, please don't forget, boots and windproof clothing are essential. A final observation: when the weather is too bad for the high summits these lower routes can provide good map reading practice for the more experienced walker.

There is a small parking area near the bridge in Dockray. Take the track opposite, beside the green wooden hut, which leads through a gate onto Watermillock Common (National Trust sign). Do not follow the farm track which fords the stream but, keeping the stream on your right, strike off up the hillside towards the summit of Common Fell (SSW). There is no continuous discernible path in spite of the heavy dotted line across the 1:25000 map. These paths would be well used long ago by the early Greenside miners, tramping up to the head of the Glencoyne valley, but they are now barely visible. Keep to the left of the summit and you will arrive at a drystone wall which marks the ridge path leading up from the old quarry on the Dockray road at Aira Force. There is now a good path to follow on the right of the wall which gives excellent views of Ullswater and Place Fell beyond. In about a mile the wall, and the path, contour round into the Glencoyne valley. The path here, being very broken and indistinct, is marked by the occasional small stone cairn. If you maintain your height and aim for the head of the valley the route soon reappears, leading on to the waste heap which marks the old Glencoyne level of Greenside Mine. This was the goal of the early miners in the eighteenth century; who were responsible for the rights of way leading from here to the surrounding villages and hamlets. Below to your left, at the neck of the upper valley, note the old dam, now breached, which at one time stored water for use in the mine. This path, as it contours round under the crags below the summit of Hartside, leads one into the remote upper valley of Glencoynedale. The rugged aspect of the enclosing hills of Sheffield Pike and Stybarrow Dodd is more reminiscent of the remoter parts of the Scottish Highlands than the Lake District.

From the mine follow the path around the head of the valley as far as the hause **(H)** between Sheffield Pike and Stybarrow Dodd. From here you can look down onto the old workings, walls and dams, which litter the floor of the valley between Raise and the Dodds. This valley is the route of the Sticks Pass path linking Glenridding to St. John's in the Vale. Note the ski hut and tow on the north side of Raise; which retains snow longer than most other places in the district. From the hause follow the old miners path which climbs north up the ridge above Glencoyne Head onto the rounded grassy top of Hart Side. The deep trench dug east to west across the summit is a reminder of the last few years of mining at Greenside.

The owners knew that the rich lead vein, on which the mine had been built, was finally running out. Exploratory work was carried out in the 1950's. Alas no further ore was found and the mine finally closed in 1962. From the top of Hart Side there is no discernible path so one must descend the grassy northern face on either side of Coegill Beck to the farm at Douthwaite Head. As you approach the valley bottom look for the stiles over the drystone walls. Please do not attempt to climb over them. From Douthwaite Head **(E)** a well marked path, (yellow arrows), signposted 'Footpath to Matterdale' crosses the fields almost midway between the road and Aira Beck. If you have a large dog use the road instead as there are several ladder stiles crossing drystone walls with no holes for dogs provided. This path eventually emerges on the Dockray road half a mile from the startpoint.

Clough Head and The Dodds

Access to these northern hills of the Helvellyn Range can be gentle and long from Matterdale in the east or short and steep from the Vale of St. John in the west. The Dodds, as their name suggests, consist of a group of rounded grassy summits on a high plateau. The tops are linked by a broad meandering ridge which starts at Clough Head **(A)** and finishes at Sticks Pass **(G)**.

Skiing in the Lake District

This is a good cross-country ski area and in a hard winter is one of the few places in the Lake District where such skiers are to be found. However, in recent years there has been relatively little snow and the sport has suffered as a result. Raise, the north facing hill to the south of Sticks Pass, is one of the few

places in the area to boast a permanent ski tow, property of the Lakeland Ski Club. This also has suffered from a series of mild winters, although good downhill skiing can be had for a few days each year.

There is little to say about walking the Dodds. The terrain is rather unexciting, except in snow, but good views are to be had in all directions of the surrounding countryside. One can plan an interesting round from Douthwaite Head in Matterdale, which takes in some or all of the tops. Alternatively, one can ascend Clough Head from Bramcrag Quarry **(B)** in St John's in the Vale and follow the ridge to Stick's Pass, which then affords a scenic descent to Sty Beck Farm **(G)**. This latter route does involve rather a long road walk at the end unless you have two cars available.

Walks from Grasmere

The beautiful village of Grasmere has, unfortunately, become a victim of its own fame. In the past it was an important centre of the wool and mining industries. Now it is the centre of the tourist industry and much of the peace, quiet and romance of the area, described by Wordsworth and others, has been destroyed by the influx of those seeking these very delights. However one can still scale the surrounding heights to escape the madding throng. One possible walk which takes in a fair amount of local history and legend is detailed below.

Route 4   Fairfield via Great Rigg

Return via Grisedale Tarn
and Little Tongue Gill

Total climbing about 2570 ft (784 m)
(7 miles)

Car parking is available in the village but it could be expensive depending on the time of year. The start point for the walk is the minor road which leads up to Greenhead Gill from the Swan Hotel **(T)**. When you pass through the gate there is a choice of routes. The path to the left, between two walls, leads up onto Stone Arthur. This is the more scenic route to Great Rigg but it avoids the places of historical interest. If the gill is followed the walker can observe the concrete tunnel of the Thirlmere

The Helvellyn Range

Alcock Tarn with Windermere beyond

aqueduct, as is emerges from the hillside to cross this narrow valley (LH 7). Further up, at the sharp bend in the gill, is an open adit or mine entrance. This is the Greenhead Gill trial, an exploratory venture, which was probably trying to access the vein of the Grasmere lead mine. This is found round the corner further up Greenhead Gill at it's junction with Grains Gill. Grasmere lead mine is ancient. A short lived venture, it was opened by the company of Mines Royal about 1564 and closed in 1573.

Beyond the mine the gill is steep sided and rather an uninteresting ascent so, if you have come this way, a diversion to the right, which follows Grains Gill up onto the Rydal Fell ridge, might be preferred. However, this is a very steep route. If you would prefer to follow a path then backtrack to the bend in the gill and follow the steep track up onto Heron Pike. Having attained the ridge the remainder of the

walk to the summit of Fairfield is a pleasant stroll, at a gentle rate of ascent.

The return route on the old pack horse track via Grisedale Tarn and Grisedale Hause leads one past the old Tongue Gill iron mines. These mines were first worked in the seventeenth century but were reopened in the early 1870's for a short time when the price of iron shot up, as a result of demand due to the Franco - Prussian war. Neither mine has been worked since 1876. The red staining on the ground, due to the haematite content, is very noticeable. It is not advisable to get it on your clothes.

Leaving the mines, the track continues down and eventually fords Little Tongue Gill near the confluence of Little Tongue and Tongue Gill. It then follows the wall down to the road at Mill Bridge; which lies just north of the Traveller's Rest Inn. We now face a road walk of about a mile back to the startpoint. On a hot day a stop off at the Traveller's Rest to rehydrate is difficult to resist.

Route 5   Alcock Tarn **(V)** from Grasmere
                         (a circular route)

Total climbing about 1000 ft   (304m)
                     (3 miles)

This short walk is never the less quite taxing and gives excellent views of the mountains to the west of Grasmere. Park your car in Grasmere, wherever you can find space, and take the minor road which leads past Dove Cottage. This climbs for about one quarter of a mile to the summit of How Top, where there is a seat beside the road. A gravelled track bears off to the left at this point signposted 'Public

Rydal Mount circa 1900

Footpath Alcock Tarn.' Follow the track up the hillside as far as the gate but do not go through it. Instead take the rough path to the right of the wall enclosing the wood. Follow the wall up onto the fell where the track becomes enclosed between two substantial walls with even more substantial pillared gateways set in them. These constructions seem curiously out of place in such a remote area bounding, as they do, such a minor track. As you climb higher the views to the west gradually improve, revealing more of the Langdales and beyond. The path continues to follow the wall until a gap appears, through which you may pass to the tarn. The tarn has been dammed at its southern end and has

> A professor of physics at Rydal
> Would maintain the lakes were all tidal,
> And to this he adhered,
> Though the scientists jeered
> And assured him his theories were idle.

obviously been used as a water supply in the past. On a fine day Alcock Tarn is an ideal place for a picnic with plenty of open space for youngsters. The whole area is National Trust owned and is criss-crossed by many paths. The old ruined building, set into the hillside just west of the tarn, is possibly the site of Michael's farmstead which was made famous by Wordsworth in his poem 'Michael' (The Shepherd of Greenhead Gill) **(LH 8)**.

To return to Grasmere continue north along the tarn into the narrow defile that overlooks Greenhead Gill. The path drops steeply down into the gill to join the path from the Swan Hotel (described in **Route 4**). Notice that on the 1:25000 map, the woodland adjacent to the path is still called 'Michael's Fold.'

Route 6   Alcock Tarn from Rydal
                         Return by Heron Pike-Nab Scar
                                                   Ridge

Total climbing about 1800 ft (548 m)
                     (5 miles)

This alternative route has the advantage of a beautiful low level path from Rydal to Grasmere as well as the physical stimulation of attaining a respectable height on the Fairfield Horseshoe Ridge.

> ## Helvellyn (Hill of Willan?)
> another explanation of the name:
>
> *the hill that forms the wall
> or defence of the lake'.*
>
> This derives from the Norse **Hel** - Hill, **Gival** - Well, and **Lyn** - Lake. Literally this could be 'The hill containing the lake which is like a well.'

The Helvellyn Range

The startpoint is the cul de sac which leads to Rydal Hall and Rydal Mount **(X)**. There is usually parking space on the left side of the road, except when there is a church service in progress. Walk up the road past Rydal Mount to the point where the road branches to the left. Here a sign indicates the public footpath to Grasmere. Pass through the gate and follow the path west through wood and parkland as it contours round the lower slopes of Nab Scar. As you walk you will get glimpses through the trees of the busy main road below, carrying busloads of tourists to Grasmere, and feel relieved that you are up here in relative peace and solitude. The large stone wall set into the hillside, which you encounter along the route, is part of the Thirlmere aqueduct which occasionally appears above ground as it

The Sheep of Lakeland

The Herdwick is a small, hardy breed, ideally suited to the harsh conditions encountered in the Cumbrian mountains. According to legend their ancestors were the survivors of a flock which were washed up on the Cumberland coast from a wrecked Spanish Galleon. Another story attributes their introduction to the Vikings, who imported them from Scandinavia, when they settled here. Whatever their ancestry they are a true hill breed and very resistant to the local climate, which is persistently wet and cold. The Herdwicks form a real and lasting attachment to their native fell or *'heaf'* and will return year after year to the same grazing ground. According to a local farmer the sheep are instinctive survivors. In a blizzard they will collect at the ridge ends as they seem to know that the wind will blow the snow off these places. They avoid hollows where the snow will cover them up. A lot of them make for the farm! (Wouldn't you??)

D. LUSH

The Helvellyn Range

negotiates a ravine. The aqueduct in this area was built by the cut and fill method and the observant eye can identify its course from time to time. Eventually the path emerges from the parkland to join the minor road from Grasmere to 'How Top.' Follow the directions in **Route 5** from this point to Alcock Tarn.

The return route from the tarn follows **Route 5** into Greenhead Gill but then turn east and follow the steep winding path which climbs up to the summit of Heron Pike from the bend in Greenhead Gill. From Heron Pike just follow the ridge path south back towards Rydal. As you descend take in the views of Ambleside with Windermere beyond. Esthwaite Water and Coniston Water can also be seen from here.

*****

Lakes to visit - Grasmere, Rydal Water
Ullswater, Windermere

Nearest Towns -Ambleside, Keswick
Penrith

Places to visit -
Armitt Library, Ambleside
Rydal Mount, Ambleside
Wordsworth Museum and
Dove Cottage, Grasmere
Penrith Steam Museum
Penrith Town Museum

Country Houses -
Dalemain, near Pooley Bridge

Recommended Country Inns
(Good Ale and Good Food)

Brackenrigg, Watermillock
The Traveller's Rest Inn, Grasmere
The White Lion, Patterdale

Grasmere in 1819
from an old print

O LUSH.

Helvellyn Range, History

1. Dalton Sir John, Ascents of Helvellyn

Sir John Dalton; Father of Atomic Theory, born at Eaglesfield, near Cockermouth, ascended Helvellyn annually for forty years. His motives were partly to make meteorological observations and partly, as he expressed it, *"to bring into exercise a set of muscles which would otherwise have grown stiff."* Apparently on one occasion, when caught in a thick mist, he and his companions were trying to grope their way down the mountain holding on to each others coat tails. Suddenly the doctor stopped, exclaiming *"Not one step more! There is nothing but mist to tread on!"* When the mist cleared they found themselves on the edge of the cliff directly above Red Tarn. It is perhaps a pity that the unfortunate Charles Gough did not have a similar premonition when he journeyed over Helvellyn in 1805. (See below; Monuments of Helvellyn).

2. Echoes of Ullswater

A visitor attraction of the eighteenth century at Ullswater was to *'try the echoes.'* Vessels on the lake were armed with swivel guns and on a still evening, it was said, twenty five distant reverberations could be heard from the discharge of a swivel with only two ounces of powder. Mr Hutchinson in his 'Excursion to the Lakes,' page 65, gives the following description of such an event having landed on the shores of a bay opposite Watermillock. *"Whilst we sat to regale, the barge put off from shore to a station where the finest echoes were to be obtained from the surrounding mountains. The vessel was provided with six brass cannon, mounted on swivels. On discharging one of these pieces, the report was echoed from the opposite rocks, where, by reverberation, it seemed to roll from cliff to cliff, and return through every cave and valley, till the decreasing tumult gradually died away upon the ear."*
The practice was continued in more recent times. Behind the Patterdale Hotel is a crag known at one time as Nell Crag. In the eighteen thirties a cannon was occasionally fired from here to the great delight of the visitors.

3. Greenside Mine Disasters

In its long life Greenside Mine only suffered two major accidents, both occurring towards the end of the mine's life. The first of these was due to a fire which started in the north shaft over the weekend causing carbon monoxide to diffuse into the workings. On Monday 7th July 1952 a group of miners were driven back by strong fumes as they approached the lift shaft, but not before hearing the shouts of miner Leo Mulyran, who had already descended to the bottom of the shaft. In the subsequent attempt to rescue him three men died, as did Mulyran himself. The heroic rescue attempt was recognised by justly deserved medals and commendations. The second fatal accident occurred in 1960 when the mine was about to close. The Atomic Energy Authority arranged to explode two charges of TNT, one of 500 lbs and the other of 250 lbs, in order to conduct seismic tests. The data was needed to calibrate instruments which would be used to monitor underground nuclear explosions. The charges were fired electrically from the surface but only the larger one went off. After the explosion the mine was ventilated and declared safe but two men, who later went in, were asphyxiated by an isolated pocket of gas trapped in one of the stopes. At the time the secrecy surrounding the project, and the involvement of the Atomic Energy Authority, led to rumours that a small atomic bomb had been exploded in the mine.

4. Keppel Cove Dam Flood
At 1.30 a.m. on Saturday, 29th October 1927, after a period of exceptional rainfall, the earthen wall of Keppel Cove Tarn Dam burst, causing a great wall of water to descend on Glenridding far below. The size of the deluge was such that it left a gap in the dam 80ft wide by 60ft deep. The flood rushed down Glenridding Beck carrying away Rattle Beck bridge, flooding houses alongside the beck and Eagle Farm to a depth of five to six feet. Debris, including dead sheep and a tea hut, was deposited on the other side of the lake near Side Farm. The basement bedrooms

Kepple cove and Dams
(from the Helvellyn Ridge above Brown Cove)

of the Glenridding Hotel were flooded and four sleeping girls floated up to the ceiling on their mattresses. One of these had a near escape as she was swept through a window but was then saved by one Ernest Thompson. The peninsula at Glenridding, which is now the site of the steamer pier, was formed as a result of this flood which also brought down a mass of large rocks with it. The rocks were used to build up this strip of land which is now a popular recreation area for visitors.

The Keppel Cove earth dam was replaced by a rough concrete dam which also burst, but less spectacularly, in 1931. The second dam is still to be seen complete with large hole in the base.

5. King Dunmail and Dunmail Raise
"That pile of stones heaped over brave Dunmail's bones
He who had my supreme command
Last king of rocky Cumberland"

Wordsworth's 'Waggoner'

The story of King Dunmail and his last battle at Dunmail Raise in the year 945 is steeped in Arthurean legend. There are several versions of the story, some more fanciful than others. The description here is a compilaton of these.

Dunmail was the son of Owain, one of the strongest of the Cumbrian kings who came to the throne about 920. Owain was descended from the old Ceasarian line of the kings of Strathclyde, who by this time had lost much of their power and influence due to attacks from Anglian invaders, who encroached into the Scottish lowlands. Owain ruled his kingdom from Penrith as Carlisle had been sacked by the Danes in 876 and was a ruin. The seven tombs forming the 'Giant's Grave' and the 'Giant's Thumb' in Penrith churchyard date back to this time and indicate that Penrith was an important centre. The popular tradition which says that the monuments are the tomb of a giant, 'Hugh or Owen Ceasarius,' probably records some dim memory of Owain. Owain, together with his uncle, King Constantine II of the Scots, plotted with the Vikings of Galloway and the Isles against the English King Athelstan, to whom they had previously sworn allegiance as King of all Britain. This led to a great battle on the flat topped mountain near Ecclefechan in Galloway, called Burnswark, at which the English were victorious. What happened to Owain after the battle is not recorded, but Dunmail, his son and successor, apparently did not learn from this experience. Dunmail continued his dangerous alliance with the Vikings of Galloway and the Isles. King Edmund, the Saxon king, who succeeded Athelstan on the English throne, was quick to act, sending an army across Stainmore which defeated Dunmail at a place unknown. After this battle, Edmund, with the usual barbarity of the times, put out the eyes of Dunmail's two sons and gave his country to Malcolm; King of Scotland, on condition he preserved peace in the northern parts of England. Although several sites for the battle have been suggested, including Orrest Head at Windermere, legend and popular belief portray Dunmail Raise as the battleground. The story of the battle is interwoven with legend and superstition but is a fine tale to hear. I quote from an account given in 1927 in 'Cycling' magazine by one W.T. Palmer.

The Raise has legend of one mighty battle a thousand years ago. King Edmund the Saxon was quelling the raider Britons on his border, and Dunmail of Cumberland came in for punitive attention. The armies met on this level among the hills, and a formless pile of stones marks the burial place of those who fell. Here is a pretty legend: The crown of Dunmail of Cumberland was charmed, giving its wearer a succession in his kingdom. Therefore King Edmund the Saxon coveted it above all things. When

The Cairn on Dunmail Raise

Dunmail came to the throne of the mountain land a wizard in Gilsland Forest held a master charm to defeat the promise of his crown. He Dunmail slew. The magician was able to make himself invisible save

at cock crow and to destroy him the hero braved a cordon of wild wolves at night. At the first peep of dawn, he entered the cave where the wizard was lying. Leaping to his feet the magician called out "Where river runs north or south with the storm," ere Dunmail's sword silenced him.

The story came to the ear of the covetous Saxon, who, after much enquiry of his priests, found that an incomplete curse, although powerful against Dunmail, could scarcely hurt another holder of the crown. Spies were accordingly sent into Cumbria to find where a battle could be fought favourable to the magician's words. On Dunmail Raise, in times of storm even in unromantic today, the torrent sets north or south in capricious fashion. The spies found the place, found also fell land chiefs who were persuaded to become secret allies of the Saxon. The campaign began. Dunmail moved his army south to meet the invader, and they joined battle in the pass. For long hours the battle was with the Cumbrians; the Saxons were driven down the hill again and again. As his foremost tribes became exhausted, Dunmail retired and called on his reserves - they were mainly the ones favouring the southern king. On they came, spreading in well - armed lines from side to side of the hollow way, but instead of opening to let the weary warriors through, they delivered an attack on them. Surprised, the army reeled back and their rear was attacked with redoubled violence by the Saxons. The loyal ranks were forced to stand back to back round their king; assailed by superior forces they fell rapidly, and ere long the brave chief was shot down by a traitor of his own bodyguard.

"*My crown,*" cried he, "*bear it away; never let the Saxon flaunt it.*"

A few stalwarts took the charmed treasure from his hands, and with a furious onslaught made the attackers give way. Step by step they fought their way up the ghyll of Dunmail's beck - broke through all resistance on the open fell, and, aided by a dense cloud, evaded their pursuers. Two hours later the faithful few met by Grisedale Tarn, and consigned the crown to its depths - "*till Dunmail come again to lead us.*" And every year the warriors come back, draw up the magic circlet from the depths of the wild mountain tarn, and carry it with them over Seat Sandal to where the king is sleeping his age long sleep. They knock with his spear on the topmost stone of the cairn and from its heart comes a voice. "*Not yet; not yet - wait a while my warriors.*" The cairn can still be seen in the central reservation on the summit of Dunmail Raise. Another legend says that Dunmail did not die in the battle; that he survived for thirty years in Strathclyde and died a pilgrim in Rome. Be that as it may, Edmund did not gain a successor for his throne. Four years after the battle on Dunmail Raise he was assassinated, and his kingdom went into ruin.

6. Memorials of Helvellyn

There are three memorials on Helvellyn:

(i) The first of these is encountered as one crosses Striding Edge. A white painted iron plaque marks the spot where Robert Dixon of Rookings, Patterdale, died on 27th May 1858, while following the Patterdale Foxhounds.

(ii) The second memorial, which stands on the summit plateau of Helvellyn directly above Red Tarn, records an event that has since become famous through the attentions of the Lakeland poets. A large memorial stone, set into a cairn, records the death of Charles Gough of Manchester who perished in the spring of 1805 when attempting to cross from Patterdale to Wythburn. A fall of snow had partially obscured the path and he apparently fell from the head of Red Cove onto the rocks below. His dog, which accompanied him on that fateful day, remained with the body until it was found three months later by William Harrison of Hartsop. It was this act of extreme devotion which captured the imagination of both Wordsworth and Scott. Scott's verses on *'Helvellyn'* refer to the event and below Wordsworth's *'Fidelity'* tells the tale in full:-

1. *A barking sound the shepherd hears,*
A cry as of a dog or fox;
He halts and searches with his eyes
Among the scattered rocks:
And now at distance can discern
A stirring in a brake or fern;
And instantly a dog is seen,
Glancing through that covert green.

2. *The dog is not of mountain breed;*
Its motions, too, are wild and shy;
With something, as the shepherd thinks,
Unusual in its cry:
Nor is there anyone in sight
All round, in hollow or on height;
Nor shout, nor whistle strikes his ear:
What is the creature doing here?

3. *It was a cove, a huge recess,*
That keeps, till June December's snow;
A lofty precipice in front,
A silent tarn below !
Far in the bosom of Helvellyn,
Remote from public road or dwelling,
Pathway, or cultivated land;
From trace of human foot or hand.

4. *There sometimes doth a leaping fish*
Send through the tarn a lonely cheer;
The crags repeat the raven's croak,
In sympathy austere;
Thither the rainbow comes - the cloud -
And mists that spread the flying shroud;
And sunbeams; and the sounding blast,
That if it could, would hurry past;
But that enormous barrier binds it fast.

5. *Not free from boding thoughts, a while*
The shepherd stood; then makes his way
Towards the dog, o'er rocks and stones,
As quickly as he may;
Not far had gone before he found
A human skeleton on the ground;
The appalled discoverer with a sigh
Looks round to learn the history.

6. *From those abrupt and perilous rocks*
The man had fallen, that place of fear!
At length upon the shepherds mind
It breaks, and all is clear:
He instantly recalled the name,
And who he was, and whence he came;
Remembered, too, the very day
On which the traveller passed this way.

7. *But hear a wonder, for whose sake*
This lamentable tale I tell!
A lasting monument of words
This wonder merits well.
The dog which still was hovering nigh,
Repeating the same timid cry,
This dog had been through three month's space
A dweller in that savage place.

8. *Yes, proof was plain that since the day,*
When this ill-fated traveller died,
The dog had watched about the spot,
Or by his master's side:
How nourished here through such long time
He knows who gave that love sublime:
And gave that strength of feeling great
Above all human estimate.

Charles Gough's remains are buried at Tirril between Pooley Bridge and Penrith. There is speculation how the dog, a terrier bitch named Foxey, survived for three months on the mountain. Some say the dog fed on rabbits, or sheep, or stray birds. But one thing is certain, the flesh on the man's legs was completely eaten and nothing left but the bones.

Canon Rawnsley in his book *'Literary Associations of the English Lakes'* disputes the suggestion that Foxey ate the remains of her master. He quotes a letter dated Yanwath 30th of Eighth month 1805 which contains a brief note of the incident. In that letter, written only six months after the event, it is stated that *'his bones were bleached white though covered with his clothes, and his skull was separated and found at a distance from the rest. --- His faithful dog had attended his relics between three and four months, but how it had subsisted itself is difficult to suppose, though it appeared to the people who collected his remains that it eat grass'* Foxey gave birth to pups during her vigil which were found dead. Further evidence says Rawnsley that Foxey survived only on grass and carrion mutton which did not provide enough sustenance to support her pups.

(iii) The third memorial on Helvellyn is to be found a hundred yards or so south of the summit shelter beside the path leading towards Wythburn. A recently re-erected plaque records the first landing of an aircraft on the summit of an English mountain. On the 22nd December 1926, pilots John Leeming and Bert Hinkler landed an Avro 585 Gosport aeroplane on the summit plateau. After a short stay they then flew back to Woodford in Cheshire. (Woodford is very near the present Manchester Airport).

7. Thirlmere and Manchester

In 1894 Thirlmere had the dubious distinction of being the first lake in the district to be converted into a reservoir by Manchester Corporation. Prior to the building of the dam, Thirlmere, formerly known as Leathes Water or Wythburn Water, consisted of two parts connected by a narrow and shallow channel. The hamlet of Armboth on the west side was connected by a bridge over this channel to Dale Head Park and the Keswick road. Armboth or *'City,'* as it was known to the lead miners of Helvellyn, was to disappear for ever with the raising of the water level. Manchester had originally wanted to extract water from Ullswater but, due to local opposition, they were diverted from this course and eventually settled on Thirlmere where there were fewer influential landowners to deal with. One other problem with

Ullswater was the presence of Greenside Lead Mine. It was incorrectly supposed that the lead workings would contaminate the lake water. Similar fears at Thirlmere led to the closing of Helvellyn Mine in 1880.

The later schemes at Haweswater and Ullswater were required to blend in with the natural environment and not to alter the natural beauty of the area. The Thirlmere scheme, however, was not bound by such tight constraints. As a result, for many years access was denied to the lake and visitors were discouraged. Unsightly notices prohibiting trespass on water board land were commonly encountered. Happily this is no longer the situation. The signs have disappeared and North West Water has constructed paths and stiles giving easy access to the lake and the surrounding woods. Thirlmere will, however, never look a natural lake. Its height goes up and down with the season and

Charles Gough Memorial

the demand for water. At times of drought the exposed white rocky shores contrast sharply with the conifer forest above, emphasising that it is no longer a natural lake. Whatever one thinks of the spoiling of the area by these 19th century engineers, one can only admire their vision and engineering skills. The aqueduct that carries Thirlmere's water the 96 miles to Manchester is a series of tunnels, buried channels and pipelines which utilise gravity alone to keep the water moving.

8. The Shepherd of Greenhead Ghyll

This pathetic tale is related by Wordsworth in his poem *'Michael,'* which is too long to reproduce in full here.

I will relate a brief synopsis of the tale:

Long ago a shepherd called Michael was married to a wife, Isabel, twenty years his junior. They were blessed late in life with an only son called Luke. From the age of ten Luke worked with his father, who was then sixty six, day in and day out. In the evening they would rest in their cottage which was high on the side of Greenhead Ghyll and could be seen from Grasmere and the surrounding vale. Every night Isabel lit a lamp to see them home which, as it

Dove Cottage, Grasmere
from an old guide book

stood in the window of the cottage, could be seen by the whole valley. This light became famous and was named *'The Evening Star'* by the residents of Grasmere Vale.

Unfortunately, due to the misfortune of his brother's son who failed in business, Michael, who had agreed to be bound in surety for his nephew, had to give up half of his living to cover the debt. The farm could no longer support both he and his son. Luke, who was eighteen years old at this time, had to leave and live with a relative in the city who agreed to try and find work for the lad. Before Luke left, his father and he

laid the foundations of a new sheepfold beside the ghyll which, Michael promised, would be ready for his son's return, when his fortune was made. While his son was away Michael added to the sheepfold in his spare moments, ever looking forward to Luke's eventual return. Alas it was not to be. Luke soon became influenced by city life and turned to drink,

Wordsworth's Grave
in Grasmere Churchyard

gambling and coarse living. The old man lost heart when he heard the news and realised that Luke was not coming back. Michael finally died at the age of ninety one, with the sheepfold still unfinished. Isobel survived a further few years before the estate was sold and went into a stranger's hand.

Wordsworth relates how the cottage which was named the *'Evening Star'* has gone, a ploughshare has been through the ground on which it stood. Yet the oak is left that grew beside the door. A possible site for the cottage is immediately west of Alcock Tarn where the remains of a house built into the hillside is to be seen. A few yards further down the slope to the right of the cottage are the rotten remains of a large tree stump. The view from this point is just as the poem describes, encompassing Grasmere vale, Easedale and Dunmail Raise.

9. Wordsworth - the brothers' parting stone

The inscribed stone which stands just off the path, a short distance east of Grisedale Tarn, marks the spot where William bade goodbye to his brother John for the last time. William would see his brother on his way, accompanying him as far as Grisedale Tarn. Unfortunately, shortly after this last parting, John was to perish in the loss of his ship, the East Indiaman, the *'Earl of Abergavenny.'* The ship was wrecked on The Shambles off the Portland Bill through the incompetency of the pilot, on Friday night, February 5th 1805. Wordsworth records this sad happening in a poem of lament, composed at the parting stone. There follows a short excerpt :

I
The sheep boy whistled loud and lo!
That instant, startled by the shock,
The buzzard mounted from the rock
Deliberate and slow:
Lord of the air, he took his flight:
Oh! could he on that woeful night
Have lent his wing, my brother dear,
For one poor moment's space to thee
And all who struggled with the sea
When safety was so near.

III
Here did we stop and here look round,
While each into himself descends,
For that last thought of parting friends
That is not to be found.......

Queen of the Mountains

Helvellyn and her companions while not exactly within the inner sanctum are yet not subsidiary to Scafell. If Scafell is thought of as the King of the Lake mountains, then Helvellyn is more like the Queen than the Prince. (Perhaps burly Skiddaw, the only other peak to over - top 3,000 ft. is the Prince). She is of equal importance with King Scafell in the general scheme and below her spreads like a train the beautiful lake of Ullswater. She is more accessible, too, as a Queen should be, than Scafell, and on her Striding edge, that famous dizzy walk, she offers the adventurous tourist the slightly spurious thrill of a danger that looks greater than it is ....

E.F. Bozman, The English Countryside (1939)

Wythburn Water in 1819
Helvellyn is in the distance

74

East of Ullswater

General

The group of fells bounded by Haweswater and Ullswater provide a good variety of walking. The terrain in the north of the area ranges from the rounded rolling tops immediately west of Haweswater, to the steep sided remote valleys of Boardale and Martindale. To the south is a wild area of craggy mountains joined by high ridges, which give dramatic views of the valleys and lakes below. In spite of its remoteness man has made his mark on this area. In Roman times the Roman road of High Street was constructed to provide a high level but convenient route from north to south. Earlier this century Manchester Corporation flooded the Mardale valley to satisfy its thirst for water and, more recently, the North West Water Authority has extended this extraction to Ullswater. At least the most recent developments have been made with an eye to conservation, so that pipelines and plant are hidden and do not intrude on the natural grandeur of the area.

Walking

One can devise many fine ridge routes of varying length and difficulty depending on your start point. A selection of possible routes are described below based on start points at Martindale **(B)**, Haweswater **(N)**, Patterdale **(I)**, Kirkstone Pass top **(P)**, and Hartsop **(K)**

Walks from Martindale

The secluded valleys of Martindale and Boardale can only be reached by car via Pooley Bridge and Howtown; along the east side of Ullswater. The journey culminates in a steep climb with hairpin bends, until the hause is reached just below Hallin Fell. The start point for this walk is the car park on the lower slopes of Hallin Fell, which is opposite Martindale New church at the top of the hause **(B)**.

Route 1   Boardale Hause via Beda Fell
                                                     Ridge
            return via Place Fell
      Total climbing about 2500 ft, 762 m
                          (8 miles)

            return via Boardale Valley
      Total   climbing about 1580 ft, 482m
                          (7 miles)

Leaving the car park follow the road south down into the village, bearing left at the junction. As you make your way towards the old church of St. Martin, **(E) (LH7)**, notice the

The Nab

conical hill in the middle distance. This is the Nab which marks the point where Bannerdale branches off to the right of Martindale. The Nab and the area above and around it form the Martindale Deer Forest. The fell to the right of the Nab is Beda Fell, our immediate goal.

The old church with its ancient Yew tree is steeped in history and well worth a visit. On leaving the church cross the Christy bridge and, in about fifty yards, a carved slate sign in the wall indicates the path to Boardale. Ignore this and continue along the road for a further two hundred yards or so. At the end of the wall **(G)** follow the grassy track which climbs steeply up to the hause between Raven Crag and Winter Crag. On reaching the ridge between Martindale and Boardale turn left and follow the ridge path south towards the craggy top of Beda Head. As you approach the top, note how the path wends its way up through a rocky defile. This well graded route, whilst appearing natural, has surely been altered at

some time by man. Perhaps it was once an alternative pack horse route from Martindale to Patterdale.

From the vantage point of Beda Head the views in all directions are magnificent. To the east the long flat top of High Street runs from north to south, where it merges with the tops of Thornthwaite Crag and Stony Cove Pike. To the west is Place Fell with the Helvellyn range beyond. The well marked track slanting down the western side of Place Fell from Boardale Hause marks the path of a water pipeline carrying water from Hayeswater to Penrith. This path is your descent if you wish to avoid

Dunmallet Hill from Beda Head

climbing Place Fell on the second half of the walk. Turning to the north you can survey the long reach of Ullswater with the pimple of Dunmallet Hill (a Roman signalling station) marking Pooley Bridge at the head of the lake.

As you leave Beda Head and follow the ridge path south, notice the red roofed building in Martindale below the Nab. This is 'The Bungalow,' the shooting lodge of the 'Yellow Earl.' who entertained the Kaiser there in 1895. Continue on as far as Beda Fell Knotts **(H)**, where the packhorse route, from Dale Head to Patterdale, crosses the ridge. Turn right onto this track (at the small cairn) and continue down to Boardale Hause. Here you must decide which way to return. You may follow the cairns down into Boardale or strike out for the top of Place Fell to complete the round. If you take the former route listen for the rushing sound of water in the pipeline beneath your feet as you start the descent into Boardale. The noise emanates from the water board's 'Break Pressure Tank' situated just to the left of the path near the top of the pass. If it is very windy on Boardale Hause perhaps you should wear a safety helmet. Mrs Little records in 'The Chronicles of Patterdale' how, on one very windy day in 1951, a corrugated iron garage belonging to the White Lion Hotel in Patterdale was blown to bits and pieces of the corrugated iron were scattered in and around the village. One piece soared higher than the rest and came down on Boardale Hause having travelled a distance of about half a mile and achieved a vertical ascent of at least eight hundred feet.

The path up Place Fell is steep and worn but the top, with its trig point, is soon attained. If the day is clear, good views are to be had to the east of Helvellyn and the Grisedale and Glenridding valleys. Note the grassed over spoil heaps of Greenside lead mine; once the richest lead mine in the north of England. Our route now crosses the broad top of Place Fell, dropping gently down to the sheep fold at Low Moss **(D)**. It is easy to lose your way here in mist or snow. Keep to the ridge and walk in a northeasterly direction. At the sheep fold the path forks into two. The left hand track passes to the left of High Dodd, as it contours down towards Sandwick, whilst our track goes to the right and continues along above the Boardale Valley. In about a mile one can leave the ridge by following the path which drops down to the ford and footbridge at Garths Head in Boardale **(C)**. The last mile of the walk takes us along the road back to our start point.

Route 2 - Boardale Hause via Place Fell
Return by lakeside path between
Patterdale and Sandwick
Total climbing about 1640 ft, 500 m
(8 miles)

Park your car at Sandwick **(A)** and follow the bridle path south towards Patterdale for about half a mile. On reaching a large drystone barn the path to Patterdale bears right and drops down towards the footbridge over Scalehow Beck. Leaving the bridle path at the barn, follow the path bearing SSW which climbs up the eastern side of Scalehow Beck, past the waterfalls and pools. This path takes you round High Dodd, past the disused quarry to the sheepfold at Low Moss where we join Route 1. Turn right here and follow the path SW which climbs gently up the shoulder of Place Fell to the trig point on the summit. Our path now continues almost due south across the summit plateau and down the shoulder to Boardale Hause where we turn right and follow the path around the side of the fell towards Patterdale. As you reach the lower slopes avoid going down to the road and follow the fellside path past the old quarries which lie just above Side Farm campsite. This route will take you back to Sandwick along the elevated lakeside path, which traverses the juniper wooded lower slopes of Place Fell. There are two paths at this point a lower and an upper one. The upper path passes through a small pass **(F)** to the right of Silver Crag whilst the lower path follows the lakeshore to the left of Silver Crag. Both paths become one north of the crag. As you follow the lakeside path towards Sandwick note the long stretch of Ullswater to your left. It was here on July 23rd 1955 that Sir Donald Campbell broke the world water speed record **(see page 122)**. He travelled at an average speed of 262.32 mph over a measured mile in his jet powered boat Bluebird. Continuing north, the path eventually bears right and you will rejoin your outward route after crossing the footbridge over Scalehow Beck.

Low Level Walks

Combined Cruise and Walk

During the tourist season the lakeside path walk, just described, can be combined with a steamer trip between Glenridding and Howtown, to make a delightful day out for a family. Remember to allow plenty of time for the walk which is about 8 miles from Howtown Pier to Glenridding. The Ullswater Navigation and Transit Company **(LH8)** run regular services from Easter to the end of October. Take the boat from Glenridding to Howtown pier, a 30 minute journey. The lakeside path can then be followed from Howtown, round the west side of Hallin Fell, to Sandwick and on to Side Farm, Glenridding. Turn right at the farmhouse and follow the track across the field to Glenridding village. Of course if you are based in the Howtown area there is no reason why this trip should not be planned in the reverse direction.

Hallin Fell
        Total climbing about 525 ft (160 m)
                    (1 mile)

This is a short grassy but steep walk, popular with young families and the less energetic hill walker. Starting from the car park at the base of Hallin Fell **(B)** the path climbs straight to the summit on which there is a large cairn. This is a fine viewpoint giving extensive open views of the two longest stretches of Ullswater.

Walks from Patterdale
Route 2 (above) can be tackled from Patterdale. Parking is available in the village just north of the White Lion Hotel.

On leaving your car follow the road south past the White Lion to the sharp bend in the road. Take the small road to the left here which crosses Goldrill Beck and leads to several houses at the foot of the fell. At the houses take the left fork and, in 100 yards or so, you will reach a gate across the road. Turn right here, through another gate signposted 'fell

path', and follow the well worn path which leads south east and rises steeply to Boardale Hause. From here you can follow route 2 in reverse to the barn near Sandwick and return via the lakeside path.

Route 3   Hayeswater via Boardale Hause
                        and Angle Tarn
            Return via Hartsop and
            the bridle path to Patterdale.
        Total climbing about 1600 ft,   490 m
                    (8 miles)

This is a very picturesque but relatively easy route which gives rise to excellent panoramic views in spite of the moderate height attained. This walk is at its best in winter when the tarns are frozen and the fells are bedecked with snow. Park your car in Patterdale, as described in the previous walk, and follow the same route to Boardale Hause. At the Hause take the path which climbs south up the shoulder of Dubhow Crag towards Angle Tarn. The path eventually drops of the shoulder passing through the gap between Dubhow Crag and Stony Rigg **(J)**. From here the main path skirts round Angletarn Pikes to reveal Angle Tarn below. However, in my opinion, the small path which goes over the pikes gives a more imposing view of the tarn and the surrounding fells. The path then skirts round

Angle Tarn

the boggy eastern side of the tarn before rising gently to the plateau above Prison Crag. From Prison Crag the track bears off in a southeasterly direction, following a fence as it traverses the upper slopes of Rest Dodd. Hayeswater with its dam will soon be seen in the valley to your right. The steep path down to the dam leaves the path you are on as it starts to rise again towards the summit of the Knott. In mist this can be hard to find but, as long as you have crossed two major streams in your walk from Prison Crag towards the Knott, you will be past the crags and can safely descend the fell to Hayeswater.

From Hayeswater a good road leads quickly down to Hartsop farm and hamlet. As you approach Hartsop the path crosses over Hayeswater Gill, which bears left to join Pasture Beck, flowing out of Threshwaite Cove. At the confluence of the two becks **(L)** are the ruins of Low Hartsop Mine which has not been worked since 1878. A thirty foot water wheel was erected to drain the mine which suffered badly from flooding. The stone piers which you can see are the remains of the watercourse supports and beyond is the wheelpit, with a tree growing out of it.

From Hartsop village follow the access road towards the main Kirkstone Pass road but, before reaching it, turn right along the farm access road leading north to Patterdale. This soon becomes a meandering track which eventually brings you back to Patterdale.

Walks from Hartsop (K)

There is a car park at the end of the public road leading to the hamlet of Hartsop.

Route 4   Thornthwaite Crag Beacon
via Gray Crag
Return via Thresthwaite Mouth,
Stony Cove Pike and Hartsop Dodd

Total Climbing about 2400 ft (750m)
(6 miles)

Take the path up to Hayeswater through the gate from the car park. As you proceed note the old mine workings high on the side of Hartsop Dodd to your right. The return route will bring you over the top of the Dodd and it is important that you stick to the ridge path on

the right of these workings. Above the spoil heaps there is an open shaft with a vertical drop of 25 ft which leads to another shaft 200 ft in depth.

In just over a quarter of a mile you will cross the bridge over Hayeswater Gill **(L)** as the path

View from Thornthwaite Beacon

traverses the lower slopes of Gray Crag. Follow the path up the hill and through the gate. In a short distance you must bear right up the steep shoulder of Gray Crag. The path here is indistinct and difficult to see lower down. Use the remains of the drystone wall to lead you up the first part of the climb. This is a long hard pull but at least it is encountered at the beginning of the walk. Your effort will be well repaid by the views that will greet you when the ridge is attained. The long almost flat ridge stretches to the south in front of you, providing easy walking in dry conditions. The impressive Thornthwaite Beacon cairn is a mile and a half away at the end of the ridge on Thornthwaite Crag. As you approach the crag, the narrow col between it and Stony Cove Pike will be seen at the head of the valley to your right. If short of time, Thornthwaite Crag can be bypassed by dropping down onto this col as the final ascent to the crag begins. The beacon at Thornthwaite Crag **(M)** is very large and well worth a visit. The view to the south, of Morecambe Bay and beyond, is most impressive on a clear day. It is said that Blackpool Tower is visible on occasions but I have yet to see that.

On leaving the beacon take the path leading northwest down onto Threshthwaite Mouth and then up onto Stony Cove Pike. From here the return journey is a pleasant stroll, almost due north, along the shoulder of Stony Cove Pike, which culminates in Hartsop Dodd directly above Hartsop. Be careful to keep to the well worn path down the shoulder of the Dodd, thus avoiding the mine shafts previously mentioned.

Route 5   Thornthwaite Crag Beacon
        via Hayeswater, The Knott
                    and High Street
    Return via Gray Crag (7 miles)
    Return via Stony Cove Pike (8 miles)

    Total Climbing about 2400 ft (750 m)

These are variations on the last route which give accesss to the southern end of the Roman road across High Street. From Hartsop take the track up to the Hayeswater reservoir and, turning north cross the footbridge just east of the spillway. A steep climb of approximately 850 ft then follows up onto the summit of the Knott where there is a mountain rescue post. The path now leads almost due south, climbing gently along the broad summit ridge of High Street. The path here splits into two almost parallel routes one of which follows the eastern edge of the ridge giving fine views into Riggindale and Haweswater. The other path, west of the drystone wall, traverses the ridge a little below its crest.

The summit of High Street is rather barren and featureless. In mist or snow the drystone wall which traverses the ridge north to south is a useful guide. The views from High Street are most dramatic in winter when snow highlights the crags and gullies of the adjacent fells to best advantage.

The local name of this broad top is Racecourse Hill which dates back to the 18th century

when the local farmers held annual horse races here **(LH4)**. From the summit of High Street follow the line of the Roman road which drops gradually down the ridge to the south towards the Thornthwaite Beacon, previously described.

As you rest at the beacon you must decide on your return route. If returning by Gray Crag just follow the broad ridge which falls gently away in a direction just west of north. Here we are retracing the first half of Route 4. To the right of the ridge lies Hayeswater nestling in the deep valley betwen Knott and Gray Crag and to the left is Threshthwaite Cove leading

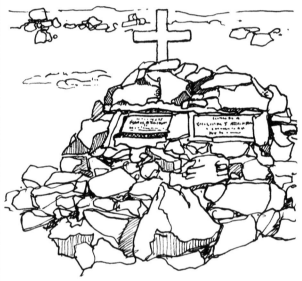

Memorial on Caudale Moor

back down to Pasture Bottom and our destination; the village of Hartsop. If returning by Stony Cove Pike take the path which descends in a northwesterly direction to Threshthwaite Mouth as described in Route 4. For the rest of the walk see Route 4.

Walks from the Summit of
Kirkstone Pass

Walks starting from here have the advantage of saving approximately 800 ft of climbing compared with starting at Hartsop. If you also finish here there is the added attraction of a 15th century coaching inn. The Kirkstone Pass Inn is a friendly welcoming place with log fires and mulled wine in cold weather **(LH5)**.

When snow lies on the ground a portable ski tow is sometimes set up here facilitating skiing

East of Ullswater

on the lower slopes of Woundale Fell which rises behind the inn. Thornthwaite Beacon and High Street are easily reached by the path which threads its way up this slope to the ridge; St Raven's Edge. Follow the ridge path north for a mile across rising peaty ground until you reach the Caudale Moor Cairn.

The cairn with the cross on it, which is situated a couple of hundred yards to the west, is a memorial to one Mark Atkinson of Kirkstone Pass Inn who died in 1930 aged 60 and, more recently, to his son Mark Ian Atkinson who was born at the inn and died in 1987 aged 83 years.

The path from Caudale Moor Cairn now bears east reaching Stony Cove Pike in half a mile. From here there is a steep drop down to Threshthwaite Mouth and an equally steep climb up the other side to Thornthwaite Beacon. With two cars, one left at Hartsop and the other at the top of the pass, it is possible to enjoy a walk which takes in part of the High Street ridge with a minimum of climbing. This can be a great benefit on short winter days.

D.LUSH.

Smallwater

Walks from Haweswater

The starting point for these walks is the head of Haweswater **(N)** where there is a car park. The journey to the head of the valley takes you past the Haweswater Dam along the new road, which was built between 1929 and 1931 before the valley was flooded **(LH6)**. As you approach the head of the lake note the island, Wood Howe, which was created when the adjacent village of Mardale was flooded by the waterworks scheme. Every few years, when an extended drought occurs, the roads, walls and bridge of the old village reappear and Wood Howe becomes a small hill in the old village once more. The resulting influx of sightseers has, unfortunately, caused serious traffic problems and damage to the remains on the lake bed. More seriously, the water birds, which nest on the island, have been disturbed by people and their dogs wandering around the area.

Route 6   High Street via Smallwater
and Mardale III Bell
Return via Riggindale Crag
and Rough Crag
Total Climbing about 1800 ft,   550 m
(6 miles)

This is a spectacular walk which circumnavigates the main watershed at the head of Haweswater. Go through the gate at the end of the road and take the path which leads southwest, round the western flank of Harter Fell, as it climbs up towards Smallwater. The path follows the line of Mardale Beck, eventually merging with it at the mouth of the small hanging valley which contains Smallwater. This is a pleasant sheltered place on a fine day and a good place to rest and look back at Haweswater.

Stepping stones cross the beck and the path circles the western shore of Smallwater as it gradually climbs up towards Nan Bield Pass; which links Harter Fell to Mardale III Bell. The final few hundred yards of this path is steep and twisty as it wends its way through the crags to the shelter on the pass. From here you can look down into Kentmere. Beyond, if the viewing is good, Morecambe Bay will be visible. Leaving the shelter we must now follow the path to the west which leads us steeply up to the plateau ridge of Lingmell End. The path then swings north as we walk the last few hundred yards to the inconspicuous summit of Mardale III Bell. This area can be difficult in mist due to the lack of any prominent markers but there is a good path visible on the ground, assuming the absence of snow. Mardale III Bell overlooks Bleawater and the Riggindale Ridge opposite. Unless very short of time, avoid the temptation to follow the edge of the ridge round to Riggindale as the ground is rough and boggy. From Mardale III Bell a broad path leads northwest onto the summit ridge of High Street. Follow this path until you reach the wall near Thornthwaite Crag (M). We now join the Roman road for about a quarter of a mile until the summit cairn of High Street is reached.

The return route down Riggindale Crag can be difficult to find in mist. Continue north for a further three hundred yards, keeping well to the right of the wall, until you see a cairn marking the path back to Haweswater. This route leads due east, dropping steeply down onto the Riggindale Ridge. Following this ridge path for a further two miles brings you back down to the lakeside at The Rigg. From here take the lakeside path south back to the car park.

An alternative descent is to leave the ridge at the plateau between Riggindale Crag and Rough Crag. An indistinct path, which drops down to the right, takes one to the dam at the head of Bleawater and from the dam a good path leads down the valley to the car park.

Route 7　　　Harter Fell via Smallwater
Return via Gatesgarth Pass
Total climbing about 1730 ft 526 m
(5 miles)

This walk follows Route 6 as far as Nan Bield Pass with its shelter (O). On reaching the summit of the pass follow the path which winds steeply up the craggy eastern shoulder of Harter Fell. In about half a mile the slope levels out as the summit plateau, with its large cairn, is reached. The path, across the rather featureless summit follows the wire fence, which runs roughly northeast above the craggy northern cliff of the fell. This fence is a useful marker in mist but, check with your compass that you are following the fence in the correct direction, or you could end up in Kentmere.

Good views can be enjoyed in all directions from this flat promontory. To the north and west the hills are steep and craggy, whilst to the south more rounded features drop away to Morecambe Bay and beyond. To the east, in the distance, can be seen Shap and the beginnings of the Lune Valley, which carries the motorway and railway past the Howgill Fells.

The path across the summit of Harter Fell follows the fence as it bends to the southeast and drops down the shoulder of Little Harter Fell. After about half a mile of gentle descent the path bears left and down onto the Gatesgarth Pass track; which links Long Sleddale to the Haweswater valley. The return route down Gatesgarth Beck gives dramatic views of Harter Fell Gully and the steep craggy northern face of Harter Fell.

Pack Horse Route
via Gatesgarth Pass
(from an old print)

Route 8　　　The Kentmere Round
Thornthwaite Beacon
from Kentmere via Garburn Pass
Yoke, III Bell and Froswick
return via Mardale III Bell,
Harter Fell and Kentmere Pike
Total climbing about 2500 ft, 762 m
(13 miles)

The southern fells east of Ullswater can conveniently be tackled from Kentmere village which is largely unspoilt and undeveloped. One disadvantage of this is that, at the time of writing, there is very little car parking space in the village. However there is some space beside Kentmere church. From the church take the road north to the beginning of the Garburn pass. A signposted track ('Garburn Road and Troutbeck') lies between two drystone walls which leads steeply up the hillside. This old packhorse route from Kendal to Troutbeck is the easiest route onto the ridge which is reached in about one mile. A drystone wall marks the line of the ridge from the top of the pass up towards the summit of Yoke, but this lies in rather boggy ground. In order to avoid most of the marshy ground, continue on the Garburn Pass track to the point where it bends sharply to the south. Turning north at this point will take you along an old quarry track marked by small cairns. In half a mile you will cross a stream and come across a large cairn. Leave the quarry track, which contours to the west at this point, and follow the cairned path which gradually converges with the wall following the ridge. Eventually the wall turns to the west leaving the ridge but our route continues ever upward to the summit of Yoke. The summit provides splendid views of the hills to the west, of Morecambe Bay to the south and of Kentmere Reservoir below and to the north east. The eastern flank of this ridge is craggy and precipitous. Do not attempt to descend on this side. In emergency either return down the ridge to the Garburn Pass or descend the western flank to Troutbeck.

From Yoke it is a gentle stroll along the ridge above Rainsborrow Cove to the summit of Ill Bell. The name Ill Bell, Hill Bell on old maps, indicates that the hill might have been used in days gone by to celebrate the fire god Bel by the lighting of fires at the festival of Beltane. From the top of Ill Bell the ridge path drops about 400 ft before rising through a height of 250 ft to attain the summit cairn of Froswick. It is not far now to the landmark of Thornthwaite Beacon approximately half way round the route which, with its panoramic views of the surrounding fells, is a good place to stop for lunch.

The second part of the journey takes us east from the beacon to hit the path which traverses the head of the Kentmere valley,

passing over Mardale Ill Bell and dropping down to the shelter at Nan Bield Pass (see Routes 6 and 7). From Nan Bield Pass take the path east up onto Harter Fell **(Route 7)** and, on reaching the summit cairn (and the fence which borders the summit plateau) turn south and follow this fence down the gently sloping ridge. In about a mile the path starts to climb again to the summit of Kentmere Pike. In good weather, as you stride down this broad ridge, the view of open countryside and distant coast makes you feel as if you are on the top of the world.

From Kentmere Pike an easy path continues gently down in a southeasterly direction for a further half mile. At this point a ninety degree turn in the fence is encountered directly above Goat Scar. Be careful in mist here. The path continues to follow this fence southwest until a ladder stile is reached which crosses a high wall. Cross the wall, turn south again and follow the well marked path which keeps to the line of the wall and the ridge, eventually arriving directly above Shipman Knotts. The path now threads its way due south down through the crags to the bridleway, which links Longsleddale with Kentmere, a drop of about 700 ft. This is a delightful part of the walk meandering as it does down through miniature valleys and knolls. In misty weather, or when the path is obscured by snow, just keep to the line of the wall. On reaching the valley, turn west and follow the bridleway

---

Lakeland Rains, and rains !

Much of the rich verdant beauty of the Lake District is derived from its frequent rains; but inexperienced tourists complain bitterly of them. For the guidance of strangers, it may be mentioned that, generally speaking, the worst months of the year, in the region, are November and December for storms; March for gales; and July for summer rains. The driest season is usually for a month or more onwards from the middle of May. September and October are often very fine months indeed.

Harriet Martineau   Guide to the Lakes
published in 1855

East of Ullswater

which will bring you in half a mile to the metalled road called High Lane. Turn left and follow this road back to your car in Kentmere.

* * * * *

Lakes to visit   Haweswater, Ullswater
Hayeswater

Nearest Towns Penrith, Ambleside
Places to visit Penrith Steam Museum
Penrith Town Museum

Country Houses   Dalemain
near Pooley Bridge

Recommended Country Inns
(Good Ale and Good Food)

The White Lion, Patterdale
The Kirkstone Pass Inn
The Haweswater Hotel
The Punch Bowl, Askham
The Helton Inn, Helton
The Queen's Head, Tirril

◆◆◆◆◆✿◆◆◆◆◆

Goldrill Bridge, Patterdale
(in 1819)

84

Kirkstone Pass and Inn (1991)

East of Ullswater, Local History

1. Border Reivers

These eastern fells provided corridors south for the marauding Scots and there are many tales of battles and skirmishes among these hills. Great Scarth Pass, Nan Bield Pass and High Street were frequently used. One such story describes how the burghers of Kendal received warning of an imminent Scottish raid. The raiders were expected to pass through Mardale by either Great Scarth or Nan Bield Pass. The men of Kendal laid a trap, posting their archers among the rocky ground on and surrounding Castle Crag on the west bank of Haweswater. When within shooting distance, the bowmen of Kendal poured volley after volley of arrows into the raiders killing them all. The Scots were buried where they fell. The archers of Kendal were famed for their bravery. Besides covering themselves with glory at Agincourt they featured in the battle of Flodden Field:

'These were the bows of Kendale bold
Who fierce will fight and never flee'

Incidentally, Castle Crag was probably no stranger to such violent happenings, like its namesake in Borrowdale, it is the site of an iron age fort.

2. Corpse Road and Mardale Church

Prior to 1728, when Mardale Church was granted a licence for burials, baptisms and marriages, anyone who died in the dale had to be transported via the old corpse road to the parish church of Shap. The corpse road wends its way across the northern slopes of Selside Pike down into Swindale Head. The dead were strapped to the backs of fell ponies for the trip, as the route is rather a rough fell path and quite unsuitable for wheeled vehicles.

A story has been handed down of one such journey when a wicked man, who had died in Mardale with an undivulged crime, was being carried over to Shap on the back of a strong young horse. During the journey a dreadful thunderstorm arose and the terrified horse bolted. For three months it roamed the fells evading every attempt at capture. Then, as is usual in such tales, the secret came to light, the horse allowed itself to be caught and the poor man was buried at Shap where, hopefully, he rests in peace.

The last body to be born over the fells for burial at Shap was John Holme of Brackenhow on 17th June 1736. The first burial in Mardale churchyard was that of John Turner in 1731. Of course since then, as a result of the water scheme, the bodies at Mardale have been exhumed and re-buried, the majority of them at Shap.

The church has been demolished and some of its fittings distributed to other churches in the county. The bell went to St. Barnabas, Carlisle, where it can still be heard today. The weather vane and various other artefacts went to Shap and the pulpit to

Borrowdale. The stonework of the windows can still be seen, as it was incorporated into the upper chamber of the water intake well on the eastern shore of the lake.

3. Hartsop Hamlet

The earliest record of the name Hartsop was in a document dated 1245. The name means 'the hill of the red deer' and deer still roam wild on the hills above the village. Although now a sleepy hamlet, Hartsop long ago had a bigger population than Patterdale or Glenridding. With two mines in the area and large slate quarries on the side of Caudale Moor and Place Fell, Hartsop must have been buzzing with industry. The green slates were sledged down to Kirkstone Foot, brought on horseback to the head of the lake and then ferried down to Pooley Bridge in boats carrying between six and eight tons. The sledging of slates down the mountainside was a skilled and rather dangerous task. This was described as follows in Clarke's 'Survey of the Lakes' published in 1789.

' A man will carry eight hundredweight at a time and go faster with it than without it: trials of that kind having been often made. The slate is laid upon a barrow, which is called a *trail barrow*; it has two inclining handles or stangs, between which the man is placed, going like a horse before the weight, and has nothing more to do than keep it in its tract, and prevent it from running too fast. Those who are dexterous will not sometimes set a foot on the ground for ten or twelve yards together; but the barow will often run away with an unskilful person, which was my case when I made an attempt. The length that is so carried is here about half a mile; the ascent so steep that to many persons it is easier than the descent'.

4. High Street

High Street probably derives its name from the 'strata' or Roman road which, following the course of an earlier British track, leads along its ridge at more than 2000 ft above sea level. In the Middle Ages this path was used by the Border Reivers on their forays into the district and was known as 'The Scots Rake'.

This rather inhospitable place was surprisingly well frequented by the local inhabitants in times gone by. Over 150 years ago, on holidays and feastdays, horse race meetings were held on the broad flat top above Blea Water. Hence the name Racecourse Hill. Clarke

in his 'Survey of the Lakes,' describes how, on the 10th of July each year the shepherds of the area assembled here for:

'horse racing, wrestling, and other such like country diversions: hither, likewise, every one brings the stray sheep he has found during the preceding year, that they may be owned: they also at this time amuse themselves with fox hunting.'

He goes on to describe how at one such hunting a man called Dixon fell about 1000 ft from the top of Blea-Water Crag. Although he hit the rocks several times on his way down, he had no broken bones, but

Horse Racing on High Street
over 150 years ago

was terribly bruised and was almost completely scalped. Dixon, a resident of Kentmere, survived to tell the tale and Clarke relates that the only hair on his head was a small tuft above one ear. The place on the crag where this unfortunate event occurred became known as Dixon's Three Jump.

5. Kirkstone Pass and Inn

The name Kirkstone (church stone) refers to the church-like rock standing at the head of the pass overlooking Brotherswater below. It was Wordsworth no less who immortalised this rock with the words:

'This block-and yon, whose church-like frame
gives to this savage pass its name'.

The Kirkstone Pass Coaching Inn dates back to the 15th century. It was built in 1496 by a priest from the Troutbeck valley, - *'in order for workers and travellers alike to stop and rest away from the harsh weather which comes without warning.'*

The Kirkstone

6. Mardale, the drowned valley

It is now over 50 years since Manchester Corporation, in its thirst for water, flooded the Mardale valley and ended a way of life for ever. The inhabitants were moved out and the hamlet of Mardale, farmsteads, pub, church and field walls were demolished.

Lying as it does on the old packhorse route from Kendal towards Penrith by way of Longsleddale and Gatesgarth Pass, this remote corner of lakeland had been inhabited for hundreds if not thousands of years. Its inhabitants had survived the rigours of severe winters, the harassment of border raiders and other natural and manmade calamities only to be eventually vanquished by Manchester Corporation.

As in Patterdale one family settled and remained in the valley for generations. A one Hugh Holme arrived in the valley in the reign of King John. By long ownership of property and by residence at Chapel Hill his descendants became known as '*The Kings Of Mardale*.' The last male Holme was Hugh Parker Holme who died in 1885 aged 34. The last person with the name Holme to live in the valley was his aunt, Mrs T Holme, who died in 1915 aged 90.

In 1919 the Manchester Corporation obtained parliamentary sanction to convert Haweswater into a reservoir. By 1925 they had bought out the landowners and taken possession of the land around the lake. However preparation and construction took a further sixteen years. The reservoir was brought into service in October 1941 and overflowed for the first time in December 1942.

The dam raised the level of Haweswater by 96 ft, trebling its surface area and increasing its capacity to 18,660 million gallons. The total cost of the dam was £476,948.

Unique in its day, the Haweswater dam is a hollow concrete buttress type of dam. It makes use of the immense compressive strength of concrete and was cheaper to build and is easier to maintain than the more traditional solid gravity dam. It can be inspected and maintained from within. Possible movement of the dam is monitored by a massive plumb bob hanging inside to indicate the vertical. This marker deflected one twentieth of an inch from the vertical when the dam first filled to overflowing in 1942.

Hugh Parker Holme
Born July 12th 1851
Died Nov. 27th 1885

The last King of Mardale and sole male survivor of a long line commencing with Hugh Holme in the year 1208

Since that time Manchester's thirst for Lake District water has not abated, but the developments at Ullswater and Windermere have reflected the immense public concern to protect the National Park. Ullswater and Windermere pumping stations are underground, soundproofed and completely hidden. Both stations are remotely operated from the treatment works at Watchgate, north of Kendal. The Ullswater station, near Pooley Bridge, pumps water up the fellside to Tarn Moor tunnel from where it flows to Heltondale and on to Haweswater. The Windermere station pumps water to a balancing reservoir at Banner Rigg from where it flows to Watchgate.

7. Martindale Church

Written records show that the old church of Martindale dates back to at least 1541. The ancient yew tree in the churchyard, now known to be 1300 years old, indicates that there has been a church on this site for a very long time. Although not used for regular services since 1881 the church is well kept and open to view. The pulpit bears the date 1634 and the flagged floor was laid in 1714 to replace the earthen floor. The font is believed to have been a roman altar brought down from the Roman road of High Street about 500 years ago. It was originally

used as a holy water stoup and later as the font. The deep scratches on the side of the font were made many centuries ago in the sharpening of tools.

Clarke, in his Survey of the Lakes, remarks on the smallness of the stipend paid to the curate in days gone by. In spite of this Mr Richard Birkett, who served the curacy for sixty seven years, amassed a considerable fortune. Being the only person in the parish who could write, he transacted all the legal affairs of his 200 parishioners. Whenever he lent money he deducted interest at two shillings in the pound. Whenever he wrote a receipt he charged two pence and for a promissary note, fourpence. He also served as parish clerk and was the local schoolmaster. In addition to his school fees he had a fortnight's free board and lodging at the house of each of his scholars and at Easter was paid in eggs. These he collected himself, carrying with him a board with a hole in it to

---

The Name of Ullswater

The name is possibly due to the fact that the lake is situated among mountains 'hul' in ancient Saxon signified a mountain.

However, it is more likely that the name came from the Celtic 'Ulle', meaning the bend or elbow.

King of Patterdale

Among the cottages of this village (Patterdale) there is a house belonging to a person of somewhat better condition; whose little estate, which he occupies himself, lies in the neighbourhood. As his property, inconsiderable as it is, is better than that of any of his neighbours, it has given him the title of *King of Patterdale,* in which his family name is lost. His ancestors have long enjoyed the title before him. We had the honour of seeing this prince and he took the diversion of fishing on the lake; and I could not help thinking, that if I were inclined to envy the situation of any potentate in Europe, it would be that of the King of Patterdale. The pride of Windsor and Versailles would shrink in comparison with the magnificence of his dominions.

William Gilpin - 1772

The old Church at Martindale

serve as a gauge and politely declining to accept any egg which would pass through the hole. Although the living was only worth seventeen pounds a year, through his enterprise and economies the Reverend Birkett was able to leave his wife twelve hundred pounds when he died. This custom of taking board and lodging from parishioners was common in former times, as church livings were so poor, and was known as 'Whittle Gate.' *Whittle* (or knife) and *Gate* (free board) at every farm or other house in the parish, turn and turn about for a week together. The parson also took casual employment, sheep shearing, hay making, teaching etc..

8. Ullswater Navigation and Transit Company

For over one hundred years two nineteenth century steam yachts have provided a regular service on the lake. 'The Lady of the Lake,' the smaller of the two vessels, was launched in 1877 followed by 'The Raven' in July 1889. The Raven, built at Rutherglen near Glasgow by Joseph Seath and Company, was carried in sections by rail to Penrith and then by horse dray to Pooley Bridge, where she was assembled. During the 1930's both vessels were converted to oil burning. A famous passenger on the Raven in the early 1900's was the German Kaiser, who was a guest of the famous Yellow Earl; Lord Lonsdale of Lowther Castle.

The company provide a scheduled daily service from early Spring to late Autumn between Pooley Bridge, Howtown and Glenridding. In addition, one hour cruises, cruise and lunch and special charters are available.

The Raven at Glenridding Pier

Great Gable from Great End

The Scafell Area

General

Scafell Pike, the highest mountain in England, can be visualised as sitting at the centre of a wheel, the spokes of which radiate outwards in the shape of the valleys of Eskdale, Langdale, Borrowdale, Ennerdale and Wasdale. The mountains surrounding the heads of these valleys form the highest and possibly the most popular wild area in the Lake District. The scenery here is magnificient, having a profusion of craggy steep sided mountains towering over narrow valleys. In contrast there are also wide expanses of broad ridgeland leading down from the high ground, such as at Burnmoor (LH9) and Ullscarf. There are many popular climbing faces on the crags of these mountains and several of the hills, such as Great End and Lingmell, are scarred by steep gullies which can provide good snow and ice climbing in a hard winter. This, unfortunately, does not occur often nowadays.

Walking

The paths are many and, due to the pressure of visitors, invariably well worn. Recently much work has been done by the National Trust pathbuilders to mitigate and forestall this erosion. Visitors to these high fells can help conserve the landscape by keeping to the marked path wherever there is one. The remoteness of most of the high tops from the valley base makes for longer more demanding expeditions than in some other parts of the district. The selection of routes that follows includes most of the major tops in the area.

Route 1   Scafell Pike from Seathwaite (A)
               via Grains Gill and Great End
               return via Lingmell and
               the Corridor Route
               (9 miles)

    Total Climbing about   3110 ft. (947 m)

The start point of this walk is Seathwaite Farm. There is parking space along the road to the farm but, in high season, or a good day in the winter, all of the space is often taken up by 10.00 a.m.. On leaving your car set off along the road through the farmyard towards Stockley Bridge. To your right, high on the hillside, notice the spoil heaps of the famous

The Scafell Area

Seathwaite Plumbago mine, which originally produced the pencil lead for the Keswick pencil industry (LH10).

Seathwaite has the unenviable reputation of being the wettest place in England with the highest annual rainfall. In 1954 the recorded annual rainfall at Sprinkling tarn above Seathwaite was 257 inches (6527 mm) making it the wettest place in the United Kingdom that year.

A mile along the track, Stockley Bridge is reached; this ancient packhorse bridge was washed away in floods twenty years ago but it has since been restored to its original style. After crossing the bridge, go through the gate and turn sharp left along the wall onto the path leading up Grains Gill. The path, gentle at first, gradually steepens as it follows the line of the gill. The mountain lying immediately ahead is Great End and, as it is approached, the well known features of Central and Cusp Gullies become visible. These can be exciting snow climbs in winter. A mile and a half above Stockley Bridge the Grains Gill path joins the path from Styhead and continues upwards and around the southern corner of Great End. It is only a short diversion to the summit of this fine mountain which, on a good day, is well worth the effort.

This vantage point provides magnificient views of Great Gable to the northwest with Glaramara to the northeast framing Borrowdale and Keswick in the distance. To the west the Isle of Man and its mountains should be visible with the Galloway coast bounding the Solway Firth further to the north.

Continuing on, the path to Scafell Pike now leads southwest over the shattered rocky terrain of Ill Crag and Broad Crag. This can be a confusing place in mist and the path can easily disappear in snow, but it is fairly well marked with cairns. In clear weather occasional excellent views are to be had from this path down onto Wasdale Head; home of the famous Will Ritson (LH6). The summit cairn of Scafell Pike lies directly ahead, apparently not much higher than our present position. Unfortunately for the legs, before that goal is reached, the path descends about 130 ft to cross a narrow cove which separates Broad Crag from Scafell Pike. The path then climbs steeply up the final three hundred feet

of shattered rock to the summit of England's highest mountain. The massive summit cairn on Scafell Pike affords both shelter from the wind and a platform for the view. To the west on the Solway plain are the cooling towers of Calder Hall, part of the Sellafield complex, intruding somewhat into an otherwise superb

Scafell Pike
(approaching the summit via Broad Crag)

view, with the Isle of Man in the background. To the north, east and south however the Lake district lies before you with almost every major peak being visible from here. Usually it is too busy to loiter here for long. Care must be taken when deciding in which direction your return route lies. Because of the rocky nature of the summit the paths, marked by small cairns, all look alike and in mist it would be sensible to take a compass bearing.

Return via Lingmell and the Corridor Route

The path down to Lingmell from the summit cairn lies on a magnetic bearing of 295° and is marked by small cairns to the edge of the summit plateau. A fairly steep descent follows down on to the col between Lingmell and Scafell Pike. Before reaching the col our path joins the track from Wasdale, which eventually becomes the Corridor route. If there is time it is well worth a detour to the top of Lingmell in order to peer down into the rocky depths of

Piers Gill, a truly spectacular ravine. The return path, via the corridor route, is well worn and easy to follow with one or two interesting rock scrambles along the way. The path effectively traverses the northwestern slope of Great End until it emerges at the bottom of The Band, just above Styhead Tarn. The path back to Seathwaite from Styhead splits not far below the tarn. The main packhorse route keeps to the south of Styhead Gill as it wends its way down to Stockley Bridge and hence to Seathwaite Farm. The minor path to the north of the gill affords a pleasant alternative route past the 140 ft. waterfall, Taylor Gill Force. This route does entail some interesting rock scrambling as it passes through the ravine, which only adds to the interest of the path. From the foot of the falls a rather indistinct and wet path meanders over the rough fellside on the western side of the gill, leading back to the bridge at Seathwaite Farm, where the tea room beckons.

Route 2.   Great Gable from Honister Pass via Drum House
Total Climbing about 2220 ft (677 m)
Return by the same route
(6 miles)
including the Gable Girdle
(9 miles)

This is the most popular, the shortest, and the least demanding route to the summit. Because it is relatively short for a day trip I have included the Gable Girdle as an option to extend the walk without much additional climbing. Park your vehicle in the park behind the Youth Hostel at the summit of Honister Pass. This elevated start point saves about 600 ft of climbing compared with the valley bottom. Honister Pass was the scene of a great battle between the Graeme's; a notorious family of Scottish Reivers, and the English Borderers (**LH5**). It is also the site of a famous lakeland quarry, now alas finally closed, which produced Honister green slate for over three hundred years. According to local legend the quarries were first worked by one Moses Rigg, a notorious whisky smuggler (**LH8**). The path to Gable passes through the quarry yard, past the sheds housing the large slate saws, and on up the old tramway which was used to carry slate to Honister from Dubs

Quarry on the side of Fleetwith Pike. In half a mile the drumhouse is reached. This is the highest point on the tramway.

The drumhouse used to house the winding gear which pulled loaded tubs up from Dubs and then lowered them under gravity to Honister. The path to Gable turns south at the drumhouse, as it leaves the tramway and circumnavigates the crags of Grey Knotts. About half a mile after leaving the drumhouse our path intersects the route from Haystacks to Brandreth, part of the Ennerdale Horseshoe. We will follow this route as far as the summit of Great Gable. Turn left here and follow the path to the top of Brandreth. From Brandreth continue south by descending to the minor col of Gillercomb Head before climbing again to the top of Green Gable. In summer the top of Green Gable is generally green unlike the rocky dome of Great Gable facing us across the narrow col of Windy Gap. A steep well worn path leads down onto the col before climbing, in a southwesterly direction, up the rocky front of Gable. The path here is really a rock scramble through a chaotic terrain of loose stones, slates and rock steps, but is easy to follow as it is so well worn. Care must however be taken with younger members of the family who may find parts of the route rather daunting. In a short time the path levels out as the summit plateau is approached. The cairned route across the rather featureless top of this sugar loaf mountain leads directly to an outcrop of large rocks where the summit cairn is to be found.

Set into the side of one of the rocks is the Fell and Rock Climbing Club War Memorial which consists of a bronze relief map of the fells in the area of Gable. A service has been held here on Remembrance Sunday every year since its dedication in 1924. This event has become an annual pilgrimage for many and it is not uncommon to have several hundred people attend, even in poor weather conditions. Great Gable is an ideal platform for surveying the surrounding fells but by far the best view to be had is that down the Wasdale Valley from Westmorland Cairn. The cairn lies directly above Westmorland Crags, on the edge of the summit plateau, about 130 metres southwest of the memorial. Westmorland Cairn was built in 1879 by two brothers from

The view from Westmorland Cairn

Honister follows the stone wall which climbs over the summit of Grey Knotts before descending towards the car park on Honister Pass. The last quarter of a mile of this path is quite steep and eroded. If time is available the day can be extended by including the **'Gable Girdle'** in the route. From the top of Gable retrace your steps back to Windy Gap; the narrow col between Green and Great Gable. Turn right at the col and follow the path beside the beck down to Styhead Tarn. Turn right again when you arrive at the tarn and follow the old packhorse route southwest towards Wasdale. The beautiful remote pass via Styhead is thankfully still just that. There was once a proposal to put a road through here from Borrowdale to Wasdale. Luckily the plan was opposed and shelved before it even got off the drawing board. On reaching the Mountain Rescue Stretcher Box at Sty Head, the path into Wasdale drops steeply down into the valley. The Girdle path, however, bears to the right, climbing gently to pass beneath the crags of Kern Knotts. The path tends to split and rejoin rather confusingly as it traverse round under the crags. Eventually the Great Napes are reached, flanked by the stone chutes of Little Hell Gate and Great Hell Gate. The Napes is a popular climbing area made famous by the Abraham Brothers of Keswick at the turn of the century. Their early climbing photographs did much to popularise the new sport of rock climbing and have become classics of their time. Perhaps their most famous photograph is that of an ascent of the Napes Needle, the large spire of rock which lies below the Napes Crags.

The Needle, which was first climbed in June 1886 by Walter Parry Hasket Smith, does not stand out when seen from the path below and is best seen from the 'Dress Circle'; a ledge on the opposite side of Needle Gulley to the Needle. If climbers are on the rock this is the ideal place to sit and watch. For those, like myself, too timid and too inexperienced in the art of rock climbing to attempt to climb the needle, there is a lesser alternative, namely to thread the needle. The process of threading the needle is to climb through the narrow gap between the needle and the Napes crags. This is an interesting but not too difficult little gully scramble with plenty of good holds. The

Penrith of that name who were of the opinion that it marked the best mountain viewpoint in the area. Many would agree with them, depending on the weather of course. If the weather is fine and you have time to linger you may wish to look for the smugglers hut perched high on a small plateau below the summit on Gable Crag (**LH8**).

The return route is just the reverse of the outward journey. However a variation can be introduced if desired. On reaching the summit of Brandreth an alternative path back to

93

summit of Gable can be regained from this point on the traverse if desired. Little Hell Gate and Great Hell Gate provide steep and stony access to the ridge which terminates above the Napes. From here there is a good path up to the summit. However, less energy will be expended if we continue on our traverse. On leaving the Napes the path contours round to the north, as it crosses the steep and stony western face of the mountain, eventually arriving at Beck Head; the source of Gable Beck. Several paths meet at Beck Head due to its position on the col between Ennerdale and Wasdale. The most famous of these is 'Moses' Trod' which is said to be the route by which

Napes Needle

Moses Rigg smuggled his contraband whisky, from his illegal distillery in the quarries, down into Wasdale. The shortest way back to Honister from here is to follow Moses' Trod eastwards, as it contours round Stone Cove and across the flatter ground under Green Gable Crag. It is quite easy to get lost here, particularly in poor visibility, as paths lead towards both Ennerdale and Honister. The path back to the Drum house contours round the southwestern side of Brandreth. It is broad and easy to follow. Alternatively one may wish to complete the girdle by sticking to the higher path, which traverses under the northern crags of Gable as it gradually rises to the col of Windy Gap.

Route 3   Haystacks via Scarth Gap
               return via Fleetwith Pike
Total Climbing about 2080 ft   (634 m)
                    (5 miles)

This interesting short walk gives excellent views along the Buttermere Valley, takes one over the aptly named rocky summits of Haystacks and gives a glimpse into the past with a visit to the upper workings of the Honister Crag Slate Quarry. The startpoint for the walk is Gatesgarth Farm (see Derwent map). There is a small car park adjacent to the road (£2 charge). Take the footpath through the gate by the bridge, which bypasses the farmyard, and follows the wall across the field at the head of the lake. The well worn path to Scarth Gap climbs up the steep lower slopes of Buttermere Fell. It then turns due south as it makes a beeline for Scarth Gap Pass. On reaching the pass, which leads into Ennerdale, take the steep path to the left which climbs up through the crags onto the summit of Haystacks. This is yet another section of the marathon lakeland walk, the Ennerdale Horseshoe. Care needs to be taken here in misty weather. Haystacks is an extended chaotic summit of crags and small tarns. The path over its popular and well- walked top splits and rejoins many times, as it circumnavigates the many small rocky outcrops on its way down to Innominate and Black Beck Tarns. From Black Beck Tarn the path turns northeast as it drops down towards Dubs Quarry. Before reaching the quarry our path joins the old pony track from Gatescarth to Dubs. The most direct route to the summit of Fleetwith Pike from here is straight up the hill, due north, from this junction. However, you may wish to visit the old quarry first. The one remaining building, which is still used as a climbing hut, used to be the stable for the quarry ponies. Metal rings set into the inner walls of the building betray its original use. There is no obvious path up to the summit of Fleetwith Pike from Dubs. Just make your way, as previously stated, due north straight up the hill. As you approach the summit you will join the path which traverses the summit of Honister Crag. If you have time this is a place worth exploring. Some of the oldest workings at Honister are to be found at the top of the crag. Here you will find carefully constructed walls and staircases of slate and areas where the slate was split and dressed before being led down the crag. About 300 years ago the slate was taken along Moses' Trod (or sledgate) which crossed Dubs Moor, Brandreth and the head of Ennerdale and thence down to Wasdale.

Having explored the old surface workings of Honister Crag continue west along the ridge path to the summit of Fleetwith Pike. From here a well worn path snakes its way down the rocky contours of Fleetwith Edge leading back to Gatesgarth. The descent is tricky in places, particularly when wet, so care should be taken. The consequences of not being careful are amply illustrated by the white cross situated near the base of the ridge, which is easily seen from the road. This is the memorial to Fanny Mercer who died here in 1887 after falling over the crag on her way down the edge **(LH3)**. The path has recently been diverted around this final crag on the edge in order to reduce erosion. From Fanny Mercer's Cross it is only a short distance back to Gatesgarth farm, which was renowned in the old guide books as an excellent place to take board and lodging.

Route 4　　Red Pike via Yewbarrow
return via Scoat Fell and Haycock
Total Climbing about 2930 ft (893 m)
(9 miles)

The starting point for this walk is the car park at Overbeck Bridge **(M)** on the northern shore of Wastwater. The path up Yewbarrow follows Over Beck for about 300 yards before

Wastwater, looking northeast

turning sharp right up the well defined southern ridge of this fine mountain. In half a mile the path becomes a rock scramble. This is in order to negotiate the broken ground of Dropping Crag, as it climbs up through the 'Great Door.' The summit cairn of Yewbarrow is soon reached from where the surrounding mountains and tarns can be viewed.

Burnmoor Tarn can be seen to the south lying high on the plateau of Eskdale Moor. To the east lies Lingmell with Great End beyond, overshadowed by the great mass of Scafell Pike and Scafell to the southeast. The path now continues north along the ridge for half a mile until a subsidiary summit is reached, just above Stirrup Crag. A steep scrambly descent now leads down onto the col of Dore head between Yewbarrow and Red Pike. From here the path to the summit of Red Pike climbs steeply to the northwest as it skirts above Bull Crags and Black Crag, which overhang the Mosedale valley between Red Pike and Kirk Fell. In about a mile the summit cairn of Red Pike is reached. At 2710 feet (826 m) this is almost as high as we go. Seven hundred foot

The Scafell Area

below us to the west lies Scoat Tarn, with Haycock beyond. The path continues for another half mile or so across Scoat Fell until it meets the main ridge route between Pillar and Haycock, yet another section of the Ennerdale Horseshoe. We now follow this path west towards Haycock. On this section of the route one can only marvel at the skill and fortitude of the drystone wall builders. The massive wall which traverses this ridge from Steeple to Crag Fell, just above Ennerdale Water, is a fitting monument to their endeavours. It can also be a life saver in mist, as the main ridge route follows it for over five miles across this rather featureless section of the Ennerdale Horseshoe. However, we need only follow the wall to the point just before Haycock, where the ridge path meets the path from Ennerdale to Wastwater. You now have a choice of either taking the path down the valley to the west of Scoat Tarn, which follows Nether Beck to Netherbeck Bridge, or going on to Haycock. From the summit of Haycock you can then stay high and visit the lower summit of Seatallan before dropping down to the path beside Nether Beck. It is only a short walk along the road from Netherbeck Bridge back to the car park at Overbeck Bridge. If you descend from Haycock on a fine evening, with the sun low in the west, the view of Wastwater with its famous scree slopes falling steeply down to its southern shore can be truly unforgettable.

Wastwater Screes

D. LUSH

Some Thoughts On Wasdale

"There is a lake, hid far among the hills,
That raves around the throne of solitude,
Not fed by gentle streams or playful rills,
But headlong cataract or rushing flood.

There gleam no lovely lines of hanging wood-
No spot of sunshine lights her sullen side-
For horror shaped the wild in wrathful mood,
And o'er the tempest heaved the mountain's pride. "
Christopher North *(see LH 6)*
(Poet and Philosopher, friend of **Will Ritson**)

"Oh Wasdale, where are thy charms,
That poets have found in thy face;
Better dwell in the midst of alarms,
Than stay in this watery place."
Miss Knowles
July 12th 1869
"Nor have these eyes by greener hills
Been soothed in all my wanderings
(Two entries in the Wasdale Hotel)
(Visitors' Book)
quoted by **Edmund Bogg**

Above: A sea of clouds seen from Allen Crags
Below: Ascending the greasy slates of Hopegill Head from Ladyside Pike (see page 11)

Above: Blencathra in winter (December 1993) Courtesy of Phil Towers
Below: Ascending Robinson in winter sunshine

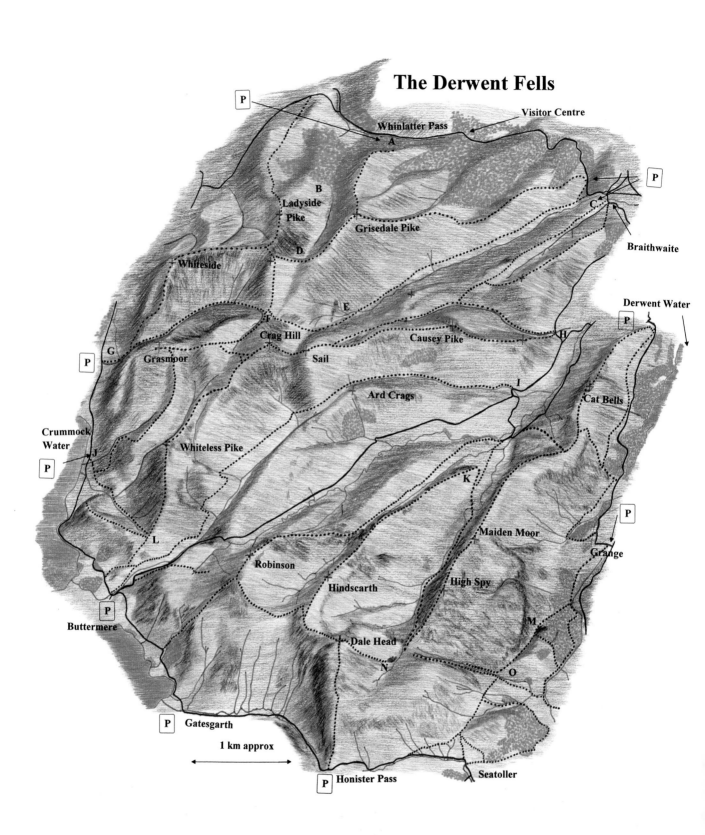

The Derwent Fells

Whinlatter Pass

Visitor Centre

A

B
Ladyside Pike

Grisedale Pike

D

Whiteside

C

P

Braithwaite

E

F

Crag Hill

Causey Pike

H

Derwent Water

G

Grasmoor

Sail

P

I

Cat Bells

Crummock Water

Ard Crags

J

P

Whiteless Pike

K

P

L

Maiden Moor

Grange

Robinson

High Spy

P

Buttermere

Hindscarth

M

Dale Head

N

O

P
Gatesgarth

1 km approx

P
Honister Pass

Seatoller

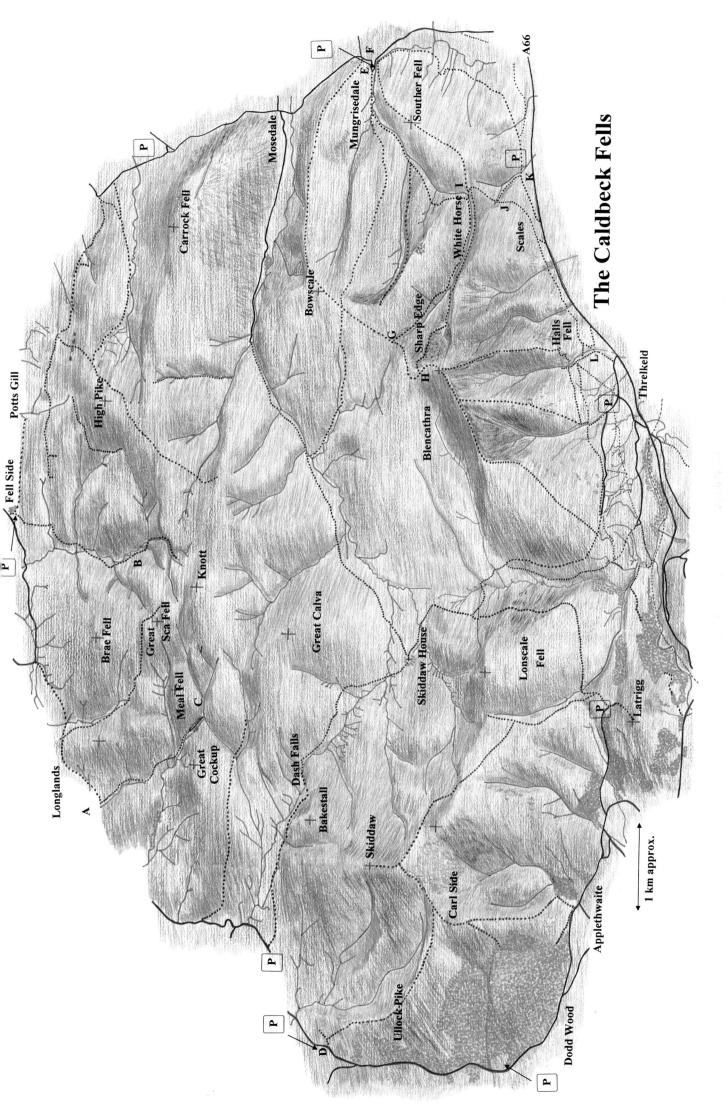

The Caldbeck Fells

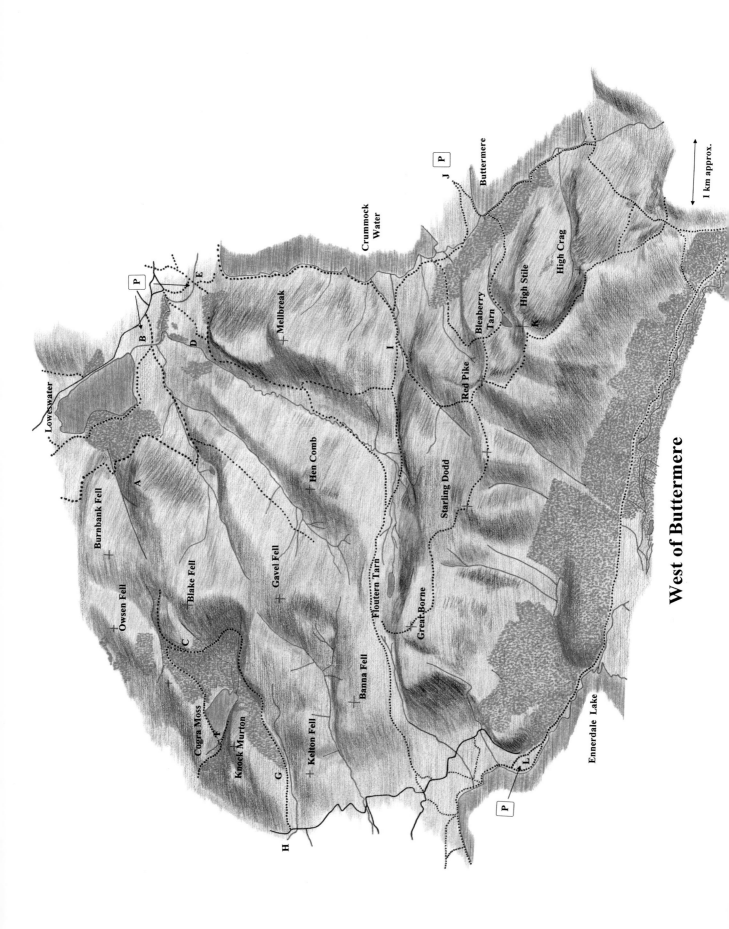

West of Buttermere

Loweswater

Burnbank Fell

Owsen Fell

A

Blake Fell

B

P

D

E

Mellbreak

Cogra Moss

C

F

Knock Murton

Gavel Fell

Hen Comb

Crummock Water

I

G

Kelton Fell

H

Banna Fell

Floutern Tarn

Great Borne

Starling Dodd

Red Pike

Bleaberry Tarn

High Stile

K

High Crag

J

P

Buttermere

L

P

Ennerdale Lake

1 km approx.

North of Whinlatter

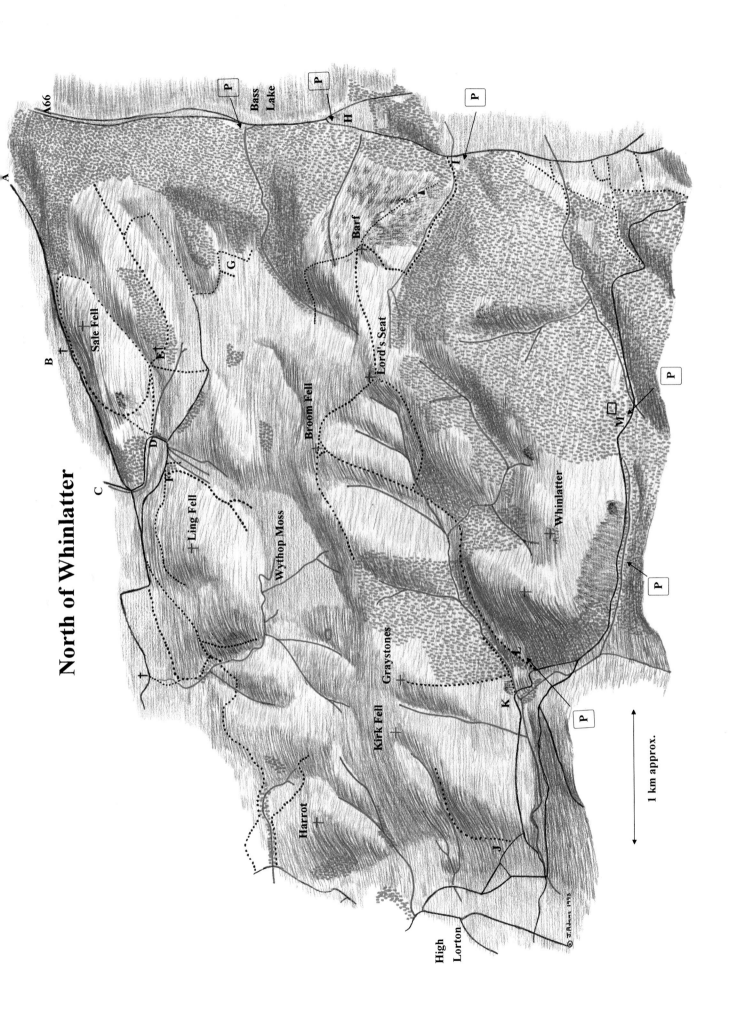

1 km approx.

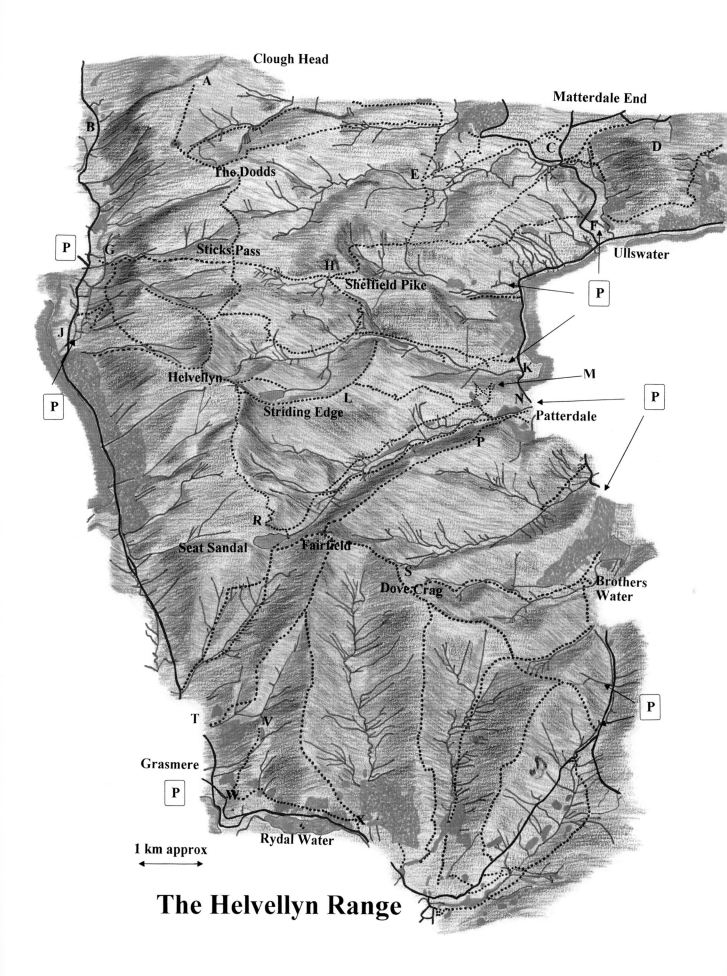

The Helvellyn Range

Clough Head

Matterdale End

A

B

The Dodds

C

D

E

F

Ullswater

P

G

Sticks Pass

H

Sheffield Pike

P

J

K

Helvellyn

M

L

N

Patterdale

P

Striding Edge

P

P

R

Seat Sandal

Fairfield

S

Dove Crag

Brothers Water

T

V

Grasmere

P

W

X

Rydal Water

P

1 km approx

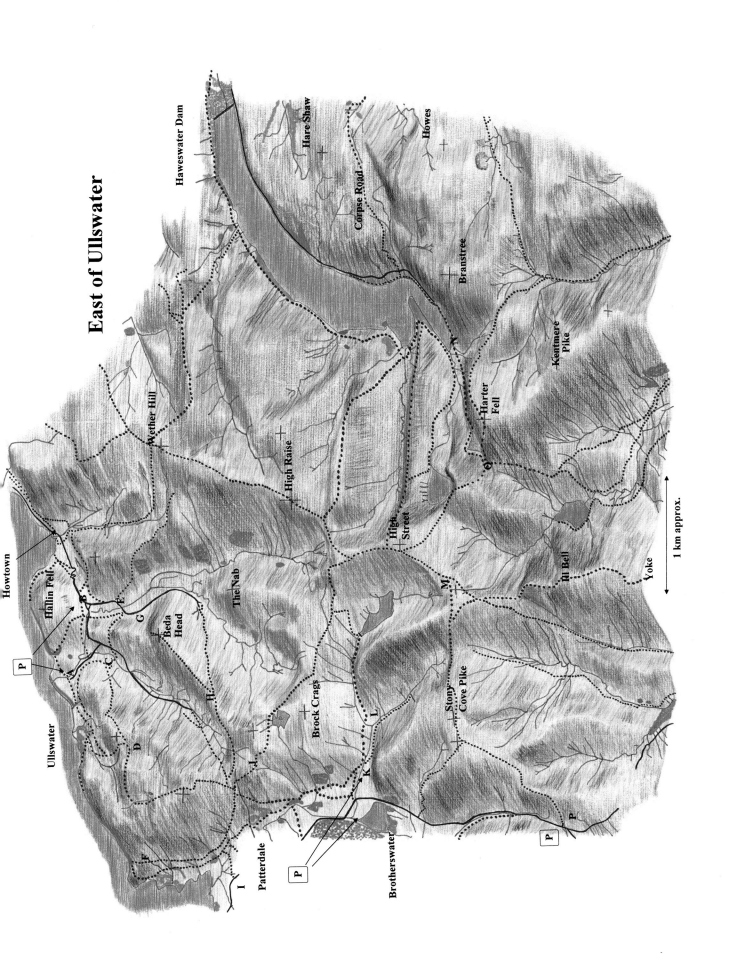

East of Ullswater

Howtown

Ullswater

Hallin Fell

P

Patterdale

I

F

D

C

E

G

Beda Head

The Nab

H

J

Brock Crags

K

L

P

Brotherswater

P

Wether Hill

High Raise

High Street

M

Stony Cove Pike

Ill Bell

Yoke

P

Haweswater Dam

Hare Shaw

Corpse Road

Howes

Branstree

Kentmere Pike

Harter Fell

N

O

1 km approx.

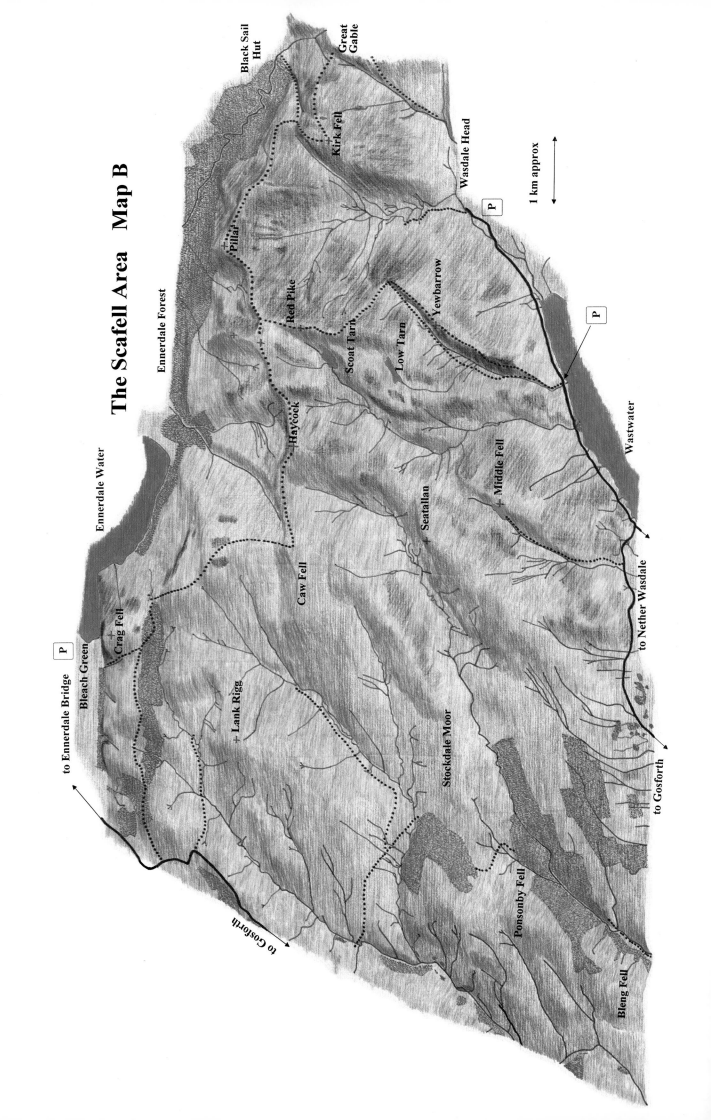

The Scafell Area   Map B

Black Sail Hut

Great Gable

Kirk Fell

Wasdale Head

Pillar

Ennerdale Forest

Red Pike

Scoat Tarn

Low Tarn

Yewbarrow

Haycock

Ennerdale Water

Middle Fell

Seatallan

Wastwater

Caw Fell

Crag Fell

Bleach Green

Lank Rigg

Stockdale Moor

to Nether Wasdale

P

to Ennerdale Bridge

to Gosforth

to Gosforth

Ponsonby Fell

Bleng Fell

P

P

1 km approx

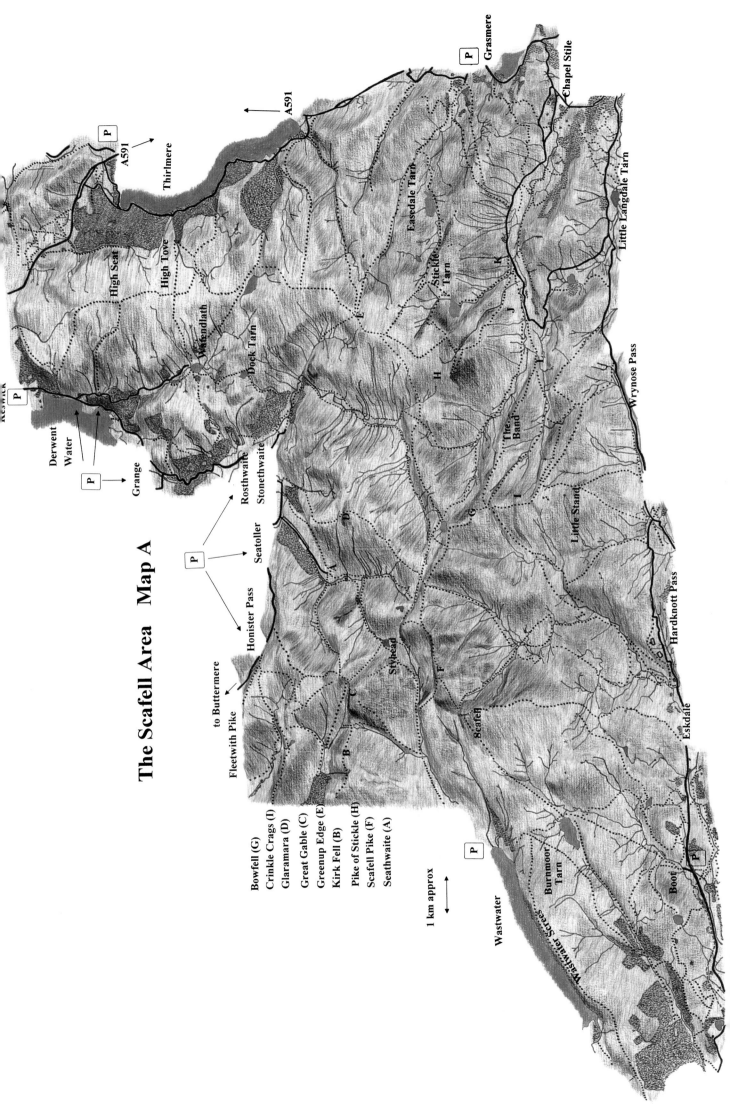

The Scafell Area   Map A

Bowfell (G)
Crinkle Crags (I)
Glaramara (D)
Great Gable (C)
Greenup Edge (E)
Kirk Fell (B)
Pike of Stickle (H)
Scafell Pike (F)
Seathwaite (A)

1 km approx

Grasmere

Chapel Stile

Little Langdale Tarn

Easedale Tarn

Stickle Tarn

Wrynose Pass

The Band

Little Stand

Hardknott Pass

Eskdale

Boot

Wastwater

Wastwater Screes

Burnmoor Tarn

Scafell

Styhead

Fleetwith Pike

to Buttermere

Honister Pass

Seatoller

Rosthwaite
Stonethwaite

Dock Tarn

Watendlath

High Tove

High Seat

Thirlmere

A591

A591

Derwent
Water

Grange

Keswick

The Coniston Fells

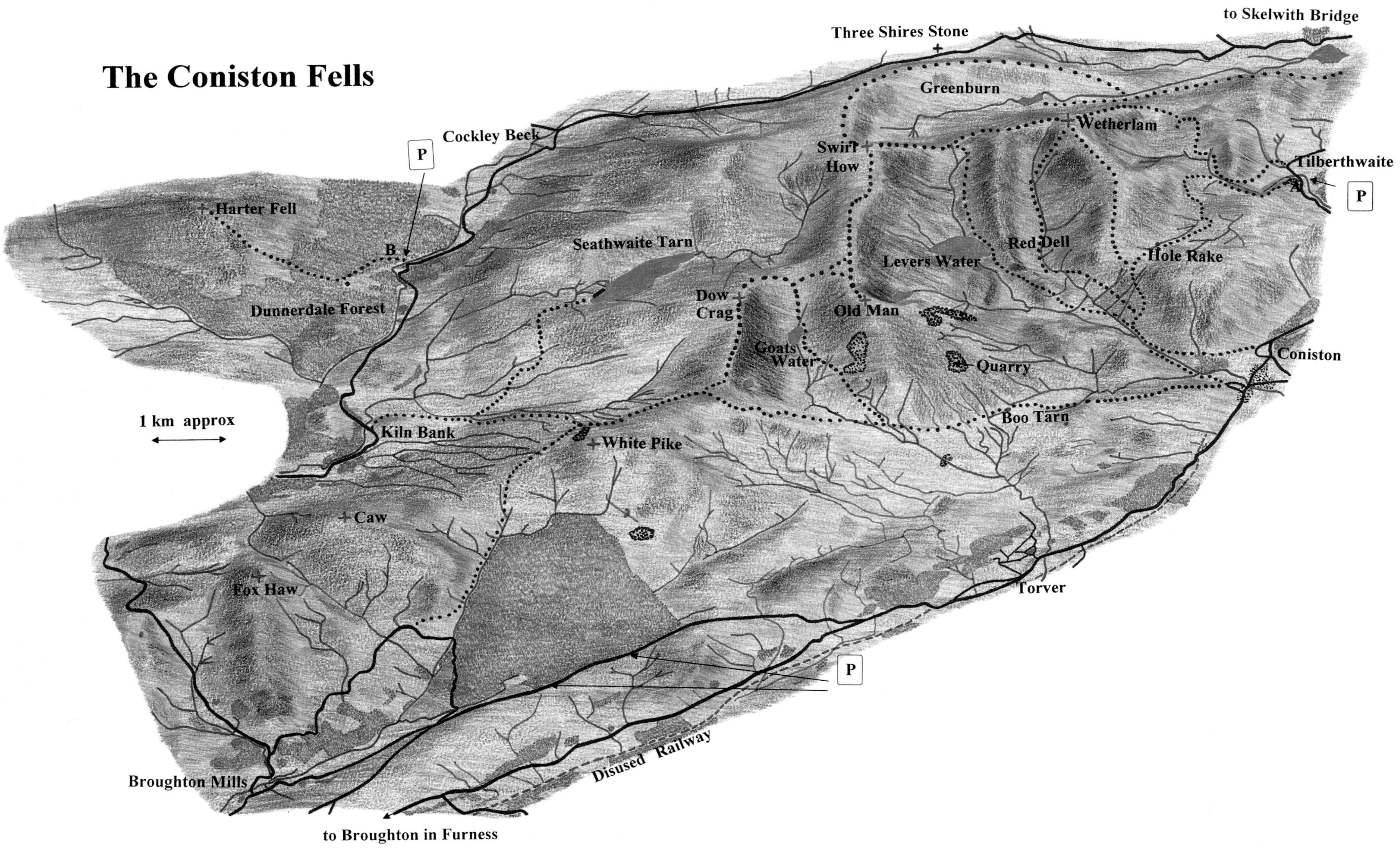

to Skelwith Bridge

Tilberthwaite

P

Coniston

Hole Rake

Wetherlam

Red Dell

Greenburn

Three Shires Stone

Levers Water

Swirl How

Old Man

Quarry

Boo Tarn

Torver

Goats Water

Cockley Beck

Seathwaite Tarn

Dow Crag

White Pike

P

Disused Railway

P

B

Harter Fell

Dunnerdale Forest

Kiln Bank

Caw

Fox Haw

Broughton Mills

1 km approx

to Broughton in Furness

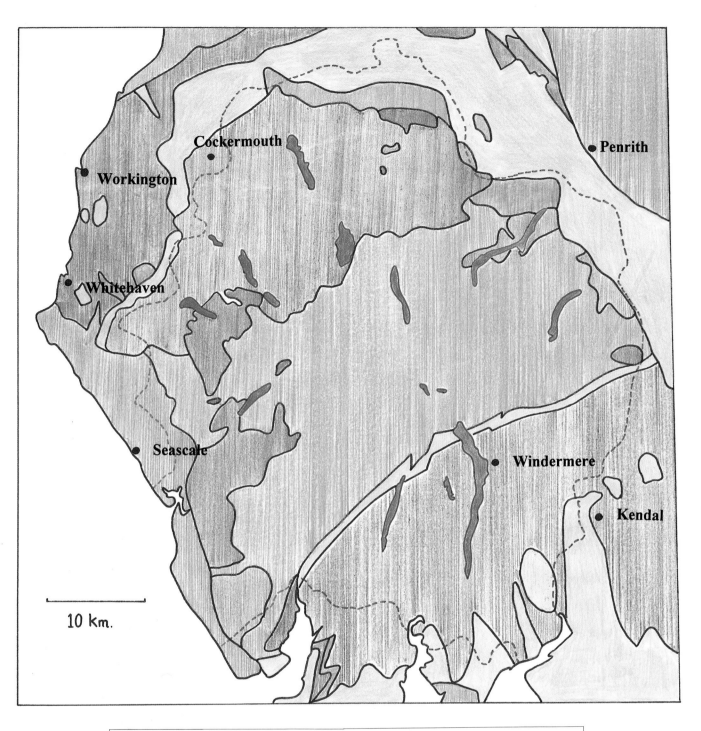

Simplified Geological Map of the English Lake District

(with thanks to Tom Shipp)

The boundary of the National Park on the map is shown thus: — — — — —

Succession of rocks in the Lake District

Geological Period	Age (million years)	Key to the Map	Geological events and principal rock formations	Environmental / climatic conditions
Pleistocene _____ 1			Ice Ages	Periodic temperature fluctuations; cooler then warmer
			Gentle folding and faulting of Lake District Rocks	Major erosion by glaciers. Probably a hilly landscape.
	100		Rocks formed at these times are not found in the district.	A warm climate, alternating between land and shallow sea
	200		St Bees Sandstone	River plain deposits formed in a semi - arid climate.
Triassic _____ (New Red Sandstone)			St Bees and Eden shales including beds of gypsum.	Periodic flooding of a desert basin.
Permian _____	300		Penrith Sandstones and Brockrams	A hot and windy desert terrain.
Upper Carboniferous _____ (including Coal Measures)			Considerable folding and faulting Coal Measures	
Lower Carboniferous _____ (mainly limestones)			Millstone Grit and Carboniferous Limestones	Forested swamp with a tropical climate. River deltas discharging sand from the north
Devonian _____ 400 (Mell Fell Conglomerate)			Mell Fell Conglomerate	into shallow tropical seas. Rapid erosion of mountainous terrain under a hot semi-arid climate.
Silurian _____ (Windermere group)			Main phase of granite emplacement. Caledonian mountain-building.	Major collisions between continental masses.
Upper Ordovician _____ (Coniston group)			Marine mudstones and sandstones.	Layers of sediments formed in a marine trough.
Mid Ordovician _____ 500 (Borrowdale & Eycott volcanic groups)			Marine mudstones and sandstones	Sea engulfing an eroded volcano. Volcanic island develops.
Lower Ordovician _____ (Skiddaw group)			Marine mudstones and sandstones	Early volcanic eruptions. Sediments deposited off the edge of the former continent.
Igneous Intrusions (deep granitic magma)				

Above: Crossing the Crinkles in winter (December 1993)
Below left: The Embleton Sword (see page 52)

Below right: Skiddaw with a mantle of Spring snow

Above: Helm Crag, Grasmere on a winter's morning

Above: A hungry sheep with an eye on my sandwiches (see page 25)
Below: Morning mist over Ullswater

Above: A winter reflection on Fleetwith Pike
Below: Summer sunset over Ullswater

Above: Trinity School Staff Friday Night walking group
                     on a chilly September evening in the Caldbeck Fells

Below: Butty time at the summit of Place Fell on a fine summer evening

Above: Rainbow over Outerside

Below: Winter sunbeams over Souther Fell

Below: John Adams setting out for an underground walk in the Lake District

The Scafell Area

Walks from Great Langdale

Route 5   Crinkle Crags **(I)** via Oxendale **(L)**
return via the Band

or return via Bowfell **(G)**
(the hill with the bow shaped shoulder)

Total Climbing about 2630 ft (801 m)
(9 miles)

The start point for this walk is the car park at the old Dungeon Ghyll Hotel **(J)**. Leaving the car park walk back to the junction with the main road. Take the footpath, leading west across the fields towards Stool End, which starts at the gate near the junction. Before reaching Stool End Farm the path to Oxendale leads off to the left. The path follows Oxendale Beck for half a mile until a footbridge is reached. From here our route leads almost due south as it rises steeply to the col between Pike of Blisco and Great Knott. The jagged ridge of Crinkle Crags can be seen beyond against the skyline. The ridge surprisingly derives its name from the Norse 'Kringla' or circle and not from its jagged appearance. In Norse times it must have been known as the 'Circling' or perhaps 'Encircling Crags.' On reaching the col below Red Tarn the path turns sharply west, as it contours round the summit of Great Knott onto the start of Crinkle Crags. The route across the Crags threads this way and that as it negotiates the rocky pinnacles and can be confusing, particularly in mist. The main route is well worn and reasonably easy to follow. Generally it is better to follow the line of the ridge than to try and bypass the summits. The path over the summits is straightforward, involving a little scrambling except for a large rock which blocks the path at the first pinnacle. This might test the less experienced walker. There are two ways past this obstacle, up and over the adjoining rock face to the right, (there are many easy scrambling holds), or through the hole under the large rock. This latter route still involves a scramble up the rock face on the far side of the large rock.

On a clear day the view from the Crinkles is excellent. To the northwest lie Scafell, Scafell Pike and Great End and to the north, Bowfell,

with Esk Pike beyond. From this viewpoint these high mountains are seen to their best advantage as their steep rugged crags drop away to the wild head of Mosedale. Continuing on along the shattered rock summit ridge of the Crinkles the path eventually drops down to the col of the three tarns; which lies between the Crinkles and Bowfell. To return down the broad ridge of The Band, take the path which contours to the northwest under Bowfell before it eventually drops onto the

Langdale Pikes from the Band

White Stones ridge. This route gives excellent views of the Langdale Pikes and the Langdale valley as it drops directly down to Stool End and our outward path.

If continuing over Bowfell, take the steep scree path which leads directly north to the summit ridge of this fine mountain. The path along the narrow summit plateau leads west before turning sharply north towards ore gap and Esk Pike. Ore or 'Ure' Gap was used in days gone by to lead iron ore over from Eskdale to the smelter or 'bloomery' which was sited in the Langstrath valley north of Bowfell **(Page 100)**. On reaching Ore Gap, between Esk Pike and Bowfell, turn north and follow this ancient trade route down to Angle Tarn above which you will encounter the popular path to Scafell from Langdale via Rossett Gill. Turning east along this path takes us back to Langdale. As you descend via Rossett Gill you may observe

The Scafell Area

"The Old Woman's Grave" on a grassy mound to the right of the path **(LH4)**. The path has been recently repaired by the National Trust but luckily the grave, being situated somewhat off the path, has not been disturbed. On reaching the bottom of the Gill our path merges with the Stake Pass route (part of the Cumbria Way) which takes us along Mickleden, beneath the Langdale Pikes, back to the Old Dungeon Ghyll Hotel.

Route 6   **'The Langdale Pikes'**
(the pikes of the long dale)

Pike of Stickle **(H)**
via Pavey Ark and Harrison Stickle

Total Climbing about 2390 ft   (729 m)
(5 miles)

The start point for this walk is The New Dungeon Ghyll Hotel **(K)** in Great Langdale. In high season it is advisable to arrive early as the car parks soon fill up in this very popular valley. The walk described is quite short, suitable for a cold short winter's day, when finding a place to park may be easier. The route starts at the north end of the car park beside the hotel. Go through the National Trust gate and follow the recently reconstructed path, which follows Stickle Gill up to its source, namely Stickle Tarn. The path follows the left hand side of the Gill until a wooden footbridge over the gill is reached. The path now continues on the right hand side of the gill until the reconstructed path comes to an end just below Tarn Crag. From here there is a choice of routes up either side of the gill. However the path on the right is to be recommended. As it wends its way up to traverse the lower slopes of the crag there are some fine rock steps, giving a foretaste of what is to come on Pavey Ark. On reaching the tarn, formerly a water supply for the gunpowder works at Elterwater, the impressive crags of Pavey Ark, which cradle the tarn's northern shore, are seen to best advantage.

The most adventurous walking route to the summit of Pavey Ark, 700 ft above the tarn, is of course 'Jack's Rake,' a narrow path which can be seen following a diagonal groove from east to west across the face of the crag. Described as a 'safe natural' path' by the pioneer climber Owen Glynne Jones in 1900, Jack's Rake has suffered from many millions of vibram clad feet since then, but it is still an enjoyable scramble. These great cliffs of Pavey Ark are deeply cut by two gullies. These have been popular with climbers for many years. The right hand gully, namely 'Great Gully,' was first climbed by Haskett Smith in 1882 and the first ascent by a lady was made in 1887, thus showing that the female rock climber is no new phenonemon. The lefthand gully, 'Little Gully,' was also a first for Haskett Smith in June 1886.

For those less adventurous, or who dislike feeling exposed on narrow ledges, alternative routes to Jack's Rake are available, namely Easy Gully and North Rake. Easy Gully and Jack's Rake both start at the same point at the base of the buttress which rises at the east end of Stickle Tarn.   If ascending by Jack's Rake or Easy Gully follow the path round the western side of the tarn to the base of the eastern buttress of Pavey Ark. The grassy slope to the left leads up into the groove of Jack's Rake whereas to the right is the grass

Ascending Jack's Rake

98

and scree incline of Easy Gully. Near the top the gully is choked with large rocks which must be overcome before one emerges about halfway up the North Rake. To make the full ascent via the North Rake, thus avoiding the rocks at the top of Easy Gully, take the path round the east side of the tarn which follows the east bank of Bright Beck. About 300m north of the tarn the path crosses the beck and leads upwards to the foot of the Rake.

North Rake is an easy grassy stroll and is in no way to be compared with the airiness of Jack's Rake. However, if you have your dog with you, and he is of the large less agile variety, he would more than likely prefer you to take him up the North Rake.

If you are ascending by Jack's Rake the route starts off rather steeply but soon becomes a more gentle slope. Much of the route involves clambering over rock steps, but as you tend to be in a groove much of the time, there are only a few places where the feeling of exposure may affect the meeker walker unduly. The Rake crosses Great Gully about 100 ft from the top. Here one must watch out for descending rocks dislodged by careless, or panicking climbers in the gully above. The traffic here can be very heavy in summer. At this point there is an awkward scramble, with some exposure, in order to get onto the last section of the rake, which then crosses Little Gully about 50 ft from the summit. Emerging at the summit of Pavey Ark is rather an anticlimax after the rigours of Jack's Rake. Less than half a mile distant lies Harrison Stickle which is not very impressive seen from here, as its summit rises a mere 50m or so above the floor of Harrison Combe. Further to the west is Pike of Stickle whose characteristic cone shaped summit is still recognisable from this viewpoint. The path to Harrison Stickle circumnavigates the neck of Harrison Combe before climbing gently to the rocky ridge forming the summit. The views from here are impressive. In particular the view down into Great Langdale from the southern end of the summit ridge should not be missed.

From Harrison Stickle a broad well worn path leads westward to the rocky dome of Pike of Stickle, the ascent of which involves a little rock scrambling. This is the turning point for the walk and would make an excellent lunch

stop while you survey the surrounding hills, valleys and tarns.

It was in this area of the Langdale Pikes where much scientific interest was generated forty or fifty years ago with the discovery of several

Pike O' Stickle
from Harrison Combe

stone age axe factory sites. Unfortunately the subsequent publicity led to considerable damage being caused by souvenir hunters. As a result I do not intend to reveal the exact locations of any of these sites in this book. The return route from Pike O' Stickle is a well worn path which leads southeast down the ridge over Loft Crag and Raven Crag. This route is quite spectacular in places as it wends its way down through the craggy sections to arrive finally at the New Dungeon Ghyll Hotel Car Park, where of course liquid refreshment is generally available.

Route 7   Glaramara and Allen Crags

return via Langstrath
(the long valley)

Total climbing about 2800 ft (853 m)
(10 miles)

To find the start point for this walk follow the road to Seatoller from Stonethwaite as far as

The Scafell Area

the old quarrymens' cottages at Mountain View. Immediately before the bridge there is a farm track to the left which follows the river. Follow this track for about two hundred yards when you will see some level ground on the right hand side of the road. Pull off the road and park here. Walk back along the road to the bend and you will see the path up onto the Glaramara ridge through a gate on the right. The path curves gently round, leading up through the wood and emerging on the northern ridge of Thornythwaite Fell. The path now follows this broad ridge rather uneventfully all the way to the a point just below the summit of Glaramara.

The path may be rather boring but the views certainly are not. To the right is Honister with the tramway clearly visible leading up to the drumhouse. Straight ahead the hanging valley above Seathwaithe can be seen, surrounded by the crags of Base Brown. To the left and ahead lies Dovenest Crag with its natural, but dangerous, caves. These craggy cliffs which guard the northern slopes of this mountain give the mountain its name. Glaramara appeared in a document of 1211 as *Gleuermerghstele* and probably comes from the old Norse *Glaefra-merki* which, roughly translated, means 'the boundary mark of the chasms or cliffs.'

The last section of the route to the summit of Glaramara is an interesting rock scramble, which leads one into a small col between two hillocks. The summit lies to the right. From here the path continues south dropping gently towards the high pass between Allen Crags and Glaramara, where several small tarns are to be found, the source of Allen Gill. This is not a good place to be in very windy weather. I have seen a twelve stone man lifted off his feet here while trying to cross this col. From the tarns a further half mile of steady climbing brings one to the summit of Allen Crags. From here it is downhill all the way home.

The return path drops steeply down to the southwest towards Esk Hause. Turn left at the hause onto the *'motorway'* route which leads southeast towards Langdale. In about half a mile the path down into Langstrath drops away to the left following Allencrags Gill. Initially the path down is steep and rather tortuous, but it soon becomes a gentle if

boggy walk beside the gill; which eventually becomes Langstrath Beck. On a hot day this valley is a marvellous place to cool off. At the junction with Stake Beck near the footbridges the water has worn out some deep pools. These are ideal for bathing in hot weather and, as they are some three miles up the valley from Stonethwaite, they do not get so crowded as the more accessible pools further down the valley. Continuing on, the path follows Langstrath Beck down to its junction with Greenup Gill, where it turns left down to Stonethwaite. The ruined old building near the end of the valley was once an inn known as *'Auld Jwonny Hoose.'* Johnny ran the inn around the beginning of the nineteenth century. Continue through the village and on past Stonethwaite Primary School. Beyond the school take the road to the left which leads past the church and through the farmyard, then follow the marked footpath which eventually brings you onto the road half a mile northwest of Mountain View Cottages. From here it is a short road walk back to the start point.

Langstrath Bloomery

In Elizabethan times a bloomery or iron smelting furnace was to be found near here, just where the path begins to ascend the stake. The smelter was sited here in order to use the local forest for fuel and ore from miles around would be smelted here. Iron ore would be brought over Stake Pass through *'Ure Gap'* or Ore Gap from the mines in Eskdale and it is likely that the ore from Castle Crag in Borrowdale was processed here. The bloomery had a major effect on the environment as it denuded the landscape of trees leaving it as it is today. Ancient charcoal heaps are still to be found around the old bloomery site.

Route 8   Watendlath and Dock Tarn
from Rosthwaite

Return via Stonethwaite Beck

Total Climbing about 1100 ft (336 m)
(4 miles)

The Scafell Area

This short walk is ideal for a family on a warm summer's day. Park at the car park in Rosthwaite village, which is down the track just opposite the village shop and post office. The track over to Watendlath follows the access road to Hazel Bank Hotel as far as the bridge over the beck (Hazel Bank was the mythical home of Rogue Herries in the Hugh Walpole novels about the Herries dynasty).

The route now bears round to the left of the hotel grounds and climbs quite steeply up onto the lower slopes of Grange Fell. In about half a mile the gradient lessens as the highest point of Puddingstone Bank is reached before the path drops down again towards the hamlet of Watendlath. From here Watendlath can be seen nestling at the head of its small tarn.

In the past this was an important staging post for the pack horse drivers of old, as several routes cross here. Now, apart from the hill farm, the inhabitants of this beautiful hamlet rely on the constant stream of tourists in their cars to add to their income. The name *'Watendlath'* describes well its situation, stemming from the Norse *'Vaten Lath'* or 'Lake Farm Buildings.' Watendlath is an excellent watering place for those who like afternoon tea on a fine summer's day. One can descend to Watendlath, to partake of tea, and then take the track along the western edge of the tarn towards Dock Tarn. Alternatively, if feeling rather lazy or not wishing to meet hordes of people, you can take the signposted path which leads due south from the top of the bank across the moss towards Dock Tarn.

To avoid damage to the rather delicate terrain here, part of the path has been marked with wooden posts. Please keep to the marked path and protect the fauna and flora around you. In about half a mile the path climbs out of the wet boggy ground up through a miniature canyon onto the undulating top of Great Crag. In August this area is beautiful; as the route winds round a series of craggy outcrops bedecked in purple heather. Eventually Dock Tarn is reached, covered in a carpet of water lilies. This name can also be traced back to its Norse origins as *'the lily covered lake'*. The route continues round the west side of the tarn and then begins a curving descent down into the Stonethwaite valley. The views from here straight up the Langstrath Valley and also

The Borrowdale Sop
from the Watendlath Path
(See Page 20)

towards Greenup Edge are excellent. A steep descent now follows through the wood beside Willygrass Gill to emerge on the path along the north side of Stonethwaite Beck. Continue along this path back to Rosthwaite.

The Ennerdale Horseshoe

This marathon length walk effectively circumnavigates Ennerdale Water and the head of the Ennerdale Valley. It therefore takes in fells described in the 'West of Buttermere' section of this book as well as some of those in this section. The walk is about twenty two miles in length and is best done on a fine day in May or June when one has adequate daylight to complete it.

Separate parts of the walk are mentioned on the following pages:

Page 39 (First seven miles of **Route 2**)
Page 40 (First two miles of **Route 3**)
Page 93 (Scarth Gap to Haystacks)
Page 92 (From Haystacks to Gable)
Page 96 (From Pillar to Haycock)

In my opinion the best way round the route is to start from the Forestry Commission car park at Bowness Knotts in Ennerdale. This means that the majority of the climbing is done in the first six hours or so of the walk. The remainder of the walk from Pillar onwards is over more featureless terrain which gradually descends

The Scafell Area

towards Crag Fell at the foot of Ennerdale Water.

In case of fatigue one can cut the walk short by descending down the ridge from Steeple to the head of Ennerdale Water.

In case of mist one can follow the stone wall, which leads from Scoat Fell almost to the summit of Crag Fell.

The fell tops covered by the walk are:
Great Borne - Starling Dodd - Red Pike - High Stile - High Crag - Seat - Haystacks - Brandreth - Green Gable - Great Gable - Kirk Fell - Looking Stead - Pillar - Little Scoat Fell - Great Scoat Fell - Haycock - Caw Fell - Crag Fell

The path down from Crag Fell follows the ridge above Revelin Crag. It then drops steeply down through the crags to the foot of Ennerdale Water near the weir.

Lakes to visit
Derwentwater, Thirlmere, Grasmere, Wastwater

Nearest Towns
Ambleside, Egremont, Keswick

Places to visit
Armitt Library, Ambleside
Rydal Mount, Ambleside
Wordsworth Museum and Dove
Cottage, Grasmere
Cars of the Stars (Motor Museum), Keswick

Recommended Country Inns
Good Ale and Good Food
Scafell Inn   Rosthwaite
Old Dungeon Ghyll Hotel   Langdale
New Dungeon Ghyll Hotel   Langdale
Langstrath Hotel   Stonethwaite

Scawfell Pikes, from Styhead, Cumberland
from an old print (1833)

102

Ald Will outside Rowfoot (from an old postcard)

Scafell Area, Local History

1. Lanty Slee, Quarryman and Whisky Distiller
Lancelot Slee lived at Elterwater, about a hundred years ago and worked at the Elterwater slate quarry. He was a colourful character who became famous for his clandestine whisky distilling and his ability to avoid the excise men. Much of the whisky distilling took place in a small cave high up on Lingmoor above Little Langdale. Lanty's exploits have probably become embroidered and enlarged on with time but there is no doubt that he was quite successful in his illegal pursuits.

His cave high up on the hillside was close to a stream which provided his water supply. Here he could distil his spirit in relative safety, relying on the wind and mist to disguise the occasional emissions of steam. Apparently this was only one of several locations where Lanty distilled his whisky. He is reputed to have had a still under the floor of his kitchen at Low Arnside Farm. The tell-tale steam from this device was led underground through a long pipe to emerge inside a hedge in the adjoining field. Having produced his whisky he had to market it. This was achieved by smuggling the spirit out at dead of night by packhorse across Slater's bridge and up the fellside to another cave high on the slopes of Wetherlam. From here he could watch the road over Wrynose and choose his time to make his run for Ravenglass and the sea. Smuggling was a favourite pastime for many at this time. Duty free contraband

run ashore along the coast could be bartered for illicit whisky and locally poached salmon. In spite of his abilities and his local knowledge Lanty was not always successful in escaping detection and, every now and again, he would end up before the magistrates at Hawkshead. However this did not appear to deter him, possibly because these same magistrates were some of his best customers. Lanty ranged far and wide in the district having stills and whisky caches in many remote places. Perhaps one of these was in the area of Lanty's Tarn near Glenridding. I know of no other reason for the name.

2. Scafell - the name
The name Scafell is Norse and gives a hint that, in former times, it may have looked completely different to its appearance now. In the eighteenth century the mountain was called Scofell or Scowfell, which implies the Norse name Skogo-fjall or the wooded hill. It does not appear likely that Scafell Pike was wooded, even in Norse times, but it is quite probable that Scafell, particularly on its broad southwest slopes down to Burnmoor, was wooded in pre-sheep farming days. Most of the names in the area are of Norse origin but some derive from Celtic names borrowed by the Norse. The Norse word *'barrans'* derives from the Celtic *Boirean* meaning land covered with rocks or stones. Burnmoor or *Barransmoor* is a place where several prehistoric

103

stone circles are to be found **(LH9)**. An interesting mountain name is that of Base Brown, just above Seathwaite Farm. The 'brown' is from the Celtic *Boirean* mentioned previously, while the 'base' is probably the Norse *bass* or cow shed. Base Brown probably means 'the rough ground by the cow shed.'

3. An Early Mountain Accident

The white painted cross, which can be seen on the lower section of Fleetwith Edge from the road beside Gatesgarth Farm, is a memorial to Fanny Mercer; accidentally killed in 1887. Fanny was an 18 year old servant visiting the lakes with the family of her employer. On the day of the accident Fanny, and two other servants, were given the day off and set out for a walk over the fells. They eventually arrived on Honister Crag and decided to return to Buttermere via Fleetwith Pike and Fleetwith Edge. It was on their descent, as they neared the road, that the accident happened. Fanny, who was at the rear, apparently jumped off the ledge on which she was standing, using her alpenstock for support. The effect was to propel her up and outwards so that she fell a considerable distance and, unfortunately, struck her head on a rock. Fanny suffered severe head wounds

Fanny Mercer's Memorial

The Old Woman's Grave

and was carried down to Gatesgarth Farm, alas to no avail. A messenger was sent for a doctor from Cockermouth but, by the time he arrived several hours later, Fanny had died.

4. The Old Woman's Grave

Beside the path about half of the way up Rosset Gill is *'The Old Woman's Grave.'* The grave is now marked by a stone cross, pointing southeast, on a raised flat area to the left of the path. Originally it was a row of flat stones, according to an account of 1851:

"High up above the vale of Great Langdale we came to the Old Woman's Grave. Tradition relates that a Westmoreland woman, who was in the practice, for many years, of going over into Cumberland to receive an annuity, perished in the mountains. She was buried on the spot, and a row of flat stones marks her grave. My guide pointed to the hollow, a few yards below, where the body is said to have been found."

Alfred Wainwright mentioned the grave in his book on the Southern Fells. His story is at variance with

Hudson's account of 1851. Wainwright said that, according to Mr H Mounsey of Skelwith, the old woman was a *'pack woman,'* who called at Langdale Farms about one hundred and seventy years ago selling her wares until, one fateful day, she perished on the hills. The account by Hudson was written about fifty years after the event and his informant was his guide, the son of a Langdale farmer. I do not know the source of Mr Mounsey's version. The story has obviously become altered in the telling over the years. Which version is the more accurate I do not know. You must decide for yourself.

5. The Border Freebooters

On Honister Crag lie buried the bones of the young Graeme, leader of one of the most notorious families of Border Reivers. The Graemes were renowned and feared for their predatory excursions into this remote corner of England. On one such raid they infiltrated the Lake Country by coming in small numbers by devious routes and joining together at a pre-arranged rendezvous. They then captured and drove away all the cattle and sheep they could find, via the Borrowdale - Honister route. Word spread quickly and the Dalesmen were soon in hot pursuit of the Graemes. The Graemes split into two groups, one party pushing forward with the captured booty while

Honister Pass in 1897

the rest waited in ambush in the rocks of Yew Crag and Honister, at the summit of the pass. The ambush party was led by the young Graeme and his aged father. When the English reached the neck of the pass the young Graeme sprang to his feet and waved his claymore to the enemy. Immediately volleys of musketry rang out from the crags and arrows flew through the air. In the melee that followed the English leader was killed by a musket shot and fell from his white horse. Furious at the loss of their leader, the troopers wheeled their horses round and stormed the crags on which the Graemes, and a few of their followers, were standing. Before help could arrive from the rest of their band the younger Graeme and several of his men were cut down. The English then dashed on down the pass, away from the ambush point, still in pursuit of their sheep and cattle. The older Graeme was devastated at the loss of his son and heir. They laid his body to rest in an opening in the hillside and built a cairn of stones on top to mark the grave. Young Graeme's bonnet, shield and claymore were supposedly placed on top of the cairn *'that neither friend nor foe should thereafter pass it with irreverence.'*

6. Will Ritson of Wasdale

Will Ritson or *'Ald Will'* as he was better known was born at Row Foot, Wasdale in 1808. He lived his whole life in the valley, becoming a guide to the many visitors who, thanks to Wordsworth and other early writers of Lake District guides, now *'discovered the sublime beauties of the crags and precipices of that wonderful valley.'* Will was renowned for his ready wit and soon became very popular with the tourists who placed themselves in his charge. His remark to a clergyman who he was conducting to the top of Scafell Pike was typical of this humour. As they neared the summit he said *'Tha'lt ne'er be nigher t' heaven than now.'* Will eventually married and set up as an innkeeper at Row Foot. The house was enlarged about 1850 and became known as The Huntsman's Inn. Will obtained an excise licence to sell liquor in 1856, although he had probably been dealing in smuggled, under the counter, liquor for several years previously. Auld Will became very friendly with Professor Wilson, alias *'Christopher North'* the poet. Wilson was Professor of Moral Philosophy at Edinburgh University. The pair became renowned for their practical jokes and rough behaviour. Wilson was a strong, athletic man who enjoyed all sports, was fond of rude horseplay and at the same time was full of kindness and good humour.

Mc Intyre relates an amusing description that Ritson wrote of his friend's first visit to Wasdale :-

"First time as Professor Wilson cam t' Wasdale Head he had a tent set up in a field, an' he gat it weel stockt wi' bread an' beef, an' chees, an' rum, an' ale, an' sech like. Then he giddered up my granfadder, an' Thomas Tyson, an' Isaac Fletcher, an' Joseph Stable, an' Robert Grave, an' some mair, an' there was gay deed amang 'em. Then nowt would sarra but he would hev a boat an' they must all hev a sail. Well, when they gat into t' boat he tell'd em to be particularly careful, for he was liable to get giddy i' t' head, an' if yan of his giddy fits sud chance to come he mud happen tumble into t' watter. Well, that pleased 'em all gaily weel, an' they said they'd tak varry girt care on him. Then he leaned back an' called oot that they must pull quicker. So they did an' what does Wilson do then but tipples ower eb'm of his back i' t' watter wi' a splash. Then there was a girt cry: 'Eh Maister Wilson's i' t' watter!' An' yan clickt an' anudder, but nean o' them could get hod on him. An' there was sic a scrow as nivver was. At last yan o' them gat him round the neck as he popped up, at t' teal o' t' boat, an Wilson toad him to keep a good hod, for he mud happen slip

back agean. But what, it was nowt but his bits o' pranks - he was smirkin' an' laughin' all t' time."

Auld Will was noted as a Cumberland Wrestler and on one occasion he tried a friendly wrestling bout with the Professor and won two falls out of three. As he modestly explained, however, his opponent had walked forty miles before the encounter. *"Not"* he added, *"that forty miles tewd him, for I've known him tramp ower seventy an' put six hours fishin' forbye into the twentyfour hours. He was a varry bad un to lick."* It must be added that Wilson was twenty years older than Will. The professor achieved a certain notoriety with the irreverance of some of his poetry. For example, the death of Charles Gough in 1805 on Helvellyn inspired Wordsworth and others to write poems about the faithful fox terrier who guarded her master's body through three winter months. Christopher North's light hearted tale of that event talked about *'The Red Tarn Club'* of ravens who were fabled to have set to work on the Quaker's remains. This upset many people who preferred to believe the noble tale of the faithful fox terrier bitch guarding her master's body from all predators. Canon H. D. Rawnsley described the professor as *"that rough jester Christopher North"* in his book on the Literary Associations of the English Lakes, in which he puts forth evidence in support of Wordsworth's version of the tale. During his long life Will Ritson became friend and guide to many of the great mountaineers who developed their skills in this valley before venturing abroad to make their mark in the Alps. In old age Will retired, with his wife, to a house at the foot of Buckbarrow where he died in 1890. He was buried in the churchyard of Nether Wasdale, in the valley where he had spent the whole of his long and active life.

Ald Will Ritson of Wasdale Head

A Poem said on the Summit of Scafell in 1851

I said my vent'rous foot should press
The monarch mountain's brow;
And on that high aspiring spot,
Behold me standing now!

But while I gladly look around,
This thought calls forth a sigh,
We are not always nearer Heaven,
When nearest to the sky.

7. An Early Mountain Rescue

The following cautionary tale from *'A Handbook to the English Lakes,'* 1856 edition, shows that the guide writers of the time were becoming aware of the dangers associated with hill walking:-

"It is needful here to remark that the ascent of these fells is not unattended with danger, on account of their sometimes being rapidly encircled with mists. In the month of July, 1847, a party from Manchester, amongst whom was a foreigner, commenced the ascent of the Langdale Pikes, and when about half the distance, this gentleman feeling fatigued, agreed to rest himself till the return of his comrades. Observing the clouds touching the mountaintops, and thinking his friends might have miscalculated their return, he began to retrace his steps, as he thought in the right direction, but soon found the brow of the mountain becoming steeper, and at last came to the brink of a precipice nearly forty yards high. He still thought it might be possible to descend gradually by the help of a tree growing out of the rock, and, to aid in his descent, he stripped, took of his shirt, cut it up into shreds, which he tied together, fastened to the tree, and, after weighing the chances of danger as to going down or up, he deliberately chose the former, as the safer of the two courses, and lowered himself down to a ledge a good number of feet below the edge! But when there he saw the impossibility of further progress either way. It was now about seven o' clock, the clouds were descending the mountains , and his situation had become most alarming. He endeavoured to attract attention by shouting and waving his vest and handkerchief, though neither house nor person was in sight. His strength gradually gave way under the exertion and long continued excitement. His footing was as nothing, and he was, from his situation, incapable of moving. Most providentially, his alarm had been heard in the vale below, and his signs observed. After a long interval of dread suspense and dire foreboding he had the unspeakable pleasure of observing, at a great

---

Cumberland

used to be called *'the nursery of the Alps'.* The title has been more than justified. Men who first learnt the use of hand and foot-hold on the steep cliffs of Scawfell, or the swing of an ice-axe on the slippery, slanting slopes of Great End, have left honourable records upon the greatest mountains in the world.

Abraham   "British Mountain Climbs" (1909)

---

distance below him, six figures wending their way up a distant shoulder of the hill. Their steps seemed directed towards him; and soon he became sure of this, as he observed they carried a something which he could not at first make out; this turned out to be a large coil of rope. One of the six was let down by his fellows, with the rope round his body. He fastened an end round the almost sinking wanderer, and he was immediately hoisted up in safety, and conducted by his deliverers to a farm house, where the greatest attention was paid him by the good people there. "

8. The Smuggler's Hut on Great Gable

Moses Trod, the well known route which leads from Dubs Quarry to Great Gable and then down into Wasdale, has been associated with various forms of smuggling over the years. The path was used to ferry green slate on packhorses from Dubs to Wasdale and thence to Ravenglass for export. Moses Rigg, one of the quarrymen who used this route, was reputed to bring back a return load of smuggled goods from overseas for sale to the local populace. Another tale relates how Moses operated an illegal whisky still at Dubs and used this route to export his product to his customers on the west coast. Yet another story says that stolen wad from the Seathwaite mine, a very valuable commodity in the eighteenth century, was carried along this track into Wasdale. Whatever the truth in these tales if smuggling did indeed occur it follows that a remote, safe hideaway to store the goods en route would have been very useful. There were rumours that Moses had such a hideout on Gable but nobody knew where it was. In 1890, according to Lakeland author O.S. MacDonell writing in Cumbria Magazine, pioneer climber W. P. Haskett-Smith and two friends, made a first ascent up the middle of Gable Crag. Near the top they came upon a stone building which they later named *'The Smuggler's Shelter.'* The hut is situated on a wide ledge below the summit, accessible with care from above but with great difficulty from below. The siting of the hut is such that it is almost impossible to see from anywhere but above and then only if you descend part of the way down the crag at the appropriate place. Today the hut is roofless and consists of a rectangular drystone wall built up against a rockface. Its purpose was possibly a safe store for smuggled goods which could be lowered without too much difficulty from the summit of the crag. In particular, wad, which had been pilfered from the mine at Seathwaite in small amounts by individuals, could be accumulated here until there was sufficient

Smuggler's Shelter on Gable Crag

for a packhorse run along Mose's Trod to Ravenglass. This would be a very lucrative business as wad commanded a price of three thousand nine hundred and twenty pounds a ton in 1804. Another possible use of the hut, suggested by Graham Sutton in his book *'Fell Days,'* was as a Jacobite refuge. If so it was rather a remote refuge and it would have been rather difficult to keep the incumbent supplied with food, fuel and other necessary comforts for an extended stay.

9. Burnmoor - Beltane, Corpse Road, Ghosts and Stone Circles

Burnmoor has long featured in the local history and folklore of the district and relics of its former importance are still to be found. In spite of its remoteness Burnmoor was populated at a very early period. Evidence for this is provided by the large number of stone barrows or burial mounds. On Burnmoor the remains usually consist of stone circles. The largest of these circles consists of forty one stones and has a diameter of a hundred feet. It encloses five burial mounds, each of which is said to have contained a box built up of five stones which contained burnt bones together with horns of stags and other animals. According to McIntyre, the small size and irregular setting of the stones of these circles would indicate that they were merely boundaries or *'taboo rings'* to mark the limits of the sepulchre, or to

keep the ghost of the departed from wandering from his tomb to haunt the living. Such circles are to be found at Brat's Hill, Low Longriggs and Acre How on Burnmoor.

Of course there are many stone circles in the district, some built for astronomical purposes, some for religious or other reasons. Many are in better condition than those on Burnmoor. Other similar stone circles can be seen at Gunnerkeld, Oddendale, Seascale, and Kinniside. More famous and better preserved monuments are to be found at Castlerigg, near Keswick, at Swinside, five miles west of Broughton in Furness, and also at Little Salkeld near Penrith (Long Meg and her daughters).

Burnmoor was reputed to be a great meeting place long ago. At the feast of Beltane in May each year the men from the neighbouring valleys of Wasdale, Eskdale and Mitredale would meet to light their fires and celebrate Beltan. They would drive their stock through the smoke for 'good luck,' to drive out the devil and see an end to the winter. (The smoke would probably have a useful effect on the parasites on the animals as well). Several hills in the district contain the name *'Bell.'* This name probably originates from the lighting of fires on these hills at the feast of Beltane. There is an old corpse road over Burnmoor which dates back to the time before the churchyards of Wasdale had been consecrated. Over this road came the funeral corteges of the dale with the coffin strapped upon the back of a horse. The road led from Wasdale to St. Catherine's Church at Boot. On one such journey, at the funeral of a young man, the horse took fright and bolted, being lost by the mourners in the mist. The young man's mother fretted and died, and at her funeral, which took place on a snowy day, the horse bearing her coffin was lost like that which bore her son. The searchers, following the tracks in the snow, subsequently found the first horse and duly carried out the son's funeral. The mother's corpse, however, was never recovered, and her weary spirit still haunts the hillside. So, if walking over Burnmoor in the mist, do not be surprised if a galloping horse suddenly appears with a dark object on its back. It is only the poor lad's mother trying to find a resting place for her soul. Careful readers will note that in other parts of this book I have mentioned two other corpse roads, one of which had a similar ghostly story attributed to it. The writer cannot vouch for the truth or otherwise of these tales. I can only say that they have been passed down from generation to generation over the years and I record them here for posterity.

10. The Seathwaite Wad Mine

Records indicate that graphite or *'wad'* was first mined commercially at Seathwaite in the latter half of the 16th century. The wad had been used before that by local farmers to colour or mark their sheep. There was a good market for graphite even in the 16th century when prices ranged from five to thirteen pounds per ton. The mine was worked irregularly over many years, partly because of the random distribution of the graphite *'pipes'* and the difficulty of finding them, but mainly to keep the price up by introducing an artificial rarity. Later in the seventeenth century the price shot up even more, reaching an astonishing level of three thousand nine hundred and twenty pounds per ton in 1804. The original uses of the mineral which was variously known as Black Cawke, Wad, Black Lead and Plumbago were for marking sheep, rust proofing stoves and, when taken with ale, as a panacea for a variety of ailments. The main industrial uses however, were in crucible and refractory mould construction, as a separating agent in metal casting and, of course, pencil making. The Cumberland Pencil Company at Keswick have a fine museum attached to their premises which details the history of graphite mining in Borrowdale. The artificially high price of graphite in the eighteenth century led to problems at the mine. Pilfering was endemic and miners were undressed and inspected internally on leaving the mine. The theft problem became so severe that in 1752, following an armed attack on the mine, an Act was passed in Parliament declaring illegal entry into, or stealing from a wad mine to be a felony. Punishment for infringement was a public whipping plus one year's hard labour, or seven years transportation. Presumably this Act must have been some deterrent but clearly wasn't wholly effective, for as late as 1771 there are reports of rogues using gunpowder during the night. In the nineteenth century graphite mining in Borrowdale slowly ground to a halt. The price of graphite plummeted as methods were developed by which inferior graphite could be ground up and mixed with kaolin to produce uniform pencil leads of varying hardness. There was no longer any need to use the pure Borrowdale graphite. Pencil making still continues at Keswick but now, of course, the raw materials are imported.

(Factory and Museum visit available. See page 16 - Places to visit).

Lunch on Scafell Top

Here, in one of the grandest spots in England, with the snow and rocks of the Scafell chasms beneath us on either hand, a tumult of mountains around us, and a distance of fertile valleys, glistening lakes and azure sea, our first thought is, sad to confess, of lunch.

Pockets are soon emptied: bread and butter, potted meat, raisins, chocolate, crystallised ginger and brandy - a queer mixture, and no doubt the three tourists lunching quietly at the hotel would have pitied us as much as we pitied them.

Lehmann J. Oppenheimer - 'The Heart of Lakeland' (1908)

**'Schofell' on Wast Water
in 1814**

D. LUSH.

The Coniston Fells

General

The extensive and rather remote area between Ravenglass to the west and Coniston Lake to the east has a lot to offer the visitor. In the east Wetherlam and The Old Man of Coniston dominate the scene, whilst in the west the lower hills of Birkby Fell and Whitfell enclose the wilderness area of the Ulpha Fells, with its wide expanses of rolling moor. This region was obviously of importance to our ancestors as it is littered with cairns, barrows, stone circles, field systems and other such evidence of former habitation. Separating this moorland wilderness of the west from the higher hills to the east is the craggy rather chaotic terrain of the Dunnerdale Fells. The geographical remoteness from the centre and the limited road access to this corner of Lakeland have helped it to retain its peace and charm. Even in high summer one can walk in seclusion if desired.

Walking

The walking around Wetherlam and Coniston Old Man is superb. Here there are high ridges with extensive views in all directions. In addition the area abounds with evidence of its industrial past, in particular that of the copper and slate mining industries. Wheel pits, old reservoirs, water leats, mine entrances and old quarry workings are frequently encountered. With the passage of time these artifacts of a bygone age have weathered into the scenery and do not intrude unduly on the eye. On the contrary they add to the interest of a walk, as one tries to visualise the hustle and bustle of those times and what life must have been like for the miners who lived and worked here. The attraction of the hills around Devoke Water in the west lies in their remoteness and the broad expansive nature of the terrain, rather than their height. In this area as well there are old mine workings and other earlier signs of habitation to capture one's imagination.

Route 1 Wetherlam and Coniston Old Man

(a) Wetherlam from Tilberthwaite
return via Red Dell and Hole Rake
Total Climbing about 2000 ft (610 m)
(5 miles)

(b) Coniston Old Man via Wetherlam
return via Stubthwaite Crag and Hole
Rake
Total Climbing about 2660 ft (810 m)
(9 miles)

Route 1(a) is ideal for a 'pottering' day when one has plenty of time to stop and inspect the

110

The Coniston Fells

industrial relics of this mining area. Parking is available beside the bridge and adjacent to the old Penny Rigg slate workings at Low Tilberthwaite **(A) (LH5)**. From the bridge follow the road north to the small row of cottages where the road bends. Take the path which leads past the front and round the back of the

Cottage with Spinning Gallery
Low Tilberthwaite

cottages onto Blake Rigg. In a short distance the path branches into two directions. Take the lefthand branch which follows the course of Tilberthwaite Gill, round the southern flank of Blake Rigg. To the right of the path you will encounter a boarded up mine level, one of many you will see on this walk. This one is different in that zinc was mined here rather than copper; the main product of Tilberthwaite Mine. To your left there is a precipitious drop down into the deep ravine, which has been cut out by Tilberthwaite Gill over many thousands of years.

Follow the path round into the valley where you will see the *'waterfall'* level of Tilberthwaite mine just on the other side of the gill. Our route now climbs almost due north up to *'Borlase Mine'* and *'Hellen's Mine'*; two workings situated quite high on the fellside above Tilberthwaite. Above these workings the ridge of Birk Fell is soon reached, providing an extensive view into Little Langdale and beyond. Our path now joins the track from Greenburn and climbs southwest up the steep side of Wetherlam Edge. The summit cairn of Wetherlam provides a grandstand view for this part of the district and you may wish to linger

here a while and admire the panorama of surrounding fells. To the north are the rugged crags of the Langdale Pikes, the Crinkles, Bowfell and of course Scafell. To the south lies The Old Man with Furness and Morecambe Bay beyond.

(a) Return via Red Dell

If following the shorter route **(a)** take the path leading due south from the summit. This route soon splits into two, the upper path follows the line of the ridge over Red Gill Head Moss and the lower one loses height more quickly as it drops down to Red Dell Beck. Take the lower route if you wish to visit the Red Dell workings of Coniston Copper Mine and the upper route if you intend to merely return to Tilberthwaite via Hole Rake, without first visiting the mines. Following the lower track, the old Red Dell Head workings are situated above and to your right. As you drop further down the valley observe the old stone incline

Wheel Pit near the New Engine Shaft
Coniston Copper Mine, Red Dell Workings

111

leading down to the workings near the New Engine Shaft. The large wheel pit set into the ground here once housed the giant waterwheel which drained this part of the mine. Do not venture over the fence to peer down into the shaft, as there is a vertical drop of three hundred feet down to Deep Level of the Red Dell Workings. The extended gash beyond the engine shaft marks the line of the vein and is the open top of the worked out stope from Taylor's Level, two hundred feet below. If you have a small child or a dog in this area keep it on a leash. There are many such holes in the valley and, generally, the only warning is a rudimentary fence with a keep out notice. Remember dogs and very small children cannot usually read.

Continuing on down the valley, the tall chimney like structure ahead is a support for the wooden aqueduct that led water to the overshot waterwheel, which serviced the old engine shaft. Immediately below this stone pillar the wheelpit can be seen (LH4). The path continues southeast, gradually dropping towards the entrance to the valley. To avoid unnecessary descent and re-ascent it is advisable to leave the path and bear left up the hill, before arriving at a point above and behind the row of cottages in the valley below.

Wheel pit
(Old Engine Shaft, Red Dell Workings)

This will take you up onto the return route via Hole Rake, which intercepts our path further down the valley. As you climb up the hillside look for the old cable from the overhead cableway, which is still lying where it fell when the cableway was dismantled many years ago. The path up Hole Rake takes you over a low pass and then back down towards Tilberthwaite. Near the summit of the pass the ridge path from Wetherlam Top, previously mentioned, joins the Hole Rake Path. The descent to Tilberthwaite via Hole Rake is a fine experience on a good day. The Rake is a gentle well graded path, obviously constructed to service the small slate quarries, which are encountered at intervals on the descent. Slate would be taken from here by horsedrawn sled down to the road at Tilberthwaite. The views from here are expansive to say the least.

As you near the Tilberthwaite Gorge note the spoil heap of Wetherlam Mine across the valley. Several vertical posts around the entrance make it stand out from its surroundings. Follow the path around the south side of the gorge which leads one down through the massive excavations of Horse Crag Quarry to the car park at Tiberthwaite Gill.

(b) Return via Stubthwaite Crag

From the summit of Wetherlam take the westerly path which drops down onto Keld Gill Heads and then climbs again up onto Prison Band. A hard pull eventually brings one to the summit cairn on Swirl How. To the north the ridge of Wet Side Edge curves away down to the Wrynose Pass and to the south the broad ridge of Swirl Band leads on to the small prominence of Great How Crag, before descending to Levers Hawse, directly above Levers Water. If time is short, or if you wish to visit the Paddy End Workings of Coniston Copper Mine, there is a path here which leads directly down to Levers Water (see later *). Continuing across the hause, our route follows the ridge due south for a further mile, rising gently to the summit of Coniston Old Man. From here a steep path descends to the east, taking us down to the 'copper blue' tarn of Low Water. The path continues on down under Stubthwaite Crag and across the 'mouth' of coppermines valley to the Miners'

Bridge. Crossing the bridge, take the path to the north which climbs steeply up the fell via Hole Rake. From here the route is the same as in **(a)**.

* Return via Paddy End. From the hause above Levers Water take the path which drops steeply down to the lake. Continue round the shoreline to the dam. The fenced off area to the right, just before the dam, leads down through the *'crater'* into the Middle Level of the Paddy End workings of Coniston Copper Mine. Do **NOT** attempt to investigate. These workings are dangerous and should be left to the experts. Crossing the dam, take the path which leads down the hill to the point where an old water leat bears off to the left, around Kennel Crag. This man made cut once carried a wooden aqueduct which led water to the New Engine Shaft of the Red Dell Workings; previously mentioned in return route **(a)**. Follow the leat to arrive at the New Engine Shaft. From this point follow return route **(a)** back to Tilberthwaite.

Route 2.   Hesk Fell Copper Mines from
Buckbarrow Bridge via
Buckbarrow Crag, Bowscale Beck and
Sele Bottom
Return via Whitfell

Total climbing about 2297 ft   (700m)
(9 miles)

This meandering round, over relatively low but isolated fells, gives an insight into the industrial past of the area, as well as revealing the undoubted beauty of this little known part of Lakeland.

Park your car off the unfenced road near Buckbarrow Bridge **(SD134904)**. Follow the northern bank of the beck for just under half a mile up to Whit Crags just below the waterfall. Here is the first mine of the walk, a small copper mine with one level about 130 yds long. Leaving Whit Crags, cross the beck and go through the gate in the stone wall. Climbing up the fell in an easterly direction will bring you, in about a mile, to the summit of Buckbarrow Crag; our next goal.

The views from here are magnificent. To the northeast lies Wetherlam and the Coniston Fells, whilst to the west is the Irish Sea with

Ravenglass and the Cumbrian coast stretching into the distance. From Buckbarrow drop down in an easterly direction to the lower promontory of Plough Fell. As you will see, there are few well worn paths in this little walked area, so you must pick your own way down through the scree and across the moor. Just over the summit of Plough Fell you will encounter a stone wall, which encloses the field system flanked by Bowscale and Logan Becks. Do not attempt to cross the wall but turn right and follow the wall down to Bowscale Beck; where there is evidence of past mining activity. This was a small copper mine of which little is known. There is a small spoil heap on the south bank of the beck and a few yards to the west there is a level driven into the north bank. Do not attempt to enter as there is a dangerous false floor and an 18 foot

Logan Beck Mine
Entrance to Level

113

flooded sump only a few feet in from the entrance.

To continue with the walk, cross to the north side of the beck and walk along between the wall and the fence for a short distance, until you encounter a gate in the fence at the bend in the stream. A little used track leads north from the gate for about 400 yds before another gate is encountered on the track; which leads to the farm of Whinfield Ground. Do not go through this gate but take the field gate above and to your left. Continuing north across the field the ruins of old mine buildings are soon seen (SD174916).

This is Logan Beck Copper Mine, the third mine on our walk. On the top of the large spoil heap is the collar of a 53 ft deep flooded shaft and a ruined building is seen at the foot of the heap. On the south side of this building is the entrance to a 165 yd level. This level has several flooded pits in its floor, which probably connect with deeper workings. The entrance to the workings is in a particularly good state of repair as they are currently being explored and renovated by local mine enthusiasts. Immediately north of the shaft is the old wheel pit which carried the water wheel used to drain and provide power for the mine. Water for the wheel was carried along a leat which led from a dam situated on Logan Beck just above the waterfall. The course of this leat can easily be seen and an iron bar stuck in a rock in the bed of the beck marks the position of the old dam.

Having browsed around Logan Beck Mine, continue the walk by following the beck up past the waterfalls to the top of the wood at Sele Bottom, below Whitfell. From this point follow the wall, which contours round the wood in a northerly direction along the base of Whitfell. In about two thirds of a mile, as a small ridge is traversed, the track over Whitfell, between Waberthwaite and Millbrow is crossed. Hesk Fell and its copper mines can now be seen about a mile away to the northwest, below you. On a clear day pick your own route down to Storthes, avoiding the boggy bits near the wall. If misty then follow the track down as far as the wall and then turn left along the wall (very wet) and follow the wall until you reach the mines road. This was a large mine, as is obvious from the size of the

spoil heaps, which incidentally, still yield interesting ore samples for the mineralologist. Several ruined mine buildings are still to be seen enabling one to visualise how the mine must have looked long ago.

The return route involves retracing your path to the base of Whitfell and then ascending to its summit cairn and trigpoint. From the trigpoint walk west of southwest across the summit plateau to pick up the track which leads down the side of the fell above Buckbarrow Beck. Continuing on down the track brings you back to the road a short distance north of Buckbarrow Bridge.

Route 3   Harter Fell from Dunnerdale
Forest car park **(B)**
Return by same route
Total climbing about 1620 ft (494 m)
(4 miles)

This short walk is well worth the effort for the spectacular views it provides of the surrounding countryside. Harter Fell stands alone, without immediate neighbours, and so is an ideal platform to observe this area of the district.

Park your car in the Forestry Commission car park where, incidentally, picnic tables are provided, together with a plan of waymarked forest tracks. Cross the bridge and follow the

Hardknott Roman Fort
seen from Harter Fell

The Coniston Fells

forest track which bears to the left and gently climbs up through the wood. In about a quarter of a mile, the track crosses a clearing and you will see the house called Birks below you. The path to Harter Fell turns right, leaving the forest road here and follows a boggy track between a drystone wall and the drystone sheepfolds. At the forest follow the path up the ride (avoiding the bog at the bottom by keeping to the left). A better path can be found just within the forest to the left of the firebreak. This leads you steeply up through the forest until, in a relatively short distance, you will emerge onto a grassy slope adjacent to Dropping Crag. The track now leads a meandering route towards the summit of the fell. As you climb don't forget to look back and admire the fine view of the Coniston Fells behind you, with Seathwaite Tarn Reservoir visible high on the opposite hillside. Seathwaite was the home of 'Wonderful Walker' for most of his long life (LH3). A little further up the hillside you will reach a wire fence. To continue, cross the fence, using the stile near the large rock, and, after a further couple of false summits, you will reach the complicated top of Harter Fell.

There are several craggy outcrops on the summit which are great for photographers and adventurous children who think of themselves as budding rock climbers. Among the crags are grassy areas, ideal for a picnic on a sunny day. To the west lies the isolated Devoke Water with Ravenglass and the sea beyond. Eskdale lies to the northeast, nestling under the lower slopes of Scafell. Looking north from the summit Hardknott fort can be seen in plan view, illustrating very clearly its characteristic Roman design. To the northeast and east the skyline is filled with the outlines of the mountain ridges from Langdale to Scafell. Harter Fell may be a short walk but it is certainly a satisfying one, especially on a clear day.

* * * * *

Lakes to visit
Coniston Water
Esthwaite Water
Windermere

Nearest Towns
Ambleside
Bowness on Windermere (via Ferry)
Ulverston

Places to visit
Grizedale Forestry Commission Visitor Centre
Lakeland Motor Museum, Holker Hall
Lakeside and Haverthwaite Railway
Laurel and Hardy Museum, Ulverston
Muncaster Mill
Ravenglass and Eskdale Railway
Sellafield Visitor Centre

Recommended Country Inns
Fox and Hounds, Ennerdale Bridge
Gosforth Hall Hotel, Gosforth

The Old Man
(From Wordsworth's Seat at Brantwood)

The Coniston Fells, Local History

1. "Laal Ratty"

The Ravenglass and Eskdale Railway carries tens of thousands of delighted visitors every year. It owes its origins to the iron mining that provided much needed employment in the area during the last century. In the early 1870's the Whitehaven Mining Company investigated the Haematite deposits at Boot, near the head of the Eskdale valley. The deposits were considered to be good enough to warrant the construction of a three foot gauge light railway to carry the ore from Upper Eskdale to Ravenglass, from where it could be transferred to the Furness Railway. The line was duly built and opened for mineral traffic on May 24th 1875. In 1876 it was decided to introduce a passenger service and this was opened by Lord Muncaster on 9th November of that year. The line was soon christened 'Owd (or old) Ratty' by the dalesfolk, who found it greatly improved their communications with the outside world. The railway soon became a popular tourist attraction and passenger traffic increased. Unfortunately the mines were not doing well and in 1877 the Whitehaven Mining Company failed, causing the line to be put into receivership. However the receiver continued to operate Owd Ratty, mainly as a passenger service. The line struggled on for another 34 years with a gradually deteriorating permanent way and ageing rolling stock. In 1912 the remaining iron mines at Boot closed, thus precipitating a financial crisis, which eventually led to the closure of the Ravenglass and Eskdale railway after almost 40 years.

This closure was a great loss to the local people of the dale who had no railway service for three long years. In 1915 news of the proposed re-opening of the line caused great interest. The railway was to be re-constructed with 15" gauge track and rolling stock by the Narrow Gauge Railway Company Ltd.. The anticipation and excitement of the local population at the proposed rebirth of 'Ratty' is expressed in this dialect poem written at the time.

Fer Yan We Miss

"In t' April days now at an end,
When t'buds war brusten out,
Our deale-foak aw sum time wud spend
Ta hear t'oald cuckoo shout.

Bit us oald wives up Esktle way,
Er waiten fain ta hear
Anudder sound, lost menny a day,
When Ratty will appear.

Tho' often game was meade ev it,
An at its speed we laft;
Now when its fairly stop't a bit,
It's us its shown er daft.

116

The Coniston Fells, Local History

Fer when ta Drigg we hev ta woak,
It's gaily hard on t' shanks;
An seah fer starten it them foak
Desarve our best ev thanks.

Wey, driver, oil up ivvery joint,
An warm oald Nabb Ghyll's blood,
An let us see yea round Rock Point,
Er climmen Murthet Wood.

When yea git up ta Irton Road,
Rouse t' foak theare fra ther sleep,
Bit mind aw t' way up laal Rat trod,
Doun't run ower enny sheep.

As yea gaa past Lang Yockin How,
Give t' postman yah laal whute;
Let them at Esk bank hear yer row,
Ther's nea need ta be mute.

An them at leaves near Esktle Green,
Quite glad will be again,
An say yer t' best seet they hev seen,
Aw flatch up t' grand laal train.

May him 'ats cum't ta Fishergrund,
Thy smook ga seun now spy,
Ah Know 'at he'll feel nar stunn'd
As t' loco rushes by.

Fer Stowbank foak hed nea laal train
Gaen puffen by t' back duer;
Sua when t' express gits gaen again,
It will suit him, ah's sure.

Them up at Hollin Head ano,
Will welcome ye beath back,
Altho up theare ye gaa gay slow,
Cos terble twin't is t' track.

Reet aw t' way up tull Boot laal town
We'll aw be pleast to see,
T' laal ingen puffen up and down,
Like what it used ta be.

They say ther's heeaps ev ore an stean
Still liggin in our fells;
An nobbet waiten ta be taen,
Sua now just stir yersels.

T' new maniger hes turned out fine,
As any yan can tell;
He's fittest neame fer enny line
Fer they sud aw Hastwell.*

Wheniver Ratty cums next time
Ah'll have a ride fer sport;
An now ah must just stop this rhyme,
An t' ink is running short.".

* Wilson Hastwell   SCAWFELL
(manager of the new line)
                     Frizington

In 1915 Narrow Gauge Railways Ltd. took over the line and commenced laying a 15" gauge line from Ravenglass. Within seven weeks trains were running as far as Muncaster Mill and by 1917 trains were running to Boot once more. The line soon became known as 'Laal (or little) Ratty' and both passenger and goods traffic grew very quickly. For ten years or more after the re-opening the railway provided a year round service to the people of Eskdale, carrying people, goods and the Royal Mail. One of the mainstays of the line was the transport of crushed pink granite roadstone from the Beckfoot quarries. During the Second World War the railways passenger traffic was discontinued, but it continued to haul roadstone. The quarries stopped working in 1953 and in 1960 the railway was saved from being scrapped by a group of enthusiasts. The line is now owned and operated by the Ravenglass & Eskdale Railway Company Ltd. and is supported by the thriving Ravenglass & Eskdale Railway Preservation Society.

Brantwood from the Lake

2. Ruskin and Brantwood

John Ruskin, poet, writer, artist, art critic, philosopher, social reformer, was world famous before he came to Brantwood in 1872, at the age of fifty three. He had fallen in love with the mountains of the Lake District when visiting with his parents, as a child of fourteen, in 1833. The poetry he wrote at this time showed that he missed nothing and was entranced by the beauty of the area. Canon Rawnsley in his book entitled 'Ruskin and the English Lakes,' published in 1902, describes this well. I quote:

" *-- he gazes back upon the Coniston lake, is struck by the beauty of rain-cloud and mist-hidden shores, and notes the way in which*

" The mountains all mistily softened away
Appeared like thin clouds at the dawn of the day,"

-- It is not great poetry truly, but it shows accuracy in observation, and the boy's heart is full to overflowing----"

Something of a child prodigy, John was an avid reader by the age of five and was writing his own verse and prose by the age of seven. He travelled widely in Europe in his earlier years visiting Germany, Switzerland, Italy and France. Here his love of mountains came to the fore. He marvelled and wondered at the beauty of the Alps, particularly the area around Chamonix, Mont Blanc, which featured often in his later writings. In spite of the grandeur of the European Alps he still loved the English Lake District above all else. Many books have been written about John Ruskin, his writings and lectures on art, architecture, and politics amongst other things. The influence of his ideas on social reform was immense. He was way before his time in advocating such new ideas as free schools, free libraries, town planning, smokeless zones and green belts, all of which are now accepted.

It is fitting that his memorial is in the Lake District as he, like Wordsworth, was a pioneer conservationist doing his best to protect the environment he loved, so that others in the future could enjoy it. It was mainly his inspiration that led Canon Rawnsley to put forward his paper entitled 'The Proposed Permanent Lake District Defence Society' in 1883, the first step towards the formation of The National Trust. This initiative came about as a direct result of the continued attempts by the railway companies to obtain Parliamentary permission for new lines into the

John Ruskin in 1864
drawn by Samuel Lawrence

district. These had been all strongly resisted by Wordsworth, Ruskin, Rawnsley and others. Rawnsley presented his paper shortly after the successful defeat of a proposal to build a railway from Braithwaite to Honister, known at the time as the Braithwaite - Buttermere Railway. This line would have traversed Cat Bells and Maiden Moor, passing between Castle Crag and High Spy on its way to the head of Borrowdale and the slate quarries. Thankfully like several other proposals, such as the Yanwath - Pooley Bridge line and the Ennerdale line, it was never built, due mainly to the efforts of these early conservationists.

3. Wonderful Walker

Vicars and Curates had a hard time in the eighteenth century. Livings carried very small stipends and the poor cleric depended greatly on the local population and his own wits in order to survive. One or two were so successful in this endeavour that they became part of the local folklore. One such example was the Reverend Richard Birkett, vicar of Martindale, whose story is told in the East of Ullswater section of this book. An even more famous cleric was Robert

Buttermere
from an old engraving

Walker of Seathwaite who became known as 'Wonderful Walker.'

Robert Walker is first recorded as taking up the posts of curate and schoolmaster at Buttermere in 1732. His salary was paid almost entirely in kind, as follows:

A *'Darrack'* of peats i.e. 'a day's work' of peats. This meant as much turf as he could dig upon the common moss in a day.

A *'Goose Grass.'* This was the right of putting upon the fell or common ground a goose, a gander, and their goslings for free pasture.

A *'Harden Sark.'* This was the obligation of each of his parishioners to provide the curate with a part of his clothing. A Harden Sark was a shirt of very rough and coarse linen.

The right of *'Whittle Gate.'* This has already been described as it applied to Richard Birkett in the section on Martindale Church. In Mr Walker's case he was engaged to instruct the children and perform the clerical duty of the parish, on condition that the parishioners should provide him with board and lodging. It was agreed that he should live at each of their houses for a week or a fortnight in the year. Many would have found this mode of living very arduous and uncomfortable, but not Wonderful Walker, who used it to get to know his flock, to assess their assets and failings and to remove their prejudices. These emoluments of office, however, only provided the bare essentials of life. Robert Walker was the equivalent of the modern workaholic and his devotion to his calling was praised and recorded by several people of note, including Wordsworth. The following passages from 'Seathwaite and The Wonderful Walker' by Thomas Ellwood give an idea of his lifestyle.

"In the mornings before school time, and in the evenings he laboured in manual occupations; during the day he taught school. He publicly catechised the children, and performed the whole duty, morning and afternoon on Sunday. In Summer he rose between three and four o'clock and went to the field with his scythe and his rake, and in harvest time with his sickle. He ploughed; he planted; he went on the mountains after the sheep; he sheered and salved them; he dug peat - all for hire. ---- He was an excellent spinner of linen and cotton thread. All his own clothes and afterwards those of his family were of his own spinning. He knit and mended his own stockings, and made his own shoes. In his walks he never neglected to gather the wood from the hedges and bring it home. He was also the physician and lawyer of the place; he drew up all wills, conveyances, bonds, &c., wrote all letters and settled all accounts. These labours (at all times considerable) at one period of the year, viz., between Christmas and Candlemas, when many transactions are settled in this country, were so intense that he passed a great part of the night, and sometimes whole nights, at his desk." The Torver Parish Register records that on 29th Day of December 1734 Robert took up the curacy of Torver. He stayed there just over a year before taking up the living at his native Seathwaite. Torver was a much better living with a salary of between five and six pounds a year but Walker preferred to live in his home vale. Here Robert settled, married and through his endeavours built up the reputation previously described. Robert Walker died in June 1802, in his 93rd year. His wife was born in 1707 and died in 1800 aged 92 years. Until the sickness of his wife, a few months previous to her death, his health, spirits and faculties were unimpaired. The shock of his wife's death, however, led to his rapid deterioration and death within two years.

4. Copper Mining at Coniston

Copper appears to have been mined at Coniston prior to the arrival in the Lake District of the German miners in 1564. The Germans concentrated their efforts initially at Goldscope Mine in the Newlands valley; as described in the Derwent Fells section of this book. It was not until 1605 that reference is made in documents that "a mine of copper has lately been discovered in the mountains of Lancashire called *'Furnes Fels'* at Coniston." The Germans were said to have opened *'new workings beside the old mine.'* Hence the supposition of copper being mined there

Copper Mines Valley
as it appears today

previously. Records of baptisms, marriages and burials at Hawkshead, however, indicate that German miners worked in the area from about 1599. Evidence of the workings by '*The Old Men*' is still to be found in the hand cut '*coffin levels,*' which survive in some of the more modern workings. The ore produced at Coniston was transported to Keswick for smelting as smelters were never built at Coniston, due mainly to the fact that the mines were not very profitable. Mining in the district was severely disrupted in the middle of the 17th century with the onset of the Civil War. It was at this time that the smelter at Keswick was destroyed by the Parliamentarian forces.

Deeper mining at Coniston commenced in the eighteenth century with the advent of gunpowder as a tool for driving adits. Water power was utilised to drain the mine and raise the ore to the surface. For several years the mine was quite productive but, by the end of the century, the mine was closed once again due to lack of profitability.

Most of the surface and underground workings now remaining date back to the 19th century; the most profitable era for the mine. Mining engineer John Taylor and his manager John Barret re-opened the mine around 1834. New levels were driven, new machinery was introduced, including the forty foot waterwheel at the Old Engine Shaft, and the mine began to prosper once more. The ore was transhipped by barge to the foot of the lake and then carted to Greenodd for shipment to the Swansea smelter. From 1859, when the railway arrived at Coniston, the ore was taken by rail to Barrow for transhipment to the smelter. At its height Coniston Copper Mine employed around four hundred people, mainly Irish immigrant miners and their families. The impact on Coniston must have been considerable as the company built extra housing, contributed to the parish rates, to the church and to the schooling of the village children.

Unfortunately however, in the late 19th century the increasing availability of cheap supplies of copper from abroad spelt the deathknell of the industry in this country and, by the turn of the century, copper mining had effectively ceased at Coniston.

Coniston Lake from Nibthwaite Forge

5. Slate Mining in the Coniston Area

Slate mining on a small scale has been a traditional industry in the area for hundreds of years. The slate was worked where it outcropped, often high on the fells. It was dressed on site into roofing slates and transported by packhorse and sled down to the valleys. About the middle of the last century, as a result of the industrial revolution and the consequent expansion of the big cities, there was a boom in the industry. Transport was a problem and areas, like Coniston, with relatively easy access to lake and sea benefitted greatly. Luckily for Coniston this expansion came at a time when copper mining was running down in the area, thus providing new jobs for the redundant copper miners. The giant open quarries at Tilberthwaite, Hodge Close, Moss Rigg and Coniston Old Man bear witness to this increased demand. In addition much of the best slate was found deep within the mountains. This slate had to be mined rather than quarried thus creating enormous caverns within the hills. Coniston Old Man and Honister Crag were mined extensively in this way. Cathedral Cavern at Little Langdale is a good example of such an excavation, which is relatively accessible to the

A Visit to Hodge Close

Hodge Close is well worth a visit. Take the minor road (once the main road incidentally) signposted 'Hodge Close Only' about one and a half miles north of Coniston on the A593. When you reach Hodge Close park on the vast flat waste tip area which extends on either side of the road. The main quarry is on the south side of the road and is flooded to at least half of its depth.

The cavern entrance visible down at water level is where the slate was trammed out of the quarry. A water balance was used to raise the slate from the quarry floor (see drawing). A tank of water, connected to the slate bogey by a cable and pulley system, was filled until its weight was sufficient to raise the bogey and slate clog to the exit tunnel, halfway up the quarry face. The tank was then emptied so that the weight of the bogey would be sufficient to lower itself back to the quarry floor. Today the flooded quarry is a spectacular sight. The water is extremely clear and the depth from above is very apparent. There is much to see here but be careful, especially with dogs and small children in tow.

Cathedral Cavern on the south side of Little Langdale, adjacent to Moss Rigg Wood, is also well worth a visit. Take the road to High Park, again from the A593, about four miles north of Coniston. Follow the road to its end at the old ford near Stang End. Take the path along the beck towards 'Slater's Bridge.' The quarry is in the wood on your left. It is possible to walk into the cavern through a rather wet adit (tunnel). Large caverns similar to this are to be found under Honister Crag and beneath Coniston Old Man. These two are truly hollow mountains.

The Water Balance at Hodge Close

A walk through the woods above and behind Cathedral Cavern will take you up onto the Moss Rigg workings. Man has certainly devastated this landscape in the past but, already nature has taken over and has done much to repair the damage. These impressive artificial rock faces and giant caverns are a lasting monument to the endeavours of those many miners and quarrymen, who lived and worked here so long ago.

ordinary walker. In the heyday of the industry several hundred men and boys were employed in and around Coniston.

Nowadays slate is still quarried in Lakeland, albeit on a much smaller scale. The use of slate as a roof covering has declined over the years due to the availability of a wide range of cheaper synthetic building materials. Slate has thus become a luxury building material, highly desirable due to its attractive appearance and its high durability, but too expensive for general applications. The result has been a much greater use of slate as a decorative feature on modern buildings, a trend which will surely ensure the continued survival of this ancient industry.

6. Sir Donald Campbell and Coniston

Sir Donald Campbell C.B.E. has become closely associated with the local history of the Lake District through his various attempts at world water speed records on Coniston Water and, to a lesser extent, on Ullswater.

It was January 1949 when Donald heard that Henry Kaiser was building a boat to regain the world water speed record for America. At the time the record was held by Donald's father, Sir Malcom Campbell, who had achieved a speed of 141.74 mph in August 1939, shortly before his death from a heart attack. Donald determined to follow in his father's footsteps and retain the record for Britain. In the sixteen years that followed Donald was to increase the world water speed record no fewer than seven times. During the year that followed, Donald trialled his father's old boat, Bluebird; a propellor driven hydroplane powered by a Rolls Royce aero engine capable of developing 2500 horsepower. In 1950 Stanley Sayers of America raised the record to 176 mph. Bluebird was further modified and trialled on Coniston around this time, but it soon became apparent that a complete new design was needed, if the record was to be regained for Britain. Donald then set about raising money and sponsors for a new jet powered Bluebird that would be capable of speeds well in excess of 200 mph. After many setbacks, both technical and financial, Donald's efforts paid off, when he achieved a world record speed of 202.32 mph on Ullswater in 1955. He quickly followed this success, in the same year, by increasing his record to 216.2 mph on Lake Mead in Nevada.

It was about this time, when everything was going very well, that Donald suggested the building of a Bluebird car to travel at over 400 mph and break John Cobb's land speed record of 394 mph. Within a short time initial plans for the car were drawn up, sponsors were found and the project was commenced. During this time Donald Campbell returned to Coniston Water where, during the next four years, he broke his own record four more times, raising the water speed record to 260.35 mph by 1959.

By May 1960, when the car was built, the project had cost over one million pounds. This could be compared with the twenty five thousand pound price tag of the Bluebird boat. On 16th September 1960 the car was trialled at Bonneville Salt Flats, Utah, where it crashed on its fifth run. Undeterred, Donald had the car rebuilt and took it to the sand flats at Lake Eyre in Australia. Here, after suffering many problems and delays, he finally raised the land speed record to 403 mph on 17th July 1964. Then, on the last day of the year, on Lake Dumbleyung in Australia, he broke the world water speed record once again with a speed of 276.3 mph in Bluebird. This feat made him the first person in history to have broken both land and water speed records within the space of one year. This marvellous success was not enough for Donald. A world water speed record of more than 300 mph was now within reach. Donald returned to Coniston and between November 1966 and January 1967 made several further attempts on the record. It was on the last of these, on January 4th 1967, when he tragically met his death. Donald had just completed a successful first run at well over 300 mph. He turned for the second run and, instead of waiting for the lake to settle down again, set off within four minutes of the first run. This could well have been his undoing. During the second run down the lake Bluebird rose out of the water, somersaulted and crashed. Sir Donald Campbell's body was never recovered.

7. British Nuclear Fuels and Sellafield

The modern Sellafield nuclear re-processing facility owes its origins to the need, in the late 1940's, to set up a factory for the production of fissile material, namely plutonium, to be used in nuclear weapons. Plutonium is a by-product of the fission (or nuclear burning) of uranium; which is carried out in a nuclear reactor.

Prior to 1940 the site on which the plant now lies was farmland, but during the war it was taken over and used by the Ministry of Supply. In 1946 the Ministry of Supply were looking for a suitable site for the production of plutonium. Initially they needed to build two nuclear reactors to produce the plutonium and a chemical processing plant to extract the plutonium from the fission products and the uranium.

At that time it was thought preferable to site the plant in a remote area to allow for the safe discharge of slightly radioactive cooling gases into the atmosphere, through high chimneys. In addition there had to be in the locality an abundant supply of pure water and, preferably, existing road and rail links. Sellafield, situated on the Cumbrian coast, fulfilled these criteria and, as the land was Government owned, it was easy to start operations. So, in 1947, the building of the original Windscale factory was commenced. The first Windscale re-processing plant operated from 1952 to 1964.

Meanwhile Calder Hall, hailed as the world's first full scale nuclear power station, was being constructed on a site adjacent to Windscale. Calder Hall was opened on 17th October 1956 by Her Majesty the Queen and is still operational today, producing electricity for the National Grid. This was only the beginning of a fast growing civil nuclear power programme which would require extra waste disposal and re-processing facilities.

Anticipating this extra demand, the United Kingdom Atomic Energy Authority (UKAEA), which had taken over from the Ministry of Supply in 1954, decided to build a new plant at Windscale to deal with both the military and civilian reprocessing and waste disposal needs. This new facility was commissioned in 1964, replacing the original plant.

In the late 1960's it looked as if cheap oil from the Middle East would make the nuclear industry unnecessary. However, the oil crisis of 1973 showed the need for self sufficiency in energy supply and nuclear power became 'flavour of the month' once more.

New reactors were being designed which could use re-processed fuel from the older less efficient reactors and many countries were building up stocks of used fuel which required re-processing. This eventually led to the building of the giant Thorp re-processing plant at Sellafield.

Using nuclear energy to generate electricity has always been a controversial topic, but opposition to the nuclear programme, has escalated over recent years. Fears first began to be expressed in 1957 when there was a disastrous fire in one of the reactor chimneys of the Windscale factory. This caused a large uncontrolled release of radioactivity onto the surrounding countryside, possibly the first nuclear accident. As a result the Windscale reactors were shut down permanently. Since then the accidents at Three Mile Island and Chernobyl have only served to reinforce the opposition. Nuclear reprocessing did not

Sellafield

develop as a major issue until the Windscale Inquiry in 1977 and British Nuclear Fuels plc., who now run the Sellafield Complex, have always been aware of the need to have good relations with the public. However, the increased opposition to the very existence of the industry by certain groups in recent years has caused them to spend great amounts of money on putting their side of the nuclear argument. One of the direct results of this policy has been the development of the Sellafield Visitor Centre.

The Sellafield Centre is a must for adults and children alike with its interactive displays and clever simulations of nuclear processes; such as the fission of uranium. Here one can learn about the history and development of the British nuclear power programme. The principles by which nuclear energy is produced, the impending world energy crisis and the case for nuclear power are clearly explained for the layman, using a variety of 'high tech' visual aids. Sellafield Visitor Centre is open on every day of the year except Christmas Day. Entrance is free and there is a restaurant in the Visitor Centre.

8. Muncaster Water Mill

A working water powered corn mill which was the manorial mill for the Manor of Muncaster. The present building dates from about 1700 and records tell us that a mill has occupied this site since at least 1455. Freshly milled stone-ground products are on sale to the visitor, who can combine a trip on Laal Ratty with a visit to the mill. Well worth a look !

The Geology of Lakeland

The Earth in its Youth
This is the story of the origins of the Lake District, a story which began about **half a billion** (yes, five hundred million) years ago; an unimaginably distant time. There were no trees or grass, no living creatures of any sort on land or in the air, and no fish in the sea either. The Earth at that time would have seemed an alien place to us, had we been there, but there would have been aspects of its surface processes familiar to us.

Early Landscaping
Even so long ago, the Earth possessed an atmosphere, albeit unbreathably low in oxygen, as well as oceans and continents. The sun shone, wind blew, water evaporated and fell as rain or snow. Then, as now, the land was carved by wind, water and ice into hills and valleys, cliffs and plains. Volcanoes heaved up and earthquakes shook the land. The relentless transport of weathered rock waste planed down the land and built up the sea floor.

Skiddaw Slates
It is with this scenario that the story of the Lake District starts, a story that has been pieced together by geological detective work, seeking and interpreting the clues held by the rocks and scenery of the region. The oldest rocks of the Lake District are found mainly in the north-west as the Skiddaw and

Grasmoor fells, and are known as the **Skiddaw Group**. They consist in the main of grey to bluish grey mudstones and sandstones which formed from sediments that were probably dumped in shallow seas on the edge of an ancient continent. These wet sediments periodically slumped down the underwater slopes into the deeper ocean bed to the north. Over the ages, these muddy rocks have been squeezed and hardened into poor quality slates. These now break down at the surface into small pieces forming scree, sliding down the hillsides to produce the smooth looking slopes so characteristic of the area around Skiddaw. The marine origin of these rocks is confirmed by the finding of occasional fossilised remains of **graptolites;** long extinct creatures which floated in the seas of the time. These fossils are not easily found, neither are they exciting to look at, resembling bits of broken fretsaw blade in general size and shape.

The Formation of a Volcanic Island
The tranquility of these ancient seas was shattered by a series of volcanic outbursts which erupted violently and periodically over the relatively short span of a few million years. Repeated eruptions produced a volcanic island about forty kilometres in diameter. We can visualise the Lake District at four hundred and forty five million years ago as one of a series of volcanic islands on the south western side of a wide

ocean separating *"early Scotland"* from *"southern England."*

Volcanic Ancestry of Lakeland

The worn down remains of our Lake District volcano form the tract of high craggy ground of the central part of the Lake District. Such well known features as the Scafells, the Langdale Pikes and Helvellyn lie in the region of volcanic rocks whose steepness, hardness and resistance to weathering form such an attraction for rock climbers.

It is perhaps a common misconception to suppose that all volcanic rocks have formed by the direct cooling of streams of molten lava. Recent volcanic eruptions, such as that of Mount St. Helens, have shown that in many eruptions only a small proportion of the ejected material comes out in truly liquid form as a lava stream. Volcanic eruptions depend on the explosive force of gas, mostly steam, to blast out solid or liquid material.

A look at the textures of the **Borrowdale Volcanic Group** of the Lake District will provide clues to the volcanic origins of the rocks. A sample looking rather like concrete, full of angular fragments, probably formed not far from an active vent, from lumps of solid rock shot up into the air. Sand like layers would have formed from the volcanic grit and dust blown downwind, and perhaps reworked as volcanic mud by the torrential rain produced by condensing volcanic steam. Molten lava flows tend to keep moving downslope, even though they may have formed cooled slaggy skins.

Evidence in the Rocks

Sections through many Lake District lavas show the slaggy upper and lower surfaces, often full of gas bubbles, and a compact crystalline centre. Sometimes, lava flows are found to have erupted one on top of

The Borrowdale Valley
in 1819

another, forming step like features in the Lakeland landscape. Perhaps the most intriguing type of volcanic rock in the Lake District has been formed by gassy eruptions, where the erupting gas, moving at high speed, was loaded with incandescent droplets of lava and pumice. When the droplets fell to ground, they would still have been hot enough to be squashed, giving a rock with the appearance of 'streaky bacon', known as **ignimbrite**. An eruption of this type in 1902 on the Caribbean island of Martinique rapidly obliterated a town with its thirty thousand inhabitants, and produced an ignimbrite layer a few centimetres thick. The Lake District ignimbrites are many hundreds of metres in thickness, a witness to the ferocity of the eruptions. Huge volumes; many hundreds of cubic metres, of gas, liquid and solid were thrown out and much of it came to rest on to the surrounding land. This must have caused great instability, and one of the exciting recent geological discoveries in the Lake District is an ancient fault system at the eastern end of the Wastwater Screes which seems to indicate that the *"Borrowdale Volcano"* collapsed inwards upon itself with a vertical fall of as much as a mile.

Fossil Evidence

When the activity cooled off, the collapsed stump of the volcano was engulfed by the sea, depositing first thin beds of limestone and mudstone of the **Coniston Group**. These are crowded with fossils of early sea creatures such as shellfish, corals, sea lilies and trilobites, showing that the sea was in part a shallow one. Erosion of the volcanic landscape produced vast quantities of debris which forms the thick mudstone and slate sequence of the **Windermere Group** to the south of the Ambleside - Coniston line, and extending eastwards into the Howgill Fells.

During this first hundred million year phase of the Lake District's geological story, the area predominantly existed as part of the sea bed with volcanoes forming dry land for a short period.

Collisions between Continents

in order to explain what came next, we need to remember that the Earth's thin crust moves slowly, responding to patterns of heat circulation deep down. By this process, continents are able to drift inexorably across the Earth's surface. Compared with the size of the Earth, the crust is desperately thin, about as thick as a postage stamp stuck on a football! About four hundred million years ago two of the thicker crustal plates collided, roughly along the boundary of England and Scotland. A similar but more recent collision between Asia and India has produced the impressive Himalayan mountain ranges. Thus, we can imagine the northern part of Britain of four hundred million years ago consisting of soaring mountains of folded and faulted rock layers squeezed upwards from the sea bed as the continents moved together.

Altered Rocks

Apart from crumpling and breaking, two other effects arising from continental collision are plainly seen in the Lake District. Intense squeezing has caused the rocks, particularly the marine and volcanic mudstones, to re-form into the **slates** which are still quarried in various parts of the district. It is often easy to see the original coloured sedimentary layers, but the slaty rock now splits in a regular way *across* these layers. Furthermore, the roots of these ancient mountains were injected with vast pools of hot molten rock which, unable to find its way to the surface, cooled slowly to form **granite.** It is thought that the northern half of the Lake District is entirely founded

Disused Quarry, Moss Rigg

on granite, which can be seen in Eskdale, Wasdale, Ennerdale, near Skiddaw and at Shap Fell. The Shap granite is noted for its strikingly beautiful crystalline texture, and it has been used as an ornamental stone in buildings throughout the land.

What became of these colossal early mountains? It seems that during the fifty million years following the continental collision well over five miles of vertical thickness of rock was eroded away. This left a range of low hills which slowly subsided beneath the sea. Little remains of this phase apart from some bouldery, chocolate brown rocks to be seen at Mell Fell to the north of Ullswater.

The Beginnings of Limestone and Coal

At this time, some three hundred and fifty million years ago, the region lay in the tropics. The shallow seas then were supersaturated with lime, and supported a rich variety of living organisms. The evidence for this can be seen in the **Carboniferous Limestone** which almost completely encircles the more ancient rocks of the Lake District. The light grey limestone contains fossils of shellfish, corals, sea lilies and many other creatures. The gradual silting up of these tropical seas led to the extensive growth of tropical swamp forests during the **Upper Carboniferous** period. Vast quantities of rotting vegetation were covered from time to time by layers of mud and sand to form a gigantic compost heap, and the result was **coal.** There are no coal measures in the Lake District itself, but coal has been mined for hundreds of years along the west coast of Cumbria from Whitehaven to Maryport. By the end of the carboniferous period, at two hundred and seventy million years ago, we have come nearly halfway in our gallop through the story of Lakeland rocks.

Formation of the Sandstones

Again the climate was changing as the region drifted into the desert latitudes of the present-day Sahara. Again, the region was uplifted to form ranges of hills and valleys which for nearly one hundred million years were subjected to hot desert winds and occasional rainstorms. This led to periodic flooding of a massive river system which flowed northwards from the area of northern France. The rocks of this **Permo-Triassic** period, characteristically rich red-brown in colour, are known as the **New Red Sandstone** and are to be seen at St. Bees, Maryport, Barrow, and in the Eden Valley.

At this point we are forced to leap into the present (or nearly so) since there is no direct evidence of geological events in the Lake District at the times when the rocks of Southern England, the limestones of the Cotswolds, or the chalk of the Downs, were being formed.

Mountain Carving by the Ice

We pick up the story again less than two million years ago, when the climate of the northern hemisphere became rather variable, alternating between cooler and warmer episodes, each lasting a few tens of thousands of years. At the moment we are in a warmer episode. Twenty thousand years ago, it was much cooler and wetter, with snow and ice covering most of Britain north of the Thames. The present landscape of the Lake District, with its frost-shattered fell tops, trough shaped valleys; with their oversteepened and ice-sculpted slopes, as well as the lake basins themselves, all bear witness to the powerfully erosive effects of glacier ice cover. The glaciers that moved off the higher ground have excavated the valleys of Lakeland and spread rock fragments far and wide. The rapid melting of the glaciers some fifteen thousand years ago filled the lake basins, and helped to spread the pulverised glacier waste even further afield. Plants and animals re-established themselves as the climate improved, and **Mankind** arrived.

The Future

What of the future? Clearly geology is the foundation stone of all our activities. We live on the Earth and extract all of our needs from it. Building stones, gemstones, metals, coal, oil, gas, industrial and agricultural chemicals and, of course, fresh water. All of these needs must be served, but at a price. The price is either that of wanton rape and pillage of the land, or of frugal usage sensible to the needs of our descendants. The Lake District has been fortunate to survive former exploitation. Let us ensure that future generations are enabled to enjoy its charm.

Tom Shipp

The Slate Quarries

An Alphabetical Guide to the Fells

Allen Crags

Height 581 m = 1906 ft   NY237085   **Rank 43**

There are two obvious summits on the broad band of high ground between Langstrath and Grains Gill. These are Glaramara and Allen Crags. Using the conventional approaches, which take one over Glaramara first, one can almost walk over Allen Crags without noticing. The top is covered with rocky outcrops and offers fine views.

From Stonethwaite via Langstrath and Allencrags Gill:
       Ascent 685 m = 2247 ft   *Distance 9 km = 5.6 miles*
From Seathwaite via Stockley Bridge, Grains Gill and Ruddy Gill:
       Ascent 660 m = 2165 ft   *Distance 4.9 km = 3 miles*
From the Old Dungeon Ghyll Hotel (Great Langdale) via Mickleden Beck, Rosset Gill, Angle Tarn:
       Ascent 685 m = 2247 ft   *Distance 6.4 km = 4 miles*

Adjacent Fells:	Great End	910 m = 2985 ft	Distance 4.9 km = 3 miles
	Glaramara	783 m = 2568 ft	2.4 km = 1.5 miles
	Esk Pike	885 m = 2903 ft	1.6 km = 1.0 miles

Angletarn Pikes

Height 567 m = 1860 ft   NY 414147   **Rank 149**

From Brothers Water the two rocky peaks of Angletarn Pikes are seen most clearly. The ground on which they lie is broad and sometimes boggy but certainly not lacking in interest. This is excellent walking country and the views are superb. Just below the summit nestling in a hollow is the delightful Angle Tarn.

From Patterdale via Side Farm and Boredale Hause:
       Ascent 417 m = 1368 ft   *Distance 2.6 km = 1.6 miles*
From Hartsop along the path at the foot of the fell (goes below Calf Close and Dubhow Crag) to Boredale Hause: Ascent 397m = 1302 ft   *Distance 4.3 km = 2.7 miles*
From Hartsop via Hayeswater Gill to the north end of Hayeswater then onto the path rising up to the Knott but, instead of going to the latter, turn left to Angle Tarn and the Pikes:
       Ascent 397 m = 1302 ft   *Distance 5.7 km = 3.5 miles*
From Martindale Old Church via Winter Crag, Howstead Brow, Beda Head, Bedafell Knott, Heckbeck Head:
       Ascent 377 m = 1237 ft   *Distance 5.1 km = 3.2 miles*

Adjacent Fells:	Beda Head	Height 509 m = 1669 ft	Distance 2.9 km = 1.8 miles
	Rest Dodd	696 m = 2283 ft	2.6 km = 1.6 miles
	Place Fell	657 m = 2155 ft	2.8 km = 1.7 miles

Ard Crags

Height 581 m = 1906 ft   NY 207198   **Rank 141**

Because of its lofty neighbours and its lack of connection with adjacent fells, Ard Crags tends to be neglected. It is however a good interesting walk with splendid views from the top.

From the quarry car park on the Braithwaite / Buttermere road at Rigg Beck bridge follow the beck along a short way and then take to the ridge:
       Ascent 415 m = 1362 ft   *Distance 2700 m = 1.7 miles*

Adjacent Fells:	Knott Rigg	Height 556 m = 1824 ft	Distance 1400 m = 0.9 miles

Armboth Fell

Height 479 = 1571 ft   **NY297160**   **Rank 194**

The upper reaches of the fell are flat and very boggy and little pleasure is to be gained there. The route up through the woods by the Launchy Gill waterfall is very pleasant indeed, but one can enjoy this without continuing to the summit. The only redeeming feature of the summit is that it provides good views of the more distant fells.

From the foot of Launchy Gill:

| | *Ascent 289 m = 948 ft* | *Distance 2 km = 1.2 miles* |

From Armboth up the footpath to Watendlath then turn southwest at the top of the woods:

| | *Ascent 289 m = 948 ft* | *Distance 1.6 km = 1.0 miles* |

| *Adjacent fells* | *High Tove* | *Height* | *515 m = 1689 ft* | *Distance 1.4 km = 0.9 miles* |
| | *Ullscarf* | | *726 m = 2381 ft* | *4.9 km = 3.0 miles* |

Arnison Crag

Height 433 m = 1420 ft   NY393 160   Rank 208

A low but interesting rocky hill to the south of Patterdale. To ascend follow the north / south wall which runs most, but not all, of the way to the top. Restricted but nevertheless good views.

From Patterdale (The path starts by the side of the White Lion car park):

| | *Ascent 283 m = 928 ft* | *Distance 1.2 km = 0.7 miles* |

| *Adjacent Fells* | *Birks* | *Height 622 m = 2040 ft* | *Distance 1.6 km = 2.0 miles* |

Arthur's Pike

Height 532 m = 1745 ft   **NY461207**   **Rank 164**

From the Ullswater side this fell looks impossibly steep. However beyond this facade is a gentle grassy hill sloping down, over a distance of two kilometres to Heltondale. The attraction of the fell is the exciting walk up or down the steep ravine of Swarthbeck Gill. The bed of the gill is too narrow, wet and difficult for a direct scramble but, there is a narrow path above the ravine which gives good views into it for most of its length. The view from the summit is good from the west but rather dull from the east. The route over Barton Fell is pleasant and easy but lacks excitement.

From Pooley Bridge via the lower slopes of Heughscar Hill and Barton Fell:

| | *Ascent 374 m = 1227 ft* | *Distance 5.2 km = 3.2 miles* |

From Pooley Bridge via the lakeside path to Waterside House. From here on (rather than use the road) use the system of paths over farm land. e.g. Cross Dormant to Seat Farm to Thwaitehill to Auterstone to Swarthbeck. Thence up Swarthbeck Gill:

| | *Ascent 374 m = 1227 ft* | *Distance 6.1 km = 3.8 miles* |

From Howtown via the footpath at the foot of the fell to Swarthbeck. Thence up Swarthbeck Gill:

| | *Ascent 382 m = 1253 ft* | *Distance 2.7 km = 1.7 miles* |

| *Adjacent Fells:* | *Loadpot Hill* | *Height* | *671 m = 2201 ft* | *Distance 2.6 km = 1.6 miles* |
| | *Bonscale Pike* | | *524 m = 1719 ft* | *1.2 km = 0.7 miles* |

Bakestall

Height 673 m = 2270 ft   **NY 266307**   **Rank 102**

Bakestall would be hardly worthy of mention were it not for the presence nearby of Dead Crags and Whitewater Dash waterfall. The approach from the road (Peter House Farm) follows a long and rather tedious track. However things get a lot more interesting as the crags are approached.

Bakestall (continued)

From the road (Peter House Farm) along the track and up the side of Dead Beck (care needed, steep loose ground): Ascent 461 m = 1512 ft   Distance 2.9 km = 1.8 miles

From the road (Peter House Farm) along the track and up by the waterfall. Then up Birkett Edge: Ascent 461 m = 1512 ft   Distance 3.5 km = 2.2 miles

Adjacent Fells: Skiddaw   Height 931 m = 3054 ft   Distance 1.7 km = 1 mile

Bannerdale Crags

Height 683 m = 2240 ft   **NY335290**   **Rank 100**

The east ridge makes Bannerdale Crags an interesting fell in its own right. It is a narrow, but not difficult, ridge with some good rock scenery on both sides. The fell can also be made part of the route to Blencathra. There are fair views from the top. It is possible to ascend the ridge which is steep and may not be to everyone's taste as it is very greasy in wet weather. It is better to follow the gently graded path from Mungrisedale round the north side of the Tongue to the summit. In dry weather the ridge is a good descent route.

From Mungrisedale via the east ridge: Ascent 448 m = 1470 ft   Distance 3.2 km = 2.0 miles

From Mungrisedale via the Tongue: Ascent 448 m = 1470 ft   Distance 4.2 km = 2.6 miles

From Mungrisedale along the river Glendermakin around White Horse Bent, along the old mine track and up by the old lead mine (Saddleback Old Mine): Ascent 448 m = 1470 ft   Distance 5.4 km = 3.4 miles

Barf

Height 468 m = 1535 ft   **NY 215267**   **Rank 198**

The east side of Barf is steep, rugged and most conspicuous from the Keswick/Cockermouth road, particularly so because of the white-painted rock, known as the Bishop of Barf, to be seen near the top of the scree on the southeast corner. It is possible to climb to the top via the Bishop but many will find this an awkward undertaking, maybe a little unnerving. An easier but nevertheless very pleasant route is to follow the path up the south side of Beckstones Gill and then cross over easy ground to the summit. The west side of Barf is grassy and undulating, leading down to the quiet Wythop valley. The summit views down the length of Bassenthwaite and across to Skiddaw are superb and the climb is worth it just for this.

*From opposite the Swan Hotel, straight up the southeast corner of the Bishop. This route is **not** recommended for a descent: the main difficulties are the very steep scree slope up to the Bishop and a short climb across the right hand side of the crescent shaped slab rock below the summit. An exciting route if you enjoy scrambling:* Ascent 368 m = 1207 ft   Distance 1 km = 0.6 miles

From opposite the Swan Hotel, up the south side of Beckstones Gill then across to the summit: Ascent 368 m = 1207 ft   Distance 1.2 km = 0.8 miles

From the Whinlatter Visitor Centre, along the track below Seat how and across from the edge of the wood to the summit: Ascent 158 m = 518 ft   Distance 3.1 km = 1.9 miles

From Wythop Hall Farm via the old brickworks (shown as a quarry on the map) and into the wood. Follow the forest tracks to emerge near Hagg Beck. Then follow the edge of the wood upwards: Ascent 258 m = 846 ft   Distance 2.7 km = 1.7 miles

From Beck Wythop up the forest tracks and out near Wythop Hall Farm. Thence to the old brickworks. The route is then the same as that above: Ascent 398 m = 1306 ft   Distance 3.2 km = 2.0 miles

Adjacent Fell: Lords Seat   Height 552 m =1811 ft   Distance 1.1 km = 0.7 miles

Barrow

Height 455 m = 1492 ft   **NY227218**   **Rank 201**

A small mountain with excellent views from the summit. Not much effort is needed to get to the top and therefore a walk suitable for not very enthusiastic children. A good circular walk is from Braithwaite to Barrow Door then up to the summit before dropping down to Braithwaite Lodge Farm and thence Braithwaite. The mountain has been mined for lead and the large face of scree above Uzzicar Farm is a result of these operations. A small mine tunnel entrance can also be seen at the head of Barrow Gill, just below the Barrow Door. Yet more evidence of mining activity can be found on the west side of Stoneycroft Bridge. Here a watercut has been hewn from solid rock to divert the water from the mineshaft, which lay in the natural stream bed.

From Braithwaite via Barrow Door:
          Ascent 365 m = 1197 ft   *Distance 2.8 km = 1.8 miles*
From Braithwaite via Braithwaite Lodge Farm:
          Ascent 365 m = 1197 ft   *Distance 2 km = 1.2 miles*
From Stoneycroft Bridge via Barrow Door:
          Ascent 335 m = 1099 ft   *Distance 2.1 km = 1.3 miles*
Adjacent Fell: Oughterside   Height 568 m = 1863 ft   Distance 1.7 km = 1 .1 mile

Base Brown

Height 646 m = 2119 ft   **NY225115**   **Rank121**

Base Brown is somewhat out on a limb and accordingly rarely visited as most walkers will by-pass it for Great Gable. The direct approach from Seathwaite (i.e. up Sour Milk Gill and the ridge via Hanging Stone) is certainly very steep and a little rough in places. However you do gain height quickly and the walk to Green Gable (and Great Gable beyond that) becomes quite leisurely. The views from the top are restricted but you do get a good view of the Scafells.

From Seathwaite via Sour Milk Gill and Hanging Stone:
          Ascent 521 m = 1707 ft   *Distance 1.7 km = 1.1 miles*
From Seathwaite via Sour Milk Gill and along Gillercomb then up on to the ridge to Blackmoor Pols followed by an easy walk to the summit:
          Ascent 521 m = 1709 ft   *Distance 2.7 km = 1.7 miles*
Adjacent Fells: Green Gable   Height 801 m = 2627 ft   Distance 1.5 km = 0.9 mile

Beda Head

Height 509 m = 1669 ft   **NY428170**   **Rank 179**

The summit is situated on the long ridge leading from Angletarn Pikes in the south to the base of Hallin Fell in the north. The side of the ridge is steep and grassy and drops into Boredale. The east side is more craggy and drops into the valley containing Martindale. The views from the top are of moderate quality only and the lack of features makes for fairly dull walking.

From Martindale Old Church via Winter Crag and Howstead Brow:
          Ascent   319 m = 1047 ft   *Distance 2.2 km = 1.4 miles*
From Garth Heads in Boredale via Howstead Brow:
          Ascent   319 m = 1047 ft   *Distance 1.6 km = 1.0 mile*
Adjacent Fell: Angletarn Pikes Height 567 m = 1860 ft   Distance 2.9 km = 1.8 miles

Binsey

Height 447 m   **NY225355**   **Rank 203**

A small almost conical hill that has just managed to stay within the northern border of the National Park. It is quite distinct from the rest of the northern fells which makes its top a good platform for viewing them. The

Binsey (continued)

summit gives an excellent view of Skiddaw and the Uldale Fells. Binsey has also become popular with the hang gliding fraternity.

From a track off the A591 a short distance north of Bewaldeth:
Ascent	281 m = 922 ft	Distance 1.8 km = 1.1 miles

From the Bewaldeth/ Ruthwaite road a short distance west of Binsey Lodge:
Ascent	183 m = 600 ft	Distance 1.6 km = 1 mile

Birkhouse Moor

Height 718 m = 2355 ft   NY364160   **Rank 81**

Birkhouse Moor is the broad eastern termination of the famous ridge leading up to Striding Edge and Helvellyn. Birkhouse Moor has a steep, craggy and dramatic northeast face, but the rest of it is sprawling and uninteresting. The views are fair but not outstanding. It is usually by-passed by the huge number of walkers going to the top of Helvellyn.

From Grisedale Bridge along the track to the end of the wood, across the river and up the hill by Brownend Plantation. Head straight up to the summit:
	Ascent 568 m = 1863 ft	Distance 3.2 km = 2.0 miles

From Glenridding via Rattlebeck Bridge and Mires Beck:
	Ascent 568 m = 1863 ft	Distance 3.1 km = 1.9 miles

From Glenridding via Rattlebeck Bridge and the ridge leading up to The Nab, a rather more adventurous route:
	Ascent 568 m = 1863 ft		Distance 2.8 km = 1.7 miles
Adjacent Fells:	Helvellyn	Height 950 m = 3116 ft	Distance 3.2 km = 2.0 miles
	Catstye Cam	890 m = 2919 ft	3.2 km = 2.0 miles

Birks

Height 622 m = 2040 ft   NY380144   **Rank 128**

The summit is on the ridge leading up from just south of Grasthwaite Howe to the summit of St Sunday Crag. It is probably the case that someone visiting here is on the way to the latter and possibly beyond. The walk to the top is very pleasant and, though the summit itself offers little of interest, the views are good.

From Grisedale Bridge via Thornhow End:
	Ascent 472 m = 15949 ft	Distance 2.3 km = 1.4 miles
Adjacent Fells:	St Sunday Crag Height 841 m = 2759 ft	Distance 1.7 km = 1.1 miles
	Glenridding Dodd	442 m = 1450 ft	1.6 km = 1.0 miles

Black Combe

Height 600 m = 1968 ft   SD135855   **Rank135**

A hill of great bulk dominating the southwest corner of the National Park. The terrain is largely grassland and the walking would be pleasant but unremarkable were it not for the truly magnificent views; both inland and out to sea. In common with the other fells along the west coast it is rarely visited by the tourist. The usual ascent is from Whichham Church.

From Whicham Church via the beck to the farm, Townend Knotts, Black Crag:
	Ascent 555m =1820 ft	Distance 3.9 km = 2.4 miles

From Holegill (from opposite the lane to Barfield) via Hall Foss and Little Fell:
	Ascent 570 m = 1868 ft	Distance 5.5 km = 3.4 miles

Adjacent Fell:	White Combe	Height 415 m = 1361 ft	Distance 3.8 km = 2.4 miles

Black Fell

Height 323 m = 1059 ft   NY340016   **Rank 238**

The summit is very obvious when looking to the northeast from Tarn Hows. Though not high, it is the highest hill within the considerable area of land between Windermere Lake and the A593 Ambleside / Coniston road. Accordingly the views are extensive and of high quality. The usual route is via the Iron Keld Plantation path which starts on the Borwick Lodge / Oxen Fell lane. The route can be extended by starting from Tarn Hows.

From Iron Keld Plantation:
                     Ascent 43 m = 141 ft   *Distance 1.8 km = 1.1 miles*
From Tarn Hows Car Park along the west side of the tarns, then east along Borwick Lodge / Oxen Fell lane to Iron Keld Plantation:
                     Ascent 123 m = 403 ft   *Distance 3.5 km = 2.2 miles*

Blake Fell

Height 573 m = 1879 ft   NY110197   **Rank 145**

A quiet place with some excellent views. A good circular walk including this summit is Maggie's Bridge / Gavel Fell / Blake Fell and then down the front of Carling Knott (steep) and back to Maggie's Bridge
                                        (Distance 9.7 km = 6 miles).
From Maggie's Bridge via Black Crag and Gavel Fell:
                     Ascent 448 m = 1470 ft   *Distance 5.2 km = 3.2 miles*
From Maggie's Bridge via High Nook Farm and Carling Knott:
                     Ascent 448 m = 1470 ft   *Distance 4.5 km = 2.8 miles*
Adjacent Fells   Gavel Fell   Height   526 m = 1725 ft   Distance 1.7 km = 1.1 miles
                  Burnbank Fell   475 m = 1558 ft   1.5 km = 0.9 miles

Blea Rigg

Height 540 m = 1771 ft   NY301078   **Rank 160**

Blea Rigg is a relatively small rock outcrop in the broad, long and undulating ridge between High Raise and Silver How. There is some good local scenery and, for example, it is worth making a short excursion from the summit to the edge of Blea Crag, some 200 m to the north. Excellent long distance views across to the Helvellyn range in the northeast and the Langdales (Pavey Ark and Harrison Stickle) in the west. The best ascents are from Great Langdale, but the route up the gill below Whitegill Crag entails a certain amount of scrambling and is not recommended as a means of descent.

From Millbeck (a few hundred metres to the east of the New Dungeon Ghyll Hotel) up the gill between Swine Knott and Whitegill Crag then northeast to Blea Rigg:
                     Ascent 440 m = 1444 ft   *Distance 1.6 km = 1 mile*
From the New Dungeon Ghyll Hotel via Stickle Tarn :
                     Ascent 440 m = 1444 ft   *Distance 3.1 km = 1.9 miles*
From Grasmere via Easedale Road, Easedale, Easedale Tarn and then up the east side of Blea Crag:
                     Ascent 470 m = 1542 ft   *Distance 4.8 km = 3 miles*

Adjacent Fells: Silver How   Height 394 m = 1292 ft   Distance 3.1 km = 2 miles
                  Sergeant Man   Height 730 m = 2394 ft   Distance 2.1 km = 1.3 miles

Bleaberry Fell

Height 590 m = 1935 ft   NY286196   **Rank 137**

Approached from the north the fell is pleasant easy walking. South of the summit the ground becomes boggy and not very enjoyable. If coming (or going) from (to) the north it is well worth going by Walla Crag. The views from the summit are excellent.

Bleaberry Fell (continued)

From Keswick (Moot Hall), St John Street, Ambleside Road, Springs Road, Rakefoot, Low Moss (or detour to Walla Crag). A path off Springs Road gives access to the Castlehead viewpoint:

> Ascent   510 m = 1673 ft   Distance 5.2 km = 3.4 miles

From the A591 500 m (0.3 miles) south of Dale Bottom Farm via the path along the top of the woods. Ascend by the south end of Goat Crag:

> Ascent 426 m = 1398 ft   Distance 2.7 km = 1.7 miles

From the Borrowdale Road, a footpath at the south end of the woods below Walla Crag follows Cat Gill. At the top of the gill turn southeast to the summit:

> Ascent 500 m = 1640 ft   Distance 3.2 km = 2.0 miles
>   From Keswick 5.8 km = 3.6 miles)

From Ashness Bridge follow Barrow Beck and at the waterfall change direction to the summit:

> Ascent 435 m = 1427 ft   Distance 1.7 km = 1.1 miles

Adjacent Fells: Walla Crag   Height 379 m = 1243 ft   Distance 2.4 km = 1.5 miles
                   High Seat   608 m = 1994 ft   1.6 km = 1 .0 miles

Blease Fell

Height 590 m = 1935 ft   NY312270   **Rank 31**

It is unlikely that anyone would wish to make reaching the summit of Blease Fell the sole object of a walk. It is the western end of a 1.5 mile long ridge that includes the top of Blencathra and terminates in the east at Foule Crag above Sharp Edge. The ascent of Blease Fell is a somewhat monotonous plod up a huge grassy slope and would not be considered the best way of getting to the top of Blencathra. However it is a safe way off Blencathra in wet weather, when the rocky ridges of Gategill Fell and Hall's Fell can be rather slippy.

From the Blencathra Centre:

> Ascent 514 m = 1686 ft   Distance 1.7 km = 1.1 miles

From the car park near the school building in Threlkeld Village via the enclosures above Blease Farm:

> Ascent 624 m = 2047 ft   Distance 2.3 km = 1.4 miles

Adjacent Fell: Blencathra (Saddleback) Height 868 m = 2847 ft   Distance 1.6 km = 1 mile

Blencathra

Height 868 m = 2847 ft   NY323277   **Rank 14**

The south side of Blencathra, above the Keswick / Penrith road is magnificent to see and magnificent to walk. The other side is grassy, moorish and quite different in character. All the ridges on the south side are well worth climbing, Hall's Fell possibly being the best. None of the ridges pose any difficulties in dry weather but, in wet and icy weather they can become unpleasant in places. It is possible to climb the gulleys between the ridges but much of the walking is on steep grass and loose scree and is not generally recommended. The exciting way up is via Sharp Edge above Scales Tarn. There are some exposed and slightly awkward places on the narrow but short ridge and care is needed. Sharp Edge should be avoided in wet and icy weather when it can be very dangerous. There are many ways of climbing Blencathra which is one of the reasons why the author ascends the mountain several times a year. Here are some of the better known routes.

From the car park just north of the school building in Threlkeld via Gategill Fell:

> Ascent   678 m = 2224 ft   Distance 2.7 km = 1.7 miles

From the car park just north of the school building in Threlkeld, up Blease Gill and then take the northeast branch of the stream at the 500 m contour (NY 315267) and up to the top of the ridge on Gategill Fell. (You will need good boots for this one):

> Ascent 678 m = 2224 ft   Distance 2.9 km = 1.9 miles

134

Blencathra (continued)

From the east turn off from the Keswick / Penrith road into Threlkeld via the old Threlkeld Lead Mine and
Hall's Fell Ridge: Ascent 718 m = 2356 ft　　　　　　　　*Distance 2.7 km = 1.7 miles*
From the east turn off from the Keswick / Penrith road into Threlkeld along the foot of Hall's Fell and then up
Doddick Fell:　　Ascent 718 m =2356 ft　　　　　　　　*Distance 3.3 km = 2.1 miles*
From Mousethwaite Comb via Scales Fell:
　　　　　　　　Ascent 628 m = 2060 ft　　　　　　　　*Distance　2.8 km = 1.7 miles*
From Mousethwaite Comb via the path above the Glendermakin River, up Scales Beck to Scales Tarn, then
Sharp Edge:　　Ascent　628 m = 2060 ft　　　　　　　*Distance　3.8 km = 2.4 miles*
From the car park near the Blencathra Centre and up Blease Fell (a long and totally safe grass plod):
　　　　　　　　Ascent 578 m = 1896 ft　　　　　　　　*Distance 3.2 km = 2.0 miles*
From the car park near the Blencathra Centre along the path running parallel to Glendaterra Beck, then up
Roughten Gill past the waterfalls. Eventually turn up the grassy slope leading to the top:
　　　　　　　　Ascent 578 m = 1896 ft　　　　　　　　*Distance 4.8 km = 3 miles*
Adjacent Fells :　Bannerdale Crags　　　　*Height 683 m = 2240 ft　Distance 2.5 km = 1.6 miles*
　　　　　　　　　　　　　　　　　　　　　　　　　(via source of Glendermakin River)

　　　　　　　　　Bowscale Fell　　　　　*Height 702 m = 2303 ft　Distance 3.3 km =　2 miles*

Boat How

Height 337 m = 1105 ft　　　　　　　　　　　　**NY177034**　　　　　　**Rank 233**

The summit of Boat How is a small rocky prominence situated in the midst of rather unexciting grassy moorland. The views from the top, particularly of Scafell, Great Gable and Kirk Fell serve to remind one that there are better places to be. To the southwest is an unusual cluster of stone circles and ancient cairns. These antiquities, for some, might be more than adequate justification for visiting the fell.

From Boot via the path above the west side of Whillan Beck. Turn off to the west at the stone hut
　　　　　　　　　　　　(at the 260m = 850 ft contour) and ascend the slope:
　　　　　　Ascent 277 m = 909 ft　　　　　　　　　*Distance 3.1 km = 1.9 miles*
From Boot via the ruins at NY 176 018 and the stone circles on Brat's Hill:
　　　　　　Ascent 277 m = 909 ft　　　　　　　　　*Distance 3 km = 1.9 miles*

Bonscale Pike

Height 524 m = 1719 ft　　　　　　　　　　　　**NY454201**　　　　　　**Rank 170**

Much the same as Arthur's Pike, an impressive facade of rock and scree on the Ullswater side but almost flat grass on the other. The only appeal is the steep and exciting pull up the side of the Swarthbeck Gill Ravine. Good views to the west but drab to the east.

Routes: See Arthur's Pike, the distances are much the same:

Adjacent fells :　Loadpot Hill　　Height　671 m = 2201 ft　　Distance 2.1 km = 1.3 miles
　　　　　　　　Arthur's Pike　　　　　　*532 m = 1745 ft*　　　　　　*1.2 km = 0.7 miles*

Bowfell

Height 902 m = 2959 ft　　　　　　　　　　　　**NY245064**　　　　　　**Ra nk 6**

Magnificent rock scenery, superb long distance views and a very interesting rocky summit. Highly recommended. For approaches from the north see Esk Pike.

From Boot (Eskdale) via the road to Brotherilkeld. Follow the Esk to where it splits at Lingcove Bridge.
Thence via Throstle Garth, Pianet Knott, Churn How, Three Tarns:
　　　　　　Ascent 842 m = 2762 ft　　　　　　　　　*Distance 11.2 km = 7.0 miles*

Bowfell (continued)

Alternatively at Churn How one can go via Yeastyrigg Gill to Ore Gap:

    Ascent 842 m = 2762 ft   *Distance 12.3 km = 7.6 miles*

From the Old Dungeon Ghyll Hotel, Great Langdale via Stool End, The Band, Earing Crag, Three Tarns:

    Ascent 804 m = 2638 ft   *Distance 4.9 km = 3.0 miles*

From Stonethwaite via Langstrath and Ore Gap:

    Ascent 802 m = 2631 ft   *Distance 10.1 km = 6.3 miles*

Adjacent Fells :   *Esk Pike Height 885 m = 2903 ft*   *Distance 1.7 km = 1.1 miles*

                 Crinkle Crags 859 m = 2818 ft   *1.8 km = 1.1 miles*

Bowscale Fell

Height 702 m   **NY333305**   **Rank 90**

The fairly steep north side cradling Bowscale Tarn is the best direct approach to the top. An interesting way to approach the summit is from the south via the east ridge up Bannerdale Crags. The top of Bowscale Fell is pretty flat and the views, though good, are not spectacular. Why not carry on from here to Blencathra ?

From Bowscale slowly climbing up the hill to Bowscale Tarn, then up the west side of the combe:

    Ascent 472 m = 1549 ft   *Distance 3.6 km = 2.2 miles*

From Mungrisedale and up by Bullfell Beck:

    Ascent 467 m = 1532 ft   *Distance 3.2 km = 2.0 miles*

From Carrock Tungsten Mine, straight up the hill:

    Ascent 412 m = 1352 ft   *Distance 2.5 km = 1.6 miles*

Adjacent Fells: *Bannerdale Crags*   *Height 683 m = 2240 ft*   *Distance 1.7 km = 1.1 miles*

                 Blencathra (Saddleback)   *868 m = 2847 ft*   *3.1 km = 1.9 miles*

Brae Fell

Height 586 m = 1922 ft   **NY289352**   **Rank 139**

A great sprawling grassy hill. The east side above Dale Beck is the most interesting with its mine workings and hush. (A hush is a groove cut in the topsoil from a reservoir high up the hillside. The miners did this to expose mineral veins in the rock below. The hush is opposite the confluence of Dale Beck and Birk Gill). Good long distance views to the east, north and west.

From Longlands via Turpin Hill and Charleton Gill, thence up to Little Sca Fell and along to Brae Fell top:

    Ascent 374 m = 1227 ft   *Distance 5.2 km = 3.2 miles*

From Fell side and up the deepcut Ramps Gill:

    Ascent 316 m = 1037 ft   *Distance 3.3 km = 2.1 miles*

From Greenhead, straight up (a real trudge):

    Ascent 331 m = 1086 ft   *Distance 2.2 km = 1.4 miles*

Adjacent Fells: *Great Sca Fell*   *Height 651 m = 2135 ft*   *Distance 1.5 km = 0.9 miles*

                 Knott   *710 m = 2329 ft*   *2.3 km =1.4 miles*

Brandreth

Height 715 m = 2345 ft   **NY215119**   **Rank 82**

A fairly flat and not particularly interesting place. It is, however, on the route to more interesting places such as Great Gable and Haystacks and that is why we can find ourselves here. Good views.

From Honister Hause via the Drum House:

    Ascent 365 m = 1197 ft   *Distance 2.7 km = 1.7 miles*

From Honister Hause via Grey Knotts (a harder route than the above):

    Ascent 365 m = 1197 ft   *Distance 2.1 km = 1.3 miles*

Brandreth (continued)

From Gatesgarth Farm via Warnscale Bottom and Dubs Bottom:
   Ascent 987 m = 1962 ft   Distance 4.2 km = 2.6 miles

Branstree

Height 713 m = 2339 ft   **NY478100**   **Rank 84**

The fells on the south side of Haweswater tend to be neglected by most walkers. They may lack drama but, with their numerous undulations and rocky outcrops they are interesting to walk. Of all the fells Branstree is probably one of the most interesting underfoot. There are some good views to be had, but you will have to wander about the broad summit to see them. The feature shown as *'Pillar'* on the O.S. map is a twin pronged stone tower that was constructed for surveying purposes when the Haweswater aqueduct was being driven.

From the car park at Mardale Head to Gatescarth Pass, thence to the summit:
   Ascent 461 m = 1512 ft   Distance 2.6 km = 1.6 miles
From the point where Rowantreethwaite Beck crosses under the lakeside road and up the north ridge (runs parallel to Hopgill Beck):
   Ascent 433 m = 1421 ft   Distance 2.1 km = 1.3 miles
From Sadgill, along the valley and up Gatesgarth Pass:
   Ascent 513 m = 1683 ft   Distance 4.6 km = 2.9 miles

Adjacent Fells :	Harker Fell	Height	778 m = 2552 ft	Distance 2.7 km = 1.7 miles
	Selside Pike		655 m = 2148 ft	1.7 km = 1.1 miles
	Tarn Crag		664 m = 2178ft	2.5 km = 1.6 miles

Brim Fell

Height 796 m = 2611 ft   **SD271986**   **Rank 38**

The summit lies on the ridge between Swirl How and Coniston Old Man. Accordingly a visit here is likely to be the result of a journey to some other place. The top itself offers little interest and the Seathwaite Tarn side of the ridge is rather drab. The eastern side of the ridge, however, is packed with fascinating detail, crags, scree, Levers Water, Low Water and the extensive surface workings of the long abandoned Coniston Copper Mines. Thus, if one wishes to visit the top directly, then the ascent from Coniston is most rewarding. The ascent from the Duddon Valley is long, boggy and lacking in interest.

From Coniston via Coppermines valley, Levers Water, Gill Cove, Brim Fell rake :
   Ascent 736 m = 2415 ft   Distance 4.1 km = 2.5 miles
From the Duddon Valley (car parking near Hinning House) via the path along the north side of Seathwaite Tarn, Little Pikes, Goat's Hawse:
   Ascent 606 m = 1988ft   Distance 5 km = 3.1 miles

Adjacent Fells:	Coniston Old Man	Height 803 m = 2634 ft	Distance 0.8 km = 0.5 miles
	Swirl How	802 m = 2631 ft	2.2 km = 1.4 miles

Brock Crags

Height 561 m = 1840 ft   **NY419137**   **Rank 150**

The fell is situated immediately behind the attractive and tiny hamlet of Hartsop. The summit consists of a number of rocky outcrops but, apart from these, the immediate surroundings lack interest. The long distance views from the top are good, particularly that of Brotherswater to the southwest. The ridge route from Rest Dodd to Angletarn Pikes is nearby and the walk could be usefully extended by joining it.

From Hartsop along the path to Hayeswater. Just before it crosses Hayeswater Gill join the path to the filter house. Once clear of the enclosures, ascend:
   Ascent 391 m = 1283 ft   Distance 1.7 km = 1.1 miles

Brock Crags (continued)

Adjacent Fells:	*Rest Dodd*	*Height*	*696 m = 2283 ft*	*Distance 1.7 km = 1.1 miles*
	Angletarn Pikes		*567 m = 1860 ft*	*2.2 km = 1.4 miles*
	The Knott		*739 m = 2424 ft*	*2.6 km = 1.6 miles*

Broom Fell

Height 511 m = 1676 ft   **NY195270**   **Rank 177**

Just a steep grassy hill but, like other fells in this area, offers peace and solitude. Good long distance views from the top. The large flat tract of land between Broom Fell and Ling Fell is Wythop Moss, a boggy place full of hidden ditches and rusty overgrown barbed wire fences. Don't try crossing it (It's a wretched place) skirt around it.

From Wythop Mill via Burthwaite, Burthwaite Heights and up the long slope to the top:

	Ascent 411 m = 1348 ft			*Distance 3.7 km = 2.3 miles*

From near Scawgill Bridge via Darling How and up by the side of the forest:

	Ascent 288 m = 945 ft			*Distance 2.1 km = 1.3 miles*
Adjacent Fells :	*Lord's Seat*	*Height*	*552 m = 1811 ft*	*Distance 1.2 km = 0.7 miles*
	Graystones		*456 m = 1496 ft*	*2.3 km = 1.4 miles*

Brund Fell (see Grange Fell)

Brunt Knott

Height 427 m = 1400 ft   **NY 484006**   **Rank 210**

After an initial steep climb from Brunt Knott Farm one quickly reaches the top. The landscape from hereon being gently undulating moorland and not really very interesting. Solitude, however, is guaranteed. The longer distance views of the fells at the head of the Kent and Longsleddale valleys are good.

From the beginning of the track to Brunt Knott Farm:

	Ascent 227 m = 745 ft	*Distance 2 km = 1.3 miles*

Buckbarrow (near Bootle)

Height 549 m = 1801 ft   **SD 152910**   **Rank 157**

The fells to the east of Bootle are generally featureless grass but Buckbarrow is the exception, for its top is crowned with shattered rocky outcrops. Good long-distance views are to be had from here. The easiest approach is from the road which crosses Corney and Thwaites Fell, just below Stoneside Hill. An unfrequented fell.

From the fell road:	*Ascent 152 m = 499 ft*	*Distance 1.7 km = 1.1 miles*
Adjacent Fell:	*Whitfell*	*Height 573 m = 1879 ft*	*Distance 2.8 km = 1.7 miles*

Buckbarrow (above Wastwater)

Height 425 m = 1394 ft   **NY 136061**   **Rank 82**

Not a separate fell at all though it gives that impression from the road. It is simply a relatively short steep outcrop of the great sprawling mass of Seatallan. Good views of Wastwater Screes. A pleasant, easy walk.

From the road and up the side of Gill Beck:

	Ascent 310 m = 1017 ft		*Distance 1.2 km = 0.7 miles*
Adjacent Fells:	*Seatallan*	*Height 692 m = 2270 ft*	*Distance 2.6 km = 1.6 miles*

Burnbank Fell

Height 475 m = 1558 ft NY 110210 **Rank 196**

Not a very exciting hill. The approach via Holme Wood and Holme Beck is initially very pleasant but becomes less interesting as one nears the top. Another route is from Felldyke to the dam on Cogra Moss, then across the corner of the wood at the most northerly tip of the reservoir. Here a rough forest track will take you high into the wood. The quality of this track is initially poor but later improves. At NY101200 there is a very obvious fork, the track, rising up the hill, will take you to the top of the wood at Sharp Knott. The summit of Burnbank Fell is then only 1 km (0.6 miles) away.

From Maggie's Bridge via Holme Wood and Holme Beck :
  Ascent 350 m = 1148 ft *Distance 2.8 km = 1.7 miles*
From Felldyke via Cogra Moss and the pine forest :
  Ascent 270 m = 886 ft *Distance 4.6 km = 2.9 miles*

Calf Crag

Height 537 m = 1761 ft NY301104 **Rank 161**

The highest and most northerly point of a two mile long ridge that starts in the south as Helm Crag and then a little further north becomes Gibson Knott. The ascent from the Wythburn valley starts pleasantly enough but, in its later stages, becomes rather boggy. The most scenic routes are via Greenburn Bottom or Far Easedale. The view from the summit is restricted to the west by higher fells, but that to the east is quite good.

From Grasmere via Easedale Road then along Easedale to Far Easedale and Brownrigg Moss :
  Ascent 467 m = 1532 ft *Distance 6.3 km = 3.9 miles*
From Grasmere via Easedale Road, Low Mill Bridge, Greenburn Bottom :
  Ascent 467 m = 1532 ft *Distance 6.2 km =3.9 miles*
From Wythburn (Steel End) to Wythburn Head Tarns, then climb the hillside to the summit :
  Ascent 347 m = 1138 ft *Distance 3.7 km = 2.3 miles*
Adjacent Fells: Gibson Knott Height 420 m = 1377 ft *Distance 2.1 km = 1.3 miles*
  Steel fell 553 m = 1814 ft *2.5 km = 1.6 miles*

Calfhow Pike

Height 660 m = 2165 ft NY 331211 **Rank 108**

Calfhow Pike is an isolated outcrop of rock in the long grassy expanse between Clough Head and Great Dodd. To access see either of the latter.

Adjacent Fells: Clough Head Height 726 m = 2381 ft *Distance 1.5 km = 0.9 miles*
  Great Dodd 857 m = 2811 ft *1.5 km = 0.9 miles*

Carl Side

Height 746 m = 2447 ft NY 255281 **Rank 66**

The view to the east is dominated by the huge scree strewn slopes leading to the top of Skiddaw, with fair views in other directions. Once you get to the top of Carl Side you will not feel the walk is complete unless you carry on to the top of Skiddaw. So see Skiddaw !

From Millbeck via White Stones :
  Ascent 621 m = 2037 ft *Distance 2.3 km = 1.4 miles*
From Millbeck via Lyzzick Wood and Long Doors :
  Ascent 621 m = 2037 ft *Distance 2.7 km = 1.7 miles*
From the car park opposite Mirehouse and up through Dodd Wood via Skill Beck, thence to Long Doors and
up : Ascent 632 m = 2073 ft *Distance 3.2 km = 2 miles*

Carl Side (continued)

From near High Side up the side of Southerndale Beck :

	Ascent 591 m = 1939 ft		*Distance 4 km = 2.5 miles*
Adjacent Fells :	*Ullock Pike*	*Height 690 m = 2263 ft*	*Distance 1.4 km = 0.9 miles*
	Skiddaw	*931 m = 3054 ft*	*Distance 1.3 km = 0.8 miles*

Carrock Fell

Height 660 m = 2165 ft   NY 342336   **Rank 108**

The east face of Carrock Fell is a steep rough crag. It looks climbable but one soon runs into difficulties, especially if you try to ascend the gully up the middle of the face. The best way up is the very obvious path on the south edge of the crag. The hillside around the corner into the Mosedale valley is strewn with boulders and scree. Some of the boulders are quite large and made of a rough non-slipping rock called Gabbro. Accordingly children, and adults, can have a lot of fun scrambling around here. The rest of the hill is just a large grassy lump and not terribly exciting. There are good long distance views across to the Pennines from the summit but, in other directions, not much at all. Away from the crag two interesting routes up are Brandy Gill and Drygill Beck, both have been the site of lead mining activity.

From Carrock Tungsten Mine up Brandy Gill, then to Miton Hill :

Ascent 370 m = 1214 ft	*Distance 4 km = 2.5 miles*

From the ford on Carrock Beck along to Drygill Beck, then up along Red Gate and on to Miton Hill :

Ascent 400 m = 1312 ft	*Distance 5.2 km = 3.2 miles*

From the ford on Carrock Beck go straight up the hillside to the top :

Ascent 400 m = 1312 ft	*Distance 1.6 km = 1 mile*

From the road and up the south edge of the crag :

Ascent 425 m = 1394 ft	*Distance 1.6k m = 1 mile*

From Mosedale and straight up the rocky slope to the top :

	Ascent 439 m = 1440 ft		*Distance 2.4 km = 1.5 miles*
Adjacent Fells :	*High Pike*	*Height 658 m = 2158 ft*	*Distance 3.4 km = 2.1 miles*
	Knott	*710 m = 2329 ft*	*5.5 km = 3.4 miles*

Carron Crag

Height 314 m = 1030 ft   SD 325943   **Rank 241**

This hill is not very high but offers very good views. It is entirely surrounded by Forestry Commission woodland and you will need to make use of the rather complex system of tracks and paths to reach it. It is a good idea to buy the inexpensive ' Grizedale Forest Guide Map,' which will not only enable you to navigate to Carron Crag but also inform you of the whereabouts of the many other interesting features that this area has to offer. The walk starts at the Grizedale Visitors' Centre between Hawkshead and Satterthwaite. The map mentioned can be purchased at the centre.

From the Grizedale Visitors' Centre :

Ascent 209 m = 686 ft	*Distance 1.8 km = 1.1 miles*

Castle Crag

Height 290 m = 951 ft   NY 249159   **Rank 244**

Castle Crag and the wooded area around it is truly delightful. On the west side are overgrown and long abandoned excavations and tunnels from which slate used to be won. Overlooking the east side is the huge mass of Goat Crag. Castle Crag is a real mountain in miniature with crags, scree and steep winding paths and well worth the climb. Take care if accompanied by children, there are some nasty drops not far from the paths.

From Grange follow the path to the Hollows Farm camp site in Grange Wood. Take the right turn (path to Dale Head) through the gate. Follow it until you come close to the screes, which drop down to the path from the crag. A path crosses the wall and winds its way up the scree through the old slate workings :

Castle Crag (continued)

Ascent 210 m = 689 ft   *Distance 2.2 km = 1.4 miles*

From Grange follow the path to the Hollows Farm Camp Site. Take the left turn and walk through the woods. In the steep slopes below the crag are the old slate working caves where Millican Dalton lived (See the local history notes for the Derwent Fells). Try to find them and look for the inscription left by Millican. By going round to the south side of the crag you can get to the top by ascending to some old quarry tunnels and beyond

Ascent 210 m = 689 ft   *Distance 3.1 km = 1.9 miles*

There is a path from Rosthwaite which crosses the River Derwent and takes you to the south side of Castle Crag. You can then get to the top via the tunnels mentioned in the last paragraph :

Ascent 195 m = 640 ft   *Distance   2 km = 1.2 miles*

Catbells

Height 451 m = 1479 ft   **NY244199**   **Rank 202**

Not a high fell but a real gem offering marvellous views in all directions. All routes to the summit are steep but the climbing is over quickly. Accordingly this is a place to take recalcitrant children without fear of undue rebellion or collapse. There are old mine workings on Skelgill Bank near the north end of the ridge (Old Brandley Lead Mine) and also below Yewthwaite Comb and Brunt Crag (Yewthwaite Lead mine). Care should be exercised in the neighbourhood of these if you are accompanied by children or dogs. Apart from these old workings the only other hazard offered by the mountain are the steep crags on the west side of the summit.

From the road near Gutherscale farm (parking):

         Ascent 321 m = 1053 ft   *Distance 1.6 km = 1 mile*

From Chapel Bridge near Little Town Farm:

         Ascent 311 m = 1020 ft   *Distance 2.1 km = 1.3 miles*

From Grange along the road to Manesty then up to Hause Gate:

         Ascent 371 m = 1217 ft   *Distance 2.8 km = 1.7 miles*

Adjacent Fell: Maiden Moor   Height 576 m = 1889 ft   *Distance   2 km = 1.2 miles*

Catstye Cam

Height 890 m = 2919 ft   **NY348158**   **Rank 10**

The top is linked to the summit of Helvellyn by an excellent rocky ridge which falls away rapidly on its north side to the lonely hollow of Brown Cove, but descends more gently to Red Tarn on the south side. The ground around the summit is steep in all directions but becomes precipitious on the northeast side. The fell lies in magnificient country and can quite easily be included in a walk to or from its large neighbour; Helvellyn. There are good but not outstanding views from the top.

From Glenridding car park via the old Greenside Mine buildings, Keppel Cove and up the northwest ridge (at the west end of the crags) to the summit:

         Ascent 740 m = 2428 ft   *Distance 5.2 km = 3.2 miles*

From Glenridding car park via the old Greenside Mine buildings, thence to Red Tarn and up onto Swirral Edge: *Ascent 740 m = 2428 ft*   *Distance 6.2 km = 3.9 miles*

Adjacent Fells::   Helvellyn   Height   950 m= 3116 ft   *1 km =0.6 miles*

Causey Pike

Height 637 m = 2089 ft   **NY219208**   **Rank 123**

The steep slope with the nobble on the top gives Causey Pike a very characteristic and easily spotted shape. The climb from Stoneycroft is hard and steep but, if you are carrying on up to Scar Crags and Sail, the ridge beyond the summit is quite easy going. Excellent views in all directions from the top. Causey Pike is the first (or last) fell in the Coledale Horseshoe.

Causey Pike (continued)

From Stoneycroft Bridge:

         Ascent 507 m = 1663 ft   *Distance 2.2 km = 1.3 miles*

From the quarry car park at Rigg Beck. Follow Rigg Beck to the Hause between Ard Crags and Causey Pike then turn right and up onto the ridge:

         Ascent 467 m = 1532 ft   *Distance 4.7 km = 2.9 miles*

Adjacent Fells: Sail 773 m = 2536 ft   *Distance 2 km = 1.3 miles*

Caw

Height 529 m = 1735 ft   **SD230945**   **Rank 165**

An interesting fell with numerous rocky outcrops and good long-distance views from the summit. Both routes given start from Seathwaite, the one along the quarry road being the most well defined.

From Seathwaite following the path initially alongside Gobling Beck until it emerges onto open fellside near Green Pikes. Carry on to the Pikes, then to Caw:

         Ascent   426 m = 1397 ft   *Distance 3.1 km = 2 miles*

From Seathwaite along Park Head road. Turn off on to the track which leads up to the disused quarry, thence to the top: *Ascent 426 m = 1397 ft*   *Distance 2.6 km = 1.6 miles*

Caw Fell

Height 697 m = 2286 ft   **NY 132110**   **Rank 94**

It is unlikely that one would visit Caw Fell just for the sake of it as the terrain is bleak and moorlike and the views from the top aren't too good either. Caw Fell and the hills to the west of it have very broad tops. They would be very difficult to navigate in mist were it not for the convenient stone wall that runs along the top and continues for a considerable distance both east and west. Many people, including the author, have been saved from total disorientation by groping their way along it. This is part of the Ennerdale Horseshoe walk.

From the car park at Bleach Green (at the west end of Ennerdale Water) up the side of Ben Gill, behind Crag Fell and along the tops:

         Ascent 577 m = 1893 ft   *Distance 7.7 km = 4.8 miles*

From the car park below Bowness Knott across the head of the lake and up the ridge between Silvercove Beck and Deep Gill: *Ascent 567 m = 1860 ft*   *Distance 6.7 km= 4.2 miles*

From the north end of Gosforth along the path through Blengdale Forest, across Stockdale Moor and the Hause and up to the top:

         Ascent 627 m = 2057 ft   *Distance 9.2 km = 5.7 miles*

Adjacent fells:	*Crag Fell*	*Height*	*523 m = 1715 ft*	*Distance 5.6 km = 3.5 mile*
	Haycock		*797 m = 2614 ft*	*1.5 km = 0.9 miles*
	Whoap		*511 m = 1676 ft*	*5 km =3.1 miles*

Clough Head

Height 726 m = 2381 ft   **NY334225**   **Rank 76**

The summit itself is flat and grassy but the views are good. However what makes the fell of interest to the more adventurous are the numerous paths (some quite scary) that run along the top of the crags to the west. Some may be tempted by the clefts and gills that slice through the crags, but bear in mind your limitations. Fishers Wifes Rake at the south side of Wanthwaite Crag is steep but presents no special problems. Beckthorns Gill is also an exciting but not especially difficult route to the top. Sandbed Gill is tricky (very narrow and you have to climb up slimy wet rocks) and once you are on your way there is no turning back. For experienced scramblers only.

From Bramcrag quarry along the foot of the crags to the east side of Buck Castle. A diagonal path then takes you up the crags: Ascent 576 m = 1890 ft   *Distance 2.5 km = 1.6 miles*

Clough Head (continued)

From Wanthwaite along the path over Wanthwaite Bank to the east side of Buck Castle. A diagonal path takes you up the crags: Ascent 576 m = 1890 ft   *Distance 2.8 km = 1.7 miles*

From the road by Red Moss along the old coach road and ascend at Hause Well. A long walk over bleak terrain: *Ascent 311 m = 1020 ft*   *Distance 6.2 km = 3.9 miles*

Adjacent Fells: *Calfhow Pike*   *Height 660 m = 2165 ft*   *Distance 1.5 km = 0.9 miles*

                  Great Dodd   *857 m = 2811 ft*   *3 km = 1.9 miles*

Cold Pike

Height 701 m = 2299 ft   **NY263036**   **Rank 91**

Cold Pike is a continuation of the ridge on which Bowfell and Crinkle Crags are situated. It is unlikely to be the object of a walk; just a place to pass through on the way to Crinkle Crags. It has a multiple summit of three tops. There are good views to be had, particularly over the Duddon and Little Langdale valleys.

From the Three Shire Stone on Wrynose Pass:

                Ascent 311 m = 1019 ft   *Distance 2.1 km = 1.3 miles*

Adjacent Fells: *Crinkle Crags*   *Height 859 m = 2828 ft*   *Distance 2.1 km = 1.3 miles*

                  Pike 'o Blisco   *705 m = 2312 ft*   *1.7 km = 1.1 miles*

Coniston Old Man

Height 803 m = 2634 ft   **SD273978**   **Rank 32**

Very popular, being the most obvious target for those staying at Coniston. Whilst the top offers excellent views over considerable distances, the best part, in the author's opinion, is the ascent itself. The eastern side of the fell abounds with fascinating features both natural and man-made: crags, tarns, scree, hidden valleys, old mine shafts, levels, quarries, derelict buildings, water wheel pits...... and so on. Some will consider the man-made features an eyesore, others a source of fascination and speculation. Care should be taken in the vicinity of mine workings and exploration should not be contemplated unless accompanied by persons with the right knowledge and equipment. The west side of the fell is quieter but much less interesting.

From Coniston along the path on the south side of Church Beck (turns westerly just beyond the Miners' Bridge) via Colt Crags and Low Water:

                Ascent 742 m = 2434 ft   *Distance 3.7 km = 2.3 miles*

From Torver via the Moors, Tranearth, Banishead Quarry, The Cove, Goat's Water:

                Ascent 694 m = 2277 ft   *Distance 6.1 km = 3.8 miles*

From the car park in the Duddon Valley (SD235995) via Pike How, Foss How, North side of Seathwaite Tarn (boggy), Tarn Head Moss, Far Gill, Goat's Hause:

                Ascent 620 m = 2034 ft   *Distance 6 km = 3.7 miles*

Adjacent Fells :   *Brim Fell*   *Height 796 m = 2611 ft*   *Distance 0.8 km = 0.5 miles*

                  Dow Crag   *778 m = 2552 ft*   *1.7 km = 1.1 miles*

Crag Fell

Height 523 m = 1715 ft   **NY097144**   **Rank 171**

The northside of Crag Fell is imposing and dramatic and makes and interesting walk, as do the paths through the wood, a little to the west. The other side of Crag Fell is bleak moorland that stretches for miles. In the distant past a number of small exploratory iron mines (haematite) were driven into various parts of this and neighbouring fells. Although the entrances are long closed or run in you may come across the small spoil heaps which still betray their presence. There are good views from the top of West Cumbria and the hills above Ennerdale.

From the car park at Bleach Green (West end of Ennerdale Water) and up the side of Ben Gill:

                Ascent 403 m = 1322 ft   *Distance 2500 m = 1.6 miles*

Crag Fell (continued)

From the road at Scaly Moss and along the old mine track through the woods:

	Ascent 283 m = 928 ft			Distance 4 km = 2.5 miles
Adjacent Fells:	Grike	Height	488 m = 1601 ft	Distance 1.3 km = 0.8 miles
	Caw Fell		697 m = 2286 ft	5.6 km = 3.5 miles
	Whoap		511 m = 1676 ft	2.1 km = 1.3 miles

Crinkle Crags

Height 859 m = 2818 ft   **NY249049**   **Rank 17**

Very appropriately named, a jagged and contorted rocky summit ridge, precipitious on both sides, makes this a most interesting and enjoyable fell. Its character is further enhanced by superb short and long distance views. By ascending from the Wrynose Pass you can save approximately 300 m or 1000 ft of climbing.

From Cockley Beck Bridge (Wrynose Pass) via Little Stand:

Ascent 646 m = 2119 ft   Distance 3.8 km = 2.4 miles

From the Three Shire Stone (Wrynose Pass) via Rough Crags and Cold Pike:

Ascent 469 m = 1538 ft   Distance 4.1 km = 2.5 miles

Alternatively via Rough Crags, Red Tarn, Great Knott

Distance 4.2 km = 2.6 miles

From Boot (Eskdale) along the road to Brotherilkeld and then along the Esk to Lingcove Bridge. Continue along the east fork of the stream to Grinsty Gill. Follow the gill up to Adam-a-Cove and, when the stream splits, follow the north fork to the summit:

Ascent 799 m = 2621 ft   Distance 9 .6 km = 6 miles

*From the Old Dungeon Ghyll Hotel (Great Langdale) via Stool End, Oxendale Beck, Brown Howe, Red Tarn and Great Knott:*Ascent 759 m = 2490 ft   Distance 5.9 km = 3.7 miles

From the Old Dungeon Ghyll Hotel via Stool End, Oxendale Beck, Hell Gill, Buscoe Sike and the three Tarns:

Ascent 759 m = 2490 ft   Distance 5.4 km = 3.4 miles

Alternatively after Stool End follow the Band to Earing Crag thence to Three Tarns:

Distance 5.2 km =3.2 miles

Adjacent Fells:	Bowfell	Height	902 m = 2959 ft	Distance 1.8 km = 1.1 miles
	Cold Pike		701 m = 2299 ft	2.1 km = 1.3 miles
	Pike O' Blisco		705 m = 2312 ft	3.1 km = 1.9 miles

Dale Head

Height 753 m = 2470 ft   **NY223153**   **Rank 65**

Dale Head summit is most easily attained from the top of the Honister Pass (parking), a steep but fairly short walk. From anywhere else reaching Dale Head involves a good deal of walking. The part of the fell overlooking Newlands valley is steep, craggy and scree ridden, but there is a perfectly safe path up this way. Views in all directions are very good. Dale Head is roughly the midway point of an excellent horseshoe walk starting near Little Town and incorporating Hindscarth, High Spy and Maiden Moor.

From Honister Hause by the side of Yew Crag slate quarries:

Ascent 393 m = 1289 ft   Distance 1.9 km = 1.2 miles

From Seatoller via Scaleclose Gill and Launchy Tarn:

Ascent 603 m = 1978 ft   Distance 3.7 km = 2.3 miles

From Chapel Bridge near Little Town via Dalehead Tarn:

Ascent 613 m = 2011 ft   Distance 5.6 km = 3.5 miles

Alternatively using the path up Dale Head Crags:

4.7 km = 2.9 miles

Adjacent Fells:	HIgh Spy	Height 653 m = 2142 ft	Distance 2 km = 1.3 miles
	Hindscarth	727 m = 2385 ft	1.6 km = 1 mile
	Robinson	737 m = 2417 ft	2.8 km = 1.7 miles

A - Z Guide to the Fells

Darling Fell

Height 391 m = 1282 ft NY130225 **Rank 222**

All the fells north of Loweswater are unremarkable and the only thing that can really be said in their favour is that they are quiet and unfrequented. The top of Darling Fell is very soon reached and rather than bring a walk to a rapid end one usually carries on by Low Fell. Quite good views from the top, especially of Loweswater.

From the road (about half way along Loweswater) and up the track and thence to the open fell:

	Ascent 267 m = 876 ft		*Distance 1.2 km = 0.7 miles*
Adjacent fell:	*Low Fell*	*Height 423 m = 1387 ft*	*Distance 1 km = 0.6 miles*

Dodd

Height 502 m = 1646 ft NY244273 **Rank 185**

However you decide to get to the top of Dodd you are going to have to walk through a good deal of trees and it can get confusing. The best course of action is to purchase a copy of the Forestry Commission's Dodd Wood map. Not only are all the tracks and suggested walks shown on a large scale map (10 cm = 1 km or 6.3 inches = 1 mile), but there are descriptions of the various types of trees to be seen and items of historical interest. There are good views over Bassenthwaite and Derwentwater from the top. Forest walks like Dodd, Whinlatter and Grizedale are good places to take children: the variety of experience keeps their interest alive in a way that open slopes often don't.

From the car park opposite Mirehouse:

	Ascent 387 m = 1270 ft		*Distance 2.5 km = 1.6 miles*
From Millbeck via Lyzzick Wood:			
	Ascent 377 m = 1237 ft		*Distance 2.5 km = 1.6 miles*
Adjacent fells:	*Carl Side*	*Height 746 m = 2447 ft*	*Distance 1.7 km = 1.1 miles*
	Ullock Pike	*690 m = 2263 ft*	*3 km = 1.9 miles*
	Skiddaw	*931 m = 3054 ft*	*3.1 km = 1.9 miles*

Dollywagon Pike

Height 858 m = 2814 ft NY346134 **Rank 18**

The west side of Dollywagon Pike is just a steep to moderate grassy slope. The east side is much more interesting with crags, waterfalls and an enjoyable short ridge leading from Spout Crag to the summit. On both sides of the fell are to be found old and fairly small mine workings. Birkside Gill copper mine is found in the lower reaches of Birkside Gill on the west side and Ruthwaite Lodge lead mine near the Ruthwaite Lodge climbing hut on the east side. The views from the top are restricted by Nethermost Pike and Helvellyn in the north, but those in other directions are excellent.

From Grisedale Bridge, along the valley and up the packhorse track to Grisedale Tarn, then up the zig zag path: *Ascent 708 m = 2323 ft* *Distance 7.1 km = 4.4 miles*
From Grisedale Bridge, along the valley to Ruthwaite Lodge. Thence up by the north side of Spout Crag and along the Tongue:Ascent 708 m = 2323 ft *Distance 5.9 km = 3.7 miles*
From Mill Bridge on the Grasmere / Keswick road via Little Tongue Gill and Tongue Gill to Grisedale Tarn, then up the zig zag path:
Ascent 758 m = 2487 ft *Distance 5.1 km = 3.2 miles*
From Homesdale Green Bridge straight up Birkside Gill (steep), past the old mine and on to the top:
Ascent 648 m = 2126 ft *Distance 2.6 km = 1.6 miles*

Adjacent fells:	*Nethermost Pike Height*	*891 m = 2923 ft*	*Distance 1.5 km = 0.9 miles*
	Seat Sandal	*736 m = 2414 ft*	*1.7 km = 1.1 miles*

Dove Crag

Height 792 m = 2598 ft   NY375105   **Rank 39**

The west side of Dove Crag is steep and grassy and offers nothing of special interest. The east side, above Dovedale, is rough and craggy and offers excellent walking. In the north face, below the summit, is the Priest Hole Cave. This will sleep up to half a dozen people, though you might have to evict a few sheep who also find it excellent for this purpose. To access the cave you need to do a little easy scrambling. There are good views from the top.

From Cow Bridge (car park) via Hartsop Hall and up along Dovedale Beck:
          Ascent 632 m = 2073 ft   *Distance 4.5 km = 2.8 miles*
From Nook End Farm (Rydal) via Low Pike and High Pike:
          Ascent 692 m = 2270 ft   *Distance 5.5 km = 3.4 miles*
Adjacent Fells: Hart Crag   Height   822 m = 2696 ft   Distance 1.2 km = 0.7 miles
                   Low Pike   508 m = 1666 ft   2.8 km = 1.7 miles
                   Little Hart Crag   637 m = 2089 ft   1.6 km = 1 mile
                   High Pike   656 m = 2152 ft   1.6 km = 1 mile

Dow Crag

Height   778 m = 2552 ft   SD263978   **Rank 48**

The crags towering over Goat's Water on the east side are truly impressive and much loved by rock climbers. The west side of the fell is of a fairly gentle gradient and relatively uninteresting. Quite good views from the tops, particularly out to sea.

From Coniston via Walna Scar Road, Blind Tarn and Brown Pike:
          Ascent 717 m = 2352 ft   *Distance 6.5 km = 4.0 miles*
Same as above but via Goat's Water instead of Brown Pike   6.2 km = 3.9 miles
From Torver via the Moors, Tranearth, Bannishead Quarry, Walna Scar Road, Brown Pike:
          Ascent 669 m = 2194 ft   *Distance 6.2 km = 3.9 miles*
Same as above but via Goat's Water instead of Brown Pike   5.7 km = 3.6 miles
From Seathwaite via Long House, Walna Scar Road, Brown Pike:
          Ascent 675 m = 2215 ft   *Distance 5.6 km = 3.5 miles*

Eagle Crag (above Stonethwaite)

Height 525 m = 1722 ft   NY276121   **Rank 168**

Eagle Crag rises dramatically above the northern end of the Langstrath Valley. Its sheer rock face is popular with rock climbers. In order to avoid danger when descending from the crag, walk southeast for half a kilometre or so, then follow Greenup Gill down the valley. Excellent views to the north and west.

From Stonethwaite via Greenup Gill:
          Ascent 425 m = 1394 ft   *Distance 3.2 km = 2.0 miles*
From Stonethwaite via Bleak How (follow the wall) and careful navigation between Eagle and Heron Crags:
          Ascent 425 m = 1394 ft   *Distance 2.7 km = 1.7 miles*
Adjacent Fells: Sergeant's Crag   Height 571 m = 1873 ft   Distance   1 km = 0.6 miles

Eel Crag

Height 839 m = 2752 ft   NY 193204   **Rank 24**

Seen from the Coledale mine track Eel Crag is most impressive, giving the impression of being an almost vertical wall of rock and scree. The other (west) side is grassy and much less well defined. The summit is the highest point of the Causey Pike / Scar Crags / Sail ridge and a place from which many other routes can be chosen. There are very good long distance views from the tops.

Eel Crag (continued)

From Braithwaite along Coledale to Coledale Hause:
>   *Ascent 734 m = 2408 ft*   *Distance 6.7 km = 4.2 miles*

From Stoneycroft Bridge via Causey Pike, Scar Crags and Sail (half the Coledale Horseshoe):
>   *Ascent 709 m = 2326 ft*   *Distance 4.7 k m = 2.9 miles*

From the Buttermere / Braithwaite Road along Rigg Beck then up by the south side of Addacombe Beck:
>   *Ascent 679 m = 2228 ft*   *Distance 5.3 km = 3.3 miles*

From Lanthwaite Green along Gasgale Gill to Coledale Hause:
>   *Ascent 682 m = 2238 ft*   *Distance 4.8 km = 3 miles*

Adjacent fells:	*Wandope*	*Height*	*772 m = 2532 ft*	*Distance*	*1 km = 0.6 miles*
	Whiteless Pike		*660 m = 2165 ft*		*2 km = 1.2 miles*
	Grasmoor		*852 m = 2795 ft*		*2 km = 1.2 miles*
	Sand Hill		*756 m = 2480 ft*		*2.2 km = 1.4 miles*
	Sail		*773 m = 2536 ft*		*0.6 km = 0.4 miles*
	Hopegill Head		*770 m = 2526 ft*		*2.6 km = 1.6 miles*

Esk Pike

Height 885 m = 2903 ft   NY237075   **Rank 11**

Whilst offering a rocky top and fine views Esk Pike is most likely to be visited on a walk encompassing one or more of its impressive neighbours such as Bowfell or Crinkle Crags. The fell is a place one passes over en route to another hill.

From Boot (Eskdale) via the road to Brotherikeld then along the Esk to Esk Hause:
>   *Ascent 825 m = 2707 ft*   *Distance 13.4 km = 8.3 miles*

From Boot (Eskdale) via the road to Whahouse Bridge, thence Taw House, Brock Crag, Silverybield Crag, Cam Spout Crag, Esk Hause:
>   *Ascent 825 m = 2707 ft*   *Distance 12.8 km = 8 miles*

From Seathwaite via Stockley Bridge and Grains Gill thence to Esk Hause:
>   *Ascent 760 m = 2493 ft*   *Distance 5.3 km = 3.3 miles*

From Stonethwaite via Langstrath:
>   *Ascent 785 m = 2575 ft*   *Distance 9.6 km = 6 miles*

From Boot (Eskdale) via the road to Brotherikeld. Follow the River Esk to Lingcove Bridge thence via Throstle Garth, Pianet Knott, Churn How, Green Hole, Yeastyrigg Gill and Ore Gap:
>   *Ascent 825 m = 2707 ft*   *Distance 11.4 km =7.1 miles*

Adjacent Fells:	*Great End*	*Height*	*910 m = 2985 ft*	*Distance*	*2.2 km = 1.4 miles*
	Allen Crags		*785 m = 2575 ft*		*1.6 km = 1 mile*
	Bowfell		*902 m = 2959 ft*		*1.7 km = 1.1 miles*
	Scafell Pike		*978 m = 3208 ft*		*3 km = 1.9 miles*

Fairfield

Height 873 m = 2864 ft   NY359118   **Rank 13**

From Grasmere and Rydal, Fairfield lies at the top of a long grassy ridge; good walking but not dramatic. Seen from Deepdale, Fairfield is a 250 m (800 ft) wall of crags, sombre and imposing. A classic walk from the west side is The Fairfield Horseshoe, which takes in Nab Scar, Heron Pike and Great Rigg, on the west ridge, and Hart Crag, Dove Crag, High Pike and Low Pike on the east. A good approach from the east side is from Grisedale Bridge via Birks and St. Sunday Crag. A broad top with excellent views.

From Grisedale Bridge via Birks and St Sunday Crag:
>   *Ascent 723 m = 2372 ft*   *Distance 6.3 km = 3.9 miles*

From Grisedale Bridge along the valley to Grisedale Tarn and Grisedale Hause:
>   *Ascent 723 m = 2372 ft*   *Distance 7.6 km = 4.7 miles*

Fairfield (continued)

From Deepdale Bridge along Deepdale to Mossydale then up to Deepdale Hause:

          Ascent 713 m = 2339 ft   Distance 6 km = 3.7 miles

(From the end of Deepdale it is possible to ascend via Greenhow End, but this is a scramble and care is needed)

From Rydal via Nab Scar, Heron Pike and Great Rigg:

          Ascent 813 m = 2667 ft   Distance 6.4 km = 4 miles

From Nook End Farm (north of Ambleside) via Low Pike, Dove Crag and Hart Crag:

          Ascent 773 m = 2536 ft   Distance 7.8 km = 4.8 miles

From Mill Bridge via Little Tongue Gill or Tongue Gill and Grisedale Hause:

          Ascent 773 m = 2536 ft   Distance 4.3 km = 2.7 miles

Adjacent Fells:St Sunday Crag   Height   841 m = 2759 ft   Distance 2.5 km = 1.6 miles

          Great Rigg   766 m = 2513 ft   1.4 km = 0.9 miles

          Seat Sandal   736 m = 2414 ft   1.8 km = 1.1 miles

          Hart Crag   822 m =2696 ft   1.1 km = 0.7 miles

Fellbarrow

Height 416 m = 1364 ft   NY132242   **Rank 217**

Broad topped and sprawling, Fellbarrow is more of an elevated sheep pasture than a mountain. However, it is quiet and there are some good long distance views.

From Thackthwaite via Sourfoot Fell:

          Ascent 298 m = 978 ft   Distance 3.1 km = 1.9 miles

Adjacent fell: Low Fell   Height   423 m = 1387 ft   Distance 2.1 km = 1.3 miles

Fleetwith Pike

Height 648 m = 2125 ft   NY206141   **Rank 120**

The summit is easily reached from Honister Hause (car park) and the views are excellent. A more interesting route is from Gatesgarth Farm (car park) and straight up the sharp ridge past the Fanny Mercer memorial (white cross). The route from the hause takes you past the surface quarries of the Honister Slate workings: to stand in these is like being on another planet. The smooth angular slabs on the floor and walls give them a strange unearthly property. The really big workings of Honister are under Fleetwith Pike. They consist of rows of interconnecting caverns each two to three hundred feet long by eighty feet wide and up to sixty feet high. Few people get to see inside these cathedral-like workings, but those that do never forget them. Whatever you do, don't try to enter these man-made caves as they are very dangerous.

From Gatesgarth Farm straight up the ridge:

          Ascent 531 m = 1742 ft   Distance 1.7 km = 1 mile

From Honister Hause along the side of the crags above the Honister Pass:

          Ascent 298 m = 978 ft   Distance 2.1 km = 1.3 miles

Adjacent Fells: Haystacks   Height   597 m = 1958 ft   Distance 3.6 km = 2.2 miles

          Grey Knotts   697 m = 2286 ft   2.7 km = 1.7 miles

          Brandreth   715 m = 2345 ft   3.6 km = 2.2 miles

Froswick

Height 720 m = 2362 ft   NY435085   **Rank 79**

The most northerly summit of the narrow ridge starting at Yoke. The west side of Froswick is a steep grassy hill featuring a huge scree gully. A direct ascent up this side is possible, but it is hard to see why anyone would want to, as the ridge route is so interesting. The east side of the mountain is rocky and precipitious. Unfortunately the views from the top are restricted by its neighbours.

Froswick (continued)

Adjacent Fells: *Thornthwaite Crag* *Height* *784 m = 2572 ft* *Distance 1.8 km = 1.1 miles*
Ill Bell *757 m = 2483 ft* *1 km = 0.6 miles*

Gavel Fell

Height 526 m = 1725 ft NY117185 **Rank 166**

On its own Gavel Fell has little to recommend it, even the view from the top is not that good. However, a number of other fells are readily accessed from it, (see circular walk under Blake Fell). On the west side of the fell are the abandoned extensive workings of the Kelton and Knockmurton iron mines.

From Cross Rigg (by the large purple spoil heap) to Kelton Fell then along Croasdale Beck (rough underfooot) and up by Ill Gill:
Ascent 272 m = 892 ft *Distance 3.2 km = 2 miles*
From Maggies Bridge via High Nook Farm and up by Black Crag:
Ascent 401 m = 1316 ft *Distance 3.7 km = 2.3 miles*
From Buttermere via Floutern Tarn:
Ascent 414 m = 1358 ft *Distance 7.7 km = 4.8 miles*
Adjacent Fells: *Banna Fell* *Height* *411 m = 1348 ft* *Distance 1.8 km = 1.1 miles*
Blake Fell *573 m = 1879 ft* *1.7 km = 1.1 miles*

Gibson Knott

Height 420 m = 1377 ft NY320099 **Rank 215**

Gibson Knott is a rocky elevated plateau on the ridge connecting Calf Crag to Helm Crag. As a result it does not stand out as a distinct hill. The slopes on either side are steep and craggy and a descent here would be unwise. Reasonably good views from the top.

From Grasmere via Easdale Road, Goody Bridge, Gill Foot, Greenburn Bottom, Pike of Carrs:
Ascent 355 m = 1165 ft *Distance 5.7 km = 3.6 miles*
From Grasmere via Easdale Road to the quarries below Jackdaw Crag and at NY320 092 follow the path up to Bracken Hause: Ascent 355 m = 1165 ft *Distance 3.7 km = 2.3 miles*
Adjacent Fells: *Calf Crag* *Height* *537 m = 1761 ft* *Distance 2.1 km = 1.3 miles*
Helm Crag *405 m = 1328 ft* *1.1 km = 0.7 miles*

Glaramara

Height 783 m = 2568 ft NY246105 **Rank 46**

A fine fell with a fine sounding name, which derives from the Old Norse (see Scafell area, Route 7). The usual ascent is from the path opposite Mountain View on the road to Seatoller. However, the options open to the adventurous who don't need paths are manifold. Quite a number of the gills on the west side of Langstrath can be climbed and a direct ascent from above Seathwaite or Grains Gill is feasible. The south end of the fell links, via Allen Crags, to the base of the ridge which takes in Great End and the Scafell Pikes. The top is a rocky turret offering fine views; particularly over Borrowdale.

From opposite Mountain View via Combe Gill, Thorneythwaite Crag:
Ascent 678 m = 2224 ft *Distance 3.9 km = 2.4 miles*
From Opposite Mountain View via Combe Gill and along the Combe Valley to near Doves Nest Caves, thence up by the edge of the ravine to Comb Door, then Combe Head. (This is a harder route than the above):
Ascent 678 m = 2224 ft *Distance 3.8 km = 2.4 miles*
For other routes see Allen Crags.
Adjacent Fells: *Allen Crags* *Height* *785 m = 2575 ft* *Distance 2.4 km = 1.5 miles*
Rosthwaite Fell *551 m = 1807 ft* *2.6 km = 1.6 miles*
(Bessy Boot)

Glenridding Dodd

Height 442 m = 1450 ft   NY380176   **Rank 205**

Very much a case of 'small is beautiful'. It has an interesting craggy top with lovely views in all directions. It can be approached from Seldom Seen to the north, a delightful walk for the whole distance, or from Glenridding. The latter route is not particularly picturesque but gets you to the top quickly.

From Glenridding car park to the path leading to the old Greenside Mine. On reaching the mine road, continue along it past Rake cottages. Just beyond the last cottage a diagonal path rising up to Blaes Crag and thence to the top: Ascent 287 m = 941 ft   Distance 2 km = 1.2 miles
From the main road, past Seldom Seen Cottages and to the end of the wood, thence up by the side of the wood and onwards to the top:
Ascent 297 m = 974 ft   *Distance 2.7 km = 1.7 miles*

Gowbarrow Fell

Height 481 m = 1578 ft   NY407218   **Rank 193**

A well walked variegated and nobbled top lying above Gowbarrow Park, the home of Wordsworth's daffodils. Owned by the National Trust with the impressive Aira Force waterfall lying in the woods on its southwestern slopes, Gowbarrow attracts more than its fair share of visitors. However most remain on the waterfall paths, leaving the more enlightened to appreciate its summit in relative peace. Although relatively low in stature, expansive views are to be had from the summit, particularly to the south and east.

From the National Trust car park at the junction of the Pooley Bridge / Glenridding Road and the Dockray road. Take the path to Aira Force waterfall, then up the path to Hind Crag; the O.S. viewpoint above Yew Crag. Continue along to the old ruined shooting lodge. From here a path follows the wall up to the summit:
Ascent 321 m = 1053 ft   *Distance 4.1 km = 2.5 miles*

Grasmoor

Height 852 m = 2795 ft   NY175203   **Rank 20**

From Lanthwaite Green Grasmoor looks most impressive with its deeply fissured steep rock face. The most obvious gully from Lanthwaite Green is Lorton Gully which can be climbed but is difficult and potentially dangerous to all but experienced scramblers. If you wish to tackle Grasmoor's western face, the north western edge is more feasible. The way up by this route is not always well defined and there may be moments where you wonder where to go next. However it does offer excitement without danger. To the south and east Grasmoor is less exciting but the ascent is much easier. There are outstanding views from the broad top.

From Lanthwaite Green via the edge mentioned above:
Ascent 695 m = 2280 ft   Distance 1.8 km = 1.1 miles
                    (descent by this route is not recommended)
From Lanthwaite Green via Gasgale Gill, Coledale Hause and the edge of Dove Crags:
Ascent 695 m = 2280 ft   Distance 5.1 km = 3.2 miles
From Cinderdale Common (parking) via Lad Hows:
Ascent 742 m = 2434 ft   Distance 1.7 km = 1.1 miles

Adjacent Fells:		Height		Distance
Eel Crag		*839 m = 2752 ft*		*Distance 1.9 km = 1.2 miles*
Sand Hill		*756 m = 2480 ft*		*0.6 km =1.6 miles*
Hopegill Head		*770 m = 2526 ft*		*2.8 km = 1.7 miles*
Wandope		*772 m = 2532 ft*		*1.6 km = 1 mile*
Whiteless Pike		*660 m = 2165 ft*		*2.5 km = 1.6 miles*

Gray Crag

Height 699 m = 2293 ft   NY427117   **Rank 93**

The summit is at the north end of a very steep-sided and fairly narrow ridge between Pasture Bottom and Hayeswater. Though hemmed-in in almost all directions there are some very striking views.

From Hartsop village via Hayeswater Gill. Climb the north end of the ridge:
            Ascent 529 m = 1736 ft   *Distance 2.7 km = 1.7 miles*
Adjacent Fells: Thornthwaite Crag   *Height 784 m = 2572 ft Distance   2 km = 1.2miles*

Graystones

Height 456 m = 1496 ft   NY178264   **Rank 200**

A steep grassy hill and a quiet lonely place. The large track of flat ground between Graystones and Ling Fell is Wythop Moss, a wretched boggy place full of hidden ditches and rotting barbed wire. Don't try to cross it, skirt round it. The climb is steep from the Whinlatter side but easy, and rather tedious, from the Wythop side. Good (long distance) views to the north and better ones to the south.

From Scawgill Bridge and straight up by the side of the wood:
            Ascent   291 m = 955 ft   *Distance 0.7 km = 0.4 miles*
From Wythop Mill via Green Lonning and around the west edge of Wythop Moss:
            Ascent 356 m = 1168 ft   *Distance   4 km = 2.5 miles*
From High Lorton. Access the fell by Kirkfell House, up to Kirk Fell and thence to Graystones:
            Ascent 331 m = 1086 ft   *Distance 2.1 km = 1.3 miles*
From near Shatton Hall. A short distance to the south of where Gray Beck crosses under the road you will see some sheds, a wide track with several gates in it and a bungalow nearby. It looks as though you shouldn't pass through these gates, but it is a right of way and a means of getting to the top of Graystones, though not a very exciting one. There are walls and fences that can bar your way higher up so watch out for the gates:
            Ascent 338 m = 1109 ft   *Distance 3.6 km = 2.2 miles*
Adjacent Fells: Bream Fell   *Height   511 m = 1676 ft*   *Distance 2.3 km = 1.4 miles*
                    Kirk Fell   *802 m = 2631 ft*   *0.6 km = 0.4 miles*

Great Borne

Height 616 m = 2020 ft   NY124164   **Rank 131**

The steep slopes and crags below Herdus make this look a very impressive hill from the west end of Ennerdale Water. Any ascent involves steep climbing but the top is relatively flat and not as exciting as one might expect. Fair views from the top. The summit is not usually the sole object of a walk as there are progressively more exciting hills to be found by following the path to Starling Dodd and beyond. Great Borne is the first (or last) hill on the very demanding 'Ennerdale Horseshoe' walk.

From the car park at Bleach Green (west end of the Ennerdale valley) along the edge of the lake and then up to Whins. Continue up into the valley enclosing Gill Beck, then up Steel Brow to the summit:
            Ascent 501 m = 1644 ft   *Distance 5.6 km = 3.5 miles*
From the car park below Bowness Knott along the road to Whins and up into the valley enclosing Gill Beck. Then up Steel Brow to the summit:
            Ascent 476 m = 1560 ft   *Distance 5.3 km = 3.3 miles*
From Buttermere along the valley to Floutern Tarn, then up Steel Brow:
            Ascent 504 m = 1654 ft   *Distance 7.2 km = 4.5 miles*

Adjacent Fell: Starling Dodd   *Height 633 m = 2076 ft*   *Distance 2.1 km = 1.3 miles*

Great Calva

Height 690 m = 2263 ft   NY291312   **Rank 98**

Great Calva is just a big featureless hill. The views from the top are bleak and moorish. A place to go if you wish to be alone.

From a little south of Orthwaite via Horsemoor Hills, Brockle Crag, Hause Gill and up the beck by the side of Burn Tod: Ascent 455 m = 1492 ft   Distance   5 km = 3.1 miles
From Carrock Tungsten Mine (site of) along the valley and up and across Wiley Gill:
                              Ascent 400 m = 1312 ft   Distance 4.6 km = 2.9 miles
From the road (Peter House Farm) along the track to Whitewater Dash waterfall, along the edge of Candleseaves Bog and up by Little Calva:
                              Ascent 478 m = 1568 ft   Distance 4.9 km = 3 miles
Adjacent Fells: *Knott*   *Height   710 m = 2329 ft*   Distance 2.7 km = 1.7 miles

Great Carrs

Height 785 m = 2575 ft   SD270009   **Rank 43**

A craggy prominence on the long curved ridge which rises from Little Langdale (Fell Foot) to the southwest summit of Swirl How. Excellent views to the north but those to the south are restricted. It is unlikely that Great Carrs would be the target of a walk. The nearby Swirl How is a much greater attraction which offers magnificent views and a choice of four ridge routes leading from it.

From Fell Foot via Hollin Crag and Rough Crags:
                              Ascent   671 m = 2200 ft   Distance 4.3 km = 2.7 miles
From Wrynose Pass (Three Shire Stone) via Wet Side Edge:
                              Ascent   395 m = 1295 ft   Distance 2.1 km = 1.3 miles
Adjacent Fells: *Grey Friar*   *Height   773 m = 2536 ft*   Distance 1.4 km = 0.9 miles
                    Swirl How   *802 m = 2631 ft*   0.6 km = 0.4 miles

Great Cockup

Height 526 m = 1725 ft   NY273333   **Rank 166**

A sprawling isolated grassy hill; not very exciting. Like most of the hills in this area you get good views across to the Solway and beyond. In other directions the view is limited and rather bleak.

From Longlands and up by Trusmadoor:
                              Ascent 314 m = 1030 ft   Distance 3.3 km = 2.1 miles
From Orthwaite (just south of) via Horsemoor Hills and ascend up to the left when you reach Brockle Crag:
                              Ascent 291 m = 955 ft   Distance 2.7 km = 1.7 miles

Adjacent Fells: *Meal Fell*   *Height   550 m = 1804 ft*   Distance 1.1 km = 0.7 miles

Great Crag

Height 436 m 1430 ft   NY271145   **Rank 207**

Great Crag itself is nothing special at all. It is just a rocky protrusion among many. What makes this place so interesting is the land that surrounds it :- little hollows, rock outcrops, deep heather and the delightful Dock Tarn. The walk from Watendlath to Dock Tarn and White Crag and then down the steep path through the woods to Stonethwaite is superb. On your way you might just want to visit Great Crag itself, which offers some very pleasing views across Borrowdale.

From Watendlath: Ascent   176 m = 577 ft   Distance 2 km = 1.2 miles

Great Crag (continued)

From Rosthwaite via the fell path to Watendlath:

    Ascent 336 m = 1102 ft   *Distance 5.3 km = 3.3 miles*

From Stonethwaite via Stonethwaite Bridge, Lingy End and White Crag:

    Ascent 336 m = 1102 ft   *Distance 2.1 km = 1.3 miles*

Adjacent Fells: Ullscarf Height 726 m = 2381 ft   *Distance 3.6 km = 2.2 miles*

Great Dodd

Height 857 m = 2811 ft   **NY342206**   **Rank 19**

A large sprawling grassy hill. The views from the summit are good but the walking is dull. This is the kind of place you only come to on the way to somewhere else.

From High Row via Dowthwaite Head and Randerside:

    Ascent 507 m = 1663 ft   *Distance 5.3 km = 3.3 miles*

From the road via Fornside and the diagonal path up the rocky hill to Calfhow Pike:

    Ascent 697 m = 2287 ft   *Distance 3.2 km = 2.0 miles*

    (Note: instead of the diagonal path scramblers may like to try Beckstones Gill)

From the church at Legburthwaite around Castle Rock and up by the side of Mill Gill:

    Ascent 687 m = 2254 ft   *Distance 3.2 km = 2.0 miles*

Adjacent Fells: Clough Head Height 726 m = 2381 ft Distance 3 km = 1.9 miles

      Calfhow Pike   660 m = 2165 ft   1.5 km = 0.9 miles

      Watson's Dodd   789 m = 2588 ft   1.1 km = 0.7 miles

Great End

Height 910 m = 2985 ft   **NY227084**   **Rank 5**

Great End is the northern end of the undulating band of high ground that contains the Scafell Pikes. The north side of the fell is a sheer rock face; a most impressive sight from Sprinkling Tarn. Approached from Esk Hause the fell is just a fairly gentle hill. In common with the Scafell Pikes the top is very stony and can be uncomfortable underfoot. Magnificient views from the summit, particularly in a northerly direction.

From Seathwaite via Stockley Bridge, Styhead Gill, Sty Head, Sprinkling Tarn and Esk Hause:

    Ascent 785 m = 2575 ft   *Distance 7.3 km = 4.5 miles*

(Instead of Stockley Bridge, the more adventurous may like to try the path by Taylorgill Force Waterfall)

From Seathwaite via Stockley Bridge, Grains Gill, Ruddy Gill and Esk Hause:

    Ascent 785 m = 2575 ft   *Distance 5.8 km = 3.6 miles*

From the Wasdale Head Hotel (the long way) along Lingmell Beck, Sty Head, Sprinkling Tarn and Esk Hause:

    Ascent 832 m = 2730 ft   *Distance 6.8 km = 4.2 miles*

A shorter variation of the above is to turn off along Spouthead Gill (before reaching Sty Head) and join the Corridor Route at the foot of Skew Gill. Leave the Corridor route and do a direct ascent via Lambfoot Dub and Long Pike: Ascent 832 m = 2730 ft   *Distance 5.3 km = 3.3 miles*

From the Old Dungeon Ghyll Hotel, Great Langdale via Mickleden Beck, Rossett Gill, Angle Tarn, Esk Hause:

    Ascent 810 m = 2657 ft   *Distance 7.3 km = 4.5 miles*

From Boot, Eskdale, along the road to Brotherilkeld. Follow the River Esk all the way to Esk Hause:

    Ascent 850 m = 2789 ft   *Distance 14 km = 8.7 miles*

From Boot, via Wha House Bridge, Taw House, Brock Crag, Cam Spout Crag and Esk Hause:

    Ascent 850 m = 2789 ft   *Distance 12.6 km = 7.8 miles*

From Stonethwaite via Langstrath and Esk Hause:

    Ascent 810 m = 2657 ft   *Distance 10 km = 6.2 miles*

Adjacent Fells: Scafell Pike Height 978 m = 3208 ft Distance 1.7 km = 1.1 miles

      Allen Crags   785 m = 2575 ft   2.2 km = 1.4 miles

      Glaramara   783 m = 2568 ft   4.2 km = 2.6 miles

Great End (continued)

Adjacent Fells:	Seathwaithe Fell	Height	632 m = 2073 ft	Distance	3 km = 1.9 miles
(continued)	Esk Pike		885 m = 2903 ft		2.2 km = 1.4 miles
	Great Gable		899 m = 2949 ft		5 km = 3.1 miles
	Green Gable		801 m = 2627 ft		5.2 km = 3.2 miles

Great Gable

Height 899 m = 2949 ft NY211103 **Rank 7**

A magnificent mountain and very popular, you won't be alone here, even on bad days. From most start points the journey to the top will involve a good deal of walking. An exception to this is the route from Honister Hause. Here you can park the car (if you are early enough) and set off in the knowledge that you are already at a height of 350 m (1148 ft). This is cheating somewhat and, although the route isn't bad, it is certainly not the best path to the top. The sides of Gable are covered in scree and rocky outcrops with occasional runs of sheer crag; the biggest of which is Gable Crag. There is a circular route round the mountain at about the 550 m (1800 ft) contour, called the Gable Girdle. This is well worth doing as the views are terrific and there are plenty of opportunities for scrambling for those who enjoy doing this. Apart from the litter (orange peel, sandwich bits etc., biodegradable but still ugly) the views from the top are outstanding.

From Honister Hause to the Drum House, to Brandreth, to Stone Cove (or via the top of Green Gable) to Windy Gap: Ascent 549 m = 1801 ft Distance 4.7 km = 2.9 miles
From Honister Hause over into Gillercomb then up to the top of Green Gable, down to Windy Gap then up to the top: Ascent 549 m = 1801 ft Distance 4.2 km = 2.6 miles
(this route is marginally shorter but harder than the previous route)
From Seathwaite Farm to Stockley Bridge, to Greenhow Knott, to Sty Head Tarn, up Aaron Slack to Windy Gap and thence to the summit:
Ascent 774 m = 2539 ft Distance 4.7 km = 2.9 miles
(Note: by crossing to the other side of the river at Seathwaite and following the footpath along the bottom of Base Brown you can visit Taylor Gill Force; the second highest waterfall in the district. This is an exciting route, but the narrow path and long drops might upset some. The Taylor Gill route joins the previously described route just after the waterfall.)
From Seathwaite Farm across the river up by the side of Sour Milk Gill, then along Gillercomb up to the top of Green Gable, down to Windy Gap and thence to the summit:
Ascent 774 m = 2539 ft Distance 3.7 km = 2.3 miles
From Gatesgarth Farm to Scarth Gap, up to Haystacks, then over Brandreth to Windy Gap and up to the summit : Ascent 782 m = 2566 ft Distance 7.3 km = 4.5 miles
From the Wasdale Head Hotel up by Gable Beck, then up the northwest corner of the mountain between White Napes and Great Napes (a strenuous route):
Ascent 819 m = 2687 ft Distance 3.3 km = 2.1 miles
From the Wasdale Head Hotel to Sty Head Tarn up Aaron Slack to Windy Gap, thence to the top:
Ascent 819 m = 2687 ft Distance 5.3 km = 3.3 miles

Adjacent Fells :	Kirk Fell	Height	802 m = 2631 ft	Distance 2.3 km = 1.4 miles
	Green Gable		801 m = 2627 ft	0.8 km = 0.5 miles
	Brandreth		715 m = 2345 ft	2 km = 1.2 miles
	Haystacks		597 m = 1958 ft	4.8 km = 3.0 miles
	Great End		910 m = 2985 ft	5 km = 3.1 miles

Great Mell Fell

Height 537 m = 1761 ft NY397254 **Rank 161**

An egg-shaped hill that rises abruptly from almost flat surroundings. Though isolated and relatively unfrequented the fell offers pleasant woodland walking. The fell is surrounded by fenced, inaccessible, agricultural and forest land. Access is obtained opposite Brownrigg Farm. Follow the track opposite the farm

Great Mell Fell (continued)

and you will come to a National Trust sign and a stile. The ascent can be made from here or by following the track a little further to a second sign and stile. The latter route is the easier one. The strange flat, thinly grassed area on the summit is a tumulus. There are excellent long distance views from the top in all directions.

From the track opposite Brownrigg Farm go over the second stile and climb up by the south side of the wood:
        Ascent 277 m = 909 ft   *Distance 1.6 km = 1 mile*

Great Rigg

Height 766 m = 2513 ft   **NY356104**   **Rank 55**

Great Rigg is the penultimate summit on the ridge from Nab Scar, above Rydal Water, to Fairfield. As such it is unlikely to be the sole object of a walk. It is grassy and lacks any interesting features. The view from the top is good.

From Rydal via Heron Pike:
        Ascent 706 m = 2316 ft   *Distance 4.9 km = 3.1 miles*
From Grasmere via Stone Arthur:
        Ascent 681 m = 2234 ft   *Distance 3.2 km = 2.0 miles*
From Grasmere following Greenhead Gill all the way up:
        Ascent 681 m = 2234 ft   *Distance 3.3 km = 2.1 miles*

Adjacent fells :	*Heron Pike*	*Height*	*612 m = 2007 ft*	*Distance 2.3 km = 1.4 miles*
	Fairfield		*873 m = 2864 ft*	*1.4 km = 0.9 miles*
	Stone Arthur		*504 m = 1653 ft*	*1.6 km = 1 mile*

Great Sca Fell

Height 651 m = 2135 ft   **NY 291339**   **Rank 118**

A broad rather uninteresting top though there are good views to the Solway and beyond. The main appeal of the fell is that many others can be easily reached from it and there are a variety of interesting ways to the top.

From Fellside along Dale Beck and up Swinburn Gill:
        Ascent 376 m = 1234 ft   *Distance 4 km = 2.5 miles*
From Fellside along Dale Beck and up Silver Gill or Raughton Gill:
        Ascent 376 m = 1234 ft   *Distance 5.2 km = 3.2 miles*
From Longlands via Longlands Fell:
        Ascent 439 m = 1440 ft   *Distance 3.7 km = 2.3 miles*
From Greenhead via Brae Fell top:
        Ascent 396 m = 1299 ft   *Distance 3.6 km = 2.2 miles*
From Longlands via Trusmadoor and up the side of Frozen Fell Gill:
        Ascent 439 m = 1440 ft   *Distance 4.2 km = 2.6 miles*

Adjacent Fells :	*Meal Fell*	*Height*	*550 m = 1804 ft*	*Distance 1 km = 0.6 miles*
	Knott		*710 m = 2329 ft*	*1 km = 0.6 miles*
	Longlands Fell		*483 m = 1584 ft*	*2 km = 1.6 miles*
	Brae Fell		*586 m = 1922 ft*	*1.5 km = 0.9 miles*

Great Stickle

Height 305 m = 1000 ft   **SD212916**   **Rank 243**

Comparatively low lying but Great Stickle and the area around it is delightful with steep slopes, complex undulations and rocky outcrops. Indeed, it is a mountain in miniature. Good views but most people will wish to continue on over Tarn Hill to the higher Stickle Pike.

Great Stickle (continued)

From Broughton Mills turning west before Scrithwaite Farm. Thence to Hovel Knott and up the west side of the hill:

Ascent 267 m = 875 ft   Distance 2.1 km = 1.3 miles

Adjacent Fell: Stickle Pike   Height   375 m = 1230 ft   Distance 1.5 km = 0.9 miles

Great Worm Crag

Height 427 m = 1400 ft   **SD193969**   **Rank 210**

This rather remote rounded hill has little to offer except as a platform to view the surrounding more distant fells. Good long distance views in all directions. The obvious way up is straight up the hill from the fell road on its western flank.

From Brown Rigg follow the track towards Birkerthwaite, then bear right round the northern flank of Rough Crag and so up to the summit:

Ascent 189 m = 620 ft   Distance 1.4 km = 0.8 miles

Adjacent Fell: Green Crag   Height   489 m = 1604 ft   Distance 1.8 km = 1.1 miles

Green Crag

Height 489 m = 1604 ft   **SD200983**   **Rank 188**

The highest of several rocky knolls on a high remote plateau giving good views of the more distant hills. The most scenic approach is from Eskdale, using the old peat roads.

From Low Birker via the old peat track to the west of Kepple Crag and Crook Crag, then bear round to the left of Green Crag for the easiest approach to the summit:

Ascent 419 m = 1375 ft   Distance 4.2 km = 2.6 miles

Adjacent Fell: Harter Fell   Height   653 m = 2142 ft   Distance 1.8 km = 1.1 miles

Green Gable

Height 801 m = 2627 ft   **NY215107**   **Rank 36**

Green Gable is too close to, and dominated by, Great Gable to become the object of a walk. The top is broad and stony and not particularly interesting, although the views are good. Anyone visiting here will almost certainly be on their way to, or coming from, Great Gable.

From Honister Hause via the Drum House and Brandreth:

Ascent 451 m = 1480 ft   Distance 4 km = 2.5 miles

From Honister Hause via Grey Knotts and Brandreth (a harder route than the above due to the rough ground up to Grey Knotts):

Ascent 451 m = 1480 ft   Distance 3.3 k m = 2.1 miles

From Seathwaite Farm via Sour Milk Gill and Gillercomb:

Ascent 676 m = 2218 ft   Distance 3 km = 1.9 miles

From Seathwaite Farm via Stockley Bridge to Styhead Tarn then up Aaron Slack to Windy Gap (See Great Gable for the Taylorgill Force variation to this route):

Ascent 676 m = 2218 ft   Distance 4.3 km = 2.7 miles

From the Wasdale Head Hotel to Sty Head Tarn up Aaron Slack to Windy Gap:

Ascent 721 m = 2365 ft   Distance 5.2 km = 3.2 miles

From the Wasdale Head Hotel up by Gable Beck and the base of Gable Crag to Stone Cove and Windy Gap:

Ascent 721 m = 2365 ft   Distance 4.7 km = 2.9 miles

Adjacent Fells::	Great Gable	Height	899 m = 2949 ft	Distance 0.8 km = 0.5 miles
	Brandreth		715 m = 2345 ft	1.3 km = 0.8 miles
	Base Brown		646 m = 2119 ft	1.5 km = 0.9 miles
	Haystacks		597 m = 1958 ft	4.1 km = 2.6 miles
	Great End		910 m = 2985 ft	5.2 km = 3.2 miles

Grey Crag

Height 638 m = 2093 ft   NY497072   **Rank 122**

The comments used for Tarn Crag apply here, that is the fells east of Longsleddale are dull and boggy. However, Grey Crag is close enough to the valley wall to be worthwhile. There are very extensive views from the top (though not into the Lake District). The odd looking two pronged stone tower on great Hove (shown as 'Pillar' on the O.S. maps) was used in the surveying of the Haweswater aqueduct.

From Sadgill follow the walls up to Great Hove thence onward to Grey Crag:
                     Ascent   438 m = 1437 ft   *Distance 2.1 km = 1.3 miles*
Adjacent Fell: Tarn Crag   Height   664 m = 2178 ft   Distance 1.3 km = 0.8 miles

Grey Friar

Height 773 m = 2536 ft   NY260004   **Rank 51**

Seen from the long undulating and highly popular ridge route extending from Fell Foot to Dow Crag (incorporating Great Carrs, Swirl How, Brim Fell and Coniston Old Man). Grey Friar is merely a prominence to the southwest of Great Carrs. The top is a grassy dome possessing no remarkable features save a magnificent view of the Scawfell range. If ascending the fell from the Duddon Valley, the route up Tarn Head Beck is quite pleasant once the boggy ground around Seathwaite Tarn has been left behind.

From the car park near Pike How via Pike How, Fuss How, the north side of Seathwaite Tarn and up alongside Tarn How Beck:
                     Ascent   590 m = 1936 ft   *Distance 6.1 km = 3.8 miles*
Adjacent Fell: Great Carrs   Height   785 m = 2575 ft   Distance 1.4 km = 0.9 miles

Grey Knotts

Height 697 m = 2286 ft   NY217126   **Rank 94**

Other than good views from the top, the only other recommendation is that the summit can be reached quickly from Honister Hause for those who would save their legs. The path from the hause is the one behind the quarry buildings leading up through the ground, not the highly popular route to the Drum House. For those with a geological or mineralogical interest the route up from Seathwaite, which takes you through the workings of the old graphite mine, will be of particular interest. Small samples of the greasy black graphite (or wad, or plumbago) can still be found in the spoil heaps. **Beware,** there is an open shaft (120 ft deep) about half way up the workings, so take care with children, dogs and of course yourself. This graphite mine has a fascinating history which is described elsewhere in the book.

From Seathwaite Farm up by the old graphite mine workings, then carry on up the slope keeping Raven Crag to your left: *Ascent 572 m = 1877 ft*   *Distance 2.6 km = 1.6 miles*
From Honister Hause:
                     Ascent 347 m = 1138 ft   *Distance 1.2 km = 0.7 miles*

Adjacent Fells: Brandreth   Height   715 m = 2345 ft   Distance 1 km = 0.6 miles
                    Haystacks   597 m = 1958 ft   3.1 km = 1.9 miles
                    Fleetwith Pike   648 m = 2125 ft   2.7 km = 1.7 miles

Grike

Height 488 m = 1601 ft   NY085141   **Rank 189**

Like its neighbour, Crag Fell, Grike is excellent walking from the Ennerdale side, but bleak and moorish from the south side. The wood to the west of Ben Gill (at the foot of Grike) contains a number of old, very small iron ore mines. Scramblers may like to try some of the rough routes up the fell, adjacent to and including Goat Gill and Red Gill (but take good care, crumbly rock). Good views out to West Cumbria.

Grike (continued)

From the car park at Bleach Green (West end of Ennerdale Water) up the side of Ben Gill:

        Ascent 368 m = 1207 ft   *Distance 2.5 km = 1.6 miles*

From the road at Scaly Moss along the old mine track through the woods:

        Ascent 248 m = 814 ft   *Distance 2.7 km = 1.7 miles*

Adjacent Fells: *Crag Fell*   *Height 523 m = 1715 ft*   *Distance 1.3 km = 0. 8 miles*

Grisedale Pike

Height 791 m = 2595 ft   **NY198225**   **Rank 41**

Seen from Keswick, Grisedale Pike looks large and challenging. The views from the top are superb and, to the northwest, one can see over to the West Cumbrian coast. There are many ways to the top of this hill but the horseshoe route, incorporating Ladyside Pike and Hobcarton End, is probably the best. The approach along Coledale (along the mine track) seems to last forever but provides impressive views of Eel Crag and Force Crag at its end. Just below Force Crag is Force Crag Mine which has been a source of lead, zinc and barytes for hundreds of years and was worked until 1991. The approach from Braithwaite via Sleet How is good but not as good as the horseshoe route.

From the Whinlatter Visitor Centre along the road to the track by Swinside Plantation, then up onto the Ladyside Pike Ridge (For full details see ' The Hobcarton Round ' on page 11):

        Ascent   471 m = 1545 ft   *Distance 6.8 km = 4.2 miles*

                                                              (First half of horseshoe)

From Braithwaite via Kinn and Sleet How:

        Ascent   691 m = 2267 ft   *Distance 3.8 km = 2.4 miles*

From Braithwaite via Coledale, Coledale Hause and Sand Hill:

        Ascent   691 m = 2267 ft   *Distance 7.4 km = 4.6 miles*

Adjacent Fells: *Hopegill Head*   *Height 770 m = 2526 ft*   *Distance 1.6 km = 1 mile*

                Sand Hill   *756 m = 2480 ft*   *1.6 km = 1 mile*

Hallin Fell

Height 388 m = 1272 ft   **NY433198**   **Rank 223**

Small but immensely popular. For very little effort one gets magnificent views. Hallin Fell is an O.S. viewpoint. The standard route to the top is opposite the church of St. Peter's, which is situated on the hause at the entrance to Martindale, about half a mile south of Howtown. There is a footpath which circumnavigates the base of the fell and this is a very pleasant walk in its own right.

From opposite St. Peter's directly to the summit:

        Ascent 159 m = 522 ft   *Distance 0.7 km = 0.4 miles*

Hard Knott

Height 549 m = 1801 ft   **NY232024**   **Rank 157**

Roughly speaking, Hard Knott is a large (in volume) triangular - based hill bounded by the upper reaches of the river Esk, Mosedale and the Hard Knott Pass. It can be approached from almost any direction and, save for a few crags here and there, presents no special difficulties. Magnificent views of Upper Eskdale and the Scafell range are to be had from the top. The shortest route is from Raven Crag, half a mile or so from the Roman fort.

From Hard Knott Pass (east side of Raven Crag) via Border End:

        Ascent 156 m = 511 ft   *Distance 1.3 km = 0.8 miles*

A - Z Guide to the Fells

Hare Shaw

Height 503 m = 1650 ft   NY497131   **Rank 184**

Hare Shaw itself does not have a great deal to offer, however the routes to and from it are pleasant and unfrequented. For example, the walking above the woods and crags running from above the Haweswater Hotel to above Naddle Farm takes you around numerous rock outcrops and to the top of high crags. Rather bleak views from the top.

From the roadside entrance to Naddle Farm. Follow the track around to Highfield Crag then carry on to Hugh's Laithes Pike. Follow the tops of the crags then, at Kit Crag, make your way along the top of the Naddle Valley to Hare Shaw:

Ascent 283 m = 928 ft   Distance 5.2 km = 3.2 miles

For those staying at the Haweswater Hotel, there is a break in the roadside wall a short distance north of the hotel. Climb up through the old deciduous wood and continue past the head of the Naddle Valley to Hare Shaw: Ascent 243 m = 797 ft   Distance 1.6 km = 1 mile

From the point where Rowantreethwaite Beck crosses under the lake-side road. Follow the old corpse road towards Shap and then turn off for Hare Shaw near Low Birkin Knott:

Ascent 223 m = 732 ft   Distance 2.6 km = 1.6 miles

Adjacent Fells: Selside Pike   *Height*   655 m = 2148 ft   Distance 2.3 km = 1.4 miles
                      Harper Hills   419 m = 1374 ft   1.8 km = 1.1 miles

Harper Hills

Height 419 m = 1374 ft   NY508143   **Rank 216**

Low lying so the views are very restricted, except over the low ground to the northeast. Essentially a small bump on the northeast side of Hare Shaw. Rather bleak country.

From the end of the unenclosed road at the end of Swindale. Follow the path up to Scalebarrow Knott, then the track across to Harper Hills:

Ascent 181 m = 594 ft   Distance 2.1 km = 1.3 miles

Adjacent Fells: Hare Shaw   *Height*   503 m = 1650 ft   Distance 1.8 km = 1.1 miles
                      Scalebarrow Knott   335 m = 1099 ft   1.5 km = 0.9 miles

Harrison Stickle

Height 736 m = 2414 ft   NY282074   **Rank 70**

The highest of the Langdale Pikes. Magnificent views and superb rock scenery make the Langdale Pikes one of the top attractions in the Lake District. There is plenty to explore. The best approaches are from Great Langdale, the route from Borrowdale via Langstrath is relatively featureless. There are many possible routes from Grasmere taking in a variety of other fells to which the reader is referred.

From the New Dungeon Ghyll Hotel via Pike How and the east side of the Dungeon Ghyll ravine:

Ascent 705 m = 2314 ft   Distance 2.4 km = 1.5 miles

From the New Dungeon Ghyll Hotel via Stickle Ghyll and Stickle Tarn:

Ascent 705 m = 2314 ft   Distance 2.3 km = 1.4 miles

From Stonethwaite via Langstrath: (see Pike O' Stickle)

Adjacent Fells: Pike O' Stickle   *Height*   709 m = 2326 ft   Distance 1.2 km = 0.7 miles
                      Loft Crag   670 m = 2198 ft   0.7 km = 0.4 miles
                      Thunacar Knott   723 m = 2372 ft   1 km = 0.6 miles
                      Pavey Ark   700 m = 2296 ft   1.1 km = 0.7 miles

159

Hart Crag

Height 822 m = 2696 ft   NY368113   **Rank 27**

A small hump in the ridge between Fairfield and Dove Crag. The west side is a steep hill down to the valley bottom. The rough north side consists of steep crags. The proximity of Fairfield makes it unlikely that Hart Crag will be the sole object of a walk. The views from the top are rather limited.

From Nook End Farm (north Ambleside) via Low Pike and Dove Crag:
        Ascent 722 m = 2369 ft   *Distance 6.7 km = 4.2 miles*
From Deepdale Bridge via Hartsop Above How:
        Ascent 662 m = 2172 ft   *Distance 5 km = 3.1 miles*

Adjacent Fells:	Fairfield	Height	873 m = 2864 ft	Distance 1.1 km = 0.7 miles
	Dove Crag		792 m = 2598 ft	1.2 km = 0.7 miles
	Hartsop above How		580 m = 1902 ft	1.8 km = 1.1 miles

Hart Side

Height 756 m = 2480 ft   NY359197   **Rank 62**

The summit itself is not particularly interesting nor is the view particularly good. Devotees of industrial archaeology may be mildly interested in the excavations near the summit which were made to examine the northern part of the very rich Greenside silver / lead vein. These northerly trials showed the vein to be barren here. Glencoynedale, to the south of the summit, makes a very good circular walk.

From the main road via Seldom Seen, Bleabank Side, Nick Head and the top of Glencoynedale Head, an interesting route: Ascent 611 m = 2005 ft   *Distance 4.6 km = 2.9 miles*
From Park Brow through Glencoyne Park and on to Brown Hills:
        Ascent 526 m = 1726 ft   *Distance 4.3 km = 2.7 miles*
From Dockray (joins up with the above route below Swineside Knott):
        Ascent 461 m = 1512 ft   *Distance 4.6 km = 2.9 miles*

Harter Fell (Above Eskdale)

Height 653 m = 2142 ft   SD219997   **Rank 116**

Steep and covered in rock outcrops, this fell is attractive and a delight to climb. Much of its base is covered by woods which add to its charm. There are three craggy summits, two of which are easy to conquer. The middle one is somewhat harder, but not greatly so. Good views over the fells and out to sea.

From the Duddon Valley car park. Cross the river and follow the forest track to Birks, then ascend via Buck Crag (For a more detailed description see page 114):
        Ascent 470 m =1542 ft   *Distance 2.2 km = 1.4 miles*
From below Peathill Crag on the Hardknott Pass via Horsehow Crags, Demming Crag:
        Ascent 295 m = 967 ft   *Distance 2.1 km = 1.3 miles*
From Whahouse Bridge via Spothow Gill. At about the 250 m = 800 ft contour the summit path branches northeast off the gill-side path:
        Ascent 569 m = 1867 ft   *Distance 2.4 km = 1.5 miles*

Harter Fell (above Haweswater)

Height 778 m = 2552 ft   NY460093   **Rank 48**

Harter Fell is seen at its craggy best from the south end of Haweswater. From the Kentmere side it isn't so impressive. The route from the south end of Haweswater taking in Small Water and Nan Bield Pass is excellent and strongly recommended. The top is flat and not particularly interesting. The views however are superb.

From Mardale Head via Smallwater and Nan Bield Pass:
        Ascent 526 m = 1726 ft   *Distance 3.3 km = 2.1 miles*

Harter Fell (above Haweswater) (continued)
From Mardale Head via Gatesgarth Pass and Little Harter Fell:
        Ascent 526 m = 1726 ft   *Distance 3.5 km= 2.2 miles*
From Kentmere village via Hallow Bank Quarter, Smallthwaite Knott, Nan Bield Pass:
        Ascent 608 m = 1995 ft   *Distance 7.3 km = 4.5 miles*
From Sadgill, along the valley, to Gatesgarth Pass, Little Harter Fell:
        Ascent 580 m = 1903 ft   *Distance 5.8 km = 3.6 miles*

Adjacent Fells:	*Mardale Ill Bell*	*Height*	*761 m = 2496 ft*	*Distance 1.7 km = 1.1 miles*
	Branstree		*713 m = 2339 ft*	*2.7 km = 1.7 miles*
	Kentmere Pike		*730 m = 2394 ft*	*2 km = 1.2 miles*

Hartsop Above How
Height 580 m = 1902 ft   **NY383120**   **Rank 142**

Hartsop Above How lies on the long ridge which defines the south side of Deepdale. The ridge is pleasant to walk and it is likely that one will pass this small summit on the way to or from Hart Crag. Excellent views from the summit.

From Deepdale Bridge and up the ridge:
        Ascent 420 m = 1378 ft   *Distance 3.2 km = 2.0 miles*
Adjacent Fells: *Hart Crag*   *Height 822 m = 2696 ft*   *Distance 1.8 km = 1.1 miles*

Hartsop Dodd
Height 618 m = 2027 ft   **NY411118**   **Rank 130**

The north ridge is an excellent walk, steep, rocky and with excellent views. There are two mine levels on the ridge, these being connected internally by a 180 ft deep shaft. There are other mine workings at the confluence of Hayeswater Gill and Pasture Beck. The row of stone columns nearby used to support a wooden trough carrying water to a waterwheel. This used to drive the pumps to dewater the mine.

From Hartsop village up the north ridge:
        Ascent 448 m = 1470 ft   *Distance 1.8 km = 1.1 miles*
Adjacent Fell: *Stony Cove Pike Height* *763 m = 2503 ft*   *Distance 2 km = 1.2 miles*

Haycock
Height 797 m = 2614 ft   **NY145107**   **Rank 37**

Haycock marks the transition from the rather dreary ground to the west and the rugged and dramatic fells to the east. However you choose to get to this hill you will have quite a long walk. Good views in most directions.

From the car park below Bowness Knott to the head of the lake, then across and up the ridge between Silvercove Beck and Deep Gill:
        Ascent 667 m = 2188 ft   *Distance 7.2 km = 4.5 miles*
From the car park below Bowness Knott to the head of the lake, then across and up the fire break to Lingmell and Tewit How: Ascent 667 m = 2188 ft   *Distance 7 km = 4.3 miles*
From Netherbeck Bridge Wasdale (car park nearby) along Netherbeck and up by Little Lad Crag:
        Ascent 727 m = 2385 ft   *Distance 5.3 km = 3.3 miles*
From Greendale (Wasdale) via Greendale Gill, Greendale Tarn, Winscale Hows, High Pikehow and up by the side of Garden Crag:
        Ascent 717 m = 2352 ft   *Distance 5.6 km = 3.5 miles*

Adjacent Fells:	*Scoat Fell*	*Height*	*841 m = 2759 ft*	*Distance 1.7 km = 1.1 miles*
	Caw Fell		*697 m = 2286 ft*	*1.5 km = 0.9 miles*
	Seatallan		*692 m = 2270 ft*	*2.6 km = 1.6 miles*

A - Z Guide to the Fells

Haystacks

Height 597 m = 1958 ft   NY193132   **Rank 136**

Haystacks is one of the most interesting and popular of fells. This is mainly due to its broad rapidly undulating top, which is dotted with rocky outcrops, tarns, bogs, miniature crags and patches of heather. Don't, however, expect to find solitude here.

From Gatesgarth Farm (car park) via Scarth Gap:
Ascent 480 m = 1575 ft   Distance 2.7 km = 1.7 miles
From Gatesgarth farm via Warnscale Common and Blackbeck Tarn:
Ascent 480 m = 1575 ft   Distance 3.7 km = 2.3 miles
From Honister Hause via Dubs Quarry and Blackbeck Tarn:
Ascent 247 m = 810 ft   Distance 3.6 km = 2.2 miles

Adjacent Fells:	High Crag	Height	744 m = 2440 ft	Distance	2 km = 1.2 miles
	Grey Knotts		697 m = 2286 ft		3.1 km = 1.9 miles
	Brandreth		715 m = 2345 ft		3.1 km = 1.9 miles

Helm Crag

Height 405 m = 1328 ft   NY325093   **Rank 220**

The combination of relatively easy walking, interesting terrain and close proximity to the busy village of Grasmere makes this one of the more popular Lake District fells. The top is crowned with large rock slabs and pinnacles, a fascinating place to explore. With a little help from the imagination these can take on all kinds of familiar shapes. At the northwest end of the summit ridge is a group of rocks called 'The Old Woman Playing the Organ'. The justification for this name can be sought by viewing Helm Crag from Far Easdale or Dunmail Raise. The rock cluster at the southeast of the ridge is called 'The Lion and the Lamb,' when viewed from the road near the Swan Hotel in Grasmere. There are good views from the top. Helm Crag is not an isolated top. It forms the end of the ridge which starts a little to the east of Calf Crag.

From Grasmere via Easdale Road:
Ascent 384 m = 1261 ft   Distance   3 km = 1.9 miles
Adjacent Fell: Gibson Knott   Height   420 m = 1377 ft   Distance 1.2 km = 0.7 miles

Helvellyn

Height 950 m = 3116 ft   NY342151   **Rank 3**

Helvellyn is immensely popular, even in winter, and not only because it is one of the highest fells but also because the views are magnificent. The sheep up here are used to visitors and don't display any of their normal shyness. In fact they can be downright intrusive and annoying, pulling at your rucksack and stealing sandwiches from your hand. However, don't be too hard on them, what would you do in the same situation if the only alternative was tough mountain grass ? The quick way up and down Helvellyn is from the Thirlmere side, but the route is rather boring. The classic routes are from the eastern side with its ridges, crags and valleys. The top itself is interesting with its shelter and monuments. Striding Edge offers excitement but is quite safe in good weather.

From the car park by 'The Swirls' up by Helvellyn Gill to Lower Man. A fast but rather dull route to the top:
Ascent 735 m = 2411 ft   Distance 3.6 km = 2.2 miles
From the clearing in the wood up the old incline to Helvellyn Lead Mine, thence to Brownrigg Well and the top (A very direct route down, but there is no car parking at the bottom. There is, however, a very pleasant path through the forest that takes you to the car park near the Swirls):
Ascent 760 m = 2493 ft   Distance (from bottom of clearing) 2.3 km = 1.4 miles
(from Swirls car park)   4.3 km = 2.7 miles

Helvellyn (continued)

From Wythburn car park through the wood and via Comb Crags and near to the top of Nethermost Pike (why not visit it on the way?):

Ascent 765 m = 2509 ft   Distance 3.7 km = 2.3 miles

From Grisedale Bridge along the metalled road into Grisedale as far as the gate, then right across Grisedale Beck and up the well worn path on to the ridge towards the 'hole in the wall'. Thence to Striding Edge and the top: Ascent 800 m = 2625 ft   Distance 5.7 km = 3.5 miles

From Glenridding across Rattlebeck Bridge, up Mines Beck to the ridge path which leads to Birkhouse Moor, then along to Striding Edge and up to the top:

Ascent 800 m = 2625 ft   Distance 5.8 km = 3.6 miles

From Glenridding and up to the old Greenside Mine buildings. Carry on to the path along Red Tarn Beck, then up onto Swirral Edge:

Ascent 800 m = 2625 ft   Distance 6.2 km = 3.9 miles

(Note: Instead of going up the mine road to Greenside Mine you can cross the Glenridding Beck at Rattlebeck and walk up the hill path opposite the mine track. This alternative route joins the other track just above the mine).

Adjacent Fells:	Whiteside	Height	863 m = 2831 ft	Distance 1.9 km = 1.2 miles
	Nethermost Pike		891 m = 2923 ft	1.1 km = 0.7 miles
	Catstye Cam		890 m = 2919 ft	1.1 km = 0.7 miles

Hen Comb

Height 509 m = 1669 ft   NY132181   **Rank 179**

Except for quiteness Hen Combe does not have much to offer. It is essentially a long high grassy hill surrounded by very wet bog. The north end, however, can be made part of a circular walk taking in Blake Fell and Carling Knott. Good views to the east and south from the top.

From the Kirkstile Inn via Little Dodd:

Ascent 388 m = 1273 ft   Distance 3.1 km = 1.9 miles

From Maggies Bridge via High Nook Farm, the old lead mine and Little Dodd:

Ascent 384 m = 1260 ft   Distance 4.2 km = 2.6 miles

From Buttermere follow the Scales Force path to the waterfall. Continue on towards Floutern Tarn until opposite Hen Comb, then turn right and climb up to the summit:

Ascent 397 m = 1302 ft   Distance 5.9 km = 3.7 miles

Adjacent Fells:	Mellbreak	Height	512 m = 1679 ft	Distance 3.5 km = 2.2 miles
	Gavel Fell		526 m = 1725 ft	3 km = 1.9 miles

Heron Pike

Height 612 m = 2007 ft   NY356083   **Rank 132**

This marks the beginning of the long ridge up to Fairfield. Here the ridge is broad and grassy and dotted with rock outcrops. Very good views to the west and not much effort is needed to get here.

From Rydal via the road past Rydal Mount and up onto the ridge:

Ascent 552 m = 1811 ft   Distance 2.6 km = 1.6 miles

From Grasmere (A591) via the lower part of Greenhead Gill, then up the path near Rowantree Gill:

Ascent 532 m = 1745 ft   Distance 2.1 km = 1.3 miles

Adjacent Fells:	Great Rigg	Height	766 m = 2513 ft	Distance 2.3 km = 1.4 miles
	Nab Scar		442 m = 1450 ft	1.1 km = 0.7 miles

A - Z Guide to the Fells

Hesk Fell

Height 477 m = 1564 ft   SD176947   **Rank 195**

This remote, massive and rounded grassy mound has little to tempt one to climb to its summit except the distant views of the Scafell range. However, the southern slope is the site of Holehouse Gill (or Hesk Fell) copper mine with its three levels, cluster of ruined mine buildings and large spoil heaps. Mineral collectors may wish to note that there is a good deal of chalcopyrite and arsenopyrite to be found in the dumps of the middle and top level.

From the road at Woodend Bridge, follow the track towards Woodend Farm then, keeping outside the enclosures, leave the track and follow the wall up the ridge until it bears west. At this point leave the wall and continue up the ridge to the summit:
        Ascent 247 m = 810 ft   *Distance 2.4 km = 1.5 miles*
This hill could be visited along with several other of the remote minor fells in this area by following **Route 2** *on page 113.*
Adjacent Fell: *Whitfell Height 572 m = 1877 ft*   *Distance 1.5 km = 0.9 miles*

High Crag

Height 744 m = 2440 ft   NY181140   **Rank 67**

Like High Stile, its neighbour, this mountain looks most impressive from Buttermere and is well worth the ascent. The views from the top, though excellent, are not quite as compulsive as those from High Stile. However both summits can be enjoyed quite easily as they are joined by a short and delightful narrow ridge. From the Ennerdale side the fell is less dramatic, being only a very steep hill dropping down into the valley with wooded lower slopes.

From Buttermere via the Lakeside path to the south end of the lake then up to Scarth Gap and Gamlin End:
        Ascent 632 m = 2073 ft   *Distance 5.8 km = 3.6 miles*
From Gatesgarth Farm via Scarth Gap and Gamlin End:
        Ascent 627 m = 2073 ft   *Distance 3.3 km = 2 miles*
From Black Sail Youth Hostel via Scarth Gap:
        Ascent 454 m = 1489 ft   *Distance 2.7 km = 1.7 miles*
Adjacent Fells: *High Stile*   *Height* *807 m = 2647 ft*   *Distance 1.5 km = 0.9 miles*
               Haystacks   *597 m = 1958 ft*   *2 km = 1.2 miles*

High Hartsop Dodd

Height 519 m = 1702 ft   NY393108   **Rank 173**

From Brothers' Water it looks like an impressive peak, but it is, in fact, part of the ridge coming down from Little Hart Crag. The ascent is steep and there are dangerous crags near the summit.

From Cow Bridge via Hartsop Hall:
        Ascent 361 m = 1184 ft   *Distance*   *3 km = 1.9 miles*
Adjacent Fells: *Little Hart Crag Height* *637 m = 2089 ft*   *Distance 0.8 km = 0.5 miles*

High Knott

Height 270 m = 885 ft   NY454001   **Rank 245**

A grassy knoll surmounted by a memorial cairn. High Knott is a fine vantage point to view the Kentmere valley.
From Browfoot farm, follow the road southwest to the junction then turn left towards Hugill. In a short distance, as you ascend the hill, a gate to the left gives access to the fell. Follow the path which leads up to the summit: *Ascent 120 m = 394 ft*   *Distance 1.2 km = 0.8 miles*

A - Z Guide to the Fells

High Pike (near Caldbeck)

Height 658 m = 2158 ft   NY319350   **Rank 111**

A sprawling grassy lonely hill with good long distance views spanning from West Cumbria to the Pennines in the east. High Pike and the area surrounding it is of great interest to geologists as there are many old mine workings encircling it e.g. Driggith (lead and zinc), Roughton Gill (lead and zinc), Carrock (tungsten), Brandy Gill (lead), Dry Gill (lead), Potts Gill and Sandbeds (barytes) and Hay Gill (copper). Care should be taken in the ground to the north of the top for there are many subsidence holes above the old workings and more open up each winter. Some of the pits contain drops of over 100 ft, however, most are fenced and those that are not are pretty obvious. For your own safety keep out of them.

From Calebrack along the track that turns north to the large spoil heaps (west from Driggith and Sandbeds Mines) then up the hill to the top:
        Ascent 358 m = 1175 ft   *Distance 3.6 km = 2.2 miles*

From the ford along Carrock Beck then, before reaching Drygill Beck, turn north up the valley leading to the old Driggith mine workings. At the head of the workings turn left onto the track which leads to the head of the valley and traverses round High Pike. Bear right of this track to reach the summit cairn:
        Ascent 393 m = 1270 ft   *Distance 3.5 km = 2.2 miles*

From Nether Row follow the footpath straight up the gill, past the old mine workings and up to the top:
        Ascent 398 m =1306 ft   *Distance 3.1 km = 1.9 miles*

From Fell Side across the top of Ingray Gill along Short Grain and up to High Pike:
        Ascent 388 m = 1273 ft   *Distance 3.1 km = 1.9 miles*

Adjacent Fells: *Knott   Height   710 m = 2329 ft*   *Distance 3.1 km = 1.9 miles*
                 Carrock Fell   660 m = 2165 ft   *3.4 km = 2.1 miles*

High Pike (near Grasmere)

Height 656 m = 2152 ft   NY374088   **Rank 113**

High Pike lies on the long ridge running up from Ambleside to the top of Fairfield. Accordingly High Pike is usually crossed rather than deliberately visited. South of High Pike the ridge is relatively narrow but, to the north it rapidly broadens as one approaches Dove Crag. The views from the top are quite good but restricted.

From Nook End Farm along the ridge via Low Pike:
        Ascent 556 m = 1824 ft   *Distance 3.9 km = 2.4 miles*

Adjacent Fells: *Low Pike   Height   508 m = 1666 ft*   *Distance 1.2 km = 0.7 miles*
                 Dove Crag   792 m = 2598 ft   *1.6 km = 1 mile*

High Raise (above Haweswater)

Height 802 m   NY448134   **Rank 33**

There are good extensive views from the top, though for real drama the Straits of Riggindale and Kidsty Pike nearby have far more to offer. The approaches from the north (i.e. starting from Martindale or Burnbanks) are long and can be rather tedious.

From Patterdale via Side Farm, Boredale Hause, Angle Tarn, Satura Crag, The Knott, Rampsgill Head:
        Ascent 652 m = 2139 ft   *Distance 7.8 km = 4.8 miles*

From Martindale Old Church via Brownthwaite Crag, Keasgill Head, Raven Howe:
        Ascent 602 m = 1975 ft   *Distance 6.1 km =3.8 miles*

From Burnbanks via The Forces (waterfalls), Old Boundary Stone on Bampton Common, Keasgill Head, Raven Howe: *Ascent 587 m = 1926 ft*   *Distance 8.6 km = 5.3 miles*

High Raise (above Haweswater)(continued)

From the car park at Mardale Head via The Rigg, Kidsty Howes and Kidsty Pike:

      Ascent 550 m = 1804 ft   *Distance 5.6 km =3.5 miles*

From the car park at Mardale Head via The Rigg, Randale Beck, top of Whelter Crag, Low Raise:

      Ascent 550 m = 1804 ft   *Distance 5.7 km = 3.5 miles*

From Hartsop Village via Hayeswater Gill and The Knott:

      Ascent 632 m = 2073 ft   *Distance 4.8 km =3 miles*

Adjacent Fells:	*Kidsty Pike*	*Height*	*780 m = 2559 ft*	*Distance 1.2 km = 0.75 miles*
	The Knott		*739 m = 2424 ft*	*1.8 km = 1.1 miles*
	Wether Hill		*670 m = 2198 ft*	*3.5 km = 2.2 miles*
	High Street		*828 m = 2716 ft*	*2.9 km = 1.8 miles*
	Rampsgill Head		*792 m = 2598 ft*	*1 km = 0.6 miles*

High Raise (above Langstrath)

Height 762 m = 2499 ft   **NY281095**   **Rank 57**

The rounded grassy dome of High Raise limits the quality of the view from the summit, however it is an airy place with a backdrop of mountains in all directions. The routes to the summit from Borrowdale, Grasmere and Langdale will be found to be much more dramatic and interesting than the summit dome itself.

From the New Dungeon Ghyll Hotel via Stickle Gill Stickle Tarn and Bright Beck:

      Ascent 670 m = 2198 ft   *Distance 4.8 km = 3 miles*

From Grasmere, take the Easedale road west from the centre of the village (opposite the bookshop). At Easedale House turn right and follow the path up Far Easdale towards Borrowdale. On reaching Greenup Edge turn left up the ridge to the summit:

      Ascent 662 m = 2172 ft   *Distance 9.6 km = 6 miles*

From Stonethwaite in Borrowdale follow the path up Greenup Gill, towards Grasmere, as far as Greenup Edge. Turn right at the edge and follow the ridge up to the summit:

      Ascent 662 m = 2172 ft   *Distance 6.4 km = 4 miles*

Adjacent Fells:	*Ullscarf Height*	*726 m = 2382 ft*	*3.8 km = 2.4 miles*
	Harrison Stickle	*736 m = 2414 ft*	*2.6 km = 1.7 miles*
	Pike O' Stickle	*709 m = 2326 ft*	*3 km = 2 miles*

High Rigg

Height 354 m = 1161 ft   **NY309220**   **Rank 231**

High Rigg and Low Rigg constitute the lenticular mass which separates the Naddle Valley and St. John's in the Vale. Low Rigg is essentially rough pasture land whereas High Rigg is a complex mix of outcrops, hollows, crags and rough gills. There are few paths and exploration can be fun. Rising up the east flank of Low Rigg is a road which terminates at the Youth Centre and little church of St. John's in the Vale (although a rough track continues across towards the Keswick-Ambleside road). From the church the ascent to the summit cairn is a short and easy walk. A much rougher but more interesting route is from Dale Bottom Farm and involves a scramble up William's Beck. There are many ways up this complex mound, as hard or as easy as you wish to make them. Good views from the top.

From the church of St. John's in the Vale:

      Ascent 136 m = 446 ft   *Distance 0.6 km = 0.4 miles*

From Dale Bottom Farm on the A591 via William's Beck:

      Ascent 194 m = 636 ft   *Distance 1.7 km = 1.1 miles*

A - Z Guide to the Fells

High Seat

Height 608 m = 1994 ft   NY287180   **Rank 134**

The lower slopes of the fell are pleasant enough but the upper ones are boggy and thoroughly unpleasant underfoot. The superb views from the top may prove adequate compensation for wet feet.

From Ashness Bridge via Barrow Beck and Ashness Gill:
          Ascent 453 m = 1486 ft   *Distance 2.7 km = 1.7 miles*
From Watendlath via High Tove:
          Ascent 348 m = 1142 ft   *Distance 3.1 km = 1.9 miles*
From Armboth (car park) via High Tove:
          Ascent 413 m = 1355 ft   *Distance 3.3 km = 2.1 miles*

Adjacent Fells:	*High Tove*	*Height*	*515 m = 1689 ft*	*Distance 1.6 km = 1 mile*
	Bleaberry Fell		*590 m = 1935 ft*	*1.6 km = 1 mile*

High Spy

Height 653 m = 2142 ft   NY234162   **Rank 116**

The summit of High Spy is usually surmounted by those going to or from Dalehead Tarn via Maiden Moor and Cat Bells. The ground immediately west of the summit is steep and dangerous and should be avoided. Good views are to be had in all directions, particularly those of the Newlands valley, with the Causey Pike Ridge beyond.

From Grange straight up the hill overlooking Grange (avoiding the crags):
          Ascent 573 m = 1880 ft   *Distance 2.8 km = 1.8 miles*
From Grange via The Hollows and Riggindale Slate Quarrie:
          Ascent 573 m = 1880 ft   *Distance 4.7 km = 2.9 miles*
From Chapel Bridge near Little Town and along the Newlands valley via Dale Head Tarn:
          Ascent 513 m = 1683 ft   *Distance 5.3 km = 3.3 miles*

Adjacent Fells:	*Maiden Moor*	*Height*	*576 m = 1889 ft*	*Distance 2 km = 1.2 miles*
	Dale Head		*753 m = 2470 ft*	*2 km = 1.2 miles*

High Stile

Height 807 m = 2647 ft   NY170148   **Rank 29**

To see High Stile from Buttermere is to see one of the finest of all Lakeland views. The north side of the mountain is magnificent whereas the south side, though steep and rocky in places is essentially just a steep slope. The views from the top are magnificent. A straightforward approach is along the ridge from Red Pike and High Crag. It is, however, possible to make a direct ascent from the valley embracing Bleaberry Tarn or from Burtness Comb via the north side of Grey Crag. These latter routes are patchy and involve some rough scrambling. Though not difficult they will not be to everybody's taste.

From Buttermere via Bleaberry Tarn, the Dodd and Red Pike:
          Ascent 695 m = 2280 ft   *Distance 4.3 km = 2.7 miles*
From Buttermere via Bleaberry Tarn and up the east end of Chapel Crags:
          Ascent 695 m = 2280 ft   *Distance 3 km = 1.9 miles*
From Buttermere via Comb Beck, Burtness Comb and the north end of Grey Crag:
          Ascent 695 m = 2280 ft   *Distance 3.8 km = 1.9 miles*
From Gatesgarth Farm via Comb Beck, Burtness Comb and the north end of Grey Crag:
          Ascent 690 m = 2264 ft   *Distance 3.2 km = 2 miles*
From Gatesgarth Farm via Scarth Gap and High Crag:
          Ascent 690 m = 2264 ft   *Distance 4.9 km = 3 miles*

Adjacent Fells:	*Red Pike*	*Height*	*755 m = 2477 ft*	*Distance 1.3 km = 0.8 miles*
	High Crag		*744 m = 2440 ft*	*1.5 km = 0.9 miles*

High Street (Racecourse Hill)

Height 828 m = 2716 ft   NY441110   **Rank 25**

The west side of the fell is just a steep hill above Hayeswater Gill and the top is broad, flat and nothing special at all. The east side, however, is magnificent, offering some of the best walks in the Lake District. There are two classic approaches. One is the 3 km (2 mile) ridge starting from the Rigg on the edge of Haweswater. The second is the path to Smallwater, then up to Nan Bield Pass and Mardale Ill Bell. The first route is especially good, the ridge getting progressively more narrow as it gets higher and the views down into Riggindale are truly memorable. Excellent views from the beacon on the summit. Warning ! the crags on the east side above Blea Water are precipitate and, when descending in mist, the top of the narrow ridge of Long Stile can be difficult to find. Look for the cairns.

From the car park at Mardale Head follow the lakeside footpath to the foot of the long ridge (the Rigg), then left and up the ridge and onwards towards the summit:
        Ascent 576 m = 1890 ft   *Distance 4.6 km = 2.9 miles*
From the car park at Mardale Head along the path to Blea Water, up on to the ridge at Caspel Gate, then straight along the ridge and onwards towards the summit:
        Ascent 576 m = 1890 ft   *Distance 3.7 km = 2.3 miles*
From the car park at Mardale Head up to Smallwater thence up to Nan Bield Pass and across to Mardale Ill Bell: *Ascent 576 m = 1890 ft*   *Distance 4.6 km = 2.9 miles*
From the car park at Mardale Head up to Smallwater, thence up the ridge bounding the north side of Smallwater straight to the top of Mardale Ill Bell:
        Ascent 576 m =1890 ft   *Distance 3.8 km = 2.4 miles*
From Hartsop Village via Hayeswater Gill, then up to the Knott along to the Straits of Riggindale, thence to the top: *Ascent 658 m = 2159 ft*   *Dsitance 5.3 km = 3.3 miles*
From Kentmere Village via Overend then follow the path over Tongue Scar to Smallthwaite Knott and Nan Bield Pass. Then on to Mardale Ill Bell and the summit:

	Ascent 658 m = 2159 ft			*Distance 8.6 km = 5.3 miles*
Adjacent Fells:	*Kidsty Pike*	*Height*	*780 m = 2559 ft*	*Distance 2.1 km = 1.3 miles*
	Mardale Ill Bell		*761 m = 2496 ft*	*1.2 km = 0.7 miles*
	The Knott		*739 m = 2424 ft*	*Distance 1.6 km = 1 mile*
	Rampsgill Head		*792 m = 2598 ft*	*2.1 km = 1.3 miles*
	Thornthwaite Crag		*784 m = 2572 ft*	*1.6 km = 1 mile*
	Froswick		*720 m = 2362 ft*	*2.7 km = 1.7 miles*

High Tove

Height 515 m = 1689 ft   NY289165   **Rank 175**

A flat boggy top. The only thing to be claimed in its favour are some good views, particularly over the Derwent Fells. The Watendlath to Armboth path passes over the top.

From Armboth: Ascent 320 m = 1050 ft   *Distance 1.6 km = 1 mile*
From Watendlath:

	Ascent 255 m = 837 ft			*Distance 1.5 km = 0.9 miles*
Adjacent Fells:	*High Seat*	*Height*	*608 m = 1994 ft*	*Distance 1.6 km = 1 mile*
	Armboth Fell		*479 m =1571 ft*	*1.4 km = 0.9 miles*
	Ullscarf		*726 m = 2381 ft*	*5 km = 3.1 miles*

Hindscarth

Height 727 m = 2385 ft   NY216165   **Rank 75**

One usually only crosses the summit of Hindscarth if coming up or down the ridge to Scope End. This ridge is excellent walking with some very dramatic views across the Newlands Valley - strongly recommended. There are good views from the summit in all directions. The old mine at Scope End is called Goldscope Mine and

Hindscarth (continued)

was worked from Elizabethan times on and off until the early 1920's. The minerals sought were lead and copper.

From Chapel Bridge near Little Town:

	Ascent 587 m = 1926 ft			*Distance 4.2 km = 2.6 miles*	
Adjacent Fells:	*Dale Head*	*Height*	*753 m = 2470 ft*	*Distance 1.6 km = 1 mile*	
	Robinson		*737 m = 2417 ft*	*2.8 km = 1.7 miles*	

Hollow Moor

Height 426 m = 1397 ft   **NY469040**   **Rank 212**

Hollow Moor is the rough pasture hill which overlooks Kentmere. The terrain to the south of the summit is boggy with tufted grass, making walking difficult, and the area is crossed with walls and fences. The only reason for visiting it is the magnificent view it provides of the Kentmere valley. There are two routes up, one short, steep and relatively dry, the other longer and more gentle, but boggy and difficult in the latter stages.

From Kentmere Church (parking for about 10 cars). Follow the road back to Low Bridge and turn left up the fine leafy lane leading to Green Quarter. The road walk can be shortened somewhat by taking the second public footpath on the right which follow Kill Gill. At the road junction (signposted) take the track east marked 'Public footpath to Longsleddale,' which follows Nunnery Gill. After passing beyond the buildings and through the gate, turn right up the hill for the summit, passing through the gate in the wall when you reach the top of the field: *Ascent 260 m = 853 ft*   *Distance 2 km = 1.3 miles*

From Kentmere Church follow the road back to Low Bridge and turn up the lane towards Green Quarter. Take the first footpath on the right (steps set into wall) across the field, through two gates to Lowfield Lane. Turn left and walk back a few yards to the gate signposted 'Bridle Path to Longsleddale via Cocklaw Fell.' Follow this track, through many gates, to Skeggles Water. Turn left up the hill for the summit (difficult terrain):   *Ascent 260 m = 853 ft*   *Distance 2.8 km = 1.7 miles*

Holme Fell

Height 317 m = 1040 ft   **NY315 006**   **Rank 239**

This craggy little mountain perched at the head of Yewdale has much to offer. One can combine a woodland walk with an open summit and see relics of an industrial past. The giant Hodge Close slate quarries scar its northern slope and around its summit are several reservoirs used in the past to supply water for the slate workings. The summit of Holme Fell is said to be the best vantage point for viewing the whole length of Coniston Water. Parking near the road is difficult in this area, but there is ample parking at the old Hodge Close quarries. Follow the road from High Yewdale, signposted Hodge Close only, over Shepherd Bridge and up through the woods until it emerges on the open quarry site.

From Hodge Close quarry (ample parking, see above), take the old quarry road which starts at the south end of the giant hole containing the lagoon. Pass through two gates and continue along the track which follows the drystone wall on the right. About 20 m (66 ft) before the third gate take the well worn track which leads off to the left up the fell. Follow this track until it emerges from the wood and continue up to the summit: *Ascent 147 m = 482 ft*   *Distance 1.4 km = 0.9 miles*

Hopegill Head

Height 770 m = 2526 ft   **NY186222**   **Rank 54**

Whilst usually not the sole object of a walk, Hopegill Head summit has a number of interesting features. Immediately to the east of the summit is the steep and shattered face of Hobcarton Crag. There is a direct route to the top of the crag from the valley floor, but it will be too rough and steep for the majority of walkers. Immediately to the north of the summit is a fairly steep slope of crumbling slate slabs. To the west is

Hopegill Head (continued)

the delightful narrow ridge leading to Whiteside and in the opposite direction is the path to Grisedale Pike. There are very good views from the top.

From Hope Farm and up Hope Gill:
        Ascent 605 m = 1985 ft   *Distance 3.2 km = 2 miles*

From the fellwalkers car park in Swinside Plantation along the forest track to the ridge leading up to Ladyside Pike (add another 2000 m = 1.2 miles if you start at Whinlatter Visitor Centre):
        Ascent 517 m = 1696 ft   *Distance 3.7 km = 2.3 miles*

From Lanthwaite Green via Gasgale Gill and Coledale Hause:
        Ascent 613 m = 2011 ft   *Distance 4.4 km = 2.7 miles*

From Braithwaite via Coledale and Coledale Hause:
        Ascent 665 m = 2182 ft   *Distance 6.2 km = 3.9 miles*

Adjacent Fells:	*Whiteside*	*Height*	*719 m = 2358 ft*	*Distance 1.3 km = 0.8 miles*
	Grisedale Pike		*791 m = 2595 ft*	*1.7 km = 1.1 miles*
	Ladyside Pike		*703 m = 2306 ft*	*0.6 km = 0.4 miles*

Ill Bell

Height 757 m = 2483 ft   **NY436077**   **Rank 61**

Ill Bell is the middle summit on the steep-sided ridge linking Yoke in the south to Froswick in the north. The east side of the fell is precipitous and the views down into the Kentmere valley are superb. Some excellent long distance views can be had from the summit. Usually the top will be approached via the ridge (see Froswick and Yoke), but it is possible to make direct ascents. These are listed below.

From Hagg Bridge along the track up Hagg Gill to the ford, then up the zig-zag path to the old quarry in the west side of the mountain. Continue upwards and join the ridge mid-way between Yoke and Ill Bell:
        Ascent 627 m = 2057 ft   *Distance 2.5 km = 1.6 miles*

From the north end of Kentmere Reservoir, follow the north east ridge to the top (steep but not difficult in good weather):   *Ascent 457 m = 1500 ft*   *Distance 1.2 km = 0.8 miles*

Adjacent Fells:	*Froswick*	*Height*	*720 m = 2362 ft*	*1 km = 0.6 miles*
	Yoke		*706 m = 2316 ft*	*1.1 km = 0.7 miles*

Illgill Head

Height 609 m = 1998 ft   **NY169049**   **Rank 133**

Illgill Head is better known as Wastwater Screes and is the ideal platform for viewing Wasdale Head. The summit is smooth and grassy, dropping away gently to the southeast into the high valley containing Burnmoor Tarn. To the northwest, however, the summit ridge plunges precipitiously down the famous screes into the lake. Extensive views in all directions.

From Brackenclose at the head of the lake (parking) up through Fence Wood on the old corpse road to the col. Then turn right and follow the ridge up to the summit:
        Ascent 544 m = 1785 ft   *Distance 5 km = 3.2 miles*

From Boot along the old corpse road, past Burnmoor Tarn to the col, then turn left and up the ridge to the summit: *Ascent 549 m =1801 ft*   *Distance 8.4 km = 5.3 miles*

Adjacent Fells:	*Whin Rigg*	*Height*	*535 m = 1755 ft*	*Distance 2 km = 1.3 miles*
	Boat How		*337 m = 1105 ft*	*2.3 km =1.4 miles*
	Sca Fell		*964 m = 3162 ft*	*5.5 km = 3.5 miles*

A - Z Guide to the Fells

Kelton Fell

Height 311 m = 1020 ft   NY095181   **Rank 242**

The main attraction of this little hill is its industrial past. Kelton Fell is on the site of the old Kelton and Knockmurton Iron mines and is littered with old workings, levels and spoil heaps. This is not a very scenic place unless you are a mining history enthusiast.

From the road at Cross Rigg (parking for two cars), straight up the west ridge to the summit:
> Ascent 57 m = 187 ft   *Distance 1.1 km = 0.7 miles*

Adjacent Fell: *Knock Murton Fell*   *Height 447 m = 1466 ft Distance 1.5 km = 0.9 miles*

Kentmere Pike

Height 730 m = 2394 ft   NY465078   **Rank 73**

The east side falls precipitously into Longsleddale whereas the west side, though steep and craggy, is nothing like as dramatic. The top itself is fairly broad and lacking in interest. Reasonable views to the west but nothing much to the east.

From Kentmere village follow the path rising above Hallow Bank to Withered How and beyond:
> Ascent 560 m = 1837 ft   *Distance 4.4 km = 2.7 miles*

From Sadgill follow the path up below Sadgill Wood. At the 350 m contour (1150 ft) turn north of the main path up to Wray Crag, then Shipman Knotts:
> Ascent 532 m = 1745 ft   *Distance 4.6 km = 2.9 miles*

Adjacent Fells: *Harker Fell*   *Height   778 m = 2552 ft*   *Distance   2 km = 1.2 miles*
                     Shipman Knotts   *587 m = 1925 ft*   *1.7 km = 1.1 miles*

Kidsty Pike

Height 780 m = 2559 ft   NY447126   **Rank 47**

The approach from the car park at Mardale Head via Bowderthwaite Bridge and Kidsty Howes is excellent and gives magnificent views across Riggindale to the rocky and steep sided ridge leading up to High Street from The Rigg. The approach from the west is relatively poor. If starting from Mardale Head a good circular walk is to include the east ridge of High Street. See **The Knott** for western approaches.

From Mardale Head via The Rigg, Bowderthwaite Bridge and Kidsty Howes:
> Ascent 528 m = 1732 ft   *Distance 4.2 km = 2.6 miles*

From Mardale Head via the long east ridge to the top of High Street (i.e. Swine Crag to Long Stile):
> Ascent 528 m = 1732 ft   *Distance 6.2 km = 3.9 miles*

Adjacent Fells: *High Street*   *Height   828 m = 2716 ft*   *Distance 2.1 km = 1.3 miles*
                     High Raise   *802 m = 2631 ft*   *1.2 km = 0.8 miles*
                     The Knott   *739 m = 2424 ft*   *1.1 km = 0.7 miles*
                     Rampsgill Head   *792 m = 2598 ft*   *0.7 km = 0.4 miles*

Kirk Fell

Height 802 m = 2631 ft   NY195105   **Rank 33**

With Pillar to the west and Great Gable to the east nobody takes much notice of Kirk Fell, unless it is crossed over to get from one to the other. The Gable side is rocky but easy walking. The side above Black Sail Pass (Kirk Fell Crags) is steep and, on descending this for the first time, one would think that the route is going to become impossibly steep (it doesn't but care is needed in places). The top of Kirk Fell is fairly flat and unremarkable, although the views are good.

From the Wasdale Head Hotel, up the east side of Mosedale Beck to Black Sail Pass, then up by Kirkfell Crags: Ascent 722 m = 2368 ft   *Distance 4.5 km = 2.8 miles*

Kirk Fell (continued)

From the Wasdale Head Hotel along Mose's Trod (a path) up to Beck Head, then to Kirkfell Top:

	Ascent 722 m = 2368 ft			*Distance 4.1 km = 2.5 miles*
Adjacent Fells:	*Pillar*	*Height*	*892 m = 2926 ft*	*Distance 3.6 km = 2.2 miles*
	Great Gable		*899 m = 2949 ft*	*2.3 km = 1.4 miles*
	Green Gable		*801 m = 2627 ft*	*2.6 km = 1.6 miles*
	Brandreth		*715 m = 2345 ft*	*3.2 km = 2 miles*
				(crossing below Gable Crag)

Knott

Height 710 m = 2329 ft   **NY296330**   **Rank 85**

Knott is a great sprawling heather covered hill. There are good long distance views to the Solway, but otherwise the outlook is rather dreary. There are some interesting ravines which one can include in the journey and these can make the trip worthwhile. These ravines are Roughton Gill (note the old mine workings), Frozen Fell Gill, Trusmadoor and Charleton Gill.

From Longlands via Trusmadoor and Frozen Fell Gill:

> *Ascent 498 m = 1634 ft*   *Distance 4.7 km = 2.9 miles*

From Greenhead via Holborn and Charleton Wath ford, along the west side of Charleton Gill to Little Sca Fell, then Great Sca Fell:

> *Ascent 465 m = 1526 ft*   *Distance 5.7 km = 3.5 miles*

From Fell Side along Dale Beck and up the Roughton Gill ravine:

> *Ascent 430 m = 1411 ft*   *Distance 5.1 km = 3.2 miles*

From Carrock Tungsten Mine via Coomb Height:

	Ascent 420 m = 1378 ft			*Distance 3.2 km = 2 miles*
Adjacent Fells:	*Great Calva*	*Height*	*690 m = 2263 ft*	*Distance 2.7 km = 1.7 miles*
	Great Sca Fell		*651 m = 2135 ft*	*1 km = 0.6 miles*
	Brae Fell		*586 m = 1922 ft*	*2.3 km = 1.4 miles*
	High Pike		*658 m = 2158 ft*	*3.1 km = 1.9 miles*
	Meal Fell		*550 m = 1804 ft*	*1.7 km = 1.1 miles*

Knott Rigg

Height 556 m = 1824 ft   **NY197189**   **Rank 151**

This can be considered as a subsidiary summit to Ard Crags. The comments on the latter apply to this fell.

From Newlands Hause (parking here):

	Ascent 223 m = 732 ft	*Distance 1.2 km = 0.7 miles*

From Keskadale: Ascent 306 m = 1004 ft   *Distance 1.6 km = 1 mile*

> *(A rather more demanding variant of this walk is to go up Ill Gill, the distance is much the same)*

Adjacent Fell: Ard Crags   Height   581 m = 1906 ft   Distance 1.4 km = 0.9 miles

Ladyside Pike

Height 703 m = 2306 ft   **NY185227**   **Rank 89**

Quite unremarkable. Hopegill Head is only 600 m (0.4 miles) away and 67 m (220 ft) higher. See Hopegill Head.

Lank Rigg

Height 541 m = 1774 ft   **NY092120**   **Rank 159**

Isolated, lonely, bleak, there is not much reason to recommend a special visit here. Other than long distance views across West Cumbria there is not much of interest to see from the top.

Lank Rigg (continued)

From the car park at Bleach Green at the west end of Ennerdale, up by the side of Ben Gill and along the track over Revelin Crag and Crag Fell. From Crag Fell top drop down through the wood, then leave the track and bear right up to Whoap, then on to Lank Rigg:

Ascent 421 m = 1381 ft	*Distance 5.7 km = 3.5 miles*

From the road by Castley Hill, across the ford just south of Monk's Bridge, then either straight up the hill to the top (or the leisurely route, which takes you along Worm Gill, then up by Hope Gill):

Ascent 321 m = 1053 ft	*Distance 4.1 km = 2.5 miles*
	(long route 7.2 km = 4.5 miles)

From the road along the path between Blakeley Rise and Burn Edge, up the valley by the side of Whoap Beck and around the top to Lank Rigg:

Ascent 251 m = 823 ft		*Distance 4 km = 2.5 miles*	
Adjacent Fells: Whoap	*Height 511 m = 1676 ft*	*1.2 km = 0.7 miles*	

Latrigg

Height 368 m = 1207 ft   NY279247   **Rank 227**

If you don't like walking but would like to get to the top of a fell which has magnificent views, then Latrigg is for you. The road up from Applethwaite will take you to within 600 m (0.4 mile) of the top with a foot climb over easy grass of only 173 m (568 ft). There are harder ways of getting to the top, see below:

From Threlkeld (the shop) along the disused railway line path towards Keswick. Eventually leave this route for the path to Brundholme, then up onto the ridge and hence to the top:

Ascent 208 m = 682 ft		*Distance 4.9 km = 3 miles*	
Adjacent Fells: Skiddaw Little Man	*Height 865 m = 2837 ft*	*3.7 km = 2.3 miles*	
Skiddaw	*931 m = 3054 ft*	*5.3 km = 3.3 miles*	
Lonscale Fell	*715 m =2345 ft*	*3.7 km = 2.3 miles*	

Latterbarrow

Height 244 m = 800 ft   SD367991   **Rank 246**

This small bare topped hill in the midst of forest is a fine viewpoint for the surrounding area and the more distant hills. Latterbarrow is owned by the National Trust and is served by several good paths.

From just north of the Loanthwaite Lane Junction on the road from Sawrey to Wray (parking for one car only just past the gate giving access to the fell). A signposted path leads straight up the fell. At the junction take either path, although the left fork is the more direct, shorter and steeper route:

Ascent 124 m = 407 ft	*Distance 0.6 km = 0.4 miles*

Ling Fell

Height 373 m = 1223 ft   NY180286   **Rank 226**

Ling Fell is, visually, not particularly attractive, nor is it on the route to any hill. It lies in a very quiet part of the Lake District, so you don't find many people climbing it. It is rather a trudge to the top but the views are good. There are many ways to the top. One possibility is set out below.

From Wythop Mill to Burthwaite, then straight up the side to the top:

Ascent 275 m = 902 ft	*Distance 2.1 km = 1.3 miles*

Lingmell

Height 807 m = 2647 ft   NY209082   **Rank 29**

The north and east sides of the mountain provide a truly impressive spectacle of crag and scree. In particular there is the magnificent L - shaped ravine of Piers Gill on the east side. There is a path alongside the south side of Piers Gill (the bottom of the gill is impossible) and from this, or the Corridor Route the fell is seen at its

Lingmell (continued)

its most magnificent. A high level saddle, Lingmell Col, connects the summit to the summit of Scafell Pike. Accordingly most people tend to take in Lingmell on the way to or from the Pike. The other sides of the fell are essentially grass dotted with scree and displaying rocky outcrops here and there. The views from the summit are magnificent.

From Seathwaite via Stockley Bridge, Styhead Gill, Styhead Tarn, Spout Head and along the Corridor Route:
       Ascent 682 m = 2238 ft   *Distance 6.7 km = 4.2 miles*
Note: if instead of taking the Corridor Route one continues to the foot of Piers Gill, then up by the side of the Gill, the total distance is the same. Instead of going to Stockley Bridge, the more adventurous walker may like to take the path alongside Taylor Gill Force Waterfall.
From the Wasdale Head Hotel, along Lingmell Beck, then turn south at the 250 m (820 ft) contour and follow the path alongside Piers Gill to Lingmell Col:
       Ascent 729 m = 2392 ft   *Distance 5.3 km = 3.3 miles*
From the Wasdale Head Hotel take the road, then the footpath across to Lingmell Gill, then northeast following the path to the top:
       Ascent 729 m = 2392 ft   *Distance 4.3 km = 2.7 miles*
Adjacent Fells: *Scafell Pike*   *Height   978 m = 3208 ft*   *Distance 1.3 km = 0.8 miles*

Lingmoor Fell

Height 469 m = 1538 ft   **NY302 046**   **Rank 197**

Lingmoor Fell is the crescent shaped ridge which separates Little Langdale from Great Langdale. It is a varied hill with woods, crags, heather slopes and many scars from past quarrying activity. Its central position makes it a fine vantage point to view its loftier surrounding neighbours. Excellent views in all directions.

From Bleatarn House on the road between Great and Little Langdale (parking). Follow the path up by the wall to Brown Howes , then left for the summit:
       Ascent 269 m = 883 ft   *Distance 1.8 km = 1.1 miles*
From Elterwater along the white road from the hotel past Elterwater Hall, then along the old quarry road to Bank Quarry. Take the path which leads up the hillside from the right hand side of the quarry as far as the summit ridge, then turn right for the summit cairn:
       Ascent 399 m = 1309 ft   *Distance 3.4 km = 2.1 miles*
Adjacent Fell: *Pike O' Blisco*   *Height 705 m = 2312 ft*   *Distance 4.3 km = 2.7 miles*

Little Hart Crag

Height 637 m = 2089 ft   **NY387100**   **Rank 123**

Little Hart Crag lies approximately midway between the higher hills of Dove Crag and Red Screes on a broad connecting ridge. The north side is precipitous and to the east it is still very steep. The ground to the south (Scandale Fell) lacks interest. The summit consists of two rocky nobbles and offers restricted but good views.

From Cow Bridge via Caiston Glen and Scandale Pass:
       Ascent 479 m = 1572 ft   *Distance 5.2 km = 3.2 miles*
Note: it is possible to reduce the length of the route quite considerably by starting from the bottom of the Kirkstone Pass. However, if you have a car to park this could be difficult.
From Cow Bridge via Dovedale and Hoggett Gill. This is a steep, more demanding, though more interesting, route than the above:
       Ascent 479 m = 1572 ft   *Distance 4.7 km = 2.9 miles*
From Ambleside via Scandale Beck and Scandale Bottom:
       Ascent 537 m = 1762 ft   *Distance 5.7 km = 3.5 miles*
                   (easy but lacking in interest)

Little Hart Crag (continued)

From Cow Bridge via High Hartsop Dodd (steep):

	Ascent 479 m = 1572 ft		*Distance 3.8 km = 2.4 miles*
Adjacent Fells:	*High Hartsop Dodd*	*Height 519 m = 1702 ft*	*0.8 km = 0.5 miles*
	Dove Crag	*792 m = 2598 ft*	*1.6 km = 1 miles*
	Red Screes	*776 m = 2545 ft*	*1.9 km = 1.2 miles*

Little Mell Fell

Height 505 m = 1656 ft   NY423240   **Rank 182**

Like Great Mell Fell, its neighbour, this is an unfrequented and isolated hill. Unlike the former, however, it is drab and uninviting. Most of it is enclosed land, a landscape of boggy fields, muddy tracks and barbed wire fences. There are only two easy access points, a footpath starting by the covered reservoir at The Hause and another starting from a cluster of houses in the valley bottom at Lowthwaite.

From The Hause: *Ascent 135 m = 443 ft*   *Distance 0.5 km = 0.3 miles*
From Lowthwaite: *Ascent 205 m = 673 ft*   *Distance   1km = 0.6 miles*

Loadpot Hill

Height 671 m = 2201 ft   NY457181   **Rank 104**

At Loadpot Hill the ridge carrying the Roman Road High Street, which is so well defined further south, has widened into a sprawling hill. The west side above Fusedale is steep and rough in places, but the east is mainly easy gradients, almost indiscernibly merging into farmland. This is an unfrequented place. Good long distance views to be had from the summit.

From Howtown. Get onto the path that starts at Mellguards and rises diagonally up the fell side to Brock Crag: *Ascent 491 m = 1611 ft*   *Distance 2.2 km = 1.4 miles*
From Howtown, along the valley then up by the side of Dodd Gill:
        Ascent 521 m = 1709 ft   *Distance 3.2 km = 2 miles*
From Cockle Hill (above Heltondale Beck) a path leaves the unenclosed road some 75 m north of Rough Hill Tarn: *Ascent 355 m = 1165 ft*   *Distance 4.6 km = 2.9 miles*
See also Arthur's Pike and Wether Hill for other routes

Adjacent Fells:	*Arthur's Pike*	*Height 532 m = 1745 ft*	*Distance 2.6 km = 1.6 miles*
	Wether Hill	*670 m = 2198 ft*	*1.5 km = 0.9 miles*
	Bonscale Pike	*524 m = 1719 ft*	*2.1 km = 1.3 miles*

Loft Crag

Height 670 m = 2198 ft   NY277072   **Rank 105**

A prominent but minor peak on the ridge descending from Pike O' Stickle to Dungeon Ghyll. See Pike O' Stickle for route.

Adjacent Fells	*Pike O' Stickle*	*Height 709 m = 2326 ft*	*Distance 1 km = 0.6 miles*
	Harrison Stickle	*736 m = 2414 ft*	*0.8 km =0.5 miles*

Long Side

Height 734 m = 2408 ft   NY248284   **Rank 72**

See Ullock Pike (which is only 0.3 miles distant) and Skiddaw

Longlands Fell

Height 483 m = 1584 ft   NY276354   **Rank 191**

A grassy hill that is usually by-passed by walkers heading for Knott, Brae Fell or one of the larger hills. There are good views across to the Solway, but the low height of the fell limits the view to the south. Very easy walking.

From Longlands: Ascent 271 m = 889 ft   *Distance 1.2 km = 0.7 miles*
Adjacent Fells: Knott   Height   710 m = 2329 ft   *Distance 3.4 km = 2.1 miles*
*   Great Sca Fell   651 m = 2135 ft*   *2.5 km = 1.6 miles*

Lonscale Fell

Height 715 m = 2345 ft   NY285272   **Rank 82**

The east side of this fell is magnificent, steep crags down to Glenderaterra Beck. All other sides lack interest, just being part of the huge base of Skiddaw. It is possible to scramble up the crags in a number of places but, if this is not to your taste, you can climb up the grassy slope above Lonscale or up the Glenderaterra valley for about one and a half miles and up by Brunt Horse. The lazy way up is from the end of the road above Applethwaite (near the top of Latrigg). This route, however, lacks interest. Access to the Glenderaterra valley can be gained by driving to Threlkeld or, nearer still, the Blencathra Centre. Alternatively why not walk the old railway line or the forest track through Brundholme Wood (This will add approximately two and a half miles to the distances from the Blencathra Centre).

From the end of the road above Applethwaite (near the top of Latrigg) and straight up:
*   Ascent 420 m = 1378 ft*   *Distance 2.7 km = 1.7 miles*
From the Blencathra Centre across the river and up the crags (don't descend this way):
*   Ascent 425 m = 1394 ft*   *Distance 3.2 km = 2 miles*
From the Blencathra Centre across the river and up the grassy slope above Lonscale:
*   Ascent 425 m = 1394 ft*   *Distance 2.7 km = 1.7 miles*
From the Blencathra Centre along the river, cross over to Brunt Horse, then up:
*   Ascent 425 m = 1394 ft*   *Distance 4.7 km = 2.9 miles*
Adjacent Fells: Skiddaw Little Man   Height 865 m = 2837 ft Distance   2 km = 1.2 miles
*   Blencathra   868 m = 2847 ft   4.5 km = 2.8 miles*

Lord's Seat

Height 552 m = 1811 ft   NY204266   **Rank 153**

An easy climb from the Wythop Valley because you will already have gained most of your height. From most other directions the walking is steep and meandering, the latter due to the presence of woods. The most direct and probably the best route is from opposite the Swan Hotel (on the old Keswick/Cockermouth road) and up the south side of Beckstones Gill (You don't have to take in the top of Barf, but it will be worth it if you do). Lords Seat is just a steep grassy hill but there are some excellent views from the top. A place of peace and solitude.

From Wythop Hall and straight up the Hagg Beck Valley to the top:
*   Ascent 342 m = 1122 ft*   *Distance 2.2 km = 1.4 miles*
From opposite the Swan Hotel on the Keswick/Cockermouth old road and up by the south side of Beckstones
Gill: Ascent 453 m = 1486 ft   *Distance 1.8 km = 1.1 miles*
From near Scawgill Bridge via Darling How and then across the upper reaches of the forest:
*   Ascent 329 m = 1079 ft*   *Distance 3.1 km = 1.9 miles*
From the Whinlatter Visitor Centre and up through the forest:
*   Ascent 227 m = 745 ft*   *Distance 2.6 km = 1.6 miles*
Adjacent Fells: Barf   Height   468 m = 1535 ft   *Distance 1.1 km = 0.7 miles*
*   Brown Fell   511 m = 1676 ft*   *1.2 km = 0.7 miles*

A - Z Guide to the Fells

Loughrigg Fell

Height 335 m = 1099 ft   NY347051   **Rank 235**

Loughrigg is well known for the scenic view of Grasmere and Dunmail from the terrace above the lake; which forms part of the footpath from Ambleside to Grasmere. Its summit is less well frequented and consists of many confusing humps, making it quite difficult at times to find the true summit. Once there the view in all directions is excellent. The fell is criss-crossed by many paths and there are many different ways up. Only two will be described here.

From Grasmere (parking at a price) follow the Red Bank road round the lake towards Elterwater. Climb Red Bank as far as the Loughrigg Terrace path, go through the gate and follow the path through the wood. On emerging at the open terrace turn right and follow the path straight up the hill to the summit:
            Ascent 270 m = 886 ft   *Distance 3.8 km = 2.4 miles*

From Rothay Park, Ambleside. Walk through the park, over the bridge onto the back road towards Rydal. After crossing the cattle grid turn left on the farm track up past Browhead Farm and on to the open fell. At the Lily Tarn take the path that leads up to the summit ridge:
            Ascent 285 m = 935 ft   *Distance 4 km = 2.5 miles*

Low Fell

Height 423 m = 1387 ft   NY 136223   **Rank 214**

The main reasons for climbing Low Fell are that it is unfrequented and the excellent view down Crummock Water to Rannerdale Knotts and the fells around.

From the road (about halfway along Loweswater) up the track and then on to the open fell. Go via Darling Fell top: *Ascent 299 m = 981 ft*   *Distance 2.2 km = 1.4 miles*

From Foulsyke via Whinny Ridding and Pottergill:
            Ascent 293 m = 961 ft   *Distance 1.7 km = 1.1 miles*

From Thackthwaite via Sourfoot Fell:
            Ascent 305 m = 1001 ft   *Distance 2.8 km = 1.7 miles*

Adjacent Fell: *Darling Fell* *Height* *391 m = 1282 ft*   *Distance 1 km = 0.6 miles*

                  Fellbarrow   *416 m = 1364 ft*   *2.1 km = 1.3 miles*

Low Pike

Height 508 m = 1666 ft   NY374078   **Rank 181**

The first named peak on the long ridge leading up to Dove Crag and Fairfield beyond. Not usually the object of a walk, but pleasant enough if one is short of time or energy. The views are somewhat limited by the higher hills nearby but, nevertheless, they are quite good.

From Nook End Farm (Ambleside):
            Ascent 408 m = 1339 ft   *Distance 2.7 km = 1.7 miles*

Adjacent Fells: *Dove Crag*   *Height* *792 m = 2598 ft*   *2.8 km = 1.7 miles*

                   Little Hart Crag   *637 m = 2089 ft*   *3.7 km = 2.3 miles*

                   High Pike   *656 m = 2152 ft*   *1.2 km = 0.7 miles*

Maiden Moor

Height 576 m = 1889 ft   NY237182   **Rank 143**

Maiden Moor summit is a place one crosses on the way to Catbells or High Spy. The view from the top is excellent in all directions. The ground to the west of the summit is precipitous and offers no safe routes, whereas that to the east is steep but grassy and can be climbed. It is usual to approach the top from Hause Gate, below Catbells, or from High Spy.

From Grange, along the road to Manesty and then up to Hause Gate:
            Ascent 496 m = 1627 ft   *Distance 3.7 km = 2.3 miles*

Maiden Moor (continued)

From Chapel Bridge near Little Town via Hause Gate:

       Ascent 436 m = 1430 ft   *Distance 2.6 km = 1.6 miles*

From Grange straight up the hill overlooking Grange (but not on the crags):

       Ascent 496 m = 1627 ft   *Distance 2.5 km = 1.6 miles*

Adjacent Fells: *Catbells Height   451 m = 1479 ft*   *2 km = 1.2 miles*

              High Spy   *653 m = 2142 ft*   *2 km = 1.2 miles*

Mardale Ill Bell

Height 761 m = 2496 ft   **NY448101**   **Rank 60**

Although the east side of the mountain displays some of the best scenery in the Lake District, it is unlikely that this summit would be the sole object of a walk. Usually crossed on the way to High Street, Harter Fell or Thornthwaite Crag. The west side of the fell is just a very steep hill. The summit lacks interest and the views are fairly restricted. However the views across to Froswick and Ill Bell are magnificent.

From Mardale Head car park via Smallwater and Nan Bield Pass:

       Ascent 509 m = 1670 ft   *Distance 3.2 km = 2 miles*

(Note: an alternative route from the waterfall at the east end of Smallwater is to walk up the ridge above Piot Crag, this saves about 500 m (0.3 miles) on the previous route).

From Kentmere village via Hallow Bank Quarter, Smallthwaite Knott and Nan Bield Pass:

       Ascent 591 m = 1939 ft   *Distance 7.2 km = 4.5 miles*

Adjacent Fells: *High Street*   *Height   828 m = 2716 ft*   *Distance 1.2 km = 0.7 miles*

              Thornthwaite Crag   *784 m = 2572 ft*   *1.7 km = 1.1 miles*

              Harter Fell   *778 m = 2552 ft*   *1.7 km = 1.1 miles*

Meal Fell

Height 550 m = 1804 ft   **NY283337**   **Rank 155**

Meal Fell top lies at the end of a short ridge running from the west side of Great Sca Fell. Fair views to the Solway but not much else. If not going via Great Sca Fell the quickest route is from Longlands towards Trusmadoor. The fell can then be ascended from its base in a variety of ways.

From Longlands: Ascent 338 m = 1109 ft   *Distance   3 km = 1.9 miles*

Adjacent Fells: *Great Sca Fell   Height   651 m = 2135 ft*   *Distance   1 km = 0.6 miles*

              Great Cockup   *526 m = 1725 ft*   *1.1 km = 0.7 miles*

Mellbreak

Height 512 m = 1679 ft   **NY149186**   **Rank 176**

Though isolated and therefore not leading easily to other places, Mellbreak makes a splendid though rather short walk. A good way to take it in is to go up the rocky north end by Raven Crag (some scrambling is necessary). About two thirds of the way up the north end, at a bend in the path, one can look over to the eastern side for an exceptional view along Crummock Water towards Honister. Having reached the north summit descend to the dip in the centre and drop round to the west to meet a high level path returning above Mosedale to the start point. This circular walk can be started from The Kirkstile Inn or Low Park and, in both cases, is about 5 km (3 miles) long.

From Lowpark via Flass Wood:

       Ascent 401 m = 1315 ft   *Distance 1.6 km = 1 mile*

From the Kirkstile Inn, up by Raven Crag to the north summit:

       Ascent 388 m = 1273 ft   *Distance 2.1 km = 1.3 miles*

           (Distance from the north summit to the south summit = 1.1 km (0.8 miles)

Melbreak (continued)

From Buttermere via Scale Knott to the south summit:

Ascent 400 m = 1312 ft   *Distance 4.2 km = 2.6 miles*

Adjacent Fells: Hen Comb   Height   509 m = 1669 ft   *Distance 3.5 km = 2.2 miles*

(from south summit)

Middle Dodd

Height 654 m = 2145 ft   NY397096   **Rank 115**

Middle Dodd is essentially a small mound punctuating the ridge up to the summit of Red Screes. The obvious route is the direct route, straight up the edge of the ridge, but some may find it too steep for their liking. It is unlikely that anyone would ever choose Middle Dodd as the sole object of a walk, but for those who must visit it, and who don't like steepness, the easiest way is by descending from the summit of Red Screes. restricted but good views.

From Cow Bridge via Hartsop Hall and Caiston Glen, then straight up the ridge:

Ascent 496 m =1627 ft   *Distance 4.1 km = 2.5 miles*

Middle Fell

Height 582 m = 1909 ft   NY151072   **Rank 140**

A rough crag and rock strewn hill. The ascent from the road at Greendale is quite straightforward and quick. It is rewarded by some excellent views of the Wastwater Screes.

From the road at Greendale. Follow the path near the Gill as far as the fork at the 270 m (900 ft) level. Take the right fork to the summit:

Ascent 504 m = 1654 ft   *Distance 2.2 km = 1.4 miles*

Adjacent Fells: Haycock Height   797 m = 2614 ft   *Distance 3.7 km = 2.3 miles*

Seatallan   692 m = 2270 ft   *2.6 km = 1.6 miles*

Nab Scar

Height 442 m = 1450 ft   NY356071   **Rank 205**

Nab Scar is the rough craggy face above Rydal Water. It marks the beginning of the long ridge leading up to Fairfield. The view from the top is limited but, like the curate's egg, good in parts. An easy but not especially interesting walk from Rydal.

From Rydal: Ascent 383 m = 1257 ft   *Distance 1.5 km = 0.9 miles*

Adjacent Fell: Heron Pike   Height   612 m = 2007 ft   *Distance 1.1 km = 0.7 miles*

Nethermost Pike

Height 891 m = 2923 ft   NY344142   **Rank 9**

Nethermost Pike is too close to Helvellyn to attract much attention, which is a pity. The west side above Thirlmere is fairly steep and, though there are rocky outcrops in a number of places, it is generally grassy. The east side is wild and craggy with a narrow ridge dropping down to terminate on Eagle Crag; a favourite haunt of climbers and the site of a very old lead mine. There is some good walking on this side. The view from the top is restricted by Helvellyn but, apart from that, it is good.

From Wythburn through the wood and up by Comb Gill and Comb Crags:

Ascent 706 m = 2316 ft   *Distance   3 km = 1.9 miles*

From Grisedale Bridge along Grisedale to Nethermost Beck, thence up the beck to the ridge and so to the top:

Ascent 741m = 2431 ft   *Distance 5.7 km = 3.5 miles*

Adjacent Fells: Helvellyn   Height   950 m = 3116 ft   *Distance 1.1 km = 0.7 miles*

Dollywagon Pike   858 m = 2814 ft   *1.5 km = 0.9 miles*

A - Z Guide to the Fells

Orrest Head

Height 238 m = 780 ft   **SD414993**   **Rank 247**

Orrest Head, although of modest height, has long been famous as the balcony from which the high mountains of the district can be surveyed. Indeed it is mentioned in Victorian Guide books as a place which must be visited.

From the road in front of Windermere Station, follow the signposted route up the road opposite the station:
           Ascent 98 m = 322 ft   *Distance 1.2 km = 0.8 miles*

Outerside

Height 568 m = 1863 ft   **NY211215**   **Rank 148**

From Coledale Outerside looks very substantial, though not particularly inviting (just an unremittingly steep grassy slope). From the Stoneycroft Gill it looks quite inviting but is usually bypassed in one's eagerness to get to Sail and the high hills adjacent to it. Braithwaite to Outerside via Barrow Door makes quite a pleasant walk for children. The views from the top are good but restricted to the west and south by the huge bulk of Eel Crag and Causey Pike.

From Braithwaite via Barrow Door:
           Ascent 478 m = 1568 ft   *Distance 3.3 km = 2 miles*
From Stoneycroft Bridge:
           Ascent 438 m = 1436 ft   *Distance 2.5 km = 1.6 miles*
Adjacent Fells: *Barrow Height   455 m = 1492 ft*   *Distance 1.7 km = 1 mile*
                    Sail   773 m = 2536 ft   *2.1 km = 1.6 miles*

Pavey Ark

Height 700 m = 2296 ft   **NY284079**   **Rank 92**

Pavey Ark is spectacular when seen from Stickle Tarn with its near vertical ramparts enclosing the northwestern perimeter of the tarn. However its summit comprises a series of craggy outcrops on the high plateau leading up to High Raise. There are several well known and popular rock climbs on its southeastern cliffs, including the 'easy' traverse of Jack's Rake.

From The New Dungeon Ghyll Hotel via Stickle Ghyll and Stickle Tarn, follow the path eastwards around the tarn then up Jack's Rake and round to the summit (an exciting scramble in dry conditions):
           Ascent 610 m = 2000 ft   *Distance 3 km = 1.9 miles*
or   via Bright Beck and round to the summit cairn:
           Ascent 610 m = 2000 ft   *Distance 4 km = 2.5 miles*
Adjacent Fells: *High Raise   Height 762 m = 2499 ft*   *Distance 2 km = 1.3 miles*
                    Harrison Stickle   736 m = 2414 ft   *0.6 km = 0.4 miles*

Pike O' Blisco

Height 705 m = 2312 ft   **NY271042**   **Rank88**

Very well known though probably more for its name than its topographical features. From Great Langdale it rises as a cone dotted with many crags. From other directions its full height is not seen. The summit is a small ridge with good views, particularly of Bow Fell, Crinkle Crags and the Langdale valley.

From the Old Dungeon Ghyll Hotel (Great Langdale) via Wall End and Redacre Gill:
           Ascent 605 m = 1985 ft   *Distance 3.2 km = 2 miles*
From the Old Dungeon Ghyll Hotel via Stool End, Brown Howe and Red Tarn:
           Ascent 605 m = 1985 ft   *Distance 3.9 km = 2.4 miles*
From Wrynose Bridge via Wrynose Beck:
           Ascent 431 m = 1413 ft   *Distance 1.7 km = 1.1 miles*

Pike O' Blisco (continued)

| Adjacent Fells: | Cold Pike | Height | 701 m = 2299 ft | Distance 1.7 km = 1.1 miles |
| | Crinkle Crags | | 859 m = 2818 ft | 3.1 km = 1.9 miles |

Pike O' Stickle

Height 709 m = 2326 ft   **NY274 074**   **Rank 86**

The sugar lump top of Pike O' Stickle characterises the Langdale Pikes and is visible from most areas of the district. From Great Langdale the mountain is seen at its most dramatic rising sheer from the valley floor to its rounded summit. However from the high plateau of Harrison Combe the appearance is far less dramatic. The views in all directions are excellent.

From the New Dungeon Ghyll Hotel via Mark Gate and Loft Crag:
            Ascent 619 m = 2031 ft   Distance 3.1 km = 1.9 miles
From the Old Dungeon Ghyll Hotel across the road, through the gate and along the valley bottom towards Rossett Gill (Cumbria Way). After 1 km (0.6 miles) bear right on the path that climbs towards the stone chute between the summit and the floor of Harrison Combe. Climb the stone chute (hard) then left and up to the summit: Ascent 619 m = 2031 ft   Distance 3.4 km = 2.1 miles

| Adjacent Fells: | Loft Crag | Height | 670 m = 2198 ft | Distance | 1 km = 0.6 miles |
| | Harrison Stickle | | 736 m = 2414 ft | | 1 km = 0.6 miles |

Pillar

Height 892 m = 2926 ft   **NY171121**   **Rank 8**

From the Ennerdale side Pillar is truly magnificent. In the author's opinion a direct approach up to Pillar Rock from Ennerdale and then around the side of it is one of the best walks in the Lake District. Note, however, that the ground in places is steep and rough. The south side of Pillar is more of a scree ridden and rather steep hill. It provides good walking but lacks the drama of the north side. The route from Bowness Knott car park in Ennerdale involves a good deal of rather tedious road walking. A better route is from Gatesgarth Farm at the east end of Buttermere. This involves a climb over Scarth Gap and a descent into Ennerdale. This extra effort is adequately repaid by the varied views en - route. Magnificent views from the top.

From Gatesgarth Farm (car park) up the hill to Scarth Gap and on into Ennerdale. Take the west path (i.e. to your right) as you descend into Ennerdale. This leads along the top of the forest and then drops steeply down through it. Cross the river, climb through the forest to a point below Pillar Rock. Climb up to the rock and then go to the left of it (east side). This will bring you onto a path which will take you along the short ridge joining Pillar Rock to the summit of Pillar:
            Ascent 772 m = 2533 ft   Distance 5.4 km = 3.4 miles
A suitable route back to Gatesgarth is Pillar, Black Sail Pass, around the wood to Black Sail Youth Hostel, Scarth Gap and Gatesgarth: Distance   7 km = 4.3 miles
From the car park at Bowness Knott along the floor of the valley and then up to Pillar Rock and Pillar as detailed above: Ascent 762 m = 2500 ft   Distance   9 km = 5.6 miles
From the Wasdale Head Hotel along the east side of Mosedale Beck. At the fork in the track take the path to the left which leads up the hill to Wind Gap between Green Crags and Elliptical Crag:
            Ascent 812 m = 2664 ft   Distance 4.2 km = 2.6 miles
From the Wasdale Head Hotel along the east side of Mosedale Beck, then take the right fork in the path up to Black Sail Pass and then on to the summit of Pillar:
            Ascent 812 m = 2664 ft   Distance 5.9 km = 3.7 miles

| Adjacent Fells: | Scoat Fell | Height | 841 m = 2759 ft | Distance 1.5 km = 0.9 miles |
| | Kirk Fell | | 802 m = 2631 ft | 3.6 km = 2.2 miles |

A - Z Guide to the Fells

Place Fell

Height 657 m = 2155 ft   NY406169   **Rank 112**

The real attraction of this hill is the beautiful walk along its base between Scalehow Wood and Side Farm. The craggy western face of the fell is imposing and, whilst climbable in a number of places, is not easy going and probably not to most peoples taste. The usual route via Boredale Hause is fairly straightforward hillwalking, pleasant but not exciting. The same is true of the approach from Boredale. The views from the summit are good in all directions.

From Patterdale via Goldrill Bridge, Boredale Hause and Round How:
> Ascent 507 m = 1663 ft   Distance 3.1 km = 1.9 miles

From Patterdale via Side Farm, then along the top path going north over the top of Silver Crag. Follow the lakeside path round to the footbridge below Scalehow Force. Take the path up the east bank of the beck past the waterfalls to High Knott thence over Low Moss and up onto the summit:
> Ascent 507 m = 1663 ft   Distance 7.5 km = 4.7 miles

From Sandwick via High Knott and Low Moss:
> Ascent 497 m = 1631 ft   Distance 3.4 km = 2.1 miles

From Garth Heads in Boredale via Low Moss:
> Ascent 467 m = 1532 ft   Distance 3.2 km = 2 miles

Ponsonby Fell

Height 315 m = 1033 ft   NY082071   **Rank 240**

A bleak and dreary place. The only reason for visiting it is to say that you have been to one of the most boring hills in the Lake District. There are views into West Cumbria but nothing remarkable in other directions. There are many obvious ways displayed on the O.S. map of getting onto this hill. Perhaps the best route is to start from Wellington and stay in Blengdale forest for as long as you can.

From Wellington and through the forest:
> Ascent 245 m = 804 ft   Distance   4 km = 2.5 miles
> (depending on the route taken through the forest)

Adjacent Fell: Swainson Knott   Height   345 m = 1131 ft   Distance 1.4 km = 0.9 miles

Potter Fell

Height 337 m = 1105 ft   SD506995   **Rank 233**

This sprawling boggy mound on the extreme edge of the National Park is worthy of mention because of its remoteness and natural features. Its extended summit is sprinkled with a string of beautiful tarns interspersed with heather, bracken and grassy knolls.

From the back road between Staveley and Garnett Bridge, starting at Garnett Bridge. Take the fellside track up to East View and on up to the tarns. Skirt the eastern side of Gurnal Dubs and make for the summit

Raise

Height 883 m = 2896 ft   NY343174   **Rank 12**

North of Raise the fells are broad topped and rounded with crags on the western slopes. However, at Raise the topography starts to change. The ridges become narrower, the slopes steeper and the approaches more interesting. The routes from Glenridding, though long, are the most interesting, taking you past fine scenery and the old Greenside lead mine workings. The routes from Thirlmere are shorter but steeper and, though they offer good views over Thirlmere, they otherwise lack interest. Immediately north of Raise is Sticks Pass, an old pack horse route from Thirlmere to Glenridding. Extensive views are to be had from the summit.

From Stanah to Sticks Pass, thence to the summit:
> Ascent 713 m = 2339 ft   Distance 3.5 km = 2.2 miles

Raise (continued)

From Thirlspot via Brund Gill:

    Ascent 693 m = 2274 ft   *Distance 3.9 km = 2.4 miles*

From Glenridding car park follow the mine road to Greenside Mine, then up the zig zag track by Lucy's Tongue and along the route of the old lead smelter chimney to Stang. Hence up the ridge to the summit:

    Ascent 733 m = 2405 ft   *Distance 5.2 km = 3.2 miles*

Adjacent Fells: *Stybarrow Dodd*   *Height 843 m = 2765 ft*   *1.7 km = 1.1 miles*

                   White Side   *863 m = 2831 ft*   *1 km = 0.6 miles*

                   (above Thirlmere)

Rampsgill Head

Height 792 m = 2598 ft   **NY443128**   **Rank 39**

Dramatic views down to Ramps Gill and magnificent views down into Riggindale, if one wanders a short distance south. The panorama from the top is superb. There are several routes up as the summit lies approximately at the confluence of three ridges.

For routes see The Knott, High Street, High Raise and Kidsty Pike

Rannerdale Knotts

Height 355 m = 1164 ft   **NY167182**   **Rank 230**

A fairly low level, short, but interesting walk. Surprisingly good though limited views from the top. A place to take children (though care must be exercised near the crags at the north end).

From near Hause Point, straight up:

    Ascent 250 m = 820 ft   *Distance 0.6 km = 0.4 miles*

From Cinderdale Common car park via Squat Beck and Low Bank:

    Ascent 245 m = 804 ft   *Distance 3.6 km = 2.2 miles*

From Buttermere (parking at a price) via Low Bank:

    Ascent 243 m = 797 ft   *Distance 2.2 km = 1.4 miles*

From near Hause Point via Squat Beck and Low Bank:

    Ascent 250 m = 820 ft   *Distance 3.2 km = 2 miles*

Raven Crag

Height 461 m = 1512 ft   **NY303187**   **Rank 199**

A great crag rising from the conifers at the northern end (west side) of Thirlmere. Above it lie the bogs of High Seat and the heather clad slope of Bleaberry Fell. From the summit there is a good view down Thirlmere.

From the path which leaves the road some 200 m (650 ft) north of its junction with the road over the dam:

    Ascent 261 m = 856 ft   *Distance 0.8 km = 0.5 miles*

Red Pike (above Buttermere)

Height 755 m = 2477 ft   **NY161155**   **Rank 64**

A superb and very popular fell with excellent views from the top. The 'Red' probably comes from the presence of blood red haematite (iron ore) in the rock and scree around Dodd. All routes that keep to the steep

Red Pike (above Buttermere)(continued)

east face are excellent. The path via Scale Force is scenic as far as the top of the ravine above the waterfall, but then becomes less interesting until Lingcomb Edge is reached. The route up from Ennerdale is a trudge and is only mentioned because it is a possible way on and off. If planning a route from Buttermere do not attempt to ascend or descend via Sour Milk Gill as this is dangerously steep and slippy. Several people have died here in recent years.

From Buttermere via Scale Force:
                  Ascent 643 m = 2109 ft   *Distance 5.7 km = 3.5 miles*
From Buttermere via Burtness Wood, Bleaberry Tarn and Dodd:
                  Ascent 643 m = 2109 ft   *Distance 3.1 km = 1.9 miles*
From Buttermere via Far Ruddy Beck and Dodd:
                  Ascent 643 m = 2109 ft   *Distance 3.7 km = 2.3 miles*
From the car park below Bowness Knott to High Gilllerthwaite and straight up the hill:
                  Ascent 625 m = 2050 ft   *Distance 6.2 km = 3.9 miles*

| Adjacent Fells: | Starling Dodd | Height | 633 m = 2076 ft | Distance 2.1 km = 1.3 miles |
| | High Stile | | 807 m = 2647 ft | 1.3 km = 0.8 miles |

Red Pike (above Wasdale)

Height 826 m = 2709 ft   **NY165106**   **Rank 26**

Red Pike is the summit of a short ridge which abuts the main mountain ridge south of Ennerdale. Seen from Mosedale (above Wasdale Head) the ridge is stark and impressive, whereas from the east it falls away in rolling grassy slopes and dips containing tarns. It is a popular route for accessing the main Ennerdale ridge from Wasdale. The views to the south and southeast are impressive to say the least.

From Overbeck Bridge car park on the north shore of Wastwater (see Route 4, page 95) via Yewbarrow and Dore Head and up the ridge to the summit:
                  Ascent 746 m = 2448 ft   *Distance 6 km = 3.8 miles*
From Wasdale Head Hotel via Mosedale keeping to the left of Mosedale Beck as far as the sheepfold at the base of the screes. Scramble up Dore Head Screes to the col and then turn right to follow the ridge up to the summit: *Ascent 746 m = 2448 ft*   *Distance 4.4 km = 2.8 miles*

Adjacent Fells:	Yewbarrow	Height	628 m = 2060 ft	Distance 2.6 km = 1.7 miles
	Scoat Fell		841 m = 2759 ft	1.6 km = 1 mile
	Haycock		797 m = 2614 ft	2.3 km = 1.4 miles
	Pillar		892 m = 2926 ft	2.8 km = 1.8 miles

Red Screes

Height 776 m = 2545 ft   **NY396088**   **Rank 50**

Red Screes is the large craggy and scree covered hill on the west side of Kirkstone Pass. The views from the summit are magnificent. From the north end near Brotherswater or the south end rooted in Ambleside the journey to the summit is long and arduous including well over 2000 ft of ascent. The easy way to the top is from the car park opposite the Kirkstone Pass Inn. The path is steep but short and soon over.

From the Kirkstone Road near Ambleside, follow the broad ridge straight to the summit:
                  Ascent 546 m = 1791 ft   *Distance 3.9 km = 2.4 miles*
From Cow Bridge (parking) via Brotherswater, Hartsop Hall and the foot of High Hartsop Dodd, then straight up the ridge to Middle Dodd (steep):
                  Ascent 618 m = 2028 ft   *Distance 5.1 km = 3.2 miles*
or from Cow Bridge via Brotherswater, Hartsop Hall and then up Caiston Glen instead (much easier than the ridge). At Scandale Pass cross over to the summit:
                  Ascent 618 m = 2028 ft   *Distance 5.7 km = 3.5 miles*

Rest Dodd

Height 696 m = 2283 ft   NY432137   **Rank 96**

An uninteresting hill and the views are not a great deal better.

From Hartsop Village via Hayeswater Gill to the north end of Hayeswater and up on to the saddle linking The Knott and Rest Dodd:

Ascent 526 m = 1726 ft	*Distance 3.6 km = 2.2 miles*

From Patterdale via Side Farm, Boredale Hause, Angletarn Pikes and Satura Crag:

Ascent 546 m = 1791 ft			*Distance 5.3 km = 3.3 miles*
Adjacent Fells:	*The Nab*	*Height 576 m = 1889 ft*	*Distance 1.7 km = 1.1 miles*
	The Knott	*739 m = 2424 ft*	*1.1 km = 0.7 miles*
	Angletarn Pikes	*567 m = 1860 ft*	*Distance 2.6 km = 1.6 miles*

Robinson

Height 737 m = 2417 ft   NY202169   **Rank 69**

A rather flat and unexciting summit but the views are good in all directions. Perhaps the most interesting approach is from Chapel Bridge via Low Snab, along the east side of Scope Beck and up into Little Dale. Notice the old pond and dam below Littledale Crags; this used to supply the waterwheels at Goldscope Mine. Buttermere Moss to the west of the summit is wet and not particularly pleasant to cross. Another route, interesting in the lower stages but much more steep, is from above Hassness. The walk from Newlands Hause is short and not very exciting.

From Chapel Bridge via Low Snab, Scope Beck and Little Dale:

Ascent 597 m = 1959 ft			*Distance 4.4 km = 2.7 miles*

From Newlands Hause (keep to the edge of the bog):

Ascent 404 m = 1325 ft			*Distance 1.6 km = 1 mile*

From Buttermere and across the Moss:

Ascent 625 m = 2050 ft			*Distance 2.8 km = 1.7 miles*

From Hassness and up by the east side of the ravines:

Ascent 607 m = 1991 ft			*Distance 2.2 km = 1.4 miles*
Adjacent Fells:	*Hindscarth*	*Height 727 m = 2385 ft*	*Distance 2.8 km = 1.7 miles*
	Dale Head	*753 m = 2470 ft*	*2.8 km = 1.7 miles*

Rosset Pike

Height 651 m = 2135 ft   NY249076   **Rank 118**

Rosset Pike lies on the main route to Bowfell and Scafell Pike from Great Langdale. The views from the summit are restricted by the surrounding larger fells, but it is a good place to look back along the Mickleden Valley and to view the impressive crags of Bowfell.

From The Old Dungeon Ghyll Hotel along Mickleden, up Rosset Gill to Angle Tarn, hence to the summit from

the north side:	*Ascent 561 m = 1841 ft*		*Distance 6.4 km = 4 miles*
Adjacent Fells:	*Bowfell Height 902 m = 2959 ft*		*Distance 1.7 km = 1 mile*
	Esk Pike	*885 m = 2903 ft*	*2.1 km = 1.3 miles*

Rosthwaite Fell (Bessyboot)

Height 551 m = 1807 ft   NY258125   **Rank 154**

From valley level this rocky fell is attractive and there are many ways of getting to the top. However, almost all of these are pathless and involve steep gradients and, quite often, scrambling. The top is broad undulating, craggy and quite pleasant, though not in the same class as nearby Glaramara. The views are fair.

Rosthwaite Fell (continued)

From above the campsite a little to the east of Stonethwaite. Follow Big Stanger Gill through the wood and between Hanging Haystack and Alisongrass Crag all the way to the top:

Ascent 441 m = 1447 ft	Distance 1.6 km = 1 mile

From opposite Mountain View (on the Seatoller road) and up Combe Gill. At the 240 m (800 ft) contour a path branches off in a southeast direction and goes up to Tarn at Leaves. Bessyboot is a short distance north of this:

Ascent 446 m = 1463 ft	Distance 2.3 km = 1.4 miles
Adjacent Fells: Glaramara Height 783 m = 2568 ft	Distance 2.6 km = 1.6 miles

Sail

Height 773 m = 2536 ft NY198203 **Rank 51**

Sail is the penultimate top of the Causey Pike/Scar Crags/Eel Crag ridge. Its south side is very rough and steep but its north side is easily approached via the well worn path above Long Comb. Views from the top are good, but Eel Crag blocks the west.

From Stoneycroft Bridge via Causey Pike and Scar Crags:

Ascent 643 m = 2110 ft	Distance 4.2 km = 2.6 miles

From Braithwaite / Buttermere road and along Rigg Beck:

Ascent 603 m = 1978 ft	Distance 4.1 km = 2.6 miles

From Stoneycroft Bridge up by Stoneycroft Gill to Long Comb (old mine road):

Ascent 643 m = 2110 ft	Distance 4.2 km = 2.6 miles

From Braithwaite via Barrow Door and then the old mine road:

Ascent 668 m = 2191 ft	Distance 5.2 km = 3.2 miles
Adjacent Fells: Eel Crag Height 839 m = 2752 ft	0.6 km = 0.4 miles
Scar Crags 672 m = 2204 ft	1 km = 0.6 miles

Saint Sunday Crag

Height 841 m = 2759 ft NY369134 **Rank 22**

The northwest side of the fell is steep, craggy and impressive, whilst the southeast side is much gentler in gradient and appearance. The approach from Grisedale Bridge is a pleasant one, particularly in the early stages. The views from the summit are good but much better if you wander the 300 m (1000 ft) or so to Gavel Pike. A good circular walk is to continue to Fairfield, thence down to Grisedale Hause and back along the valley bottom.

From Grisedale Bridge via Thornhow End and Birks:

Ascent 691 m = 2267 ft	Distance 4 km = 2.5 miles

From Grisedale Bridge via the valley bottom to Grisedale Hause, Fairfield, Cofa Pike:

Ascent 691 m = 2267 ft	Distance 10 km = 6.2 miles
Adjacent Fells: Fairfield Height 873 m = 2864 ft	Distance 2.5 km = 1.6 miles
Birks 622 m = 2040 ft	1.7 km = 1.1 miles

Sale Fell

Height 359 m = 1177 ft NY194297 **Rank 229**

Sale Fell with its undulating top and very good views is a most pleasant fell to walk. A good place to exercise children. A good circular walk from Wythop Mill is to follow the road to Brumston Bridge then, a few yards further on, ascend the fell by the side of the wall. Walk along the top until you reach Lothwaite, then down to the track and back via Kelswick (6300 m = 3.9 miles).

From Wythop Mill via Brumston Bridge and Dodd Crag:

Ascent 254 m = 833 ft	Distance 2.1 km = 1.3 miles

From Wythop Mill via Kelswick and Lothwaite:

Ascent 254 m = 833 ft	Distance 4.2 km = 2.6 miles

Sallows

Height 516 m = 1692 ft   NY436040   **Rank 174**

Rather flat and the wiry vegetation hinders walking. There are some good extensive views from the top, but the fell has no other attractions.

From Kentmere village via the Garburn Pass:
        Ascent 326 m = 1070 ft   *Distance 2.5 km = 1.6 miles*
From the A592 via Limefitt Park and the Garburn Pass:
        Ascent 386 m = 1266 ft   *Distance 2.7 km = 1.7 miles*
Adjacent Fells: *Yoke*   *Height*   *706 m = 2316 ft*   *Distance 2.8 km = 1.7 miles*
                Sour Howes   *483 m = 1584 ft*   *1.5 km = 0.9 miles*

Sand Hill

Height 756 m = 2480 ft   NY187219   **Rank 62**

So close to the much more interesting Hopegill Head that a description is not really merited. Hopegill Head is 14 m (46 ft) higher and 400 m (0.2 miles) to the north.

Scafell

Height 964 m = 3162 ft   NY207065   **Rank 2**

Although Scafell Pike obliterates some of the view from the summit, the remainder is excellent, as one would expect from a mountain of this height. Some of Scafell's finest features, however, are to be found below the summit. Mickledore is one of the Lake District's magic places, the huge walls of rock giving it an enclosed, cathedral like quality. Magnificent too are the crags overlooking the river Esk to the east and those in the north facing Lingmell. That part of the fell occupying the quadrant between the west and south direction is grass with a dusting of scree and offers little of interest. To get from Mickledore to the summit (without a long detour) there are two ways. One of these is Broad Stand, a rock structure which looks easily climbable from a distance, but is seen to be a difficult (for most) undertaking from close to. The other route is Lord's Rake; an obvious gully which is to be found downhill in a northwest direction from Mickledore. This gully is a stone chute that has been scoured clean of stones by countless sliding boot soles. The Lord's Rake route is exciting but not usually dangerous, except to the inexperienced in ice and snow.

From Boot in Eskdale via Whillan Beck, Burnmoor Tarn, Hardrigg Gill:
        Ascent 904 m = 2966 ft   *Distance 6.7 km = 4.2 miles*
From Boot along the road to Brotherilkeld, then follow the River Esk to below Cam Spout Crag. Take the path up to Mickledore and access the summit by means of Lord's Rake (If you do not want to use Lord's Rake it is possible to follow the base of the crags below the summit around to Foxes Tarn. From the tarn one can get to the summit without too much difficulty):
        Ascent 904 m = 2966 ft   *Distance 11.8 km = 7.3 miles*
A variant of the above is from Boot then along the road, turning off just before Whahouse Bridge. From there to Taw House, Brock Crag, Silverybield Crag, Cam Spout Crag and up to Mickledore:
        Ascent 904 m = 2966 ft   *Distance 11.1 km = 7 miles*
From the Wasdale Head Hotel take the road then the footpath across to Lingmell Gill, thence up to Mickledore and the summit via Lord's Rake:

Adjacent Fells: *Scafell Pike*   *Height*   *978 m = 3208 ft*   *Distance 1.4 km = 0.9 miles*
                Slight Side   *762 m = 2499 ft*   *1.7 km = 1.1 miles*
                Illgill Head   *609 m = 1998 ft*   *4.8 km = 3 miles*

A - Z Guide to the Fells

Scafell Pike

Height 978 m = 3208 ft   NY215072   **Rank 1**

Scafell Pike is the highest of the three Scafell Pikes, which additionally consist of Broad Crag 931 m (3054 ft) and Ill Crag 935 m (3068 ft). The pikes lie on a long ridge that may be considered as starting at Great End and terminating at Slight Side, with a deep gash at Mickledore, separating Scafell from Scafell Pike. Perhaps the best route to the top of the pike is the Corridor route (or Guide's Route as it was once known). It starts at Spout Head above Sty Head Tarn and rises steadily up the northwest flank of the mountain. The views of Great Gable and Lingmell (with its huge ravine, various gulleys and other rock scenery), which unfold as one travels the route, are truly magnificent.

The route across the tops of Great End and the Pikes is pretty hard going because of the ankle twisting stones, which are scattered thickly and extensively. Moreover, the tops are fairly broad in most places so one tends to miss out on the perspective-bending downward views. The southeast flank above the river Esk is impressive to behold, but the paths are unremittingly steep. The Wastwater side is relatively dull; the cluster takes on the appearance of a huge, rock strewn, but essentially grassy hill.

If you visit the Pike you must also visit Mickledore. The rock walls towering above the cleft give the place a strange cathedral-like quality. Unless you are a fairly competent rock climber you will not be able to cross Mickledore and go directly up Scafell. The way is barred by a rock structure called Broad Stand which looks easy from a distance, but most ordinary walkers change their mind when directly confronted by it. Instead it is possible to drop down the northwest side of the cleft and climb the very obvious gully called 'Lord's Rake' which appears on your left. The scramble up Lord's Rake is exciting but quite safe (some may disagree!).

From Seathwaite via Stockley Bridge, Styhead Gill, Styhead Tarn, Corridor Route:
        Ascent 853 m = 2799 ft   Distance 6.7 km = 4.2 miles
(Instead of going via Stockley Bridge the more adventurous may like to take the path by the side of Taylor Gill Force waterfall. This will not appeal to those who suffer from vertigo).
From Seathwaite via Grains Gill, Ruddy Gill, Esk Hause, Broad Crag:
        Ascent 853 m = 2799 ft   Distance 6.7 km = 4.2 miles
From the Old Dungeon Ghyll Hotel, Great Langdale via Mickleden Beck, Rossett Gill, Angle Tarn, Esk Hause and Broad Crag: Ascent 878 m = 2881 ft   Distance 8.4 km = 5.2 miles
From the Wasdale Head Hotel along Lingmell Beck. At the 250 m (820 ft) contour take the south split in the beck to the ravine of Piers Gill at the foot of the crags of Lingmell. Take the path which runs along the south side of the ravine and follow to the top of the ravine (don't try to walk the bed of Piers Gill!), then on to Lingmell Col: Ascent 900 m = 2953 ft   Distance 5.4 km = 3.4 miles
From Boot (Eskdale) via Brotherilkeld along the east side of the river Esk to Great Moss then straight up to Mickledore: Ascent 926 m = 3039 ft   Distance 11.9 km = 7.4 miles
A variant on the above is from Boot then along the road turning off just before Whahouse Bridge. From there continue to Brock Crag, Silverybield Crag, Camspout Crag and up to Mickledore:
        Ascent 926 m =3039 ft   Distance 11 km = 6.8 miles
From Stonethwaite via Langstrath and Esk Hause:
        Ascent 878 m = 2881 ft   Distance 11 km =6.8 miles

Adjacent Fells:	Lingmell	Height	807 m = 2647 ft	1.3 km = 0.8 miles
	Scafell		964 m = 3162 ft	1.4 km = 0.9 miles
	Great End		910 m = 2985 ft	1.7 km = 1.1 miles
	Esk Pike		885 m = 2881 ft	11 km = 6.8 miles

Scalebarrow Knott

Height 335 m = 1099 ft   NY 518152   **Rank 235**

Like Harper Hill, another bump on the northeast side of Hare Shaw. Views highly limited and uninspiring.
From the end of the unenclosed road at the mouth of Swindale:
        Ascent 97 m = 318 ft   Distance 1.5 km = 0.9 miles

Scalebarrow Knott (continued)

Adjacent Fells: Harper Hills   Height   419 m = 1374 ft   Distance 1.5 km = 0.9 miles

Scar Crags

Height 672 m = 2204 ft   NY208207   **Rank 103**

The summit is on the ridge connecting Causey Pike to Crag Hill. On the north side of the summit is Long Comb and, in the late 1840's, a small and totally unsuccessful cobalt mine was opened up in the crags above the comb. In fact the long track from Stoneycroft Bridge to Long Comb was created to service this mine. On the south side of the summit, situated on rough scree is a very ancient and rather stunted oak wood. Good views, particularly to the east, from the top.

From Stoneycroft Bridge via Causey Pike:
    Ascent 532 m = 1745 ft   Distance 3.2 km = 1.9 miles
From the Braithwaite /Buttermere road and up Rigg Beck (below Ard Crags):
    Ascent 502 m = 1646 ft   Distance 3.7 km =2.3 miles
From Stoneycroft Bridge up the mine road (below Outerside) to Long Comb:
    Ascent 532 m = 1745 ft   Distance 3.8 km = 2.3 miles
From Braithwaite via Barrow Door and the old mine road:
    Ascent 567 m = 1860 ft   Distance 4.7 km = 2.9 miles
Adjacent Fells: Causey Pike   Height   637 m = 2089 ft   Distance 1.2 km = 0.7 miles
     Sail   773 m = 2536 ft   1.0 km = 0.6 miles

Scoat Fell

Height 841 m = 2759 ft   NY160114   **Rank 22**

Getting to the top involves a good deal of walking from any direction but the views are good and several other hills are in easy reach and so it is worthwhile. The OS map uses unnecessarily bold letters for Steeple, a little to the north of the top. Steeple is not a distinct fell but a broad spire of rock grafted onto the side of the ridge which drops down to Ennerdale. From some directions it looks nothing much at all, from others it can be quite imposing.

From the car park below Bowness Knott to the head of the lake then up the fire break to Lingmell and Tewit How:
    Ascent 711 m = 2333 ft   Distance 7.8 km = 4.8 miles
From Netherbeck Bridge, Wasdale (car parking at Overbeck Bridge just along the road). Follow the path up Netherbeck and then via Little Lad Crag:
    Ascent 771 m = 2529 ft   Distance   6 km = 3.7 miles
Adjacent Fells: Red Pike   Height   826 m = 2709 ft   Distance 1.2 km = 0.7 miles
    Steeple   819 m = 2686 ft   0.6 km = 0.4 miles
    Haycock   797 m = 2614 ft   1.7 km = 1.1 miles
    Pillar   892 m = 2926 ft   1.5 km = 0.9 miles

Seat How

Height 496 m = 1627 ft   NY213256   **Rank 187**

This bare prominence in the middle of Thornthwaite Forest is well served by the myriad of forest trails starting from Whinlatter Visitor Centre. A Forestry Commission map is available from the visitor centre which shows in detail all of the marked trails in the forest.

Seat Sandal

Height 736 m = 2414 ft   NY344115   **Rank 70**

The east side of the fell is rough and craggy with scree and the ascent from Grisedale Hause is short but pleasant. The rest of the fell is essentially a large grassy mound with no special features. The top is broad and grassy with good views to the west.

Seat Sandal (continued)

From Grisedale Bridge along the valley via the old packhorse track to Grisedale Hause, then up the craggy path to the top: Ascent 586 m = 1923 ft   Distance 7.2 km = 4.5 miles

From Mill Bridge (just north of the Travellers Rest Public House) via Little Tongue Gill or Tongue Gill to Grisedale Hause then up the craggy path to the top:

Ascent 636 m = 2087 ft   Distance 3.7 km = 2.3 miles

From Dunmail Raise up Raise Beck:

Ascent 491 m = 1611 ft   Distance 2.4 km = 1.5 miles

Adjacent Fells: Dollywagon Pike Height   858 m = 2814 ft   1.7 km = 1.1 miles
                Fairfield   873 m = 2864 ft   1.8 km = 1.1 miles

Seatallan

Height 692 m = 2270 ft   **NY140084**   **Rank 97**

A large sprawling hill. Rather dreary from the west side, but better (though not terribly exciting) from the east. It does not lie on any major route and therefore is usually by-passed by walkers. Some good coastal and southerly views from the top, but not much else.

From Greendale up by Greendale Gill, then turn left before reaching Greendale Tarn and head straight up the hill: Ascent 612 m = 2008 ft   Distance 3.2 km = 2 miles

From Netherbeck Bridge (car park at nearby Overbeck Bridge) and up Nether Beck. Follow Lad Crag Beck out of the valley, then turn up to Seatallan at the Pots of Ashness:

Ascent 622 m = 2041 ft   Distance 4.4 km = 2.7 miles

From Harrow Head on to the track that leads round to Raven Crag and start climbing whenever you are ready. A long trudge:

Ascent 562 m = 1844 ft   Distance 3.4 km = 2.1 miles
                                            (minimum)

See also Buckbarrow (above Wastwater)

Adjacent Fells: Buckbarrow   Height   425 m = 1394 ft   Distance 2.6 km = 1.6 miles
                Haycock   797 m = 2614 ft   2.7 km = 1.6 miles

Seathwaite Fell

Height 632 m = 2073 ft   **NY227097**   **Rank 126**

Seathwaite Fell is the tongue of land separating Grains Gill from Styhead Gill. Although the heights and grid references quoted above are for the highest point on the fell, the true top may be considered to be a little further north at NY229102 with a height of 601 m = 1972 ft. Few people visit this hill as they will almost certainly be continuing on to Gable or the Scafells. The views from the craggy top are limited by the large fells nearby, but nevertheless they are quite good.

From Seathwaite via Stockley Bridge, Styhead Gill, Sty Head Tarn and Sprinkling Tarn:

Ascent 507 m = 1663 ft   Distance 5.7 km = 3.5 miles

From Seathwaite via Stockley Bridge, Grains Gill, Ruddy Gill and Sprinkling Tarn:

Ascent 507 m = 1663 ft   Distance 4.8 km = 3 miles

Direct Route. From Seathwaite via Stockley Bridge, Black Waugh and the west side of Aaron Crags:

Ascent 507 m = 1663 ft   Distance 3.3 km = 2.1 miles

Adjacent Fells: Great End   Height   910 m = 2985 ft   Distance   3 km = 1.9 miles
                Scafell Pike   978 m = 3208 ft   4 km = 2.5 miles
                Esk Pike   885 m = 2903 ft   2.9 km = 1.8 miles

Selside Pike

Height 655 m = 2148 ft   NY490111   **Rank 114**

Like all of the fells south of Haweswater the fell is unfrequented and, whilst it lacks the drama of High Street, it is not without its charms (e.g. good views across the High Street range, down into Swindale and across the Pennines. The northeast side of the fell falls away very steeply to Dodd Bottom at the head of Swindale).

From where Rowantree Beck crosses under the lakeside road, up the old Corpse Road, then turn off near High Birkin Knott and follow the ridge to the summit:

   Ascent 375 m = 1230 ft   *Distance 3 km = 1.9 miles*

From the end of the unenclosed road at the mouth of Swindale along the track to Swindale Head, then up the old Corpse Road. Turn off near High Birkin Knott and follow the ridge to the summit:

   Ascent 416 m = 1365 ft   *Distance 5.2 km = 3.2 miles*

Adjacent Fells: *Branstree* *Height* *713 m = 2339 ft*   *1.7 km = 1.1 miles*

      Hare Shaw   *503 m = 1650 ft*   *2.3 km = 1.4 miles*

Sergeant Man

Height 730 m = 2394 ft   NY286089   **Rank 73**

Sergeant Man is just a subsidiary top of High Raise which is only 0.7 km = 0.4 miles distant. See High Raise for routes distances etc..

Sergeant's Crag

Height 571 m = 1873 ft   NY274114   **Rank 147**

Sergeant's Crag is a rocky outcrop on the eastern ridge above the Langstrath Valley; a north western buttress of High Raise. Below here is the site of the ancient Langstrath Bloomery, evidence of the industrial history of this remote area. The view from the summit cairn up the Langstrath Valley is excellent and good views are to be had to the west and north.

From Stonethwaite into Langstrath and up the valley to Blackmoss Pot. Cross the beck here and climb to the lower ridge between Bull Crag and Blea Crag, then left to the summit:

   Ascent 461 m = 1512 ft   *Distance 6.5 km = 4 miles*

Adjacent Fell: *Eagle Crag* *Height* *525 m = 1722 ft*   *Distance 1 km = 0.6 miles*

Sheffield Pike

Height 675 m = 2214 ft   NY369182   **Rank 101**

On the south side of Sheffield Pike are Glenridding Screes and the huge spoil heap of Greenside Lead Mine. Greenside Mine closed in 1962 after 200 years of almost continuous operation. During this time it yielded some 2.4 million tons of lead ore and 2 million ozs of silver. The north side overlooks the quiet Glencoyne valley. Fair, but not particularly good views, from the top.

From Glenridding Car Park and along to the last cottage (Rake Cottages) on Greenside Road. Climb up behind the cottages via The Rake and onto the ridge to Heron Pike, hence to the summit:

   Ascent 520 m = 1706 ft   *Distance 2.5 km = 1.6 miles*

From Glenridding Car Park via Greenside Mine and up the path to Stang End, then across to Sheffield Pike (a route for those who wish to see the old Greenside workings at close hand):

   Ascent 520 m = 1706 ft   *Distance 4.5 km = 2.8 miles*

From the road at Mossdale Bay and up the track by Seldom Seen (miners cottages), then to Bleabank Side and Nick Head: *Ascent 530 m = 1739 ft*   *Distance 3.2 km = 2 miles*

A variation on the above route, not shorter but more interesting, is to start climbing the fell before you come under Black Crag. Carry on to Heron Pike, then to the summit.

A - Z Guide to the Fells

Shipman Knotts

Height 587 m = 1925 ft   NY472063   **Rank 138**

This is essentially the south end of the broad ridge below Kentmere Pike. The ground is covered in rock outcrops which make for interesting walking. Good views to the south, but those to the north are restricted. This is quite a pleasant place to visit in its own right, but most people will just be passing through on the way to Kentmere Pike.

From Sadgill. Follow the path below Sadgill Wood, then turn off at the 350 m (1150 ft) contour up to Wray Crag: Ascent 390 m = 1280 ft   Distance 2.9 km = 1.8 miles
From Kentmere village via Nunnery Beck to the 350 m contour (1150 ft) thence up to Wray Crag:
          Ascent 377 m = 1237 ft   Distance 3.3 km = 2.1 miles
Adjacent Fells: Kentmere Pike   Height   730 m = 2394 ft   Distance 1.7 km = 1.1 miles

Silver How

Height 394 m = 1292 ft   NY325 066   **Rank 221**

Silver How rises above Grasmere, its sides rich in vegetation and trees giving a lovely backdrop to the village. Its undulating summit consists of grassy humps, many with their own cairns. Fine views are to be had from the top of Dunmail, Grasmere Vale and Rydal.

From the road near the hire boat landing at Grasmere. Take the public path which climbs up onto the fell, passing under the summit crags. When the track and adjacent wall reach their highest point, bear right and follow the track leading straight up the hill through a 'V' shaped gap to the summit:
          Ascent 330 m = 1082 ft   Distance 2 .1 km = 1.3 miles
From Grasmere village along the road to Allan Bank (signposted Silver Howe). Follow the road which skirts the property until a gated track onto the fell turns off to the left (Signpost Goody Bridge, Silver Howe). For the summit keep to the path which bears up and left, and crosses Wray Gill:
          Ascent 330 m = 1082 ft   Distance 2.5 km = 1.6 miles

Skiddaw

Height 931 m = 3054 ft   NY260291   **Rank 4**

Skiddaw is more of a very large hill than a mountain, but large expanses of scree and a complex shape give it a special grandeur when seen from most directions. The easiest way to the top is to take the road up from Applethwaite and park at the top, however the path from here is rather an unexciting plod. The interesting routes are from Millbeck and from High Side near Bassenthwaite Village. Care should be taken if climbing down the side of Dead Beck near Dead Crags, as it gets very steep. Marvellous long distance views from the top.

From the end of the road above Applethwaite (near the top of Latrigg), up by Whit Beck and via Little Man to the top: Ascent 636 m = 2087 ft   Distance   5 km = 3.1 miles
From Millbeck via White Stones to Carl Side, thence up the scree slope path to the top:
          Ascent 806 m = 2644 ft   Distance 3.7 km = 2.3 miles
From Millbeck via Lyzzick Wood and Long Doors to Carl Side, thence to the top:
          Ascent 806 m = 2644 ft   Distance   4 km = 2.5 miles
From the car park opposite Mire House and up through Dodd Wood via Skill Beck. Thence to Long Doors, Carlside and the top:
          Ascent 817 m = 2680 ft   Distance 4.3 km = 2.7 miles
From the Orthwaite Road (car parking near High Side House). Take the path starting next to the layby up onto The Edge and then via Ullock Pike and Carl Side to the summit:
          Ascent 771 m = 2529 ft   Distance 5.1 km = 3.2 miles
From Peter House Farm to Dead Beck at the foot of Cockup, then up the side of Dead Beck to the top:
          Ascent 721 m = 2365 ft   Distance 4.2 km = 2.6 miles

Skiddaw (continued)

Adjacent Fells:	*Carl Side*	*Height*	*746 m = 2447 ft*	*Distance 1.3 km = 0.8 miles*	
	Skiddaw Little Man		*865 m = 2837 ft*	*1.5 km = 1 mile*	
	Ullock Pike		*690 m = 2263 ft*	*2.4 km = 1.5 miles*	
	Lonscale Fell		*715 m = 2345 ft*	*3.5 km = 2.2 miles*	
	Bakestall		*673 m = 2207 ft*	*1.7 km = 1 mile*	

Skiddaw Little Man

Height 865 m = 2837 ft   NY267278   **Rank 15**

The top itself is not particularly interesting but the views are terrific. If you have got this far, you will almost certainly want to continue to the top of Skiddaw.

From the end of the road above Applethwaite (near the top of Latrigg) and up Whit Beck:
        Ascent 570 m = 1870 ft   *Distance 3.5 km = 2.2 miles*
From Applethwaite, up Howgill Tongue:
        Ascent 727 m = 2385 ft   *Distance 2.8 km = 1.7 miles*

Adjacent Fells:	*Skiddaw*	*Height*	*931 m = 3054 ft*	*Distance 1.5 km = 1 mile*	
	Lonscale Fell		*715 m = 2345 ft*	*2 km = 1.2 miles*	
	Latrigg		*368 m = 1207 ft*	*3.7 km = 2.3 miles*	

Slight Side

Height 762 m = 2499 ft   NY210050   **Rank 57**

Whereas Great End marks the northern end of the high ground on which Scafell and the Scafell Pikes sit, Slight Side marks the southern end. The summit is a well defined cluster of rocks and, although the views to the north are rather restricted, those in other directions are magnificent. The walk along the edge of the crags to Scafell is excellent.

From Boot (Eskdale) via Eel Tarn and Stony Tarn:
        Ascent 702 m = 2303 ft   *Distance 6 km = 3.7 miles*
From opposite Wha House via Bull How, Dawsonground Crags and Cat Crag, then on to the path of the previous route: *Ascent 686 m = 2250 ft*   *Distance 4.7 km = 2.9 miles*
Adjacent Fells: *Scafell 964 m = 3162 ft*   *Distance 1.7 km = 1.1 miles*

Sour Howes

Height 483 m = 1584 ft   NY428032   **Rank 191**

Like its close neighbour, Sallows, Sour Howes offers some good long - distance views but very little else.

From the A592 via Limefitt Park and the old quarry above Garburn Road:
        Ascent 353 m = 1158 ft   *Distance 1.7 km = 1.1 miles*
Adjacent Fells: *Sallows Height 516 m = 1692 ft*   *Distance 1.5 km = 0.9 miles*

Souther Fell

Height 522 m = 1712 ft   NY355291   **Rank 172**

Pronounced 'Sutra'. An isolated grassy hump best known for its association with 'The Spectre Army' seen on its summit in 1735 (see page 37). Good views of Blencathra and across the plain to Penrith.

From Mousthwaite Comb (park at Comb Beck Bridge on the minor road from The White Horse Inn):
        Ascent 282 m = 925 ft   *Distance 2.5 km = 1.6 miles*
From Mungrisedale (park near the telephone kiosk). Go through the gate leading to Bannerdale and follow the path beside the River Glendermakin towards White Horse. On rounding the corner of Souther Fell, cross the river and climb the northern ridge to the summit:

Souther Fell (continued)

Ascent 287 m = 942 ft	*Distance 2.6 km = 1.7 miles*	
Adjacent Fell: *Blencathra (via Sharp Edge) Height 868 m = 2847 ft*	*4.6 km = 2.9 miles*	

Stainton Pike

Height 498 m = 1633 ft   **SD152943**   **Rank 186**

Stainton Pike is the high point of the craggy ridge of high ground rising out of the bleak moorland south of Devoke Water. The summit provides good views to the south and west but, like the neighbouring hills of Whitfell and Hesk Fell, its main attractions are the historical remains, in this case stone circles and cairns rather than mines. An interesting natural feature on the route up the fell are the waterfalls of Rowantree Beck.

From the fell road south of Broad Oak at the junction with Fell Lane (car parking on verge only). Take the public footpath which leads over the moor, passing across Waberthwaite Fell and between Stainton Pike and Whitfell on its way to Ulpha. Follow the path for about 3 km (2 miles) until the ravine of Rowantree Gill, with its waterfalls, is seen to the left. Leave the path here to view the falls and continue up the beck, crossing it when possible to reach the wire fence. Follow the fence round and up the fell until a gate is reached giving passage to the summit:

	Ascent 400 m= 1312 ft	*Distance 5.6 km =3.5 miles*	
Adjacent Fells:	*Whitfell*	*Height 573 m = 1879 ft*	*2.2 km = 1.4 miles*
	Hesk Fell	*477 m = 1564 ft*	*3 km = 1.9 miles*

Starling Dodd

Height 633 m = 2076 ft   **NY142158**   **Rank 125**

Starling Dodd will usually be visited by walkers travelling between Red Pike and Great Borne on the Ennerdale Horseshoe round. The top is flat and uninteresting. Good views across to Pillar.

From Buttermere via Scale Force Waterfall and Little Dodd (a very pleasant walk as far as the top of the waterfall, thereafter it is less interesting):

Ascent 521 m = 1709 ft	*Distance 6.2 km = 3.9 miles*

From the car park below Bowness Knott along to High Gillerthwaite and up the break in the forest to Little Dodd (some awkward rock strewn ground):

	Ascent 503 m = 1650 ft	*Distance 6.1 km = 3.8 miles*	
Adjacent Fells:	*Great Borne*	*Height 616 m = 2020 ft*	*Distance 2.1 km = 1.3 miles*
	Red Pike	*755 m = 2477 ft*	*2.1 km = 1.3 miles*

Steel Fell

Height 553 m = 1814 ft   **NY319111**   **Rank 152**

Steel Fell is the ridge that runs along most of the west side of Dunmail Raise. To the north it is cut off from adjacent fells by the Wythburn valley and to the south by Greenburn Bottom. The only high fell connnection with neighbouring fells is a 300 m (1000 ft) wide ridge leading to Calf Crag. The views from the top are good in all directions.

From Dunmail Raise, through the gate in the wall at the northern end of the dual carriageway section of road, then up onto the north ridge and hence to the summit:

Ascent 313 m = 1027 ft	*Distance 1.3 km = 0.8 miles*

From Ghyll Foot, up the private road to Helm Side, through the gate (Greenburn NT) and up the southeast ridge: *Ascent 453 m = 1468 ft*   *Distance 2.6 km = 1.6 miles*

From Grasmere village centre via Easedale Road and Goody Bridge and up the south east ridge:

	Ascent 453 m = 1468 ft	*Distance 5.4 km = 3.4 miles*	
Adjacent Fell:	*Calf Crag*	*Height 537 m = 1761 ft*	*2.5 km = 1.6 miles*

A - Z Guide to the Fells

Steel Knotts

Height 432 m = 1417 ft   **NY440181**   **Rank 209**

Steel Knotts is the grassy fell with rock outcrops forming the low ridge overlooking Martindale Old Church from the east. The summit is rarely visited as the well used footpaths from Martindale to High Street pass along either side of it. However the view of Martindale from the summit is excellent and good views are to be had of the more distant fells to the north and west. Steel Knotts makes an interesting short evening walk from Martindale Hause, where there is adequate parking (See below).

From the Hause (opposite Martindale New Church) follow the path between the church and the wall round to the foot of the ridge at Steel End, then follow the path through the bracken up the craggy ridge to the summit:
            Ascent 284 m = 932 ft   Distance 3 km = 1.9 miles
*From Martindale Old Church (Christy Bridge), up the track starting behind the church (**the higher track which passes between three very large rocks**) almost to Brownthwaite Crag, then backtrack up the Steel Knotts ridge, hence to the summit:*
            Ascent 232 m = 761 ft   Distance 2.6 km = 1.6 miles
(The two routes above, combined with the public footpath between the churches, make a pleasant short round.)

Steeple

Height 819 m = 2686 ft   **NY157117**   **Rank 28**

Steeple is not so much a fell as a rocky protuberance grafted onto the north ridge leading up to Scoat Fell. Steeple is 600 m (0.4 miles) from the top of Scoat Fell. See the latter for routes and distances.

Stickle Pike

Height 375 m = 1230 ft   **SD212928**   **Rank 225**

One of the miniature mountains of Dunnerdale. Like many of its neighbours Stickle Pike is dramatic in appearance but low in stature. This lack of height is more than compensated by the interesting terrain. Stickle Pike has an interesting rocky summit with good views as well.

From Broughton Mills (Green Bank) take the path north climbing above Red Moss Beck to Hare Hall, hence to the summit: Ascent 325 m = 1066 ft   Distance 2.9 km = 1.8 miles
From Hoses on the road to the east of the summit, up by Stickle Tarn to the summit:
            Ascent 175 m =574 ft   Distance 0.8 km =0.5 miles
Adjacent Fell: Great Stickle   Height   305 m = 1000 ft   1.5 km = 0.9 miles

Stone Arthur

Height 504 m = 1653 ft   **NY347 092**   **Rank 183**

A rock outcrop on the southwest spur below Great Rigg. The view from the top is limited by the higher hills, but in other respects is good. A pleasant short climb from Grasmere if one has not got much time to spare.

From Grasmere (A591) up the small road adjacent to the Swan Hotel, through the gate and onto the fell, turn sharp left and follow the path up onto the ridge:
            Ascent 424 m = 1391 ft   Distance 1.7 km = 1.1 miles
Adjacent Fell: Great Rigg   Height   766 m = 2513 ft   1.6 km =   1 mile

Stony Cove Pike

Height 763 m = 2503 ft   **NY418100**   **Rank 56**

Like its close neighbour Thornthwaite Crag, Stony Cove Pke is the meeting place of several routes. The top itself is flat and uninteresting, but by wandering around the summit one can see some excellent views. The quick route up is by the path starting at the Kirkstone Inn, but this is a pretty poor route. All other listed routes are good. Note that the quarry below Caudale Head and the adit on Hartsop Dodd north ridge contain

Stony Cove Pike (continued)

deep and dangerous shafts. The route passing through the quarry is highly recommended, as it gives an excellent insight into the extent of the industry in the area many years ago. (See page 86 : **Hartsop Hamlet**).

From the A592 (100 m north of Caudale Bridge), up the ridge following Caudale Beck, then along the ridge path and down to the old mine workings. From the top of the workings climb back up to the ridge path and continue on along Rough Edge to the summit:

Ascent 573 m = 1880 ft	Distance 4.8 km = 3 miles

From Kirkstone Inn via St Raven's Edge, Pike How, John Bell's Banner:

Ascent 313 m = 1027 ft	Distance 3.2 km = 2 miles

From Hartsop via the north ridge of Hartsop Dodd (some steep ground here):

Ascent 593 m = 1946 ft	Distance 3.9 km = 2.4 miles

From Troutbeck via Ing Lane and Troutbeck Park. Keep to the west side of the The Tongue and then, near the head of the valley, follow the stream to Broad How. From there follow the wall to Doup Crag and the summit:

Ascent 613 m = 2011 ft	Distance 7.2 km = 4.5 miles

Adjacent Fells:	Hartsop Dodd	Height	618 m = 2027 ft	2 km = 1.2 miles
	Thornthwaite Crag		784 m = 2572 ft	1.6 km = 1 mile

Stybarrow Dodd

Height 843 m = 2765 ft   NY343189   **Rank 21**

This fell is grassy and sprawling and, apart from the summit view, offers little of interest. About 700 m (0.4 miles) south of the summit is Sticks Pass; a popular crossing route from east to west.

From High Row via Dowthwaitehead, Deepdale and Middle Tongue:

Ascent 493 m = 1617 ft	Distance 6.1 km = 3.8 miles

From Stanah and directly up alongside Stanah Gill:

Ascent 673 m = 2208 ft	Distance 2.8 km = 1.7 miles

Adjacent Fells:	Watson's Dodd	Height	789 m = 2588 ft	1.1 km = 0.7 miles
	Raise		883 m = 2896 ft	1.7 km = 1.1 miles
	Hart Side		756 m = 2480 ft	2.3 km =1.4 miles
	Sheffield Pike		675 m = 2214 f t	3 km = 1.9 miles

Swainson Knott

Height 345 m = 1131 ft   NY080083   **Rank 232**

Like its close neighbour Ponsonby Fell, bleak, dreary and probably not worth the trouble. The walking can be more tolerable by keeping, as far as possible, to forest tracks. In which case the two preferred starting points are Wellington in the south or Castley Hill in the north.

From Wellington: Ascent	275 m = 902 ft	Distance 5.5 km = 3.4 miles
From Castley Hill	135 m =443 ft	1.4 km = 0.9 miles

Swirl How

Height 802 m = 2631 ft   SD273005   **Rank 33**

Swirl How lies at the junction of two popular ridge routes and so is often visited, albeit inadvertently. Good long distance views from the summit.

From Coniston via the Miners' road to Coppermines Valley, up past the Youth Hostel to Levers Water. Follow the path round the western side of the Reservoir, past the 'crater' (see page 113) along to the north end of the lake and up the path to Levers Hause. From here it is an easy stroll along the ridge to the summit:

Ascent 734 m = 2408 ft	Distance 6.2 km = 3.9 miles

Swirl How (continued)

*From Low Tilberthwaite (ample parking) via Tilberthwaite Gill, Birk Fell Man, Wetherlam Edge and Prison Band (see page 110 **Route 1(b)** for more detail):*

	Ascent 654 m = 2146 ft			Distance 6.4 km = 4 miles
Adjacent Fells:	Wetherlam	Height	762 m = 2499 ft	Distance 1.7 km =1.1 miles
	Coniston Old Man		803 m = 2634 ft	2.9 km = 1.8 miles

Tarn Crag (above Easedale Tarn)

Height 550 m = 1804 ft   NY301093   **Rank 155**

Tarn Crag and Slapestone Edge tower ominously above Easedale Tarn. This craggy prominence is an ideal viewpoint for the Easedale Valley and Grasmere. The view in other directions is limited.

From Grasmere via Easedale Road and the Sour Milk Gill path to Easedale Tarn, then up onto Greathead Crag. From here it is a stiff pull up the grass slope between Tarn Crag and Slapestone Edge to the summit:

	Ascent 460 m = 1509 ft			Distance 5.4 km = 3.4 miles

From The New Dungeon Ghyll Hotel, Langdale, via eastern edge of Stickle Tarn, Belles Knott, Codale Tarn and up to Tarn Crag:

	Ascent 460 m = 1509 ft			Distance 4.9 km = 3.1 miles
Adjacent Fells:	High Raise	Height	762 m = 2499 ft	2.5 km = 1.6 miles

Tarn Crag (above Longsleddale)

Height 664 m = 2178 ft   NY488078   **Rank 107**

The fells east of Longsleddale are bleak, boggy and, unless one has acquired a taste for this type of landscape, uninviting. However Tarn Crag is close enough to the craggy valley wall to offer contrasts. In common with Branstree the top possesses a pillar (the O.S. term). This is a curious two-pronged stone tower that was involved with the surveying of the Haweswater aqueduct. You will also see another one of these on Great Howe on your way up. Extensive views, though not into Lakeland, from the top.

From Sadgill. Follow the walls up to Great Howe and from there across to the summit:

	Ascent 464 m = 1522 ft			Distance 2.7 km = 1.7 miles
Adjacent Fells	Branstree	Height	713 m = 2339 ft	2.5 km = 1.6 miles
	Grey Crag		638 m = 2093 ft	1.3 km = 0.8 miles

The Knott

Height 739 m = 2424 ft   NY437127   **Rank 68**

Though there are excellent views to the west, Knott is overshadowed on the east by the fells overlooking Haweswater thus restricting the seeing in that direction. There is a pleasant but not particularly special view down to Hayeswater (Penrith's water supply). This is a place one passes through.

From Hartsop Village via Hayeswater Gill and the north end of Hayeswater:

	Ascent 569 m = 1867 ft			Distance 3.5 km = 2.2 miles

From Patterdale via Goldrill Bridge, Boredale Hause, Angle Tarn and Satura Crag:

	Ascent 589 m = 1932 ft			Distance 6.2 km = 3.9 miles
Adjacent Fells:	High Street	Height	828 m = 2716 ft	1.6 km = 1 mile
	Kidsty Pike		780 m = 2559 ft	1.1 km = 0.7 miles
	Rampsgilll Head		792 m = 2598 ft	0.8 km = 0.5 miles
	High Raise		802 m = 2631 ft	1.8 km = 1.1 miles
	Rest Dodd		696 m = 2283 ft	1.1 km = 0.7 miles
	Brock Crags		561 m = 1840 ft	2.6 km = 1.6 miles

A - Z Guide to the Fells

The Nab

Height 576 m = 1889 ft   NY434 152   **Rank 143**

The Nab is one of the few places in the district where no public footpaths exist. It is the original Martindale Deer Forest and the resident deer herd are often to be seen on the sides of The Nab or Beda Fell. Access is not encouraged. If you do wish to visit The Nab then the obvious route is to walk along the ridge from Rest Dodd, a distance of about 1.5 km (0.9 miles).

Thornthwaite Crag

Height 784 m = 2572 ft   NY431100   **Rank 45**

Thornthwaite Crag lies at the intersection of several different routes and is accordingly a very popular place. The most characteristic feature of this place is Thornthwaite Beacon, a beautifully constructed cylindrical column of stones some 13 ft high and perched on a small rock outcrop. The top is flat and you will have to move about to see the views which are good, but not outstanding.

From Hartsop Village via Pasture Bottom and Threshwaite Cove:
             Ascent 614 m = 2014 ft   *Distance 4.2 km = 2.6 miles*
From Hartsop Village via Hayeswater Gill and Gray Crag ridge:
             Ascent 614 m = 2014 ft   *Distance 4.5 km = 2.8 miles*
From Troutbeck via Trout Beck to the head of the valley, then straight up to Threshwaite Mouth:
             Ascent 634 m = 2080 ft   *Distance 7.8 km = 4.8 miles*
From Troutbeck via Hagg Gill and the Roman Road up to the ridge at Wander Scar
             Ascent 634 m = 2080 ft   *Distance 7.1 km = 4.4 miles*
From Kentmere village via Hartrigg (farm) and Kentmere Reservoir, then via the river Kent to Gavel Crag and up the east ridge of the Crag:
             Ascent 614 m = 2014 ft   *Distance 7.7 km = 4.8 miles*

Adjacent Fells:				
High Street	*Height*	*828 m = 2716 ft*	*Distance 1.6 km = 1 mile*	
Froswick		*720 m = 2362 ft*	*1.8 km = 1.1 miles*	
Stony Cove Pike		*763 m = 2503 ft*	*1.6 km = 1 mile*	
Mardale Ill Bell		*761 m = 2496 ft*	*1.7 km = 1.1 miles*	
Gray Crag		*699 m = 2293 ft*	*2 km = 1.2 miles*	

Thunacar Knott

Height 723 m = 2372 ft   NY279080   **Rank 78**

Just a small hillock 400 m (0.3 miles) from the summit of Pavey Ark. See Pavey Ark for routes, distances etc..

Top O' Selside

Height 335 m = 1099 ft   SD309919   **Rank 235**

The low hills between Coniston and Windermere are heavily forested. However, there are still some bare tops and Top O' Selside is one of them which gives surprisingly good views of Coniston and the surrounding more distant fells. There are several car parks in the woods along the eastern side of Coniston Water and a variety of different routes which can be taken. One example is given below.

From the car park between Dales Wood and Dodgson Wood, follow the track which zig zags upwards through the wood. Turn right at the junction, then via the path to Low Parkmoor. At Low Parkmoor turn south, leave the track and make your way up through the crags to the summit:
             Ascent 285 m = 935 ft   *Distance 2.3 km = 1.4 miles*

A - Z Guide to the Fells

Troutbeck Tongue

Height 364 m = 1194 ft   NY422064   **Rank 228**

The only recommendation for this fell is that it gives a good view down the valley towards Troutbeck. In other respects it has little to offer. The best approach is from the A592 by going down through the woods, crossing the stream by one of the bridges, then ascending the south ridge (pleasant scrambling). If parking is a problem one could follow the path from Troutbeck (Ing Lane), then ascend the hill in the same manner. It is possible to climb the fell from its north end, but it is hard to see why anyone would want to (bog and isolation).

From the A52, down through Hind Wood, across the stream and up the south ridge:
        Ascent 100 m = 328 ft   *Distance 1.7 km = 1.1 miles*
From Troutbeck via Ing Lane and the south ridge:
        Ascent 214 m = 702 ft   *Distance 3.1 km = 1.9 miles*
Adjacent Fell: *Thornthwaite Crag*   *Height 784 m = 2572 ft*   *3.7 km = 2.3 miles*
           (via Park Fell)

Ullock Pike

Height 690 m = 2263 ft   NY244287   **Rank 98**

Excellent views from the top and a very pleasant ridge walk from High Side to the summit. Ullock Pike is generally visited on the way to the summit of Skiddaw.

From High Side and straight up the ridge:
        Ascent 535 m = 1755 ft   *Distance 2.8 km = 1.7 miles*
Adjacent Fells: *Long Side*   *Height*   *734 m = 2408 ft*   *0.4 km = 0.3 miles*
           Carl Side   *746 m = 2447 ft*   *1.4 km = 0.9 miles*
           Skiddaw   *931 m = 3054 ft*   *2.2 km = 1.4miles*

Ullscarf

Height 726 m = 2381 ft   NY291122   **Rank 76**

The top is a broad and featureless grass dome. The views are good, but many will not consider the climb worth the trouble. It is a shame that a fell which is so interesting around its base (crags) should become so dull higher up.

From Wythburn at the southern end of Thirlmere, via Stenkin, up by West Head and round onto the fell above Nab Crags, then along the top of the crags to Greencombe and hence to the summit:
        Ascent 536 m = 1759 ft   *Distance 4 km = 2.5 miles*
From Dobgill Bridge (car park), Harrop Tarn, through the wood and up to the ridge above Blea Tarn, then left and and along the ridge path via Standing Crag to the summit:
        Ascent 536 m = 1759 ft   *Distance 4.2 km = 2.6 miles*
From Watendlath via Blea Tarn to Standing Crag and then along the ridge path to the summit:
        Ascent 458 m = 1503 ft   *Distance 5.7 km = 3.5 miles*
From Stonethwaite via Greenup Gill to Greenup Edge, then left along the ridge to the summit:
        Ascent 626 m = 2054 ft   *Distance 5.4 km = 3.4 miles*
Adjacent Fells: *Great Crag*   *Height*   *436 m = 1430 ft*   *3.6 km = 2.3 miles*
           Armboth Fell   *479 m = 1571 ft*   *4.9 km = 3 miles*
           High Tove   *515 m = 1689 ft*   *5 km = 3.1 miles*
           High Raise   *762 m = 2499 ft*   *3.3 km = 2.1 miles*

A - Z Guide to the Fells

Walla Crag

Height 379 m = 1243 ft   NY277213   **Rank 224**

The crag emerges from steep wooded slopes overlooking Derwentwater and the Rampsholme and St Herbert's Islands. It may be considered as the abrupt termination of the northwest slopes of Bleaberry Fell. Lady's Rake or Lady's Leap is a gully down the face of the crag and is said to have acquired its name when Lady Derwentwater used it to escape from the King's men in 1715. Easy to ascend and offers magnificent views.

From Keswick (Moot Hall) via St John Street, Ambleside Road, Springs Road, Rakefoot:
                    Ascent 299 m = 961 ft   *Distance 3.4 km = 2.1 miles*
                    (Note: there is a path leading off Springs Road to the viewpoint at Castlehead)
From Borrowdale Road. A footpath at the south end of the woods, below Walla Crag, follows Cat Gill and the top of the crag to the summit:
                    Ascent 289 m = 948 ft   *Distance 1.2 km = 0.8 miles*
Adjacent Fells: Bleaberry Fell   Height   590 m = 1935 ft   *2.4 km = 1.5 miles*

Walna Scar

Height 621 m = 2037 ft   SD258963   **Rank 129**

The high ridge which separates the valley of the Duddon from Coniston was frequented in the past almost exclusively by travellers and tradesmen, using the Walna Scar Pass to pass between the two valleys and by the quarrymen, who made their living up there. Nowadays walkers make the trek up to the scar mainly for the view, which is excellent, particularly to the west and north.

From The Rigg, above Coniston Village (Parking on the moor. Take the tarmac road west from the crossroads at the south end of the village and drive up until you arrive on the open moor). Follow the old Walna Scar Road (pack horse route) which leads across the moor and up to Walna Scar Pass, then turn left up to the summit: *Ascent 391 m = 1282 ft*   *Distance 3.5 km = 2.2 miles*

Wandope

Height 772 m = 25532 ft   NY188197   **Rank 53**

One would not make this the sole object of a walk as there are many other more interesting tops nearby. Good views from the summit.

From Cinderdale Common (parking) via Whiteless Breast and Whiteless Pike:
                    Ascent 662 m = 2172 ft   *Distance 4.8 km = 3 miles*
From Buttermere (parking at a price) via Whiteless Breast and Whiteless Pike:
                    Ascent 660 m = 2165 ft   *Distance 3.6 km = 1.2 miles*
Adjacent Fells: Whiteless Pike   Height   660 m = 2165 ft   *1.2 km = 0.7 miles*
*   Eel Crag   839 m = 2752 ft*   *1 km = 0.6 miles*
*   Grasmoor   852 m = 2795 ft*   *1.6 km = 1 mile*

Wansfell

Height 484 m = 1587 ft   NY394042   **Rank 190**

Wansfell overshadows Ambleside to the east and there is a good path over the fell to Troutbeck. The best views are not to be seen from the summit of Wansfell, due to its broad undulating nature. One should walk southwest from the summit to the lower prominence of Wansfell Pike for the best views.

From Ambleside up the road leading to Stick Ghyll waterfalls, past the old Grammar School building and then turn right onto the public footpath which leads up towards the summit of the fell:
                    Ascent 414 m = 1358 ft   *Distance 2.6 km = 1.7 miles*
From Troutbeck up via Nanny Lane, turning left at the bend in the lane, onto the path for the summit:
                    Ascent 344 m = 1129 ft   *Distance 2.6 km = 1.7 miles*
Adjacent Fell: Troutbeck Tongue   Height 364 m = 1194 ft   *5.3 km = 3.3 miles*

A - Z Guide to the Fells

Watson's Dodd

Height 789 m = 2588 ft   NY336196   **Rank 42**

Essentially just a grassy undulation on the long ridge which starts at Clough Head and continues on to Dollywaggon Pike. The walking is dull and the views are rather mundane. There is much more of interest nearby.

From north of Legburthwaite Church (parking), up by the waterfall and Mill Gill, bearing right as you approach the top: Ascent 619 m = 2031 ft   *Distance 2.1 km = 1.3 miles*

From Stybeck Farm (parking), via Sticks Pass , then left and up by Stybarrow Dodd and on to Watson's Dodd:

	Ascent 619 m = 2031 ft		*Distance 5.4 km =3.4 miles*
Adjacent Fells:	*Great Dodd*	*Height 857 m = 2811 ft*	*1.1 km = 0.7 miles*
	Stybarrow Dodd	*843 m = 2765 ft*	*1.1 km = 0.7 miles*

Wether Hill

Height 670 m = 2198 ft   NY456167   **Rank 105**

There is not much to recommend Wether Hill, particularly when there are so many better fells within a short distance. A wide-topped grassy hill with quite good long distance views from the summit.

From Burnbanks via The Forces (waterfalls), Low Kop, High Kop:

	Ascent 454 m = 1490 ft		*Distance 6.6 km = 4.1 miles*

From Martindale Old Church via Brownthwaite Crag and the north side of Gowk Hill:

	Ascent 470 m = 1542 ft		*Distance 3.5 km = 2.2 miles*

From Moorahill Farm (west of Bampton) via The Hause, Low Kop and High Kop:

	Ascent 345 m = 1132 ft		*Distance 5.1 km = 3.2 miles*
Adjacent Fells:	*Loadpot Hill*	*Height 671 m = 2201 ft*	*Distance 1.5 km = 0.9 miles*
	High Raise	*802 m = 2631 ft*	*3.5 km = 2.2 miles*

Wetherlam

Height 762 m = 2499 ft   NY288011   **Rank 57**

A magnificent craggy summit providing excellent views in all directions. Wetherlam is a must for all walkers. The whole area around the mountain has a rich industrial background of Copper and Slate mining. The remains of this intriguing past are there to excite our interest and imagination as we ascend the mountain by the various routes.

*From Low Tilberthwaite (ample parking) via Tilberthwaite Gill, Birk Fell Man, Wetherlam Edge to the summit (see page 110 **Route 1(b)** for more detail):*

	Ascent 614 m = 2014 ft	*Distance 3.8 km = 2.4 miles*

From Coniston via Miners Road, Miners Bridge, then follow the path which climbs below Sweeten Crag and up to Hole Rake. At the 400 m contour just below the hause of Hole Rake, turn onto the path that crosses the stream and climbs the ridge of 'Above Beck Fells' leading to the summit:

	Ascent 594 m = 1949 ft		*Distance 5.3 km = 3.3 miles*
Adjacent Fells:	*Swirl How*	*Height 802 m = 2631 ft*	*1.7 km = 1.1 miles*

Whin Rigg

Height 535 m = 1755 ft   NY152034   **Rank 163**

Whin Rigg is the prominence at the southern end of the Wastwater Screes and, like its immediate neighbour Illgill Head, is an excellent airy place to be on a good day, providing good views in all directions. Whin Rigg will normally be visited at the same time as Illgill Head and so the routes for Illgill Head apply equally to Whin Rigg.

Whin Rigg (continued)

From Boot via Bull Crag, Blea Tarn, Siney Tarn, then down and across Miterdale and up the hillside to the summit ridge:

Ascent 475 m = 1558 ft	Distance 5.4 km = 3.4 miles

From Nether Wasdale via Forest Bridge and Easthwaite to Greathall Gill, then up the eastern side of the gill to the ridge and turn left for the summit:

Ascent 482 m =1581 ft			Distance 4.2 km = 2.6 miles
Adjacent Fells:	*Illgill Head*	*Height* 609 m = 1998 ft	2.3 km = 1.4 miles
	Boat How	337 m = 1105 ft	5 km = 3.7 miles

Whinlatter

Height 525 m = 1722 ft   **NY197249**   **Rank 168**

This bare top in the centre of Thornthwaite Forest is rarely visited as the majority of the visitors to the forest follow the marked trails up to Seat How and Lord's Seat, further to the east. Good views to the south of Grisedale and Hobcarton but nothing special in other directions.

From the summit of the pass near the wall marking the boundary of the forest on the north side (parking for two or three cars beside the forest gate, or ample parking a few hundred yards away at the visitor centre). Follow the forest road up the hill, taking the second track on the left, which should bring you out on the open fell above Whinlatter Crag. From here it is a gentle stroll to the summit:

Ascent 205 m =673 ft			Distance 2.1 km =1.3 miles
Adjacent Fells:	*Graystones*	*Height* 456 m =1496 ft	2.2 km = 1.4 miles
	Lord's Seat	552 m = 1811 ft	2.7 km = 1.7 miles

White Combe

Height 415 m = 1361 ft   **SD154862**   **Rank 218**

White Combe is   the eastern buttress of the Black Combe ridge and can be accessed by a delightful horseshoe-shaped ridge walk from Black Combe via the top of Black Combe Screes and White Combe Screes. Alternatively White Combe can be ascended directly from the A595 at Beckside Farm.

From Beckside Farm on the A595, up the lane past Whicham Mill and onto the open fell. Cross the stream and climb up onto White Hall Knot, then up the ridge to the summit:

Ascent 354 m = 1161 ft			Distance 2.2 km = 1.4 miles
Adjacent Fell:	*Black Combe*	*Height* 600 m = 1968 ft	3.8 km = 2.4 miles

White Side (above Thirlmere)

Height 863 m = 2831 ft   **NY338167**   **Rank 16**

Except for a couple of hundred metres of crags, the east side of the hill, above Thirlmere, is grassy and not particularly steep. The west side is precipitous and interesting. The summit is grassy and not much higher than the ridge it lies on. Good views from the top. The most interesting approaches are from the east side.

From Thirlspot via Fisherplace Gill and Brund Gill:

Ascent 673 m = 2.2 miles	Distance 3.2 km = 2 miles

From Glenridding via the old Greenside Lead Mine and up the north side of Red Screes, near Keppel Cove:

Ascent 713 m = 2339 ft	Distance 5.9 km = 3.7 miles

From Glenridding via the old Greenside Lead Mine and up the ridge between Keppel Cove and Brown Cove:

Ascent 713 m = 2339 ft			Distance 5.7 km = 3.5 miles
Adjacent Fells:	*Raise*	*Height* 883 m = 2896 ft	1 km = 0.6 miles
	Helvellyn	950 m = 3116 ft	

Whiteless Pike

Height 660 m = 2165 ft   **NY180190**   **Rank 108**

The views from the top are superb and make this a very worthwhile walk. However, on reaching the summit you will almost certainly want to cross the ridge to Wandope and beyond (A particularly pleasant walk is **Route 5** on page 13).

From Cinderdale Common (parking) via Whiteless Breast:
     Ascent 550 m = 1804 ft   *Distance 3.5 km = 2.2 miles*
From Buttermere via Whiteless Breast:
     Ascent 548 m = 1797 ft   *Distance 2.4 km = 1.5 miles*
Adjacent Fell: *Wandope* *Height 772 m = 2532 ft*   *1.2 km = 0.7 miles*

Whiteside (above Crummock Water)

Height 719 m = 2358 ft   **NY175221**   **Rank 80**

The attraction of Whiteside is the lovely narrow ridge joining the summit to Hopegill Head. The best way to enjoy it is to walk from east to west. (see **Route 4,** page 13). The view from the summit is good; one can see across into Scotland and West Cumbria. (Whiteside and earthquakes, see page 18).

From Lanthwaite Green (parking and telephone) via Gasgale Gill, Coledale Hause, Sand Hill and Hopegill Head: *Ascent 562 m = 1844 ft*   *Distance 5.4 km = 3.3 miles*
From Beck House, straight up the hill:
     Ascent 599 m = 1965 ft   *Distance 2.3 km = 1.4 miles*
From Miller Place, follow the track round the Dodd and up to the head of Cold Gill, hence to the summit:
     Ascent 579 m = 1900 ft   *Distance 3.6 km = 2.3 miles*
Adjacent Fells: *Hopegill Head Height 770 m = 2526 ft*   *1.3 km = 0.8 miles*
       Sand Hill   *756 m = 2480 ft*   *1.6 km = 1 mile*

Whitfell

Height 573 m = 1879 ft   **SD159930**   **Rank 145**

This is fairly bleak terrain; rolling grassy tops with occasional rocky outcrops. However, Whitfell does provide airy open walking with good long distance views. To add interest, it is best included as part of a longer walk, which takes in other neighbouring remote fells and visits the relics of the mining industry in the area (see **Route 2.** page 113).

From the fell road at Buckbarrow Bridge, up by Whit Crags (old mining level) and Buckbarrow Beck to Hare Raise, hence across Burn Moor to the summit:
     Ascent 323 m = 1060 ft   *Distance 4.4 km = 2.8 miles*
Adjacent Fells: *Stainton Pike Height 498 m = 1633 ft*   *2.2 km = 1.4 miles*
       Hesk Fell   *477 m = 1564 ft*   *1.5 km = 0.9 miles*

Whoap

Height 511 m = 1676 ft   **NY173085**   **Rank 177**

A lonely moorish place with rather bleak views (see also Lank Rigg).

From the car park at Bleach Green at the west end of Ennerdale, up by the side of Ben Gill and along the track over Revelin Crag and Crag Fell . From Crag Fell top drop down through the wood, then leave the track and bear right up to the summit (This route follows part of the Ennerdale Horseshoe walk):
     Ascent 391 m = 1283 ft   *Distance 4.5 km = 2.8 miles*
From the road, along the path between Blakeley Raise and Burn Edge, then up the valley by Whoap Beck:
     Ascent 221 m = 725 ft   *Distance 4 km = 2.5 miles*

Whoap (continued)

Adjacent Fells:	Lank Rigg	Height	541 m = 1774 ft	Distance 1.2 km = 0.7 miles
	Crag Fell		523 m = 1715 ft	2.1 km = 1.3 miles
	Caw Fell		697 m = 2286 ft	5 km = 3.1 miles
	Grike		488 m = 1601 ft	2.7 km = 1.7 miles

Yewbarrow

Height 628 m = 2060 ft   NY173085   **Rank 127**

Steep, craggy and some good exciting walking. The most apparent way up is via the south ridge. However, when you reach Bell Rib it s necessary to turn left and follow the well worn path to Dropping Crag. From here a little scrambling and walking takes you to the impressive cleft of Great Door. From there on it is an easy walk to the summit. It should be noted that the path down Stirrup Crag to Dore Head at the north end involves the use of both hands and both feet in places. This can cause problems if you have a large dog or small children with you. However, it is possible to backtrack along the ridge and find a grassier and less abrupt descent through the crags on the northwest side. Good views from the top, particularly to the south.

From Overbeck Bridge (car park) up the ridge to the foot of Bell Rib, then across to Dropping Crag and up to Great Door: Ascent 563 m = 1847 ft   *Distance 2.3 km = 1.4 miles*

From the Wasdale Head Hotel via Dorehead screes and up Stirrup Crag:
Ascent 548 m = 1798 ft   *Distance 3.2 km = 2 miles*

Adjacent Fell:	Red Pike (above Wasdale) Height 826 m = 2709 ft	2.9 km = 1.8 miles

Yoke

Height 706 m = 2316 ft   NY438067   **Rank 87**

Yoke is the first (or last) summit on the Kentmere Horseshoe. To the south of the summit much of the fell is just a gently graded grassy hill. However, as one approaches the top, a well-defined and rapidly narrowing ridge starts to appear. The ground to the east and northeast of the summit is precipitous and dramatic. Good views from the top.

From Kentmere village via The Garburn Pass:
Ascent 511 m = 1676 ft   *Distance 4.7 km = 2.9 miles*
From Kentmere Village, up the craggy slope, passing by Cowsty Knotts and Castle Crag (This is more interesting than the Garburn Pass route):
Ascent 511 m = 1676 ft   *Distance 3.6 km = 2.2 miles*
From the A592 via Limefit Park and The Garburn Pass:
Ascent 576 m = 1890 ft   *Distance 5.1 km = 3.2 miles*

Adjacent Fells:	Sallows	Height	516 m = 1692 ft	2.8 km = 1.7 miles
	Ill Bell		757 m = 2483 ft	1.1 km = 0.7 miles

The End

(Two hundred and forty six fells in the list)

The English Lakes
A Selected Bibliography

A Study of Hartsop Valley	LDSPB	1976
A History of Man in the Lake District	Rollinson	1967
A Thousand Miles of Wandering in the Border Country	Bogg	1898
Beauty of Buttermere (Novel in three volumes)	Cruickshank	1841
Beneath the Lakeland Fells	Cumbria Amenity Trust	1992
Bluebirds	Campbell Gina	1968
Bye Ways in Lakeland	W T Palmer	1952
Chronicles of Patterdale	Little (W.I.)	1952
Coniston	Collingwood	1900
Country Life Magazine	October	1972
Crag and Hound in Lakeland	Benson	1902
Cumberland and Westmorland Antiquarian and Archaeological Society Transactions		
Cumbria Magazine	Dalesman	
Description of Lakes	Penny Magazine	1837
Descriptive Guide to the Lakes	Otley	1850
Descriptive Tour and Guide to the Lakes	Housman J.	1802
Dry Stone Walls	Garner L.	1984
English Lakes	Atkinson	1853
English Lakes	Martineau H.	1855
Fell days	Sutton G.	1948
Fortnight's Ramble to the Lakes	Budworth J.	1792
Gossiping Guide to Shap and Haweswater	Partington	1923
Guide to Lakes	Aust Mrs M.	1810
Guide to Lakes	Robinson	1819
Guide to Lakes	West T.	1799
Heart of Lakeland	Oppenheimer L. J.	1908
History of Cumberland	Hutchinson	1794
Kelton and Knockmurton Iron Mines	Hewer R.	1988
Lakeland and the Border Counties Vol 1 - 3	Mc Intyre	
(Articles from the Cumberland News in the 1930's)		
Lakeland Limericks	Gibbs	1942
Legends and Historical Notes of North Westmorland	Gibson	1887
Life of John Hatfield, the Keswick Impostor	Scott & Benson	1846
Literary Associations of the English Lakes	Rawnsley	1894
Memories of Dunmail Raise (Article in 'Cycling Magazine')	Palmer	1937
Mines of the Lake District Fells	Adams J.	1988
Mountain Ascents	Barrow John	1886
Observations during a tour of the Lakes	Radcliffe Mrs Ann	1795
Penny Magazine	July	1837
Pictorial Guide to the Lakeland Fells	Wainwright	1966 - 1992
Place Names of Cumberland		1940
Ratty	Gowan W.M.	1947
Records of Patterdale	Morris W P	1903
Royal Observer Corps Journal	Thomson	Feb - 1988
Ruskin and Brantwood	Whitehouse	1937
Scawfell Pike, the ascent of	Hudson	1851
Survey of the Lakes	Clarke J.	1789
The Lakes	Sanderson	1807
The Old Man - Ravings and Ramblings	Gibson	1849
Thoughts on the Parish of Caldbeck	Pool	1862
Windscale Works	UKAEA	1966
Wordsworth's Scenery of the Lakes of England	Hudson J.	1853

The English Lakes
Name Index

The English Lakes
General Index